Al-Muraja'at:
A Shi'i-Sunni dialogue

By:
Sayyid 'Abd al-Husayn Sharaf al-Din al-Musawi

Translated from the Arabic by
Yasin T. al-Jibouri

In the name of Allah, the Beneficent,
the Merciful

Contents

Author's Biography I
Birth and Upbringing II
At Al-'Amil III
His Reforms III
His Eloquence III
His Services III
His Quest for Knowledge V
His Works VI
His Lost Works VIII
His Manners and Gifts XI
His Travels XI
His Legacies and Construction Projects XIII
Introduction and Foreword XV

Letter 1
I. Greeting the Debater 1
II. Asking Permission to Debate 1

Letter 2
I. Greetings Reciprocated 2
II. Permission to Debate Granted 3

Letter 3
I. Why do Shi'as not Uphold the Majority's Sects? 5
II. The Need for Unity 5
III. Unity Achieved Only by Adhering to the Majority's Sects ... 5

Letter 4

I. Juristic Proofs Mandate Adherence to the Sect of Ahl Al-Bayt 6

II. There is No Proof for Mandating Adherence to the Majority's Sects 6

III. generations of the first three centuries Never Knew Those Sect. 7

IV. Possibility of Ijtihad 8

V. Unity can be achieved by Respecting Ahl al- Bayt's sect 9

Letter 5

I. Admitting Our Argument 11

II. Asking for Detailed Proof 11

Letter 6

I. References to Proofs Mandating Following the 'Itra 12

II. The Commander of the Faithful (as) Invites to Ahl Al-Bayt's Sect 12

III. Relevant Statement of Imam Zainul'Abidin 16

Letter 7

I. Requesting Proofs from Statements by Allah and His Messenger 19

II. Proofs from Ahl Al-Bayt are Circumventive 19

Letter 8

I. Overlooking Our Previous Statements 19

II. Error in Necessity of (Logical) Cycle 20

III. Hadith of the Two Weighty Things 20

IV. Its Tawatur 22

V. NonAdherents to the 'Itra Shall Stray 24

VI. Their Similitude to the ark of Noah the Gate of Salvation and the Security Against Religious Dissensions 25

VII. What is Meant by "Ahl Al-Bayt" in this Regard 25

VIII. Reasons for Similitude to Noah's Ark and the Gate of Salvation 26

Letter 9

Requesting More Relevant Texts 29

Letter 10

A Glimpse of Sufficient Texts...29

Letter 11

I. Admiring Our Clear Texts...37

II. Wondering at Compromising Them With the Majority's Beliefs 37

III. Asking for Clear Signs from the Book...37

Letter 12

Qur'anic Proofs..38

Letter 13

Argument Regarding These Traditions Weak...................................57

Letter 14

I. Fallacy of Opponent's Argument 57

II. Opponents do not Know Shi'as..58

III. Distinction of Emphasizing Illegality of Falsifying Hadith 59

Letter 15

I. A Flash of the Truth...61

II. Requesting Details on Sunnis Relying on Shi'a Authorities 61

Letter 16

A Hundred Shi'a Authorities Relied upon by Sunnis 61

Letter 17

I. Appreciating the debater's sentiments 141

II. Admitting There is no Objection if Ahl ul-Sunnah Rely on Shi'a Authorities...141

III. His belief in the Miracles of Ahl al-Bayt 141

IV. Dilemma at Compromising the Above with what Ahl Al-Qibla do 142

Letter 18

I. Sentiments Reciprocated 142

II. Debater's Error in Generalizing Regarding Ahl al-Qibla 142

III. The Nation's Politicians are the Ones Who Turned Away from Ahl al-Bayt 143

IV. The Imams of Ahl al-Bayt (without any argument) are not Inferior to others 144

V. Which Fair Court Judges Calling Their Followers "Strayers"?...144

Letter 19

I. No Fair Arbitrator Would Call Followers of Ahl al-Bayt Strayers 145

II. Following Their Sects is Carrying out the Responsibility 145

III. It Could be Said that They Have the Priority to Lead 145

IV. Requesting Texts Relevant to the Khilafate..................................145

Letter 20

I. A General Reference to the Texts..146

II. A Reference to the House on the Day of Warning.......................146

III. Sunni Reporters of this Hadith..147

Letter 21..............................151

Letter 22

I. Proving the Text's Authenticity 151

II. Why the Shaykhs Have Not Reported it 152

III. Whoever Knows These Shaykhs Knows Why 153

Letter 23

I. Convinced of the Authenticity of this Hadith 155
II. Unreliability Based on Non-Sequential Narration 155
III. Its Reference to Restricted Succession...155
IV. Its Rebuttal..155

Letter 24

I. Why Relying on this Hadith 156
II. Restricted Succession is Unanimously Rejected 156
III. Revocation is Impossible..156

Letter 25

I. His Belief in the Text 159
II. Requesting More Texts 159

Letter 26

I. Clear Texts Recounting Ten of 'Ali's Exclusive Merits.................159
II. Why Rely Upon it..161

Letter 27

Raising Doubts About the Status Hadith 163

Letter 28

I. The Status Hadith Stands on Most Solid Grounds 163
II. Binding Proofs 163
IV. Why al-Amidi Suspects It...166

Letter 29

I. Believing in Our Arguments Regarding the Hadith's Sanad 167
II. Doubting its General Application...167
III. Doubting its being Binding..167

Letter 30

I. Arabs Regard it General..168
II. Disproving Claim of Restriction..169
III. Disproving its Non-Binding Application..170

Letter 31
Requesting Sources of this Hadith..171

Letter 32
I. Among Its Sources: the Prophet's Visit to Umm Salim 171
II. The Case of Hamzah's Daughter 172
III. Leaning on 'Ali 173
IV. The First Fraternity 173
V. The Second Fraternity 173
VI. Closing the Doors..175
VII. The Prophet Comparing 'Ali and Aaron to the Two Stars 176

Letter 33
When was 'Ali and Aaron Described as the Two Stars?...................177

Letter 34
I. The Occasion of Shabar ,Shubayr, and Mushbir 177
II. The Occasion of Fraternity 178
III. The Occasion of Closing the Doors...181

Letter 35
Requesting Other Texts 187

Letter 36
I. Hadith by Ibn 'Abbas 187
II. 'Umran's Hadith 187
III. Buraydah's Hadith 188
IV. Hadith Recounting Ten Exclusive Attributes [of 'Ali]................191

V. 'Ali's Hadith 191

VI. Wahab's Hadith 192

VII. Ibn Abu 'Asim's Hadith 192

Letter 37

"Wali" is a Linguistic Denominator; so Where is the Text? 193

Letter 38

I. Explaining the Implications of "Wali" 193

II. Proving its Connotation 193

Letter 39

Requesting the Wilayat Verse 197

Letter 40

I. The Verse of Wilayat and its Revelation in 'Ali's Honour 197

II. Why it was Revealed 198

III. Why Using it as a Testimonial 200

Letter 41

"Mumins" is Plural; Why Apply it to the Singular? 201

Letter 42

I. Arabs Address the Singular Using the Plural Form, ... 201

II. Testimonials, ... 201

III. Quoting Imam al-Tibrisi, ... 203

IV. Quoting al-Zamakhshari, ... 203

V. What I. have Stated. 203

Letter 43

Context Denotes "the Loved one" or the Like 205

Letter 44

I. Context is not Indicative of "Supporter" or the Like, ... 205

II. Context does not Outweigh the Proofs..206

Letter 45

Resorting to Interpretation Following in the Footsteps of the Predecessors is Unavoidable 209

Letter 46

I. Believing in the Ancestors does not Require Interpretation........209

II. Interpretation is Impossible 209

Letter 47

Requesting Testimonial Traditions..211

Letter 48

Forty Ahadith Supporting the Texts...211

Letter 49

I. Admitting 'Ali's Merits 227

II. Such Merits do not Necessitate his Caliphate............................228

Letter 50

Why Interpret Texts on His Behalf as Indicative of His Imamate ..228

Letter 51

Rebutting the Arguments Through Similar Ones...........................231

Letter 52

Rejecting the Rebuttal's Premises..231

Letter 53

Requesting the Hadith Pertaining to the Ghadir Incident..............233

Letter 54

Glitters of Ahadith Relevant to the Ghadir Incident.......................233

Letter 55

Why Use it as a Testimonial if not Transmitted Consecutively?....241

Letter 56

I. Natural Laws Necessitate the Consecutive Reporting of Hadith al-Ghadir 241

II. The Almighty's Benevolence 242

III. Concern of the Messenger of Allah (s) 243

IV. Concern of the Commander of the Faithful 244

V. al-Husain's Concern 248

VI. Concern of the Nine Imams (as) 248

VII. Shi'as' Concern 249

VIII. Its Consecutive Reporting Through the Masses 250

Letter 57

I. Interpreting Hadith al-Ghadir 255

II. The Link 255

Letter 58

I. Hadith al-Ghadir Cannot be Interpreted 256

II. Pretext for its Interpretation is Speculative and Misleading 259

Letter 59

I. Truth Manifests 263

II. Evasion 263

Letter 60

Evasion Refuted 264

Letter 61

Requesting Texts Narrated by Shi'a Sources 269

Letter 62

Forty Ahadith 269

Letter 63

I. Shi'a Texts Rejected as Testimonials, ... 281

II. Why Have Others Refrained from Quoting Them? 281

III. Asking for More Texts. 281

Letter 64
I. Above Texts were Quoted upon Request 281

II. Sahihs are Proofs against the Majority 281

III. Not Quoted Because of Their Existence in Our Own Sahihs 281

Letter 65
Requesting the Ahadith Relevant to the Inheritance 287

Letter 66
Ali is the Prophet's Heir 287

Letter 67
Where is the Prophet's Will? 291

Letter 68
The Will's Texts 291

Letter 69
Argument of the Will's Deniers 297

Letter 70
I. The Will Cannot be Repudiated 298

II. Why Denied 305

III. Deniers' Arguments not Binding 305

IV. Reason and Intellect Require it 305

Letter 71
Why Reject the Hadith of the Mother of Believers and the best Among the Prophet's Consorts? 307

Letter 72
I. She Was Not the Best of the Prophet's Consorts 307

II. The Best is Khadija 308

III. A General Hint to the Reason Why her Hadith was Discarded 309

Letter 73

Requesting an Explanation to our Rejection of 'Ayesha's Hadith .311

Letter 74

I. Explaining Why We Reject her Hadith..311

II. Reason Confirms the Will 316

III. Her Claim that the Prophet Died on Her Chest is Refuted.......317

Letter 75

I. Mother of the Believers is not Ruled by Emotions........................319

II. The Pleasant and the Ugly are Denied by Reason.......................319

III. Why Oppose the Claim of the Mother of Believers?..................320

Letter 76

I. Her Yielding to Sentiment...320

II. Rationale Regarding the Pleasant and the Unpleasant...............322

III. Rejecting the Claim of the Mother of Believers..........................324

IV. Preference of Umm Salamah's Hadith over Hers.......................329

Letter 77

Why Prefer Umm Salamah's Hadith to 'Ayesha's?.........................331

Letter 78

More Reasons for Preferring Umm Salamah's Hadith 331

Letter 79

Consensus Endorses al-Siddiq's Caliphate...337

Letter 80

No Consensus...337

Letter 81

Consensus Concluded When Dispute Dissipated............................343

Letter 82

Consensus Was Not Concluded; Dissension Did Not Dissipate 343

Letter 83

Can You Compromise the Text's Accuracy With the Companions' Truthfulness? 351

Letter 84

I. Compromising the Text's Accuracy With Their Truthfulness.....351

II. Rationalizing the Imam's Reluctance to Demand his Right 354

Letter 85

Requesting Narration of Incidents Wherein They Did Not Follow the Texts of Hadith 357

Letter 86

I. Thursday's Calamity..........357

II. The Reason Why the Prophet Repealed His Order Then 362

Letter 87

Justifying and Discussing the Calamity 365

Letter 88

Pretexts Refuted..........368

Letter 89

I. Admitting the Falsehood of Such Pretexts 373

II. Requesting Narration of Other Incidents 373

Letter 90

Usamah's Regiment..........373

Letter 91

I. Justifying Their Behaviour Towards Usamah's Regiment 381

II. No Hadith Curses its Draft Dodgers..........382

Letter 92

I. Their Pretexts do not Contradict our Statement............................383

II. Al-Shahristani's Hadith is Documented..385

Letter 93

Requesting Narration of Other Incidents 387

Letter 94

His Order (s) to Kill the Renegade..387

Letter 95

Justifying not Killing the Renegade..391

Letter 96

Justification Rejected 391

Letter 97

Requesting Narration of all Such Incidents...393

Letter 98

I. Glittering Proofs...393

II. Reference to Other Incidents 394

Letter 99

I. Their Preference of the Common Interest in Those Instances.....395

II. Requesting the Rest..395

Letter 100

I. The Debater Digresses from the Subject-Matter............................395

II. Responding to His Request...396

Letter 101

Why didn't the Imam Cite the Ahadith of Caliphate and Wisayat on the Saqifa Day?..399

Letter 102

I. Why the Imam Abstained on the Saqifa Day from Citing Such Texts 399

II. Reference to his and his Followers' Arguments Despite Obstacles 402

Letter 103
Looking for His and His Followers' Arguments..............................403

Letter 104
I. A Few Incidents When the Imam Argued......................................403

II. The Argument of al-Zahra' (as) 408

Letter 105
Requesting Narration of Other Such Incidents................................411

Letter 106
I. Ibn 'Abbas's Argument 411

II. Arguments of al-Hasan and al-Husayn.......................................414

III. Arguments of Prominant Shi'ah Sahabah.................................414

IV. Reference to their Applying the Will as an Argument 415

Letter 107
When did they Mention the Will?..417

Letter 108
The Recommendation as Evidence 417

Letter 109
Why do Some Fanatics Question the Derivation of the Shi'a School of Muslim Law from the Imams of Ahl al-Bayt (as)?....................431

Letter 110
I. Shi'ah Faith is Sequentially Derived from the Imams of Ahl al-Bayt 431

II. Advancement of Shi'ahs in Recording Knowledge During the Sahabah's Epoch 434

III. Their Authors Contemporary to the Tabi'in and the Latter's Followers 438

Letter 111
Conviction 449
Letter 112
Appreciation 449
Glossary 451
Index 457

Author's Biography

Only a few names of men, who were distinguished for their gifts and genius which lifted them to the highest peaks of recognition, are etched upon the horizons of our Islamic world. Such names, like bright stars, have kept glittering in the depth of the skies.

As for those whose names are portrayed in every horizon of the Islamic world, these, indeed, are even fewer. They are a minority. They are none other than those whom nature has elevated, achieving such rare genius that made them unique throughout all Islamic lands. Among such people is our master-author, may Allah rest his soul in peace. The Supreme Will has decreed to bless his knowledge and pen, producing from them the best intellectual output. I may not exaggerate if I allow my pen to record this: the master-author is advanced through what he produced to the very front row of Shi'a scholars. The latter dedicated their entire lives to the service of their religion and school of thought. He, therefore, deservedly occupies the front seat among the Muslim world's contemporary elite.

Within such a limited undertaking, I do not find myself inclined to elaborate on what Sayyid 'Abdul-Husayn Sharafuddin had accomplished in life's spheres and undertakings. The task may have been easier had the author being discussed been someone else. It would have been easier had the author been among those men whose lives and works were limited. But a man whose calibre is as vast as this author makes it very difficult for any writer to describe and be fair to. When the writer stands for such an undertaking, he will surely feel as though he is facing an entire generation reverberating with hues of life, overflowing from all sides and directions. He can hardly refer each hue to its source except through research with full responsibilities of logic and knowledge. This may even be beyond the capacity of trustworthy historians to tackle.

Birth and Upbringing

Sayyid 'Abdul Husayn Shrafuddin, may Allah expand his shade, was born in Kazimiyya (north Baghdad, Iraq) in 1290 A.H. from good parents linked to one another by kinship and united through a family tree of good roots. His father was noble person Yousuf son of noble Jawad son of noble Isma'il. His mother was the virtuous Zahra, daughter of Sayyid Hadi son of Sayyid Muhammad 'Ali, ending in a short kinship to Sharafuddin, one of the renowned dignitaries of this good family.

He grew up in a house for which the avenues of scholarly mastership had been paved, whose pillars were erected upon renowned dignitaries of good reputation and whose favour and services are acclaimed and appreciated throughout the Islamic world.

He grew up in that lofty house, nurtured in the gardens of knowledge and ethics, ascending the heights of dignity. When he reached tender adolescence, he became fully acquainted with the causes of goodness, the following of which made him the embodiment of virtue. Upon making his first stride in the scholarly life, he was distinguished by notable accomplishments and achievements. His students and admirers kept his company. He had a reverberating voice in the learning centres of Samarra and al-Najaf al-Ashraf where he achieved distinction.

Ever since that day, his star had always been shining amidst the circles of knowledge, its light extending far and wide as his knowledge expanded. He advanced his stages until the scholarly life was cultivated for him at the hands of many a genius among the pillars of knowledge in al-Najaf al-Ashraf and Samarra such as Tabataba'i, Khurasani, FathAllah al-Isfahani, Shaykh Hasan al-Karbala'i, and many other renowned pillars of religion and imams of knowledge.

At Al-'Amil[1]

When his maturity received recognition, his star in the circles of research and meetings of debate and learning started shining, he, at thirty two, went back to the mountain of 'Amil, south Lebanon, dignified, renowned, self-satisfied, promising, articulate, glowing in brilliance. The day of his arrival was memorable. 'Amil sent her sons to welcome his arrival, so luminous in lands and skies, welcoming him in demonstrations containing men of scholarship and public leadership, up to the borders of the mountain from Syria's highway, celebrating as though it was a day of Eid.

His Reforms

A new life started in 'Amil aiming at strict implementation of religion, improvement of manners, the strengthening of right with might, kindness to the weak, the enjoining of right and the forbidding of wrong, comfort with the masters of religion and humbleness towards the men of knowledge.

His Eloquence

His eloquent lectures and succinct methods of directives had the largest share in producing the much desired reform. This comes as no surprise when we know that the Sayyid possessed such an eloquence of speech which made him the envy of Arabia's orators. Religion, scholarship and ethics were all proud of him.

He was great, besides his eloquence, in choosing the jewels of his thoughts, the garbs of his opinions which he masterly fitted and organized, breathing life into whatever he desired of arguments, explanations, logic, expositions, additions, and into all his works which are organized through harmony and equilibrium.

His Services

As regarding his contributions to the struggle against foreign colonialism, you may elaborate on these as you please. This undertaking does not allow us to go into such struggle in detail;

---

[1] Jabal 'Amil, South Lebanon

however, I may summarize it in one statement: His great services during the Turkish regime, then under the French occupation, after the post-independence, were simply extensions of the movements of liberation. He raised their level of effectiveness and directed them towards the noble objectives of securing justice and stability, thus bringing fresh hope to the masses. All authorities during these regimes, however, spared no effort to oppose him and undermine his plans through the implementation of whatever plots, persecution and harmful means they could improvise.

The calamities from which this great imam suffered while trying to make his people happy may not have been endured except by the most outstanding Arab chiefs and leaders, those who struggled heroically and suffered a great deal in the process.

I do not need to elaborate on the surprise the occupying French authorities had in store for him when they felt sick and tired of him. They instructed some of their hoodlum hardliners to assassinate him. Ibn al-Hallaj suddenly broke into his house when he, together with members of his family and kin, had none of his supporters around. Allah the Glorious and Sublime willed for him the opposite of their will. He kept their evil away from him, and they retreated in humiliation, stumbling in their failure and shame. As soon as the news of this surprise attack was broadcast in al-'Amil, crowds rushed to Sur (Tyre) from each and every direction in order to be under the command of their master as to what to do about that incident. Yet the Sayyid dispersed them after thanking them, advising them to simply overlook it.

This incident was succeeded by many, many other similar ones. The gap became wider, and dissension exploded until, eventually, the Sayyid, together with his kith and kin among the chiefs of al-'Amil, had to seek refuge in Damascus which he reached despite the French army's attempt to close the highway in his face.

The aggressive authority was chasing him with some of its armed troops in order to forbid him from reaching Damascus. When it lost hope of capturing him, it went back to set his house in Shahur on fire, leaving it in ashes strewn in the air; then it set its hands on his big house in Sur after allowing the sinful hands to plunder and loot it until they left nothing valuable or otherwise in it. The most damaging in that tragedy was the burning of the Sayyid's library with all its precious books and most distinguished works including nineteen of his own which were still handwritten manuscripts.

Then he travelled to Egypt during the climax of upheavals which inflicted the region. When he arrived there, the Egyptians warmly welcomed him and recognized him in spite of his disguise behind a kaffiyya and iqal, outfits common to the bedouins of the desert. He took in Egypt certain stands which attracted the attention of the elite among the scholars of knowledge, the pillars of literature, and the men of politics, according to the demands of his revered personality.

That was not his first visit to Egypt. Egypt knew him eight years earlier when he visited it at the close of 1329 A.H., staying in it till the year 1330 A.H. during a trip in pursuit of knowledge. He met then with the researchers and masterminds of learned Egyptians. After that, he and Shaykh Salim al-Bishri, the then rector of al-Azhar, met quite often and exchanged discussions dealing with the significant matters of Kalam (logic) and Usul (basics of jurisprudence). Among the results of those meetings are the Muraja'at with which we are dealing here.

His Quest for Knowledge

Noting the preface above, you may first get the impression that the social problems surrounding him have diverted his attention from pursuing knowledge and kept him away from literary work. In fact, anyone who is inflicted as our Sayyid was is normally diverted from attainable knowledge and authorship. The problems surrounding him would have indeed limited his chances to look into the library, or to write. But the fact is that his time is blessed, his heart is spacious, and his mind is powerful.

While dealing satisfactorily with the problems which he encountered, he also quenched his thirst for knowledge. He obtained from his library the portion of knowledge his practical life demanded. Ever since leaving al-Najaf al-Ashraf, he continuously kept researching, reading, writing and debating. During his leisure hours, he daily went to his library in order to find his peace of mind in its subjects and forget whatever busy and exhausting life lay beyond its precincts.

His Works

1) *Al Muraja'at* is but a true specimen of his writing, and I cannot tell you enough about it here. His own tongue is indeed much more eloquent and outspoken than mine. It was printed at al'Irfan Press, Saida (Sidon) Lebanon, in 1355 A.H., and all its copies were immediately sold out. It was translated into Persian, and I have heard that it has been translated into English by Dr. Zayd, an Indian, and also into Urdu.

2) *Al Fusul Al Muhimmah fi Tal'if Al Ummah* ["The Important Chapters in Unifying the Nation"] is one of the best Islamic books which deal with controversial matters regarding which Sunnis and Shi'as dispute in the light of Kalam, reason, deduction and analysis. It was finished in 1327 A.H. and was twice printed in Saida, 'Amil mountain. The text of its second edition (1347 A.H.) was increased. In its own subject matter, *Al Fusul Al-Muhimmah fi Ta'lif Al-Ummah* suffices for an entire library. It contains 192 small size pages.

3) *Ajwibat Masa'il Musa JarAllah* ["Answers to Musa Jar-Allah's Questions"]. Although small in size, this is a magnificent book of tremendous knowledge. As the title suggests, it contains answers to twenty questions put forth by Musa JarAllah to Shi'a scholars.

He thinks they include some embarrassing questions such as why Shi'as consider some companions kafir and denounce them, and the allegation that Shi'as altered the text of the Qur'an and made Jihad unlawful, and also matters like Bada' (change of destiny by Allah), mut'a (temporary marriage), bara'a (dissociation from the enemies of Allah), 'awl (a law of inheritance adopted by the Sunnis), etc. His answers were most authentic, derived from abundant knowledge and based upon proofs and logic, leaving no room for doubt. It has an Introduction about the call for unity and a conclusion regarding the ignorance of those who raise such issues and propagate such allegations about Shi'a literature, and also of the confusion which exists in some Sunni books. It is in 152 small pages, printed at al'Irfan Press, Saida, in 1355 A.H./1936 A.D.

4) *Al Kalimah Al Gharra' fi Tafdil al Zahra'* ["The Convincing Statement in Preferring al Zahra'"]. Its 40 half size pages have combined with the text of the second edition of *Al Fusul al Muhimmah*. It contains the deepest studies. It is most authentic in style and derivation. It testifies to the overflow of the writer's pen, his fountainhead.

5) *Al Majalis Al Fakhirah fi Ma'atim al'Itrah Al Tahirah* ["The Magnificent Commemorative Speeches in Honour of the Purified Progeny"]. The Introduction to this book has already been printed. The total number of its half size pages is 72. The author explains in it the philosophy of conducting commemorative Husayni ceremonies, and the secrets of the Taff martyrdom are very nicely and precisely explained.

6) *Abu Hurairah*, printed in 1365 A.H. at Al-'Irfan Press, Saida. It is a new method in authorship and a victory in the world of biographies because of its absorbant analytical style. In its depth and style, it may well be compared with the most respectable works of its category. It deals in the light of knowledge and reason with the life of Abu Hurairah, his time, circumstances, friends, traditions, and the special attention meted to him by the six *sahih* books which quote his traditions.

7) *Bughyat Al-Raghibin* ["Quest of the Willing"] is a unique family manuscript tracing the Sharafuddin family tree and close relatives. It stands as a grand, magnificent and excellent work among the literature of diaries in its own accomplished method of

classification. He narrates in it the biographies of some renowned master authors, as well as their times and circumstances. You will, therefore, find it an excellent and interesting literary book, nay, an entire history of generations and dignitaries.

8) *Thabt Al Athbat fi Silsilat Al Ruwat* ["The Ultimate Proof in the Chain of Narrators"]. In this book, the author lists his mentors among renowned Muslim sects in a sequence which goes back to the Prophet (s) and Imams (as), to works and their authors traced through various numerous avenues. He narrates some of them by way of reading or hearing, or depending on the authority of renowned men belonging to the Shi'a Ithna Ashari or Zaydi creeds, as well as from renowned Sunnis. To elaborate on all his methods here will require lengthy details; therefore, I content myself with referring to the contents of al Thabt which was twice printed in Saida.

He has authored other books not mentioned above such as *Masa'il Khilafiyya* ["Caliphate-Related Issues"] and *Risalah Kalamiyya* [Dissertation in Theological Philosophy (i.e. derived from 'ilm al Kalam).

His Lost Works

Besides all these immortal jewels, he has written other precious works. Had they not been burnt or shredded during the 1920 raid, they could have been included among the few distinguished treasures of reason and thought. But alas; these were lost during such painful events; therefore, the institute of knowledge has suffered a severe loss. I wish our master's time will extend in order to compensate by bringing them back to life anew. Here we list them as the author does at the end of his commentary on *Al Kalimah Al Gharra'* (The Precious Word):

1) *Sharh Al-Tabsirah* ["Explicating the Tabsirah Book], i.e. Proofs in Fiqh Concerning Enlightening Deductions: They are three bound volumes containing chapters on cleanliness, justice, witness and inheritance.

2) His commentary, in one volume, on the topic of *Istishab* from Shaykh al-Ansari's letters deals with the principles of jurisprudence (Usul al-Fiqh).

3) *Risalah fi Munjazat Al-Marid* ["Dissertation on A Sick Person's Road to Recovery)"] written in a rationalizing approach.

4) *Sabil Al-Muminin*, in three volumes, deals with the topic of Imamate.

5) *Al-Nusus Al-Jaliyyah* ["The Obvious Texts"] also deals with Imamate, and it contains forty texts unanimously agreed upon by Muslims in addition to forty others narrated through Shi'a ways polished by analysis and philosophy.

6) *Tanzil Al-Ayat Al-Bahira* ["Revelation of the Dazzling Verses"] also deals with the topic of Imamate. It is written in one volume based upon one hundred Qur'anic verses revealed in praise of the holy Imams (as) according to sahih books.

7) *Tuhfatul Muhaddithin fima Akhraja 'anhu Al-Sittah minal Muda''afin* ["Ornament of the Entertainers from the hadith Regarded by the Authors of the Six (*sahihs*) as 'Weak'"]. This is a book totally new in its subject matter, one the like of which has never been written before.

8) *Tuhfatul Ashab fi Hukm Ahl al-Kitab* ["The Companions' Ornament in Judging the People of the Book"].

9) *Al-Thari'a* ("The Pretext") is a book rebutting alNabahani's Badi'a.

10) *Al-Majalis Al-Fakhira* ["The Excellent Sessions"] is a four-volume book. Its first volume deals with the Prophet's biography, the second with the biographies of Amirul Muminin,

al-Zahra and al-Hasan (as), the third with the biographies of Imam Husayn (as), and the fourth with the biographies of the nine Imams, Allah's peace be upon all of them.

11) *Mu'allifu Al-Shi'a fi Sadr Al-Islam* ["Shi'a authors at the Dawn of Islam"]. Some of this book's chapters were published in Al-'Irfan magazine of Saida (see Al-'Irfan, Vols. 1 & 2).

12) *Bughyatul Fa'iz fi Naql Al-Jana'iz* ["The Winner's Quest in Coffin Bearing"]. Most of this book's text was published in Al-'Irfan.

13) *Bughyatul Sa'il 'an Lathm Al-Aydi wal Anamil* ["Quest of the Inquirer about Hand and Finger Kissing"]. This is a scholarly thesis in literary and intelligent humour containing eighty traditions from our way and the way of others.

14) *Zakat al-Akhlaq* ["Behavioural Purification"]. Al-'Irfan published some of its chapters.

15) *Al-Fawa'id wal Fara'id* ["The Benefits and the Rareties"] is a useful inclusive book.

16) His commentary on Bukhari's *Sahih*.

17) His commentary on Muslim's *Sahih*.

18) *Al-Asalib Al-Badi'ah fi Rujhan Ma'atim Al-Shi'a*: ["The Witty Methods in the Properiety of Shi'as' Commemorations"] is a book based on logical and traditional proofs, and it is, in its subject matter, a new production.

He has written introductions, besides these, dealing with different topics some of which were lost while others were resurrected and are yet to be finished.

His books are characterized by keen observation, vast investigation, inclusive research, authentic conclusion, good finish, honest quotations and interrelation of chapters in qualities which wear the critic out and challenge the mischievous.

His Manners and Gifts

He is very patient, dignified, open-minded, gentle, brave, and highly-respected. He inspires an awe which forces you to respect and love him even if you do not know him.

He does not compromise justice, nor does he admit relaxation or leniency when an effort is exerted to counter injustice or wrong-doing, yet he remains humble, generous, maintaining a pleasant countenance.

Even-handedness has such a position within him that he is fair to both strangers and kin; doing right is his motive and motto.

He is a model of piety, self-ease, clarity of conscience, and the speaking of what is right. Besides, he is wise in his views, far-sighted. He sifts people's temper and reaches the reality and depth of affairs. He cannot be deceived by appearances, nor can he be cheated out rightly. He does not deviate from accuracy nor be tempted into hypocrisy.

These good manners may have contributed to his accomplishments, influence, and true qualifications. He is, then, counted among the most eloquent Arabs when he talks, the most outspoken when he lectures, the most heart touching when he preaches, the most efficient in implementing the law, the most fair in judgment and clarity of argument, and he is the deepest in philosophy of life.

His Travels

In 1329/1330, he undertook a scholarly visit of Egypt, as we mentioned above. During that visit he met with the most distinguished intellectuals in Egypt headed by Shaykh Salim al-Bishri al-Maliki, the then rector of Al-Azhar Mosque. The outcome of meeting him and corresponding with him is this book which suffices to be the sweet fruit of that visit.

By 1338 A.H., he made his religio-political migration about which you have learned a short while ago. In it he visited

Damascus, Egypt, and Palestine. In all these countries, he reaped the fruits of knowledge and delivered invaluable lectures.

He was the first learned Shi'a to lead the thronged stampeding masses which assembled at the Haram mosque (the Sacred Mosque) in the holy precincts of Mecca for prayers. It was the first time that people in thousands openly prayed behind a Shi'a Imam without resorting to *taqiyya*.

This is why the news of his performing the pilgrimage earned such a great fame that people kept talking about it in all Muslim lands. King Husayn son of 'Ali offered him the best welcome, and they met more than once and together washed the Ka'ba.

By the close of 1355 A.H., he visited the Imams' shrines in Iraq and had a reunion with his family and kinfolk. On the day of his arrival, the Iraqi cabinet ministers, dignitaries, and chiefs, headed by his holiness Sayyid Muhammad Baqir al-Sadr, welcomed him and escorted him the entire distance from Baghdad to Falluja's bridge in motorcades. At Karbala and Najaf, he was met with a magnificent welcome from learned men as well as the general public. The similitude of that fantastic welcome is indeed rare.

I imagine him saying, when he reached the playgrounds of his childhood and youth:

> Tears overcame me when the Tawbad did I see;
> And it glorified the Merciful upon seeing me...

It was only natural that he would burst into eager tears because of his anxiety to see such heart-comforting institutes, and the latter would glorify Allah while welcoming him, ecstatic at his arrival after an absence which lasted for many long years.

Had he not left them satisfied? Had they not acclaimed him when he was filling their halls with the best that fills an institute thronged with outstanding students?

Yes, indeed. They both exchanged passion, eagerness, anxiety and greetings. Such a purely spiritual exchange was reciprocated by all elements of goodness and sincerity at Najaf,

Karbala, Kazimiyya and Samarra'. There were many merry and colourful celebrations from which time had kept him away and obstructed him from seeing them and their distinguished dignitaries.

His meetings with the distinguished pioneers of knowledge and research were full of benefits in the different scholarly branches of knowledge.

He proceeded travelling from Iraq to Iran. In the latter country, he was blessed by visiting the mausoleum of Imam Rida, peace be upon him. While he was en route, he passed by Qum and Tehran and other Iranian cities. In all of those cities, he was met with all sorts of welcome his beloved personality deserved.

His Legacies and Construction Projects

1) He inaugurated his construction projects with a waqf Husayniyya which he built so that people might meet there on different occasions and circumstances to uphold the tenets and receive religious education and spiritual guidance, and also to offer their prayers. Shi'as, when he visited Sur, did not have a mosque there.

2) He erected, in the first stages, six stores at the city's entrance. He had a spacious house built on their rooftops wherein he planned that it would hopefully be converted into the desired school. Unfortunately, the completion of the project was not possible then because of the ruling authority's opposition as well as that of seekers of self-interest who followed its line; therefore, he had to content himself with that portion, waiting for the opportune chance.

3) Over the other side of the building he had a unique club erected which he named Imam Jafar al-Sadiq Club, 22.5 meters long and 15.5 meters wide, which he reserved for celebrations, learning, religious, social and academic occasions. Then he established in 1361 A.H. a school for girls. Like the one for boys, this school implemented a curriculum which promoted the

education of useful topics that would secure a more ideal norm of life.

The location of the school and the club is the best in beauty, landscape and spacious openness. The view is the beautiful water, extending endlessly, and if you are tired of the sea and its waves, look in another direction: towards the plains and mountains embracing the villages as far as your eyes can see. Your sight will wander from here to there, active, dazzled, dreaming of that captivating and enchanting beauty of natural scenery, extending in felicity, roaming unobstructed in pleasure and joy.

If you stand by the row of all these huge adjacent buildings, you will see in them a great structure very well put together, strongly erected, inspiring an awe within you because of their engineered beauty and magnificent design. Then your awe will increasingly intensify when you come to know its fertile output which combines both abundance of quantity with goodness of quality.

All of this, in its completion and perfection, is but a seed, considering the ambition of our master author who purchased to the south of its location a vast tract of land and linked it to the institution in order to complement through it his charitable projects and achieve his Islamic objectives. He hoped that in the end he might lay the foundation of a university that would teach its students the best principles in the widest fields of knowledge. He saw that that way was the best to deal with any imminent danger, to protect the new generation descending from our own to generations which might force it to be an enemy to ours. May Allah take his hands and lead him to whatever brings forth the wellbeing of this life and religion and the welfare of Islam and Muslims; praise be to Allah, Lord of the Universe.

Murtada Al-Yasin,
Kazimiyya, Iraq
1365 A.H./1946 A.D.

Introduction and Foreword

These pages have not been written today, and these thoughts have not been born recently: they have been organized for over quarter of a century; they could have appeared in print sooner barring hostile circumstances and calamities that put strong obstacles in their way. They had, therefore, to remain waiting for a chance to gather whatever limbs they squandered and parts they lost, for the events that delayed their publication did, at the same time, alter their organization.

As for the book's idea, this has long preceded its debates. It shone within my chest ever since my young days just like lightning shining among the clouds, and were boiling in my blood enthusiastically, searching for a straight avenue to stop Muslims at a deadline terminating their chaos and lifting the veil from their vision so that they might look at life more seriously and go back to the roots of their religion as they are enjoined to do. It is only then that they will be able to make their strides to uphold the Rope of Allah all together under the banner which calls unto them to educate themselves and behave as dutiful Brethren strengthening each other.

But the sight of these brethren, who are linked to one another by one principle and one creed, has unfortunately been a violent controversy that gets heated during arguments, just as ignorant folks go to extremes, so much so that it seemed as if controversy in the methods of pursuing knowledge was an etiquette in debating, or a final resort. This, indeed, is enough reason for worry which calls for contemplation. This, indeed, invites grief, agony and sorrow; so, what is the solution? What should be done? These circumstances have been plaguing us for hundreds of years, and these calamities have been endangering us from front and back, right and left. That is a pen twisted with barrenness once and harmed by greed another; partisanship pushes it once and once it permits itself to yield to emotion, and between this and that there is reason for embarrassment; so, what should we do? What is the solution?

I have been fed up with all this, and grief has filled my heart; therefore, I reached Egypt by the close of 1329 A.H. hoping to achieve my objective. I was inspired by the hope that I would succeed in satisfying at least part of my desire and be in direct contact with someone with whom I might exchange my views. I hoped that by discussing useful advice, Allah might assist us in achieving our objectives in the land of Kinana (Egypt) and cure the persisting disease endangering Muslims with tearing them apart and plaguing their groups with dissension. I have been able, Praise to Allah, to achieve that goal, for Egypt is a country which plants knowledge and the latter grows in it nurtured by sincerity and submission to the deep-rooted Truth through the power of evidence. This distinguishes Egypt and puts it even above all its other unique distinctions.

There, my circumstances being good, my mind peaceful, my soul delighted, I was lucky enough to come in contact with one of its distinguished renowned personalities who possessed a broad mind, gentle manners, throbbing heart, vast knowledge and high honour which he rightly enjoyed due to the quality of his religious leadership.

How good are the spirits men of knowledge are known to have, how acceptable their sayings, and how prophetic their manners! As long as an 'alim is so well attired, he will always remain good and prosperous, people will be safe and blessed, and nobody will hesitate to voice his opinion or unveil his thought to him.

That was the renowned dignitary and Imam of Egypt, and such were our meetings for which we thanked the Almighty without an end or limit.

I complained to him about my worries, and he complained to me about similar worries and uneasiness, and it was a right hour for both of us to contemplate upon that which would, by the Will of Allah, unite ourselves and our nation. We have agreed, thereupon, that: both groups, i.e. the Shi'a and the Sunni, are Muslims who indeed follow the right religion of Islam, that they all are in unanimous agreement regarding the Prophet's message, that there is no basic difference among them on fundamental issues which would impair their adherence to the glorious principles of Islam, that there is really no dispute among them about the basic tenets except that which naturally occurs among mujtahids regarding some rules because of the latter's derivations from the Book or the Sunnah, the consensus, or the fourth proof, and that this does not in any way justify such a huge gap or bottomless pit. What then caused all of this dispute of which the flashes have been sparkling ever since there were two nouns: "Sunni" and "Shi'a"?

If we scrutinize the Islamic history and discern the beliefs, views and precepts which bred therein, we will come to know that the causing factor for this dissension is agitation for a particular belief, a defense of a theory, or partisanship for an opinion, and that the greatest dispute which has occurred to the nation is the dispute about Imamate, for there have never been more swords unsheathed because of an Islamic principle as they have been because of Imamate. The issue of Imamate, then, has been among the most direct factors causing such a dissension. The various generations that differed among themselves concerning Imamate became used to being fond of such fanaticism, and such partisanship was created without precautions or care. Had either of these groups looked into the explanations of the other in understanding eyes, not in those of a cursing antagonist, the truth would have then become very clear and morning light could have been noticed by all those who can see.

We have made it incumbent upon us to deal with this issue by looking into the arguments of both groups in order to thoroughly comprehend them, without being motivated by our own personal inclinations derived from environment, habit, or custom. Instead, we must be stripped of all emotions and fanaticism and aim at reaching the truth from its generally acclaimed route, and touch upon it. This may attract the attention of Muslims, bring tranquillity of mind with its decided facts from us to them and put, by the Will of Allah, a definite deadlock.

We decided, therefore, that he would present his own question in writing so that I would provide him with my written answer stating the correct conditions and supported them by either reason or authenticated quotations from both groups.

Thus were all of our debates conducted, through the help of Allah, the Sublime and Mighty. Later on, we wanted to have them published so that we could enjoy the fruits of our labour purely seeking the pleasure of Allah, the Exalted, the Sublime, but cruel days and overcoming fates discouraged us, and maybe that was, after all, for the best.

I do not claim that these pages are confined to the texts composed then by us, or that any of the forthcoming statements is not written by my own pen. The circumstances that delayed their publication also altered their organization, as we said above. But the sessions concerning the issues we debated are included herein verbatim with some necessary additions called forth by counsel and guidance, or they may have been caused by the sequence of discussion without violating our mutual agreement.

I have today the same wish I had yesterday: that this book will cause reform and goodness. If it wins the attention and acceptance of Muslims, then that is a grace from my Lord, and that is what I wish for my labour to accomplish: I want nothing but reform, as much as I can get, and my success depends upon Allah; in Him do I trust, and unto Him do I return.

I present my book to each and every man of reason who pursues knowledge, to the keen researcher who is acquainted with the intricate facts concerning the quest for knowledge, and to the learned outspoken scholar whose speech is an authority on the sayings and practices of the Prophet (s), to the philosopher who has mastered the science of speech, and to each and every educated youth who is free from all chains or shackles, who can be depended upon for the new life of freedom: if all of these accept it, realizing the advantage therein, then I am most pleased.

I have painstakingly produced this book by providing its answers in the best way from all aspects, aiming thereby at inspiring the fair-minded people with its thought and taste with evidences which do not leave out any probability, and arguments which do not permit any loophole. I have paid a special attention to the authentic evident texts and the sayings and practices of the Prophet (s), a care which has made this book suffice for a library entirely well-equipped with the most precious books on Islamic theology, traditions, biographies, and the like. The latter are all related to this most significant subject. I have applied therein a philosophy which is very well balanced and authentic, and methods which force anyone who is acquainted with such books to walk behind this work while they, I mean the lovers of the truth, are its own followers from its beginning till the last paragraph. If my book, therefore, is accepted by fair-minded readers, then this is exactly what I desire and for which I thank Allah.

As regarding my own self, I am well satisfied with this book, pleased with my life after it. It is, I believe, a work which must make me forget all that which has made me fed up: life's heavy burdens, the impoverishing worries of time, and the enemy about whom I complain to none but Almighty Allah; He alone is his Judge and Muhammad (s) his adversary. Forget about the looting called for in its own quarters...I have also endured the calamities pouring like a flood from every direction, bearing woeful presentiments, combined with uneasiness and grief. But my life, which will be immortalized through this book, is one of mercy in this life and the life to come; within it my soul has been pleased and my conscience eased. Therefore, I implore to Allah to take my labour with acceptance and overlook my mistakes and faults; my reward for this book will Insha'Allah be the benefit and guidance of believers.

> Those who believe and do good deeds: their Lord guides them through their faith; rivers flow from beneath them in the Gardens of Immortality; their prayer therein is: "Lord! Glory to Thee!" and their greeting has peace therein, and they conclude their prayers with: "All praise is due to Allah, Lord of the worlds." (Qur'an, 10:9-10)

Letter 1
Dhul Qi'da 6, 1329 A.H.

I. Greeting the Debater

Peace and Allah's mercy and blessings be upon the learned honourable Shaykh 'Abdul Husayn Sharafuddin Al-Musawi.

I have not been acquainted yet with Shi'as' conscience, nor have I tested their manners, for I have never kept company with any of them, nor come to know the traditions of their folks. But I have always been eager to debate with their renowned scholars, anxious to mix with their commoners, in order to sift their trends and attempt to know their inclinations, until Allah helped me stand by the spacious shore of your ocean of knowledge, and you let me taste of your brimful cup; Allah helped me quench my thirst. I swear by the city of Allah's knowledge, your Chosen Grandfather, and by its gate, your pleased ancestor, that I have never tasted anything so satisfying to the thirsty, and so curing to the sick, like your overflowing stream. I used to hear that you, Shi'a folks, prefer to avoid your brethren, the Sunnis, and keep away from them, and that you find your ease in loneliness, resorting to isolation, and so on and so forth. But I have found your person to be gently charming, keen in debating, courteous, strong in argument, well humoured, honest in duel, appreciated in misunderstanding, cherished in competition; therefore, I have found the Shi'a a pleasant fragrance to sit with, and the quest of every man of letters.

II. Asking Permission to Debate

While standing by the shore of your tumultuous sea, I ask your permission to swim in it and dive deeply in pursuit of its jewels. If you grant me your permission, we will dig deeply for the root causes of particulars and obscurities which have long been agitating me; if not, it is entirely up to you. In raising my questions, I do not look for a fault or a defect, nor do I oppose, nor refute; instead, I have only one quest: searching for the truth. When truth is manifest, it then deserves to be followed; if not, I am only like one (poet) who said:

We in what we have, and you in what you offer,
Are all satisfied, even when our views differ.

I will, if you permit me, confine my debate with you to two topics: one deals with the sect's Imamate, in its roots and branches,[1] and the other deals with the general Imamate, i.e. succession to the Messenger of Allah, peace be upon him and his progeny. My signature at the close of all my debates shall be "S," and let yours be "Sh." In advance, I solicit your forgiveness for every fault, and peace be with you.

Sincerely,
S

Letter 2
Dhul Qi'da 6, 1329 A.H.

I. Greetings Reciprocated

Peace of Allah be with Maulana Shaykh al-Islam, His mercy and blessings.

Your very kind letter has granted me and bestowed upon me so many graces for which the tongue can hardly thank you enough, nor can it fulfil a portion of its duty even in a lifetime.

You have placed your hopes on me and brought me your request while you yourself are the hope of anyone with a quest, the refuge of whoever seeks refuge. I myself have come to you all the way from Syria in order to relish your knowledge and seek your favours, and I am sure I will leave you strong in optimism except if Allah wills otherwise.

---

[1] Having sought permission to debate, he starts explaining the debate's subject-matter, thus demonstrating his moral accomplishments and excellence as far as the norm of debate is concerned. The use of the initials "S" and "Sh" is an obviously suitable vehicle for carrying such a debate on, since "S" denotes his name "Salim" and his being a Sunni, while "Sh" signifies the author's surname "Sharafud-Din," and his being a Shi'a.

II. Permission to Debate Granted

You have asked permission to speak up. You have the right to bid and forbid. Say whatever you will: you have the favour; your judgment is final, your verdict fair, and peace be with you.

Sincerely,
Sh

Letter 3
Dhul Qi'da 7, 1329 A.H.

I. Why do Shi'as not Uphold the Majority's Sects?

I ask you now about the reasons why you (Shias) do not follow the sect of the majority of Muslims, I mean the sect of al-Ash'ari in determining the principles of the creed, and the four sects in its branches. Muslims agreed to abide by them in each time and clime, unanimously acclaiming their founder's fairness and ijtihad, their trustworthiness, piety, renunciation of worldly riches, straightforwardness, good morals and lofty status in knowledge and deeds.

II. The Need for Unity

How great our need today for unity and uniformity is! This can be achieved through your own adherence to these sects according to the general consensus of Muslims, especially when the religion's enemies have made up their minds to harm us by all possible means. They have set their minds and hearts upon such goals while Muslims are heedless, as if they are overcome by slumber, assisting their enemies against their own selves by letting them split their own ranks and tear their unity apart through partisanship and fanaticism, leaving them disunited, divided, leading each other astray, excommunicating one another; hence, wolves preyed on us while dogs coveted our flesh.

III. Unity Achieved Only by Adhering to the Majority's Sects

Do you see other than what we state here, may Allah lead your steps to unite our ranks? Tell me, for you will be heard when you speak and obeyed when you command, and peace be with you.

Sincerely,
S

Letter 4
Dhul Qi'da 4, 1329 A.H.

I. Juristic Proofs Mandate Adherence to the Sect of Ahl Al-Bayt

1) Our adherence, in the principles of the creed, to a sect other than that of al-Ash'ari, and our following in the branches of Islam of a sect other than those four sects, has never been due to partisanship nor fanaticism, nor has it been because of doubting the ijtihad of the Imams of these sects, of their fair mindedness, trustworthiness, integrity, or loftiness in knowledge and deeds.

Juristic proofs, rather, have mandated upon us to follow the sect of the Imams from the Household of Prophethood, the cradle of the Message, and the place the angels frequent, the abode of revelation and inspiration. We have always, therefore, referred to them in order to comprehend all matters related to the creed's branches and doctrines, in the roots and in the bases of fiqh, in the knowledge of ethics, behaviour, and manners. We have done all this in accordance with the judgment of evidence and proof, following the Sunnah of the Master of Prophets and Messengers, peace of Allah be upon him and all his progeny.

Had the proofs allowed us to differ from the Imams of Muhammad's progeny, or had we been able to achieve nearness to Allah, Glory to Him, by following others' sects, we would then have followed in the general public's footsteps, asserting the friendship and strengthening the ties of fraternity. On the contrary, positive proofs stand in the believer's way, diverting him from following his own inclinations.

II. There is No Proof for Mandating Adherence to the Majority's Sects

Still, the majority cannot prove that their own sect must be preferred over those of others, let alone making it obligatory. We have looked into Muslims' pretexts as one inquiring in depth with keen eyes, but we have found no proof for your argument except what you mentioned of their ijtihad, trustworthiness, fair mindedness and loftiness.

You, however, know that ijtihad, trustworthiness, fair mindedness and loftiness of status are not a monopoly of them only; therefore, how, since the case is as such, can their sects be obligatory by your merely pointing them out?

I do not think that there is anyone who dares to advocate their preference in knowledge or deeds over our Imams who are the purified 'itra, the nation's life-boats, the Gate of Salvation, the security against dissension in religion, the flags of its guidance, the descendants of the Messenger of Allah and his remnant in his nation. He, Allah's peace be upon him and his progeny, has said: "Do not go ahead of them lest you should perish, nor should you lag behind them lest you should perish. Do not teach them, for they are more learned than you." But it is the dictates of politics at the dawn of Islam.

I wonder about your claim that the good previous generations adhered to those sects, finding them the fairest and the best of sects, and that they agreed to adhere to them in every time and clime. You say so as if you do not know that our predecessors, the good past generations that followed the progeny of Muhammad and that, literally, constituted half the Muslim population, followed only the faith of the Imams among the descendants of Muhammad, peace of Allah be upon him and his progeny. They did not find for it any substitute, and they have been this way ever since the days of 'Ali and Fatima, when neither al-Ash'ari nor any Imam of the other four sects, or even their fathers, existed, as you very well know.

III. Generations of the first three centuries Never Knew Those Sect.

The generations of the first three centuries, then, never followed any of those sects at all. Where were those sects during those three generations, the best generations ever? Al-Ash'ari was born in 270 A.H. and died in 320 A.H. Ibn Hanbal was born in 164 A.H. and died in 241 A.H. Al-Shafi'i was born in 150 A.H. and died in 204 A.H. Malik was born in 95 A.H.[1] and died in 179 A.H. Abu Hanifah was born in 80 A.H. and died in 150 A.H. Shi'as follow the sect of the Imams from the Prophet's Household, and the household surely know what their house contains. Non-Shi'as follow the sects of the learned sahabah (companions) and tabi'in; so, what makes it "mandatory" on all Muslims, after those three centuries had gone by, to follow those sects instead of the one followed before them? What made them divert their attention from those who were peers only to the Book of Allah and its own companions, the descendants of the Messenger of Allah and his trustees, the nation's ark of salvation, the leaders, the security, and the Gate of Salvation?

IV. Possibility of Ijtihad

What caused the door of ijtihad to be shut in the face of Muslims after it had been kept widely open during the first three centuries other than resorting to reluctance, comfort, laziness, the acceptance of deprivation and the satisfaction with ignorance? Who would permit himself, knowingly or unknowingly, to say that Allah, Dignity and Glory to Him, has not sent the best of His Messengers and Prophets with the best of His religions and codes, nor has He revealed unto him His best Books and Tablets, judgment and doctrines, nor has He completed His Religion for him and perfected His blessing unto him, nor has He taught him the knowledge of the past and the present, except for the sole purpose that the whole matter would end to the Imams of those sects to monopolize for their own selves? They would then forbid all others from acquiring it from any other source, as if the Islamic faith, in its Book and Sunnah, and in all other signs and testaments, a property of their own, and that they forbade faring with it in any way contrary to their own opinions... Were they the Prophets' heirs,

---

[1] In his biography of Malik, Ibn Khallikan indicates in his *Al-a'yan* that the man lingered in his mother's womb for almost three years. The same is mentioned by Ibn Qutaybah who includes Malik among wise sages on page 170 of his book *Al-Ma'arif*, recounting him on page 198 among men whose mother's pregnancy outlasted the normal period.

or had Allah sealed through them the successors and Imams, or taught them the knowledge of the past and the present, and that He bestowed upon them what He had never bestowed upon anybody else among all human beings?

No! They were just like many others, pillars and caretakers of knowledge, ministers and callers. Those who call for knowledge are far above closing its doors against others or forbidding others from reaching it. They never curb the minds, nor confine public attention only to their own selves, nor can they seal people's hearts or make others deaf, blind, dumb, handcuffed, or chained. This can never be attributed to them except as a liar's allegation, and their own statements bear witness to ours.

V. Unity can be achieved by Respecting Ahl al-Bayt's sect

Let us now concentrate on the matter to which you attracted our attention: the unity of Muslims. What I see is that this matter does not depend on Shi'as forsaking their faith, nor the Sunnis forsaking their own. Asking Shi'as to do so without asking others (Sunnis) to do likewise is to prefer without preponderance, or even to favour the less preferable. It is demanding what is beyond one's capacity as it is known from our Introduction.

Yes. Unity and uniformity can be achieved if you release Ahl Al-Bayt's sect and view it as you view any of your own sects so that the Shafi'is, Hanafis, Malikis and Hanbalis may consider the followers of Ahl Al-Bayt just as they consider each other. Only then can the unity of Muslims be achieved, and they will be unified in one fold.

The difference among Sunni sects is not less than it is between the Sunni and Shi'a schools of thought as thousands of books on the principles and branches of the creed of both groups testify; therefore, why have several people among you condemned the Shi'as for differing from the Sunnis? Why have they not, by the same token, condemned the Sunnis for differing from the Shi'as, or even for differing from one another? If sects can be four, why cannot they be five? How come it is alright to have four sects but not five? How can four sects be considered as "unifying" Muslims, and when they increase to five, unity is shattered and Muslims are divided unto themselves? I wish when you invited us to "sectarian unity" you also invited the followers of the four sects to the same. The latter will be a lot easier for you and for them. But why have you singled us out for your invitation anyway? Do you find the followers of Ahl Al-Bayt breaking the unity while the followers of others unite the hearts and determination even though their sects and minds are different, their tastes and inclinations are numerous? I think of you to be above that, knowing your love for your kinfolk, and peace be with you.

Sincerely,
Sh

Letter 5
Dhul-Qi'da 9, 1329 A.H.

I. Admitting Our Argument

Your letter has been quite clear, very well arranged, praiseworthy. It is eloquent, powerful in determination, and strong in argument. It spares no attempt to prove that it is not compulsory to follow the majority's sects in the principles and branches of religion, saving no effort to confirm that the doors of ijtihad must remain open. Your letter, therefore, is strong in both matters, correct in proving each one of them, and we do not deny your careful research in their respect, your clarification of their obscurities, although we really were not acquainted with them, and our view in their regard is identical to yours.

II. Asking for Detailed Proof

We had asked you about your reason for not accepting the sects followed by the Muslim majority, and your answer was that because of "judicial proofs," whereas you were expected to explain that in detail. Could you please yield now to explaining them with positive proofs from the Book (Qur'an) or the Sunnah which, as you mentioned, divert the believer from following his own inclinations? Thank you, and peace be with you.

Sincerely,
S

Letter 6
Dhul-Qi'da 12, 1329 A.H.

You, thanks to Allah, can be convinced by a mere hint, without the need for an explanation, and you are above doubting the very fact that the purified offspring ('itra) are superior to all others. Their case is quite clear: they have surpassed those with qualifications and have distinguished themselves from seemingly equal peers. They have carried from the Messenger of Allah, peace be upon him and his progeny, the knowledge of the prophets, and from him have they digested secular and religious jurisdictions.

I. References to Proofs Mandating Following the 'Itra

The Prophet, hence, has made them equal only to the Glorious Book and set them models of conduct for those endowed with reason, and the ark of safety when hypocrisy with its tumultuous waves overwhelms the security of the nation, safeguarding it against dissension if the tempests of division rage, the Gate of Salvation: whoever enters it is forgiven, and the strong Rope of Allah which is unbreakable.

II. The Commander of the Faithful (as) Invites to Ahl Al-Bayt's Sect

The Commander of the Faithful is quoted in sermon 86 in Nahjul Balaghah as saying:

> "'Where are you heading (Qur'an, 81:26),' and 'where are you straying (Qur'an, 6:95, 10:34, 35:3, 40:62),'since the flags are poised up high, the Signs are clear, and the lighthouse is erected? So, where are you straying? Nay! How can you be blindfolded while you have among you the household ('itra) of your Prophet? They are the reins of righteousness, the religion's flags, and the tongues of truth; therefore, accord them as you accord the Qur'an and approach them as thirsty camels approach the water. O people! Take this[1] from the last of the Prophets, Allah's peace be upon him and his progeny: 'whoever among us passes away, he is not really dead, and

---

[1] He means to say: "Learn this from the Messenger of Allah, peace be upon him and his progeny: 'When a member of the Prophet's Household dies, he in reality does not die," that is, his soul remains shining in the real world. This is also stated by Shaykh Muhammad 'Abdoh and others.

whoever disintegrates (after dying) from among us does not really disintegrate; therefore, do not say what you do not know, for there is the greatest truth in what you deny. Accept the argument of one against whom you have no argument and it is: 'Have I not dealt with you according to the Greatest Weight^2 (Qur'an)? Have I not left among you the Lesser Weight (Ahl Al-Bayt) and laid firm among you the flags of faith?'"

He, peace be upon him, said, in sermon 96 of Nahjul-Balaghah, "Behold the Household of your Prophet; emulate their example and follow in their footsteps, for they shall never take you out of guidance, nor shall they ever bring you back into destruction; halt when they halt, and rise when they rise, and do not go ahead of them lest you should stray, nor should you lag behind them lest you should perish." He, peace be upon him, has mentioned them once, as stated in sermon 237 of Nahjul-Balaghah, saying: "They are the life of knowledge and the death of ignorance; their forbearance informs you of their knowledge, and their outward appearance informs you of their conscience. Their silence indicates the wisdom of their speech. They neither differ from truth, nor do they differ among themselves about it. They are the pillars of Islam and the gateways to salvation. Through them, justice was achieved and wrongdoing was removed, and its tongue was uprooted. They comprehended the creed with care and concern, not like hearing and reporting, for the 'reporters' of knowledge are many indeed, but those who safeguard it are few." He, peace be upon him, as stated in sermon 153 in Nahjul-Balaghah, has also said, "His offspring ('itra) is the best, and his family is the best. His tree is the best of trees: it was planted in the

---

^{2} The Commander of the Faithful (as) acted upon the Greater Weighty Thing, namely the Holy Qur'an, leaving the Lesser Weighty Things, i.e. both his sons, behind. It is also said that his progeny are the models of conduct for others, as stated by Shaykh Muhammad 'Abdoh and other commentators of *Hahjul Balaghah*.

sacred place (Haram), and it grew like a vine; it has long branches and its fruit is not unattainable."

He, peace be upon him, is quoted in sermon 153 of Nahjul-Balaghah saying: "We are the banner, the companions, the trustees and the gates. Houses are not supposed to be approached except through their gates: whoever approaches them otherwise is called a thief," until he said, describing the purified offspring ('itra), "They are the vital portions of the Qur'an, and they are the treasures of the Merciful. They tell the truth when they speak, or when they remain silent; none can speak ahead of them. Therefore, let the forerunner speak the truth to his people, maintaining his reason."

He has said in sermon 146 of Nahjul-Balaghah: "You should know that you will never know guidance unless you know who abandons it, nor will you abide by the Book (Qur'an) unless you know who contradicts it, and you will never uphold it unless you know who has discarded it; so, seek that from those who possess it, for they are the life of knowledge and the death of ignorance. They are the ones whose judgment informs you of their knowledge, their silence of their power of speech, their outer appearance of their inner selves; they neither violate the religion, nor do they differ among themselves about it, while it is among them a truthful witness and a silent speaker."

There are many similarly impressive statements of his, peace be upon him, in this regard; consider this one which is excerpted from sermon 4 in Nahjul-Balaghah: "Through us you received guidance in the darkness, ascending the zenith of nobility, and through us you reached the light and dissipated the gloomy night. May the ears that do not listen to the summoner be deafened."[3] He is quoted in sermon 104 of Nahjul-Balaghah saying: "O people! Secure your light from the flame of the lamps of a preacher who

---

[3] In his commentary, Shaykh Muhammad 'Abdoh says: "The 'sarar,' pronounced like 'sahab' and 'kitab,' is the last night of the lunar month during which the moon disappears. The meaning would be: 'You entered into the dawn,' meaning 'You used to live in utter darkness, the darkness of polytheism and misguidance, till you emerged into the light through our guidance and instruction,' a reference to Muhammad, peace be upon him and his progeny, and his cousin Imam (as), the one who supported his mission.

follows what he preaches, and drink from a spring cleansed from impurity."

He has also said the following in sermon 108: "We are the tree of Prophethood, the place of the Message, the ones to whom the angels make a pilgrimage, the treasures of knowledge, the springs of wisdom. Our supporter and lover awaits the mercy, while our enemy or antagonist us awaits the wrath."[4]

Among what he has said in this regard is sermon 143 of Nahjul-Balaghah wherein he says: "Where are those who claimed to be deeply versed in knowledge other than our own selves?[5] It is a lie and a transgression against us, for Allah has raised us high while putting them down; He bestowed upon us while depriving them, and He permitted us to enter (in the fortress of knowledge) while turning them out. Through us, guidance is achieved and blindness is removed. Surely the Imams from Quraysh have been planted in Hashim's loins. Imamate can never fit anyone else, nor can government either." Then he stated: "But they preferred a speedy gain to a later one, forsaking a pure well to drink from an impure one," up to the end of his statement. He has also said at the conclusion of khutba (sermon) 189 of Nahjul-Balaghah: "Whoever among you dies on his bed knowing the rights of his Lord and knowing the rights of His Messenger and his family (Ahl Al-Bayt) dies as a martyr, and his reward will be incumbent upon Allah, and he deserves the reward of what good deeds he has intended to do: his own intention will make up for his use of his sword (in jihad)."

Also, he, peace be upon him, has said: "We are the virtuous; our descendants are the descendants of Prophets; our party is the party of Allah, the Sublime, the Glorified, while the transgressing

---

[4] See the conclusion of sermon 105, page 214, Vol. 1, of *Nahjul Balaghah*. Ibn 'Abbas has said: "We are members of the Prophet's Household whose homes are the visiting places of the angels, the Ahl al-Bayt of the Messenger of Allah, and members of the household of mercy and knowledge." He is quoted saying so by a group of most reliable Sunni traditionists and as stated at the conclusion of his chapter on the characteristics of Ahl al-Bayt (as), on page 142 of Ibn Hajar's *Al-Sawa'iq al-Muhriqa*.

[5] See also Qur'an, 3:7 and 4:162

party is the devil's; whoever equates us with our enemy is certainly not of us."⁶

Imam al-Mujtaba Abu Muhammad al-Hasan, the patient, master of the youths of Paradise (as), has said the following in one of his sermons: "Fear Allah regarding us, for we are your rulers."⁷

III. Relevant Statement of Imam Zainul'Abidin

Whenever Imam Abu Muhammad, 'Ali son of al-Husayn Zainul'Abidin, master of those who prostrate in prayer, used to recite this verse of the Almighty: "O ye who believe! Fear Allah and be with the Truthful," he would make a lengthy invocation to Allah containing his plea to be included among "the Truthful" to attain the high ranks. He would then count the calamities and innovations of the group that split from the Imams of Faith and the Tree of Prophethood. Then he would say: "Some people went as far as underestimating us, making excuses for the Qur'anic verses which seem to them to be alike, giving their own interpretation thereof, and casting doubts about the transmitted narrations in our honour," until he would say: "With whom shall people in this nation seek refuge, since the pillars of this creed have been forgotten and the nation has divided upon itself with dissension, each party accusing the other of kufr, while Allah says: 'Do not be like those who became divided and disagreed (with each other) even after receiving the Clear Evidences (Qur'an, 3:104)?'

Who can be trusted to convey the Divine proofs and interpret the Judgment other than the peers of the Qur'an and the descendants of the Imams of Guidance, the lamps amidst the darkness, those whom Allah made as His Arguments against His servants? He has never left His creation alone without a Proof. Do you know them or find them except from the branches of the

---

⁶ This statement is quoted by many authors, including Ibn Hajar at the conclusion of his chapter on the characteristics of Ahl al-Bayt (as) near the conclusion of page 142 of *Al-Sawa'iq al-Muhriqa* where he makes quite a few lies about them, being grossly unfair to them.

⁷ Refer to it at the conclusion of his chapter on the will of the Prophet (s) in their regard on page 137 of Ibn Hajar's *Al-Sawa'iq al-Muhriqa*.

Blessed Tree, the remnant of the Elite from whom Allah has removed all impurity, purifying them with a perfect purification, clearing them from sinning and decreeing their love in His Book?"

That was his own speech, peace be upon him, verbatim.[8] Look into it and into our quotations from the speech of the Commander of the Faithful; you will find them both representing the Shi'a School of Muslim Thought in this regard very clearly. Consider this much of their speech as a specimen for all such speeches of the Imams from Ahl al-Bayt. They all are unanimous in this respect, and our *sahih* books quoting them are *mutawatir* (consecutively reported), and peace be with you.

Sincerely,
Sh

---

[8] Refer to it on page 90 of *Al-Sawa'iq al-Muhriqa* where Ibn Hajar explains the meaning of the fifth verse: "And uphold Allah's rope all of you together" as one of many others which he explains in Section 1, Chapter 11.

Letter 7
Dhul-Qi'da 13, 1329 A.H.

I. Requesting Proofs from Statements by Allah and His Messenger

Bring the proofs from the statements of Allah and His Messenger bearing witness to the mandatory allegiance to the Imams among the Ahl Al-Bayt exclusively, and leave aside the speech of anyone else in this respect except those of Allah and His Messenger.

II. Proofs from Ahl Al-Bayt are Circumventive

Your Imams' statements cannot serve as arguments against their rivals, and such an argument creates a logical cycle, as you know, and peace be with you.

Sincerely,
S

Letter 8
Dhul-Qi'da 1329

I. Overlooking Our Previous Statements

We have not neglected deriving our proofs from the traditions of the Prophet, peace and blessings of Allah be upon him and his progeny. As a matter of fact, we referred to them at the beginning of our letter which clearly stated that following the Imams from Ahl Al-Bayt exclusively is mandatory. We did so when we stated that he, peace be upon him and his progeny, had compared them with the Glorious Book, setting them as a model for those endowed with reason, equating them with the ark of salvation, the nation's security, the gate of salvation - all in reference to and quotations from the well known clear texts in the *sahih* books. We have also said that you would be satisfied with the hint instead of the details, without the need for further explanations.

II. Error in Necessity of (Logical) Cycle

The statements of our Imams, then, as we have explained, do fit to be used as an argument against their opponents, and using it as such a manner cannot be regarded as a (vicious) cycle, as you yourself know.

III. Hadith of the Two Weighty Things

Take, for example, the statements of the Prophet, peace and blessings of Allah be upon him and his progeny, to which we referred whereby he struck an awe in the heart of the ignorant, calling upon the indifferent, as quoted by al-Tirmizi and al-Nisa'i from Jabir and they, in turn, are quoted by al-Muttaqi al-Hindi at the beginning of his chapter on those who uphold the Book and the Sunnah in his work *Kanzul 'Ummal*, Vol. 1, page 44, saying:

"O people! I am leaving with you the Book of Allah and my household ('itra), my family (my Ahl Al-Bayt). As long as you uphold them, you shall never go astray."

He has also said:

"I have left with you that which, as long as you uphold, you shall never let you stray after me: Allah's Book, a Rope extending from heavens to earth, and my 'itra, my Ahl Al-Bayt. These twain shall never separate from one another till they reach me by the Pool; therefore, see how you succeed me in faring with them."[1]

He, peace be upon him and his progeny, has also said:

"I am leaving among you two successors: the Book of Allah, a rope extending from heavens to earth - or between heavens and earth - , and my household ('itra) from my family (Ahl Al-Bayt);

---

[1] Al-Tirmizi quotes it from Zayd ibn Arqam. It is hadith 874 of the ahadith quoted in, on p. 44, Vol. 1, of *Kanz al-'Ummal*.

they shall never separate from each other until they reach me by the Pool."²

He, peace be upon him and his progeny, also said:

"I am leaving among you the Two Weighty Things: the Book of Allah and my Ahl Al-Bayt; they shall never separate from each other till they reach me at the Pool."³

He, peace be upon him, has said:

"Methinks I am going to be called upon and shall answer the call, and I am leaving among you the Two Weighty Things, the Book of Allah Almighty and my offspring, my Ahl Al-Bayt. The Sublime and Omniscient has informed me that they shall never part from each other till they reach me by the Pool; so, see how you succeed me in faring with them."⁴

Having returned from the Farewell Pilgrimage, he, peace be upon him and his progeny, camped at Ghadir Khumm and ordered the area underneath a few huge trees to be swept clean then said in his sermon:

"It seems as if I am going to be called upon and shall answer the call, and I am leaving with you the Two Weighty Things, one

---

² Imam Ahmad includes it among the ahadith narrated by Zayd ibn Thabit from two sources one of which is stated at the beginning of page 182, and the other at the conclusion of page 189, Vol. 5, and also by Ibn Abu Shaybah, Abu Ya'li, and Ibn Sa'd, from Abu Sa'id. It is hadith 945 on p. 47, Vol. 1, of *Kanz al-'Ummal*.

³ It is included by al-Hakim on page 148, Vol. 3, of *Al-Mustadrak*. The author comments thus: "This is one hadith the narrators of which are trustworthy according to both Shaykhs, though the latter did not transmit it." Al-Dhahabi includes it in his abridged volume of *Al-Mustadrak*, admitting its authenticity due to the endorsement of both Shaykhs.

⁴ Included by Imam Ahmad in the hadith narrated by Abu Sa'id al-Khudri from two sources one of which is mentioned on page 17, and the other at the end of page 26, Vol. 3, of *Al-Musnad*. It is also quoted by Ibn Abu Shaybah, Abu Ya'li, and Ibn Sa'd from Abu Sa'id. It is hadith 945 as listed in page 47, Vol. 1, of *Kanz al-'Ummal*.

of which is greater than the other: the Book of Allah Almighty, and my Household; so, see how you succeed me in faring with them, for they shall never separate from each other until they reach me at the Pool."

Then he (s) added the following:

"Allah, the Exalted and the Sublime, is my Master, and I am the master of every believer." Having said so, he took 'Ali's hand and said: "To whomsoever I have been a master, this 'Ali is his master. O Allah! Befriend whosoever befriends 'Ali, and be the enemy of whosoever opposes him, etc."[5]

'Abdullah ibn Hantab has said: "The Messenger of Allah (s) delivered a sermon to us at Al-Juhfa wherein he asked us: 'Don't I have authority over your own selves more than you yourselves do?' Attendants there answered: 'Yes, indeed, O Messenger of Allah!' Then he said: 'I shall then question you about these two: the Qur'an and my 'itra.'"[6]

IV. Its Tawatur

The *sahih* books which deem it mandatory to follow the Two Weighty Things are successive through more than twenty companions who all are in consensus in this regard. The Messenger

---

[5] It is sequentially quoted by al-Hakim from Zayd ibn Arqam on page 109, Vol. 3, of *Al-Mustadrak*. The author adds: "This hadith is authentic according to both Shaykhs who did not narrate it in its entirety." He quotes it from another source from Zayd ibn Arqam on page 533, Vol. 3, of his *Al-Mustadrak*, adding: "This hadith is narrated by reliable narrators, yet they (both Shaykhs) did not publish it themselves." Al-Dhahabi has included it in his *Talkhis al-Mustadrak*, admitting its authenticity.
[6] Al-Tabrani has included it, as referred to in Nabhani's *Al-Arba'in*, and in Sayyti's *Ihya'ul Mayyit*. You are aware of the fact that his *khutba*, peace be upon him and his progeny, was not confined to this much, for nobody who narrates just this much can claim that he had heard it. But politics tied many tongues of traditionists and chained the pens of many writers. In spite of all this, such a drop of the ocean suffices; praise be to Allah.

of Allah, peace be upon him and his progeny, has emphasized these things on numerous occasions: on Ghadir Khumm's Day, on the 'Arafat day of his Farewell Pilgrimage, after leaving Taif, from his pulpit in Medina, and inside his blessed chamber during his sickness, when the room was full of his companions. He said in the latter incident: "O people! I feel I am going to die very soon, and I had previously informed you as my duty, and to leave no excuse for you, that: I am leaving with you the Book of Allah, the Glorious and Mighty, and my 'itra, my Ahl Al-Bayt." Having finished, he took 'Ali's hand and lifted it saying: "This 'Ali is with the Qur'an, and the Qur'an is with 'Ali: they shall never separate from one another till they reach me by the Pool."[7]

A learned group among the majority has admitted the above. Even Ibn Hajar, quoting the tradition of the Two Weighty Things, says, "Be informed, then, that the tradition calling for upholding both of them comes through numerous ways narrated by more than twenty companions." Further he says, "Here a doubt arises about when he said so. Some traditionists say he said so at Arafat during the Farewell Pilgrimage and others that he said so in Medina when he was sick, while his room was crammed with his companions. Another group say that he made that statement at the Khumm swamp, and in yet another that he made it, by way of preaching, after having left T'aif as mentioned above." Ibn Hajar furthermore says, "There is no contradiction here, for there is no objection to his repeating it at those places, and at others, out of his own concern for the unassailable Book and the Purified 'itra," up to the end of his statement.[8]

Suffices the Imams from the Purified 'itra the fact that their rank with Allah is similar to that of the Book which falsehood

---

[7] Refer to it at the conclusion of Section 2, Chapter 9, of *Al-Sawa'iq al-Muhriqa* by Ibn Hajar, after the forty ahadith referred to in that Section on page 57.
8 Refer to it in the exegesis of the fourth chapter:
"And stop them, for they shall be questioned (Qur'an, 37:24),"
which is quoted in Section One, Chapter 11, of *Al-Sawa'iq al-Muhriqa*, at the conclusion of page 89.

cannot approach from front or from back. This must be sufficient testimony that takes people by the neck and obligates them to abide by their sect. A true Muslim does not accept any substitute for the Book of Allah; therefore, how can he deviate from the path of those who are its own peers?

V. Non-Adherents to the 'Itra Shall Stray

The gist of his saying "I am leaving unto you that which, as long as you uphold to it, shall never let you stray: the Book of Allah and my 'itra" is that anyone who does not uphold both of them spontaneously will eventually stray. This is supported by his saying, peace be upon him and his progeny, in the tradition of the Two Weighty Things, as Tabrani narrates it, "Do not go ahead of them else you should perish, and do not teach them for they are more learned than you." Ibn Hajar has said: "In his statement, peace be upon him and his progeny, 'Do not go ahead of them else you should perish, and do not teach them for they are more learned than you,' there is proof that whoever among them is elevated to high offices and religious vocations must be preferred over all others," up to the end of his statement.[9]

---

[9] Refer to it in the chapter dealing with the Prophet's will on page 135 of *Al-Sawa'iq al-Muhriqa*, then ask him why he preferred to follow al-Ash'ari in the roots of religion, and the four jurists in its branches, and how he came to consider as superior to them in the narration of hadith men like 'Umran ibn Hattan and his likes among the Kharijites, favouring over them in exegesis Muqatil ibn Sulayman, the Murji'ite who believes that Allah has a physical form, and favoured to them in the sciences of ethics, etiquette, conduct, and psychology Ma'ruf and his likes, and how he disregarded the Prophet's own brother and *wali*, the one and only executer of his will, for general caliphate and representation of the Prophet (s). Then ask him how he came to prefer to the descendants of the Messenger of Allah, peace be upon him and his progeny, the descendants of cowards. What would one who turns away from the purified progeny of Muhammad (s) in all such lofty stations and religious obligations and follows in the footsteps of those who oppose them do with the *sahihs* of the Two Weighty Things and the like? And how can he claim that he is upholding the progeny and embarking upon their Ark and entering through their Gate of Salvation?

VI. Their Similitude to the ark of Noah the Gate of Salvation and the Security Against Religious Dissensions

What makes it compulsory to follow and refer to Ahl Al-Bayt is this hadith of the Messenger of Allah, peace be upon him and his progeny: "The similitude of my household among you is that of the ark of Noah: whoever embarks upon it is saved, and whoever lags behind it is drowned,"[10] and his statement (s), "The similitude of my Household among you is that of the ark of Noah: whoever boards it is saved, and whoever lags behind it is drowned. And the similitude of my Household among you is the Gate of the Israelites: whoever enters it is forgiven."[11] Also, consider his statement, peace be upon him and his progeny, "The stars protect the inhabitants of earth against drowning, and my Ahl Al-Bayt protect my nation against dissension (in religious matters). If a tribe among the Arabs differs (regarding the commandments of Allah, the High, the Mighty) from them, they will all then differ and become the party of Satan."[12] This is fully sufficient to oblige the nation to follow them and to protect it against differing from them. I do not think that there is any language of man more clear than this hadith to support my argument.

VII. What is Meant by "Ahl Al-Bayt" in this Regard

What is meant by his word, peace be upon him and his progeny, "Ahl al-Bayt" (i.e. "Household") here is their entirety, collectively, as being their Imams, not merely their entirety inclusively, for this status is nothing but a testimony for the Proofs of Allah - particularly those who stand for His Commandments -

---

[10] Al-Hakim quotes it from Abu Tharr on page 151, Vol. 3, of his *Sahih Al-Mustadrak*.
[11] Al-Tabrani quotes it in his *Al-Awsat* from Abu Sa'id. It is hadith 18 of the 25th *Al-Arba'in* [forty] ahadith of Nabhani's *Al-Arba'in Al-Arba'in* (the sixteen-hundred ahadith), p. 216.
[12] This is quoted by al-Hakim on page 149, Vol. 3, of *Al-Mustadrak* from Ibn 'Abbas. Al-Hakim adds: "This is an authentic hadith though they (both Shaykhs, i.e. Bukhari and Muslim) did not include it (in their own books)."

as reason and scholarship would rule. A learned group among the majority has admitted the same, such as Ibn Hajar in his *Al-Sawa'iq al-Muhriqa*. Some of them have said that what is probably meant by 'Ahl Al-Bayt' who are a security are their own learned men, for they are the ones who are like guiding stars; when lost, inhabitants of the earth will get what they were ominously warned against. Ibn Hajar said: "That will be during the time when al-Mahdi (as) appears, and the tradition indicates that they will pray behind him, and the antichrist will be killed during his time; after that, unusual events will succeed one another," up to the end of his statement which is quoted in the exegesis of verse 7, in Chapter 11, page 91, of *Al-Sawa'iq al-Muhriqa*. Somewhere else he indicates that the Messenger of Allah, peace be upon him and his progeny, was asked once: "How would people live after them?" and he answered: "They will live like an ass whose spleen has been broken."[13]

VIII. Reasons for Similitude to Noah's Ark and the Gate of Salvation

You know that likening them with the ark of Noah implies that whoever resorts to them in matters related to the creed, deriving the branches and basics of religion from their virtuous Imams, will certainly be saved from the fire of hell, and whoever lags behind them is like one who seeks shelter during the flood with a mountain so that it may save him from Allah's destiny, but he will eventually be drowned in water while the first will be hurled in the inferno, may Allah protect us from it.

The reason why they, peace be upon them, are compared to the Gate of Salvation is that Allah has made that Gate a symbol of humility before His Greatness and submission to His Judgment; therefore, it becomes a reason for forgiveness. This is the reason for the similitude.

---

[13] Refer to the conclusion of his chapter on the predictions of the holy Prophet (s) of hard times following his death, near the conclusion of page 143 of *Al-Sawa'iq al-Muhriqa*. We ask Ibn Hajar: "Since this is the status enjoyed by the scholars of Ahl al-Bayt (as), why do you then turn away from them?"

Ibn Hajar, in the exegesis of Chapter 7 of the Holy Qur'an, in Chapter 11, page 91, of his *Al-Sawa'iq al-Muhriqa*, has accepted it while saying, after quoting these and other similar traditions, "The reason for their similitude to the ark is that whoever loves and highly respects them as means of thanking the One Who gave them honours, following the guidance of their learned men, will be saved from the darkness of dissension, and whoever lags behind it is drowned in the sea of ingratitude and will perish in the paths of tyranny." Then he adds the following: "As to the Gate of Salvation (meaning thereby their similitude thereto), Allah has made entering that gate, which probably was the gate of Shittim[14] or of Jerusalem, in humility, seeking forgiveness, a reason for salvation, and He (likewise) has made loving Ahl Al-Bayt a reason for this nation's salvation."[15] The sahih books are consecutive in stating that following Ahl Al-Bayt is mandatory especially quoting the purified 'itra. Had I not curbed my pen for fear of boring you, I would have elaborated in detail, but what I have stated here must suffice for the purpose, Wassalam.

Sincerely,
Sh

---

[14] The site to the east of the Jordan and northeast of the Dead Sea.

[15] Consider this statement of his, then tell me why he did not follow the guidance of their Imams in the branches and tenets of the faith, or in the principles and bases of jurisdiction, or in the sciences of the Sunnah and the Book, or in anything related to ethics, conduct, and etiquette, and why he lagged behind and thus drowned himself in the oceans of those who deny Allah's favours, ruining themselves in the avenues of oppression. May Allah forgive him for telling lies about us and unfairly assaulting our beliefs.

Letter 9
Dhul Qi'da 1329

Requesting More Relevant Texts

Do not curb your pen, and do not worry about boring me. I am all ears listening to you; my chest is wide, and in learning from you, my heart is at ease and soul in peace and tranquility. All the proofs and arguments which you have stated made me even more enthusiastic, thus removing the obstacle of boredom. Send me, therefore, more of your captivating speech and manifestations of wise genius. I find in your speech the quest of the wise, and it is thus more saturating to my heart than crystalclear cool water; so, let me have more, may Allah bless your father, and peace be with you.

Sincerely,
Sh

Letter 10
Dhul-Qi'da 1329

A Glimpse of Sufficient Texts

If you have been pleased by receiving my letter, and if you have approached it with self-satisfaction, then I have often placed my hope on you for victory and concluded my effort with success. Whoever intends well, adopting a good attitude while being humble, amiable, dignified, crowned with knowledge, well-mannered with patience, is surely worthy of being truthful in what he says and writes, while equity and integrity are in his hand and on his tongue.

It is you to whom I owe my thanks when you asked for more, for who else can be more graceful, kind and humble? In order to grant your quest and cool your eyes, I would like to state the following:

Both al-Tabrani's Al-Mujma' al-Kabir and Rafi'i's Musnad, quoting Ibn 'Abbas, state that "The Messenger of Allah, peace be upon him and his progeny, has said: 'Let whoever is pleased to live like me and die like me and inhabit Eden's Paradise which my Lord cultivated take 'Ali as his master after me, and let him obey whoever he places in charge over him, and let him follow the example of my Ahl Al-Bayt after me, for they are my progeny: they are created of my own mould and blessed with my own comprehension and knowledge. Woe unto those who reject them and separate me from them! May Allah never permit them to enjoy my intercession .'"[1]

Al-Matir, al-Barudi, Ibn Jarir, Ibn Shahin, and Ibn Mundah have all quoted Ishaq citing Ziyad ibn Matraf saying: "I have heard the Messenger of Allah saying: 'Whoever wishes to live my life and die my death and enter the Garden which my Lord promised me, the Garden of eternity, then let him take 'Ali and his progeny after him as his masters, for they shall never take you out of guidance, nor let you stray.'"[2]

---

[1] This hadith, *verbatim*, is hadith 3819 of the ones included on page 217, Vol. 6 of *Kanz al-'Ummal*. He also quotes it in *Muntakhab al-Kanz*; so, refer to the latter's text at the beginning of the footnote on page 94 of Vol. 5 of Ahmad's *Musnad*, although the author states: "They were endowed with my comprehension," rather than "comprehension and knowledge." The copier may have committed a mistake. Al-hafiz Abu Na'im, in his *Hilyat al-Awliya'*, has also quoted it, and he in turn is quoted by the Mu'tazilite scholar on page 450, Vol. 2, of his commentary on *Nahjul Balaghah*, Egyptian edition. He also quoted something similar on page 449 from Abu 'Abdullah Ahmad ibn Hanbal in both his *Musnad* and his book titled *Manaqib 'Ali ibn Abu Talib* (as).

[2] This hadith is number 2578 of the ones quoted in *Kanz al-'Ummal*, Vol. 6, page 155. It is also quoted by *Muntakhab al-Kanz*; so, refer to the latter and read the last line of the footnote on page 32, Vol. 5, that quotes Ahmad's *Musnad*. It is also quoted by Ibn Hajar al-'Asqalani abridged in the biography of Ziyad ibn Mutraf in Part One of his *Isaba*, then he adds: "This hadith is quoted by Yahya ibn Ya'li al-Muharbi, a weak traditionist." This is strange coming from al-'Asqalani, for Yahya ibn Ya'li, according to the consensus of scholars of hadith, is quite trustworthy. In his *Sahih*, al-Bukhari quotes his ahadith related to the Hudaybiya treaty. He taught hadith to Muslim Ghaylan ibn Jami'. Moreover, al-Dhahabi, in his *Mizan*, takes the man's integrity for granted, and so do many authorities held reliable by both Shaykhs as well as by others.

Similarly, Zayd ibn Arqam is quoted in one hadith saying: "The Messenger of Allah, peace be upon him and his progeny, has said: 'Whoever wishes to live like me and die my death and inhabit the perpetual Garden promised to me by my Lord, let him take 'Ali as his master, for he shall never get you out of guidance, nor shall he let you stray.'"[3]

Also, consider this tradition narrated by 'Ammar ibn Yasir: "The Messenger of Allah, peace be upon him and his progeny, has said: 'I admonish whoever believed in me and held me truthful to accept the government of 'Ali ibn Abu Talib, for whoever accepts him as the ruler accepts me as such, and whoever loves him loves me too, and whoever loves me loves Allah. Whoever hates him hates me, and whoever hates me hates Allah, the Sublime, the Almighty."[4] 'Ammar quotes others stating this hadith: "O Lord! Whoever believed in me and held me truthful, let him take 'Ali as his master, for his government is also mine, and mine is that of the Almighty Allah."[5]

He, peace be upon him and his progeny, once delivered a sermon wherein he said: "O people! Favours, honours, prestige and government are for the Messenger of Allah and his progeny; therefore, let no falsehood divert you."[6] He, peace be upon him and

---

[3] This is quoted by al-Hakim at the end of page 128, Vol. 3, of his authentic book *Al-Mustadrak*. He adds the following: "The narrators of this hadith are all trustworthy, and they (both Shaykhs) did not quote it." It is quoted by al-Tabrani in his *Al-Jami' al-Kabir*, and by Abu Na'im in his book dealing with the excellences of the *sahabah*. It is hadith 2577 of the ones included in *Kanz al-'Ummal* on page 155, Vol. 6. The author also quotes it in his *Muntakhab al-Kanz*; so, refer to the footnote on page 32, Vol. 5, of the *Musnad*.

[4] Al-Tabrani has quoted it in his *Al-Jami' al-Kabir*, and so has Ibn 'Asakir in his history book, and it is hadith 2571 of the ones included in *Kanz al-'Ummal* at the end of page 154, Vol. 6.

[5] Al-Tabrani has quoted it in his *Al-Jami' al-Kabir* as narrated by Muhammad ibn Abu 'Ubaydah ibn Muhammad ibn 'Umayr ibn Yasir who quotes his father citing his grandfather 'Ammar. It is hadith 2576 of the ones included in *Kanz al-'Ummal*, page 155, Vol. 6. It is also quoted in *Muntakhab al-Kanz*.

[6] It is narrated by Abul Shaykh in a lengthy hadith and transmitted by Ibn Hajar at the end of *maqsad* 4 of his *Maqasid* while explaining, on page 105 of his *Al-Sawa'iq al-Muhriqa*, the verse enjoining kindness to the Prophet's kin after

his progeny said: "In every generation of my nation there are members of my Household who equal only my own self and who safeguard this religion from the distortion of wrongdoers and the interpretation of the ignorant. Be informed that your Imams are your deputies to Allah; so, see who you send to Him as your deputies."[7] He, peace be upon him and his progeny, has also said: "Do not go ahead of them else you should perish, nor should you lag behind them else you should perish. Do not teach them, for they are more learned than you."[8] He, peace be upon him and his progeny, has said: "Consider my Ahl Al-Bayt among you as you consider the head of the body, and the eyes in the head, for the head is guided by the eyes."[9] He, peace be upon him and his progeny, said: "Uphold loving us, we Ahl Al-Bayt, for whoever faces Allah loving us shall enter Paradise through our intercession. I swear by the One in Whose Hands my soul is placed that the good deeds of a believer shall never avail him except through recognizing our rights."[10] And he has also said: "The knowledge of the progeny of

---

having scrutinized it, and in the supreme *maqsad* of his book *Ghayat Al-Maram*. Do not overlook his statement: "Do not accompany the wrong-doers."

[7] This is quoted by al-Malla in his *Sirat*, as in Ibn Hajar's explanation of the verse "And follow in their footsteps, for they shall be questioned" in his *Al-Sawa'iq al-Muhriqa*, page 90, suggests.

[8] This is quoted by al-Tabrani who discusses the hadith of the Two Weighty Things, and he is quoted by Ibn Hajar when the latter explains the meaning of this verse of Chapter Four: "And follow in their foot steps, for they shall be questioned," a verse which he discusses in Chapter 11 of *Al-Sawa'iq al-Muhriqa*, page 89.

[9] This is quoted by a group of authors of books of traditions from Abu Tharr, and it is transmitted by Imam al-Sabban while enUmarating the excellences of Ahl al-Bayt (as) in his work *Is'af al-Raghibin*, and by Shaykh Yusuf al-Nabhani on page 31 of *Al-Sharaf al-Mu'abbad*, and by many other authorities. It is a text which enforces their leadership and implies that guidance to righteousness can be attained only through them.

[10] This is quoted by al-Tabrani in his *Al-Awsat* as transmitted by al-Sayyuti in his *Ihya'ul Mayyit*; by al-Nabhani in his Forty Forty [ahadith]; by Ibn Hajar in his chapter discussing enjoining their love in *Al-Sawa'iq al-Muhriqa*, in addition to many other renowned authorities; so, consider his statement: 'Nobody's good deeds will avail him unless he is mindful of our rights," then tell me what these rights are, the ones that are considered by Allah as prerequisites to the

Muhammad brings salvation from the Fire, and loving Ahl Al-Bayt is walking on the Straight Path. Allegiance to the progeny of Muhammad is a security against the torture."[11] He, peace be upon him and his progeny, has said: "The feet of any servant of Allah shall never move on the Day of Judgment unless he is asked about four things: how he spent his life, what he wore his body out for, how he made and spent his wealth, and about loving us, we Ahl Al-Bayt."[12]

He, peace be upon him and his progeny, has said: "If a man stands in prayer between the Rukn and Maqam, hating Muhammad's progeny, he shall still enter Hellfire."[13] He, peace be

---

acceptance of good deeds. Is it not obeying them and attaining Allah's Pleasure through following their RIGHT PATH? What is the commandment to which both Prophethood and caliphate attach such a great significance? But we have simply been inflicted by people who do not contemplate; so, "We are Allah's, and unto Him is our return."

[11] This is quoted by the judge 'Iyaz in a chapter explaining the fact that to venerate the Prophet (s) and be worthy of pleasing him is to please his progeny and descendants, as indicated at the beginning of page 40, Part Two, of the book titled *Al-Shifa* which was printed in Istanbul in 1328 A.H. You know that "knowing" them in this text does not mean just knowing their names and persons, and that they are kin of the Messenger of Allah, for even Abu Jahal and Abu Lahab knew all of that, but it means recognizing the fact that they are the authorities after the Messenger, peace be upon him and his progeny, as he himself has said: "Whoever dies not knowing the Imam of his time surely dies the death of *Jahiliyya*," and the meaning of loving them and their *wilayat* is the love and *wilayat* that are obligatory upon "those who follow righteousness," i.e. the Imams of Truth, a fact that is quite obvious.

[12] This is so due to the fact that Allah has granted them a special status which requires obedience to them. Loving them as such is rewardable. This hadith is quoted by al-Tabrani from Ibn 'Abbas, and it is transmitted by al-Sayyuti in his *Ihya'ul Mayyit*, and by al-Nabhani in his *Al-Arba'in*, besides many other renowned authorities.

[13] This is quoted by al-Tabrani and al-Hakim, and it also exists in Nabhani's *Al-Arba'in*, in Sayyuti's *Ihya'ul Mayyit* and in others. This hadith is akin to his saying, peace be upon him and his progeny, as in one hadith which you have already heard, "By the One in Whose Hands my life is, nobody's good deeds will be of any avail without recognizing our right." If hating them is not hating Allah and His Messenger, the good deeds of those who hate them would not have been rendered vain even if they spend their life between the Rukn and the

upon him and his progeny, has also said: "Whoever dies because of his love for the progeny of Muhammad dies a martyr. Whoever dies because of loving the progeny of Muhammad dies as a believer of a perfect faith. Whoever dies for loving Muhammad's children will be given the glad tiding of entering Paradise by the angel of death, then by Munkir and Nakir. Whoever dies for loving Muhammad's descendants will be taken to Paradise like a bride taken to her groom's house. Whoever dies loving Muhammad's progeny will have two doors in his grave overlooking Paradise. Allah will make the grave of whoever dies for loving Muhammad's children a visiting place for the angels of mercy. Whoever dies for loving Muhammad's progeny dies adhering to the Sunnah and consensus. Whoever dies hating Muhammad's progeny will come on the Day of Judgment with this inscribed between his eyes: 'He should despair of Allah's mercy,'" up to the end of his unmatchable sermon,[14] the sermon whereby he, peace be upon him and his progeny, intended to divert the inclinations and whims.

The implication is that all these traditions are unanimously agreed upon, especially those narrated through the authority of the purified 'itra. Their status would not have been confirmed had they not been the obvious Proofs of Allah and the fountainhead of His Jurisprudence, the obvious Proofs of Allah, the fountainhead of

---

Maqam [of Ibrahim, as] praying and supplicating; even then, they would not have enjoyed such a status. Al-Hakim and Ibn Hayyan, in his *sahih*, as stated in Nabhani's *Al-Arba'in Arba'in* and Sayyuti's *Ihya'ul Mayyit*, from Imam al-Hasan, the Prophet's grandson, who said to Mu'awiyah ibn Khadij once: "Beware of hating us, we Ahl al-Bayt (as), for the Messenger of Allah has said: 'Whoever hates or envies us would be pushed away from the Pool [Kawthar] with whips of fire.'" The Messenger of Allah, peace be upon him and his progeny, delivered a sermon once and said: "O People! Anyone who hates us, we Ahl al-Bayt (as), will be resurrected on the Day of Judgment as a Jew." This hadith is quoted by al-Tabrani in his *Al-Awsat* as stated in al-Sayyuti's *Ihya'ul Mayyit* and Nabhani's *Al-Arba'in Arba'in* and in other books.

[14] This is quoted by Imam al-Tha'labi in his explanation of the verse enjoining the love of Ahl al-Bayt (as) in *Al-Tafsir al-Kabir* from Jarir ibn 'Abdullah al-Bijli from the Messenger of Allah, peace be upon him and his progeny. Al-Zamakhshari takes its authenticity for granted in his own exegesis of the same verse in his book *Al-Kashshaf*; so, refer to it.

His Jurisprudence, the ones who represent the Messenger of Allah in bidding or forbidding, his own deputies in the most clear terms.

Whoever loves them, therefore, is also a lover of Allah and His Messenger, and whoever hates them is an enemy of Allah and His Messenger. He, peace be upon him and his progeny, has said: "None loves us except a God-fearing and sincere believer, and none hates us except a hypocritical wretch."[15] It is for these reasons that al-Farazdaq, the poet, has said these verses in their praise:

> You are ones loving whom is belief, hating an abomination;
> Nearness to you is indeed a rescue and a salvation.
> If the pious ones are counted, you will be their Imams; it is true.
> If one asks: "Who are the best of man?" the answer will be you.

The Commander of the Faithful, peace be upon him, used to say:

> "I and the virtuous among my descendants are the best in manners when young, and the most learned when old. Through us does Allah obliterate lies, and through us does He turn the wild fox's teeth ineffective. Through us does Allah cure your barrenness, and through us does He emancipate you. Through us does Allah begin and conclude."[16]

Suffices us a reason for preferring them over others the fact that Allah, the Sublime, the Almighty, has preferred them over all others, making sending prayers unto them part of the obligatory prayers, albeit if the one saying his prayer were a Siddiq or Faruq, with one light, or two, or with numerous lights. Nay! Everyone who worships Allah by performing His obligations also worships

---

[15] Al-Malla has recorded it in the second *maqsad* of Chapter 14 of the Holy Qur'an in his own Chapter 11 of *Al-Sawa'iq al-Muhriqa*.
[16] This is quoted by 'Abdul-Ghani ibn Sa'd in his *Eizah al-Ishkal*. It is hadith 6050 of the ones included in *Kanz al-'Ummal* at the end of page 396, Vol. 6.

Him while doing so by sending blessings unto them, just as he worships Him when testifying through the two parts of the Shahadah. This, indeed, is a status before which the nation's heads were lowered, and in front of which the eyes of whoever you mentioned of the imams have submitted. Imam al-Shafi'i, may Allah be pleased with him, has said:[17]

> O Household of Allah's Messenger! Loving you is an obligation
> Which Allah has enforced in His Honored Revelation;
> Suffices you a great honour if one sends no prayer unto you all,
> It will be as though he did not say his prayers at all.

Let us now be satisfied with this much of the sacred Sunnah in testimony to the fact that following their Sunnah is compulsory; so is emulating them. In the Book of Allah Almighty, the Sublime and the Omnipotent, there are clear verses which make that, too, compulsory. It is to such verses that we would like to attract your aware conscience and sensitive reason. You can be satisfied with an indicative hint, and a signal suffices to attract your attention; all praise is due to Allah, Lord of all the world.

Sincerely,
Sh

---

[17] These two couplets of al-Shafi'i are very well-known and in wide circulation. Many trustworthy authorities have taken this fact for granted, indicating that he is the one who has composed them. Among them are: Ibn Hajar, who quotes them while explaining the verse "Allah and His angels send prayers unto the Prophet (s)," on page 88 of his *Al-Sawa'iq al-Muhriqa*; al-Nabhani on page 99 of his *Al-Sharaf al-Mu'abbad*, Imam Abu Bakr ibn Shihabud-Din in his *Rashfatul Sadi*, and by many others.

Letter 11
Dhul-Qi'da 1329

I. Admiring Our Clear Texts

I have been honoured to receive your highly esteemed letter which I found to be authentic in its mainstream, comprehensible. You have filled your bucket to the brim. The flood of your eloquence has surmounted the highest peaks. I have scrutinized your letter very carefully, and I have found you to be far in vision, firm, strong in argument, outspoken.

II. Wondering at Compromising Them with the Majority's Beliefs

Having deeply considered your argument and dug deep into your proofs, I found myself in a very dangerous situation: When I look into your proofs, I find them convincing. When I consider your explanations, I find them indicative. When I look at the Imams of the Purified 'itra, I find Allah and His Messenger commending their status, highlighting its greatness and prestige. Then when I look at the majorty of Muslims, who represent most of this nation, I find them differing from Ahl Al-Bayt, contrary to the obligation of those proofs. Now I find myself to be split in two parts: one part of me yielding to the proofs, while the other seeking refuge with the majority of Muslims. I have submitted the first to you to lead: it is tame in your hands, while the other has stubbornly rejected you.

III. Asking for Clear Signs from the Book

Could you please, therefore, overcome the latter's stubbornness with convincing proofs from the Book which could curb it and divert it from yielding to the common beliefs? Peace be with you.

Sincerely,
S

Letter 12
Dhul-Qida 1329

Qur'anic Proofs

You, praise to Allah, have studied the Book thoroughly, becoming acquainted with both its obvious and implied meanings. Has there been anyone praised therein like the Purified 'itra? Have its perfect verses described any as "purified from all uncleanness"[1] other than them? Has the verse of Purification been revealed in honour of anyone else?[2] Has the perfect Revelation commanded love for any others?[3] Has Gabriel brought the verse of Mubahala in praise of anyone else?[4]

Has "Hal Ata" been revealed in praise of others? No! I swear By the Lord Who rightly used it for them, Who is right and fair.[5]

---

[1] As it ruled in its departure therefrom according to the Almighty's statement: "Allah wishes to remove all abomination from you, members of Ahl al-Bayt (as) and purify you with a perfect purification (Qur'an, 33:33)."

[2] Nay! Nobody else can claim that at all. They have been selected for it; so, nobody can reach their station nor dream of attaining their achievements.

[3] Nay! Allah has selected them for it and preferred them over all others, saying: "Say (O Muhammad): 'I do not ask you for any reward other than being kind to my kin,' and whoever attains a good deed [being kind to them], We shall certainly increase him in goodness; verily, Allah is Forgiving [to those who are kind to them], Appreciative [of such kindness] (Qur'an, 42:23)."

[4] Nay! The verse of Mubahala was revealed specifically in their praise. Allah, the Dear One, says therein: "Say (O Muhammad): 'Let us bring our sons and your sons,... (Qur'an, 3:61)."

[5] This is a reference to the revelation of Ayat al-'Asr (Chapter of Time) regarding them and their foes, and whoever wishes to be familiar with this matter as dealt with in the verse of purification, verse of *mubahala*, the verse enjoining kindness to the Prophet's kin, and the verse of time, he must refer to our own statement in this regard, for it is the remedy for every ailment. It brings the foes back to their senses, and it provides knowledge for those who do not know, and praise be to Allah.

Are they not "Allah's Rope" concerning whom He has said: "Hold together to Allah's Rope and do not be divided (Qur'an, 3:103)"[6]? And "the truthful" concerning whom He has said: "Be ye all with the Truthful (Qur'an, 9:119);"[7] "Allah's path" about which He has said: "Do not follow different paths else they should divert you from Allah's path (Qur'an, 6:153),"[8] the ones "entrusted with authority among you (Qur'an, 4:59),"[9] the "custodians of

---

[6] In his commentary on the meaning of this verse in his *Al-Tafsir al-Kabir*, Imam al-Tha'labi quotes Aban ibn Taghlib reporting that Imam Ja'far al-Sadiq (as) has said: "We are Allah's rope about which He has said: 'And uphold Allah's rope all of you together, and do not be separated (Qur'an, 3:103)'." Ibn Hajar has included this verse among others revealed in their praise, being the fifth in the series of verses which he enUmarates in Chapter 11 of *Al-Sawa'iq al-Muhriqa*. While explaining its meaning, the author quotes al-Tha'labi, as you have heard above, citing Imam Ja'far al-Sadiq (as). Imam al-Shafi'i is quoted in Rashfatul Sadi by Imam Abu Bakr ibn Shihabud-Din as having said:

> When I saw people being carried away to the seas of misguidance and ignorance by their sects,
>
> I boarded, in the Name of Allah, the Ark of Salvation, that is, the Household of the Chosen One, the Seal of Prophets.
>
> And I upheld Allah's Rope, and it is obedience to them, as He has commanded us to uphold to the Rope.

[7] The "truthful" here are Allah's Messengers and the Imams of his purified progeny, according to our consecutive *sahihs*, and as supported by al-Hafiz Abu Na'im and Muwaffaq ibn Ahmad, and transmitted by Ibn Hajar in his explanation of Chapter 5, Section 11, of *Al-Sawa'iq al-Muhriqa*, page 90, quoting Imam Zaynul 'Abidin (as) in a statement quoted above (see Letter No. 6).

[8] Imams al-Baqir and al-Sadiq (as) used to always say: "The RIGHT PATH here is the Imam, and do not follow diverse paths (imams of misguidance) for they will divert you from His Path (and we are His Path)."

[9] In his authentic *sahih*, the trusted authority of Muslims, Muhammad ibn Ya'qub al-Kulayni, has quoted Burayd al-'Ajli saying: "I asked Abu Ja'far (Imam Muhammad al-Baqir, as) about the verse saying: 'Obey Allah, and obey the Messenger and those charged with authority among you (Qur'an, 4:59),' and he answered me by saying: 'Have you not observed those (Jews) who are given a portion of the (knowledge of the) Book? They are invited to the Book of Allah so that it might decide between them, then a party among them turns back

Revelation" about whom He says: "Ask the custodians of Revelation when you do not know (Qur'an, 21:7),"[10] the believers about whom He says: "Whoever differs from the Messenger, after guidance has been made clear to him, following paths other than those of the Believers, We shall leave him in the path he has chosen and place him in Hell, what an evil refuge (Qur'an, 4:115),"[11] and the "guides" about whom He says: "You are a warner, and for each

---

(therefrom), and they withdraw (Qur'an, 3:23),' how they believe in sorcerers and tyrants instead, and how they say to those who disbelieve that they are closer to the Straight Path than the Believers? They tell the imams of misguidance and the callers unto the Fire that their guidance is more accurate than that of Muhammad's progeny; 'Have you not seen those to whom a portion of the Book has been given? They believe in idols and false deities and say of those who disbelieve: These are better guided in the path than those who believe. Those are they whom Allah has cursed, and whoever Allah curses, you shall never find for them any helper. Or have they a share in the kingdom? But then they would not give people even the speck in a date stone (Qur'an, 4:51-53),' nor will they ever own aught of Allah's domain, that is, Imamate and Caliphate, '... or do they envy the people for what Allah has bestowed upon them of His own favours (Qur'an, 4:54)?' We are the ones who are envied because of the Imamate which Allah has bestowed upon us rather than anyone else among His creation; 'We bestowed upon the descendants of Ibrahim (Abraham) the Book and the Wisdom, and We provided them with a great kingdom (Qur'an, 4:54),' meaning He made some of them messengers, prophets, and imams; so, how can they recognize its existence to the descendants of Ibrahim while denying it to the descendants of Muhammad (s)?!" "Among them are those who believed in it, and among them are those who turned away therefrom, and Hell suffices for a torment (Qur'an, 4:55)."

[10] Explaining this chapter, al-Tha'labi quotes Jabir saying the following in his book *Al-Tafsir al-Kabir*: "When this Chapter was revealed, 'Ali (as) said: 'We are the people of remembrance,' and this is the case with all the Imams of guidance." The Bahraini scholar has quoted in Chapter 35 more than twenty authentic ahadith bearing this meaning.

[11] Ibn Mardawayh, in his explanation of this Chapter, has indicated that "... to argue with the Messenger" in this context means to dispute with him regarding 'Ali (as), and the guidance referred to in the verse "... after guidance has been made manifest to him" is the guidance provided by 'Ali, peace be upon him." In his *Tafsir*, al-'Ayyashi states something almost similar to this, and the *sahihs* are consecutive from the sources of the purified progeny in stating that "the path of the believers" is the path of their own (progeny), peace be upon them.

nation there is a guide"?[12] Are they not among those upon whom Allah has showered His blessings and to whom He has referred in the Fatiha and the Glorious Qur'an saying "Guide us unto the Right Path, the Path of those whom You have blessed,"[13] and He has also said: "These are with those whom Allah has blessed from among the prophets, the truthful, the martyrs and the righteous (Qur'an, 4:69)"?[14]

Has He not granted them the general authority? Has He not confined it only to them after the Prophet? Read: "Your Master is Allah and His Messenger and the Believers who uphold prayers and pay zakat even while prostrating; whoever takes for Master Allah and His Messenger and the Believers, then the Party of Allah are indeed the victorious (Qur'an, 5:58)."[15] Has He not made

---

[12] Explaining this verse in *Al-Tafsir al-Kabir*, al-Tha'labi quotes Ibn 'Abbas saying: "When this verse was revealed, the Messenger of Allah (s) put his hand over his chest and said: 'I am the warner and 'Ali (as) is the guide, and through you, O 'Ali, guidance is achieved.'" Many scholars of exegesis and authors of books of traditions quote Ibn 'Abbas and Muhammad ibn Muslim saying: "I asked Abu 'Abdullah (Imam Ja'far al-Sadiq (as)) about the implications of this verse and he answered: 'Each Imam is the guide of his time.' Imam Abu Ja'far al-Baqir has said the following regarding its explanation: 'The warner is the Messenger of Allah, and the guide is 'Ali,' then he adds: 'By Allah, imamate shall remain with us till the Hour approaches.'"

[13] In his exegesis of Surahal-Fatiha, al-Tha'labi, in his *Al-Tafsir al-Kabir*, quotes Abu Buraydah saying that "*al-sirat al-mustaqim* (the Straight Path) is the path of Muhammad (s) and his progeny (as)." Interpreting this *sura*, Waki' ibn al-Jarirah quotes Sufyan al-Thawri through a chain of narrators including al-Sadi, Asht, Mujahid, all quoting Ibn 'Abbas saying: "'Guide us to the Straight Path' means 'Guide us to the love for Muhammad and his progeny.'"

[14] The Imams from among Ahl al-Bayt (as) are without any argument the masters of *siddiqs*, martyrs, and the righteous.

[15] Scholars of exegesis are unanimous, as al-Qawshaji, imam of the Ash'aris, has admitted in his chapter on "*Sharh al-Tajrid*," saying that this verse was revealed in honour of 'Ali (as) when he offered charity while engaged in the ceremonial supplication performing the prayers. In his *sahih*, al-Nisa'i quotes 'Abdullah ibn Salam testifying to its revelation in honour of 'Ali (as). This view is supported by the author of *Al-Jami' Baynal Sihah al-Sitta* while explaining Surahal-Ma'idah [Chapter of The Table Spread with Food]. Al-Tha'labi has

salvation for those who repent and do good deeds dependent upon accepting their guided authority, saying: "I am most Forgiving for those who repent, believe, do good deeds, and received guidance (Qur'an, 20:82)"[16]? Isn't their wilayat part of the "trust" about which the Almighty says: "We offered the trust unto the heavens, the earth, and the mountains, but they all refused to bear it out of extreme fear, then man bore it: he is most unjust, most ignorant (Qur'an, 33:72)"?[17]

Have they not been the "peace" wherein Allah has commanded everyone to enter, saying, "O ye who believe! Enter in peace all of you, and do not follow the steps of Satan (Qur'an, 2:208)"[18]. Are they not the "blessing" concerning whom Allah the

---

indicated its revelation in honour of the Commander of the Faithful in his book *Al-Tafsir al-Kabir*, as we will explain when we discuss it.

[16] In Chapter 11, Part One, of his *Al-Sawa'iq al-Muhriqa*, Ibn Hajar states: "The guidance referred to in Chapter 8 which states: 'I am all-Forgiving for those who repent, believe, and do good deeds, then seek guidance,' according to Thabit al-Banni, means the seeking of guidance from the household of the Prophet (s).'" This is narrated from Abu Ja'far al-Baqir, too. Ibn Hajar has narrated several ahadith testifying to the salvation of those who seek and act upon their guidance, peace be upon them. He also refers to what he quotes from al-Baqir's statement referring to the conversation between Imam al-Baqir (as) and al-Harith ibn Yahya in which the Imam says: "O Harith! Have you not seen how Allah has made it clear that repentance, belief, and good deeds are not sufficient without seeking guidance from our authority?' then he, peace be upon him, quotes his grandfather the Commander of the Faithful saying: "By Allah! If a man repents, believes, and does good deeds, but he does not seek guidance from our authority, nor recognizes our rights, all of these things will be utterly in vain.'" Abu Na'im the *hafiz* quotes Awn ibn Abu Jahufah who in turn quotes his father narrating a similar tradition from 'Ali (as). Al-Hakim has published similar ahadith from Imams al-Baqir and al-Sadiq (as), and from Thabit al-Banni and Anas ibn Malik.

[17] Refer to the meaning of this verse in *Al-Safi*, and in 'Ali ibn Ibrahim's *Tafsir*, and to the traditions narrated by Sunnis explaining its meaning as compiled by the Bahraini scholar in Chapter 115 of his work *Ghayat al-Maram*.

[18] In chapter 224 of *Ghayat al-Maram*, the Bahraini scholar quotes twelve traditions from our *sahihs* testifying to the fact that this verse was revealed regarding 'Ali's government and that of the Imams among his descendants, barring the leadership of all others. In Chapter 223, he states that al-Isfahani al-Amawi narrates the same about 'Ali (as) quoting various sources.

Sublime has said, "You will be questioned on that Day about the Blessing (Qur'an, 102:8)"[19]?

Has not the Messenger of Allah (s) been commanded to convey all of this? Has Allah not emphasized conveying it in such a language which sounded like threatening, saying, "O Messenger! Convey that which has been revealed unto you, and if you do not do it, then you have not really conveyed His Message at all, and Allah shall protect you from (mischievous) people (Qur'an, 5:70)"?[20] Has not the Messenger of Allah, peace be upon him and his progeny, conveyed it on the Ghadir Day, having reached its plains and delivered the Message, whereupon Allah revealed this congratulating verse: "Today have I completed your religion for you, perfected My blessing unto you, and accepted Islam as your religion (Qur'an, 5:4)"?[21]

Have you noticed what your Lord did with the person who openly denied their authority saying, "O Allah! If this Message is

---

[19] In Chapter 48 of his *Ghayat al-Maram*, the Bahraini scholar quotes three ahadith narrated by Sunnis testifying to the fact that the "bliss" here is what Allah has blessed people through the government of His Messenger (s), that of the Commander of the Faithful and Ahl al-Bayt (as). In Chapter 49, he quotes twelve ahadith from our *sahihs* reflecting the same; so, refer to it if you wish.

[20] Only one Sunni *faqih* among the authors of books of traditions, namely Imam al-Wahidi, while commenting on Surahal-Ma'ida in his book *Asbab al-Nuzul*, quotes Abu Sa'id al-Khudri saying: "This verse was revealed on the Day of Ghadir Khumm in honour of 'Ali ibn Abu Talib (as)." Imam al-Tha'labi has included it in his *Tafsir* from two sources, and al-Hamawani al-Shafi'i includes it in his *Fara'id* from various sources from Abu Hurayrah, and it is transmitted by Abu Na'im in his book *Nuzul al-Qur'an* from two sources: Abu Rafi' and al-A'mash, both quoting 'Atiyyah. In *Ghyat al-Maram*, there are nine ahadith narrated by Sunnis and eight authentic ones by Shi'as conveying the same meaning; so, refer to it in Chapters 37 and 38.

[21] This text is stated by Imam Abu Ja'far al-Baqir (as), succeeded in narrating it by Imam Abu 'Abdullah al-Sadiq (as). According to authentic narrations, Sunnis have included six ahadith in their own books of traditions that in the end quote the Messenger of Allah, peace be upon him and his progeny, quite clearly emphasizing this very theme. Its explanation exists in Chapters 39 and 40 of *Ghayat al-Maram*.

truly from Thee, then let stones fall upon us[22] like rain from the skies, or cause a severe torment to befall upon us"? Allah hurled a Sijjil stone at him as He had done with the Fellows of the Elephant. He revealed these verses on that occasion: " A person questioned about a penalty to befall the unbelievers which cannot be warded off: (a penalty) from Allah, Lord of the Ways of Ascent (Qur'an, 70:1-2)."

People will certainly be questioned about such authority when they are resurrected as indicated in the explanation of the verse saying: "And follow in their footsteps, for they have the authority (Qur'an, 37:24)."[23] There is no room to wonder any longer, then, especially when we discern the fact that their authority has been sanctioned by Allah unto people through His prophets, providing proofs and arguments for it, as indicated by the explanation of His saying: "And ask the Messengers whom We sent before thee (Qur'an, 43:45)."[24] Nay! Allah has even taken for

---

[22] Imam al-Tha'labi has detailed the explanation of this matter in his *Al-Tafsir al-Kabir*, and it is transmitted by the Egyptian scholar al-Shiblinji who details 'Ali's biography in his book *Nur al-Absar*, page 171, where he, too, explains it in detail. Al-Halabi mentions it at the conclusion of his chapter "Hijjatul Wada'" in Vol. 3 of his book *Al-Sira al-Halabiyya*. Al-Hakim narrates it in "*Tafsir al-Ma'arij*" in his *Al-Mustadrak*, page 502, Vol. 2.

[23] Al-Daylami, as is the case with the explanation of this verse in *Al-Sawa'iq al-Muhriqa* states that Sa'id al-Khudri quotes the Prophet (s) saying: "Follow in their footsteps, for they are responsible concerning 'Ali's *wilayat*." Al-Wahidi, as is the case with the author of *Al-Sawa'iq al-Muhriqa*, explains this verse by saying: "It has been narrated regarding Allah's statement: 'Follow in their footsteps, for they are responsible....,' that the responsibility referred to here is regarding 'Ali's government and that of Ahl al-Bayt (as),'" adding: "For Allah commanded His Prophet (s) to make people aware of the fact that he does not ask them for any rewards for conveying His Message other than being kind to his kin..., that is, they will be asked if they properly submitted to their *wilayat* as the Prophet (s) had instructed them, or if they lost it and discarded it, thus becoming subject to Allah's demands and the consequences of such discarding." Ibn Hajar includes it in Chapter 11 of his *Al-Sawa'iq al-Muhriqa* among the verses revealed in their praise, being number 4 in such sequence, and he elaborates on it a great deal.

[24] Refer to what Abu Na'im al-Hafiz has quoted in his *Hilyat al-Awliya*, and to what is recorded by al-Tha'labi, al-Nishapuri, and al-Barqi regarding its

it a promise on the Day of Alasto from the souls of His creatures even before creating their physical forms, as referred to in this verse: "When thy Lord drew forth from the children of Adam - from their loins - their descendants, making them promise, asking them: 'Am I not your Lord?' They said: 'Yes! We testify!' This is so lest you should say on the Day of Judgment: 'Of this we were never mindful (Qur'an, 7:172)'."[25] Through their intercession has Allah granted forgiveness to Adam who learned the words of repentance referred to in Chapter 2, Verse 37, of the Holy Qur'an.[26]

"Allah does not expose them to torture,"[27] for they are the security of the inhabitants of earth and mankind's means towards Him. They are the ones of whom people are jealous and about whom Allah says: "Should they feel jealous of them because Allah Has granted them His favours (Qur'an, 4:54)"?[28] They are the ones who are "deeply grounded in knowledge" about whom He says: "Those who are deeply grounded in knowledge say: 'We believe

---

meaning in their own *tafsir* books, and to what Ibrahim ibn Muhammad al-Hamawini and other Sunnis have said. Also refer to what Abu 'Ali al-Tibrisi has said while explaining its meaning in his book *Mujma'ul Bayan fi Tafsir al-Qur'an*, quoting the Commander of the Faithful (as). What Chapters 44 and 45 of *Ghayat al-Maram* state in this meaning is something that dispels all doubts.

[25] Our own discourse about Ahl al-Bayt (as), while explaining this verse, testifies to this fact.

[26] Ibn al-Maghazli al-Shafi'i quotes Ibn 'Abbas saying: "When the Messenger of Allah, peace be upon him and his progeny, was asked about the words which Adam had received from his Lord and whereby his repentance was accepted, he (s) said: 'He [Adam] asked Him by the prestige He held for Muhammad, 'Ali, Fatima, al-Hasan, and al-Husayn, and thus did He accept his repentance and forgive him.'" This is what we know for a fact to be the meaning of this verse.

[27] Refer to *Al-Sawa'iq al-Muhriqa* by Ibn Hajar who interprets the verse of the Almighty: "Allah would not torment them..." as verse 7 of those revealed in their honour as recorded in Chapter 11 of the said book where the author endorses our own view stated here.

[28] This is admitted by Ibn Hajar who counts this verse among the ones revealed in their honour, numbering it 6 in Chapter 11 of his *Al-Sawa'iq al-Muhriqa*. Ibn al-Maghazli al-Shafi'i, as indicated in the explanation of this verse in *Al-Sawa'iq al-Muhriqa*, quotes Imam al-Baqir (as) saying: "By Allah, we are the ones who are envied." In Chapters 60 and 61 of *Ghayat al-Maram*, as many as thirty authentic ahadith are recorded in this meaning.

(Qur'an, 3:7)!"[29] They are the ones who will be upon the Heights and to whom Allah refers when he says, "Upon the Heights are men who know all by their marks (Qur'an, 7:48)."[30] They are the men of truth about whom He says: "Among the Believers are men who fulfilled their promise unto Allah; some of them have passed away, while others are waiting, and they have not changed in the

---

[29] This is quoted by Thiqatul-Islam Muhammad ibn Ya'qub al-Kulayni who quotes an authentic hadith from Imam al-Sadiq (as) saying: "We are a people the obedience to whom has been mandated by Allah, the Exalted and the Sublime; we are the ones who are deeply rooted in knowledge, and we are the ones who are envied. Allah Almighty has said: 'Or should they envy (certain) people for what Allah has granted them out of His own favour?'" This has also been quoted by al-Shaykh in his *Tahthib*, also quoting Imam al-Sadiq, peace be upon him.

[30] While explaining this verse in his *Tafsir*, al-Tha'labi quotes Ibn 'Abbas saying: "The 'A'raf' is an elevated place of the *Sirat* whereupon al-'Abbas, Hamzah, 'Ali and Ja'far of the two wings identify the ones who love them by the sign of the whiteness of their countenance, and the ones who hate them by its blackness." Al-Hakim, too, has quoted 'Ali (as) saying: "We shall stand, on the Day of Judgment, between Paradise and Hell, and we shall recognize those who support us by their mark and would let them enter Paradise, and we shall recognize those who hate us also by their marks." Salman al-Farsi is quoted saying: "I have heard the Messenger of Allah, peace be upon him and his progeny, saying: 'O 'Ali! You and the *wasis* from your descendants are on the A'raf.'" This is supported by the hadith quoted by Dar Qutni at the conclusion of Part Two, Chapter 9, of *Al-Sawa'iq al-Muhriqa*. It indicates that 'Ali (as) delivered a lengthy address to the six persons assigned by 'Umar to be in charge of the *shura* in which he stated: "I ask you in the Name of Allah if anyone among you has been told similarly to what I was told by the Messenger of Allah, peace be upon him and his progeny, and that is: 'O 'Ali! You are the one who will designate the destination of every person on the Day of Judgment either to Paradise or to Hell'?" They responded: "No, indeed." Ibn Hajar states the following: "The meaning of this hadith is what is narrated by Antarah from Imam 'Ali al-Rida (as) who quotes the Prophet, peace be upon him and his progeny, saying the following to 'Ali (as): 'O 'Ali! You are the one who will assign people to either Paradise or Hell on the Day of Judgment, telling Hell which one is hers and which one is not.'" Ibn Hajar says: "Ibn al-Sammak narrates that Abu Bakr has said to 'Ali (as), may Allah be pleased with both men, "I have heard the Messenger of Allah saying: 'Nobody can pass on the Sirat except the one permitted by 'Ali.'"

least (Qur'an, 33:23)."³¹ They are the ones who glorify Allah continuously. About them He has said: "He is Glorified in the early morning and during the night by men who are not diverted, by either trade or selling, from mentioning Allah, the saying of prayers, or the paying of zakat: they fear the Day when hearts and sights are overturned (Qur'an, 24:36-37)."³²

Their houses are the ones mentioned in Allah's verses saying: "In houses which Allah permitted to be elevated and His Name be

---

³¹ In Section 5, Chapter 9, of *Al-Sawa'iq al-Muhriqa*, Ibn Hajar, while discussing 'Ali's assassination, indicates that when 'Ali (as) was on the pulpit in Kufa, he was asked to explain the verse in which this phrase occurs: "Men who proved truthful to their promise to Allah," and he answered by saying: "O Lord! Forgive them; this verse was revealed in honour of myself, my uncle Hamzah, and my cousin 'Ubaydah ibn alHarith ibn alMuttalib. 'Ubaydah died a martyr in Badr; Hamzah died a martyr on Uhud; as to myself, I am awaiting a most painful death, when this shall be drenched from the blood of this," pointing with his hand to his beard and head respectively; "It is a true promise made to me by my beloved Father of alQasim, peace be upon him and his progeny." Al-Hakim, while interpreting this verse as quoted in al-Tibrisi's *Mujma'ul Bayan fi Tafsir al-Qur'an*, cites 'Umar ibn Thabit quoting Abu Ishaq quoting 'Ali, peace be upon him, saying: "On our own behalf was this verse revealed: 'Men who proved truthful to their promise to Allah....,' and I by Allah am waiting, and I have never changed aught."

³² Mujahid and Ya'qub ibn Sufyan quote Ibn 'Abbas's interpretation of the verse saying "And when they see trade or amusement, they rush to it, leaving you standing (for prayers alone)," thus: "Dahyah al-Kalbi once came from Syria on a Friday with a merchandise of foodstuff and he came to a place called Ahjar alZayt where he announced his presence by beating drums to invite people to him. People, therefore, rushed to him, leaving the Prophet (s) standing on the pulpit preaching with only 'Ali, al-Hasan, al-Husayn, Fatima, Salman, Abu Tharr, and al-Miqdad. The Prophet (s) then said: 'Allah has cast a look at my mosque on a Friday, and had it not been for the presence of these persons, He would have set the city on fire and hurled stones at its inhabitants as He did with the people of Lut.' Allah has revealed in honour of those who remained with the Messenger of Allah at the mosque the verse saying: 'Praising Him therein, during the night and at early dawn, men whom neither trade nor sale can divert.'"

recited therein."[33] Allah has made their niche, in Surah An-Nur (Qur'an, 24:35),[34] an example for His own Light:

> Allah is the Light of the heavens and the earth. The parable of His Light is a niche, within it is a Lamp: the lamp is enclosed in glass; the glass is as (bright as) a brilliant star lit from a blessed tree, an olive, neither of the east nor of the west, whose oil is well-nigh luminous, though fire scarcely touches it: Light upon Light! Allah guides whom He will to His Light: Allah sets forth parables for men, and Allah knows all things.

They are the foremost in accepting the faith and implementing it, and they are the nearest to Allah, as He indicates in Chapter 56, verses 10 and 11.[35] They are those who testify to the

---

[33] Al-Tha'labi, while discussing the meaning of this verse in his *Al-Tafsir al-Kabir*, quotes Anas ibn Malik and Burayd saying: "The Messenger of Allah (s) once read the verse saying '... in houses which Allah has desired that they should be elevated, and His Name shall be mentioned therein,' whereupon Abu Bakr stood up and said: 'O Messenger of Allah! Is this house (then he pointed to the house where 'Ali and Fatima where living) among them?' The Prophet (s) answered: 'Yes; one of their choicest." In Chapter 12 of *Ghayat al-Maram*, there are nine authentic ahadith through which the light of dawn shines.

[34] This is a reference to the verse saying: "The similitude of His Light is a Lamp..." Ibn al-Maghazli al-Shafi'i has quoted 'Ali ibn Ja'far in his *Manaqib* saying: "I asked the father of al-Hasan (Imam al-Kazim, peace be upon him) about the verse saying '... like a niche wherein a lamp...,' and he, peace be upon him, answered: 'The niche is Fatima, the Lamp symbolizes al-Hasan and al-Husayn, and 'the glass is like a shining star,' indicates that Fatima shone like a star among all the women of the world, receiving its fuel from a blessed tree, the family-tree of Ibrahim (Abraham), neither of the east nor of the west, neither Jewish nor Christian, 'its oil almost shines (by itself),' indicates that knowledge almost speaks of itself even when no fire touches it, 'light upon light,' wherein there is one Imam after anoother, 'Allah guides whomsoever He pleases to His Light,' implies that Allah guides to our *wilayat* whomsoever He pleases.'" Suffices such an interpretation to be coming from a member of the household upon whom the revelation descended.

[35] Al-Daylami, as in hadith 29, Part Two, Section 9, of *Al-Sawa'iq al-Muhriqa* by Ibn Hajar, quotes 'Ayesha, al-Tabrani, Ibn Mardawayh, all citing Ibn 'Abbas saying that the Prophet (s) has said: "The foremost in believing in the Prophets

Prophet's truthfulness (Qur'an, 4:69).[36] They are the martyrs and the virtuous. Regarding them and their followers has Allah said: "Among Our creation is a nation calling unto the right guidance through the truth, and they are most just therein" (Qur'an, 7:181).[37] Also, Allah has said the following about their party and about that of their enemies: "Inhabitants of the Fire are not equal to those of Paradise: inhabitants of Paradise are the victorious."[38] About both

---

are three men: Joshua son of Nun who was the foremost in believing in Moses (as); the one referred to in Chapter Yasin who was the foremost in believing in Christ (as), and the foremost in believing in Muhammad is 'Ali ibn Abu Talib (as)." This hadith is quoted by al-Muwaffaq ibn Ahmad and the faqih Ibn al-Maghazli, both quoting Ibn 'Abbas.

[36] Ibn al-Najjar, as in hadith 30 referred to in *Al-Sawa'iq al-Muhriqa* quotes Ibn 'Abbas saying that the Messenger of Allah (s) has said: "The *siddiqs* are three: Ezekiel, who was the foremost to believe [in Moses] from among the descendants of Pharaoh; Habib al-Najjar, who is referred to in Chapter Yasin, and 'Ali ibn Abu Talib (as)." Abu Na'im and Ibn 'Asakir, as in hadith 31 referred to in *Al-Sawa'iq al-Muhriqa* quotes Ibn Abu Layla saying that the Messenger of Allah (s) has said: "The *siddiqs* are three: Habib al-Najjar, the believer referred to in Chapter Ali Yasin as saying: 'O my people, follow the Messengers;' Ezekiel, who was the foremost to believe [in Moses] from among the descendants of Pharaoh, who said: 'Do you kill a man just for saying that his Lord is Allah?' and 'Ali ibn Abu Talib (as), who is the best of them.'" *Sahihs* are consecutively reported in stating that he is the supreme *siddiq* and the greatest *faruq*.

[37] The most distinguished among Sunni Imams, namely Muwaffaq ibn Ahmad, has quoted Abu Bakr ibn Mardawayh citing 'Ali (as) saying: "This nation will be divided into seventy-three groups; with the exception of one, all the rest will go to Hell; this (lucky) group is the one in whose honour Allah, the Exalted and the omni-Scient, has said: 'Among those whom We have created is a group that guides towards righteousness, and through righteousness (alone) do they achieve equity,' and they include me and my Shi'as."

[38] In his *Amali*, Shaykh al-Tusi correctly quotes the Commander of the Faithful saying that the Messenger of Allah, peace be upon him and his progeny, once recited the following verse: "The companions of the Fire are not equal to those who are the companions of Paradise," whereupon he explained saying: "The companions of Paradise are those who have followed me and recognized the authority of 'Ali ibn Abu Talib (as) after me." He was asked: "What about the companions of the Fire?" He answered: "These include the ones who are dissatisfied with his ('Ali's) government, those who shall violate the covenant and fight him after my demise." This hadith is quoted by al-Saduq from 'Ali,

parties He has also said: "Should We treat those who believe and do good deeds as We treat those who cause corruption on earth, or should We equal the virtuous to the corrupt (Qur'an, 38:28)?"³⁹ He has also said the following verse concerning both parties: "Do those who commit bad deeds surmise that We will treat them like We treat those who believe and do good deeds, in life and in death? Ill is their judgment."⁴⁰ About them and their supporters He has said: "Those who believe and do good deeds are the best of creation (Qur'an, 98:7)."⁴¹

About them and their adversaries Allah has said: "These are two opponents who differed regarding their Lord: those who disbelieve will be clothed with clothes of fire: boiling liquid shall be poured on their heads (Qur'an, 22:19)."⁴² Regarding them and

---

peace be upon him. Abul-Mu'ayyad Muwaffaq ibn Ahmad has quoted Jabir saying that the Messenger of Allah, peace be upon him and his progeny, has said: "By the One in whose hands my soul is, this ('Ali) and his Shi'as are the winners on the Day of Judgment."

³⁹ Refer to the meaning of this verse in 'Ali ibn Ibrahim's *tafsir* if you wish, or Chapters 81 and 82 of *Ghayat al-Maram*.

⁴⁰ This verse descended to honor al-Hamzah, 'Ali (as), and 'Ubaydah who came out to battle 'Utbah, Shaybah, and al-Walid. The believers are Hamzah, 'Ali (as), and 'Ubaydah, and the ones who committed wrong deeds are 'Utbah, Shaybah, and al-Walid. There are many authentic ahadith supporting this argument.

⁴¹ Suffices you for proof the fact that Ibn Hajar has admitted its revelation in their own honor, counting it among the verses in their favour, numbering it 11 among such verses in Part One, Chapter 11, of his *Al-Sawa'iq al-Muhriqa*; so, refer to it to see the verses we have quoted in reference to this verse in the chapter dealing with Sunnis giving credence to Shi'as in our book *Al-Fusul al-Muhimma*.

⁴² Al-Bukhari, in his explanation of the Qur'anic Chapter dealing with *hajj*, on page 107, Vol. 3, of his *sahih*, quotes 'Ali (as) saying: "I am the first to kneel down to submit a complaint before Allah on the Day of Judgment." Al-Bukhari then quotes Qays saying: "On their behalf this verse was revealed: 'These are two opponents who have brought their case before their Lord.' They are the ones who came out on Badr to battle 'Ali (as) and his two companions, Hamzah and 'Ubaydah, namely Shaybah ibn Rabi'ah and his two fellows 'Utbah ibn Rabi'ah and al-Walid ibn 'Utbah." On the same page, he quotes Abu Tharr saying that he used to swear by the verse referring to the two opponents who disputed about their Lord which was revealed in honour of 'Ali (as) and two of his companions,

their enemy, Allah has revealed these verses: "Is this who has been a believer like unto him that who has been an evildoer? They are not equal. As for those who believe and do good deeds, their abode shall be Perpetual Gardens, a reward for their good deeds. As for those who cause corruption, their abode is Hell-fire; every time they want to get out of it, they are turned back into it and is said to them: 'Taste the torment of the Fire in which you disbelieved (Qur'an, 32:19 20).'"[43]

Concerning them and those who boasted of providing water for the pilgrims and looking after the Haram mosque, Allah has revealed this verse: "Do you count the providing of the pilgrims with water and the maintenance of the Haram mosque equal to (the value of) those who believe in Allah and the Last Day and fight in the Way of Allah? They are not equal in the eyes of Allah, and Allah does not lead the wrongdoers (Qur'an, 9:19)."[44]

---

and about 'Utbah and both of his companions when they came out to duel at Badr.

[43] This verse was revealed on behalf of the Commander of the Faithful (as) *versus* al-Walid ibn 'Uqbah ibn Abu Ma'it, without any argument. This is ascertained by traditionists and endorsed by scholars of exegesis. Imam Abul-Hasan 'Ali ibn Ahmad al-Wahidi, while discussind this verse in his book *Asbab a-Nuzul*, quotes Sa'id ibn Jubayr citing Ibn 'Abbas saying that al-Walid ibn 'Uqbah ibn Abu Ma'it once said to 'Ali ibn Abu Talib (as): "I am stronger than you; my speech is more eloquent, and I am faster than you in raising an army." 'Ali (as) said: "Say no more, for you are none other than a debauchee," whereupon the verse "Is that who is a believer similar to that who is a debauchee? They certainly are not alike," was revealed, describing 'Ali (as) as the believer and al-Walid ibn 'Uqbah as the debauchee.

[44] This verse was revealed in honour of 'Ali (as), his uncle al-'Abbas, and Talhah ibn Shaybah who started thus bragging: "I am in charge of the House (Ka'ba); I have its keys, and mine is its covering cloth." Al-'Abbas said: "I am the one in charge of *siqaya* and maintenance." 'Ali (as) said: "I do not know what you both say, for I have said my prayers in the company of the one [Prophet Muhammad, S] who leads the *jihad* six months prior to anyone else among all people," whereupon Allah revealed the verse cited above. This is stated by Imam al-Wahidi while explaining the meaning of this verse in his book *Asbab al-Nuzul* citing al-Hasan al-Basri, al-Sha'bi, and al-Qurtubi. He also quotes Ibn Sirin and Murrah al-Hamadani saying that 'Ali (as) said the following to al-'Abbas once:

About their triumph in many trials and the magnitude of their patience, the Almighty says:"Among people is one who sells his life in return for Allah's Pleasure; Allah is Clement towards His servants (Qur'an, 2:207)."⁴⁵ Regarding their endeavour in the way of Allah and their toil, Allah has said: "Allah has traded the believers' lives for Paradise: they fight in the Way of Allah and they kill or get killed. It is His true Promise in the Torah, the Gospel and the Qur'an: who fulfils his promise better than Allah? Rejoice, therefore, for your bargain; that is the great victory. Those who turn (to Allah) in repentance, worship Him, and praise Him, wander in devotion to the Cause of Allah, bow down and prostrate in prayer, enjoin goodness and forbid evil, and observe the limits set by Allah (they do rejoice). So, proclaim the glad tidings to the Believers (Qur'an, 9:111-112)." "Those who (in charity) spend of their possessions by night and by day, in secrecy and in public, have their reward with their Lord: on them there shall be no fear, nor shall they grieve (Qur'an, 2:274)."⁴⁶

"Aren't you going to migrate? Aren't you going to join the Messenger of Allah, peace be upon him and his progeny?" He answered: "Do not I have a responsibility that is superior to the migration? Do not I provide water to the pilgrims of the House of Allah and maintain its Haram?" whereupon this verse was revealed.

⁴⁵ On page 4, Vol. 3, of his *Al-Mustadrak*, al-Hakim quotes Ibn 'Abbas saying: "'Ali has bartered his own life and has, indeed, put on the Prophet's garb." Al-Hakim testifies to the authenticity of this hadith according to the endorsement of both Shaykhs, although the latter did not narrate it themselves. In his *Talkhis al-Mustadrak*, al-Hakim admits the same on the said page, quoting Imam 'Ali ibn al-Husain (as) saying: "The first to barter his life for the Pleasure of Allah is 'Ali ibn Abu Talib (as) who slept in the bed of the Messenger of Allah (s)," then he quoted a few verses of poetry attributed to 'Ali (as) beginning with these:
I have safeguarded with my own life and strength
That of the best who walked on the surface of earth,
And circled the Ancient House, though alone,
And also around the [Black] Stone.

⁴⁶ Traditionists, scholars of exegesis, and authors who have written about the causes of revelation of the Holy Qur'an have all quoted Ibn 'Abbas explaining the verse reading: "Those who spend their wealth in charity at night, during the day, in secrecy, and in the open," by saying: "This verse was revealed in honour of 'Ali ibn Abu Talib (as) who had once in his possession four dirhams; he spent

They truly say only the truth. The Truthful Himself, blessed be His Name, has borne witness to that, saying: "Those who have brought forth the truth, believing therein, are indeed the God-fearing (Qur'an, 39:33)."[47] They are the faithful relatives of the Messenger of Allah (s), his kinfolk, whom Allah Has chosen for His beautiful care and great attention, saying: "And warn your near in kin (Qur'an, 26:214)." They are his relatives, and "Relatives have the priorities according to the Book of Allah" (Qur'an, 8:75; see also 33:6). On Doomsday, they will ascend to his rank and join him in the perpetual gardens of felicity as witnessed by Allah's statement:

> Those who believe and whose families follow them in faith - to them shall We join their families: We shall never deprive them (of the fruit) of aught of their deeds, (yet) each is in pledge for his deeds. (Qur'an, 52:21)[48]

---

one of them in the Cause of Allah at night, one during the day, one in secrecy, and in public also one; therefore, this verse was revealed to appreciate what he did." Imam al-Wahidi, too, has quoted this hadith of Ibn 'Abbas in his book *Asbabul-Nuzul*. He also quotes Mujahid narrating it, and he transmits it from al-Kalbi in more detail.

[47] The one who has brought forth the truth is the Messenger of Allah, and the one who has believed therein is the Commander of the Faithful (as), according to the hadith of al-Baqir, al-Sadiq, al-Kazim, al-Rida, peace be upon all of them, as well as by Ibn 'Abbas, Ibn al-hanafiyyah, 'Abdullah ibn al-Hasan, the martyred Zayd ibn 'Ali ibn al-Husayn, and 'Ali ibn Ja'far al-Sadiq (as). The Commander of the Faithful used to use this verse as a testimonial. Ibn al-Maghazli, in his *Manaqib*, quotes Mujahid saying: "The one who has brought the truth is Muhammad (s), and the one who has believed in him is 'Ali (as)." Both *huffaz*, that is, Ibn Mardawayh and Abu Na'im, have quoted it, and so have others.

[48] In his exegesis of Surahal-Tur on page 468, Vol. 2, of his authentic *Al-Mustadrak*, al-Hakim quotes Ibn 'Abbas paraphrasing the verse reading: "And those who believe and whose families follow them in faith, to them shall We join their families: nor shall We deprive them (of the fruit) of aught of their good deeds; yet each individual is pawned to what deeds he has done," by saying: "Allah shall elevate the status of a believer's descendants so that they would be able to join him in Paradise, even if they may be in a lower station," then he

They have the right dues as the Qur'an has stated: "And give the near in kin his dues (Qur'an, 17:26)," and they have the fifth: nobody's responsibility will be cleared until he defrays it: "Know ye this: whatever ye obtain of spoils, its fifth goes to Allah, the Messenger, and the (Messenger's) kinfolk (Qur'an, 8:41)." They are the ones upon whom Allah's favours have been bestowed as implied in this verse: "What Allah has bestowed on His Apostle - (and taken away) from them - for this ye made no expedition with either cavalry or camelry, but Allah gives power to His apostles over any He pleases, and Allah Has power over all things (Qur'an, 59:7)."

They are Ahl Al-Bayt addressed by Allah thus: "Allah desires to remove all abomination from you, Ahl Al-Bayt, and purify you with a perfect purification (Qur'an, 33:33)." They are the family of Yasin whom Allah greets in the Glorious Qur'an thus: "Peace be unto the family of Yasin (Qur'an, 37:130)."[49] And they are the family of Muhammad upon whom greetings and peace have been enforced by Allah Who says: "Allah and His angels send greetings unto the Prophet: O ye who believe! Send greetings unto him and many salutations (Qur'an, 33:56)."[50]

---

recited the same verse again and said: "Allah says He will not decrease their rewards aught."

[49] This is the third verse of the ones enUmarated by Ibn Hajar in Chapter 11 of his *Al-Sawa'iq al-Muhriqa*. The author goes on to say that a group of scholars of exegesis have quoted Ibn 'Abbas saying: "The implication of this verse is to send salutations unto Muhammad's Progeny (as)." Ibn Hajar says that al-Kalbi, too, has given it the same meaning, then he adds: "Al-Fakhr al-Razi has stated that the Prophet's Progeny constitutes his ['Ali's] peer in five instances: Allah has greeted him by saying: 'Peace be unto you, O Messenger, and unto the Progeny of Yasin,' in sending prayers unto him and them in *tashahhud, sadaqa*, and *tahara*, when the Almighty says: 'Taha,' that is, *tahir*, purified, and: '... purifies you with a perfect purification;' in loving them, saying: 'Follow me so that Allah may love you,' and also: 'Say: I do not ask you for any reward other than being kind to my kin.'"

[50] Al-Bukhari has quoted it in his *tafsir* of the holy Qur'an, in Vol. 3 of his *Sahih*, in a chapter dealing with the verse "Allah and His angels send salutations unto Muhammad," in his exegesis of Surahal-Ahzab. It is also quoted by Muslim in

Some people asked the Prophet, peace be upon him and his progeny, "O Messenger of Allah! We know how to greet you with peace, but how can we greet you with prayers?" He, Allah's peace and blessings be upon him and his progeny, answered, "Say: 'O Allah! Send blessings unto Muhammad and the family of Muhammad,'" according to the hadith. It was then understood then that greeting them was part of the prayers enjoined by this verse. This is why learned men have included the verse quoted above among others in their praise. Ibn Hajar has listed it in part 11 of his *Al-Sawa'iq al-Muhriqa* among verses in their praise,[51] peace be upon them. A good resort for them and a good reward: Gardens of Eden with gates wide open to receive them.[52]

> Who can compete with them? In the sun is meaning and heat,
> Parching, exerting the one who dares to compete.

Allah has chosen them for His favours, and they are the ones who are faster than all others in doing good deeds; they inherit the Book of Allah; about them He has said the following therein: "Among men is one who wrongs his own self (by ignoring the Imams), and one who seeks righteousness (by following the Imams), and one who is faster than others in doing good deeds by the Will of Allah (who is the Imam himself): this indeed is Allah's great favour (Qur'an, 35:32)."[53]

---

a chapter on sending greetings unto the Prophet (s) in his book on prayers in Vol. 1 of his *Sahih*, and it is quoted by all traditionists from Ka'b ibn 'Ajrah.

[51] Refer to the second of these verses on page 87.

[52] Al-Tha'labi, while discussing its meaning in his *Al-Tafsir al-Kabir*, quotes hadith in which the Messenger of Allhh, peace be upon him and his progeny, says: "Tuba is a tree in Paradise whose root is in my home and whose branch overshadows the residents of Paradise." Some people asked: "O Messenger of Allah! We have asked you before about it, and you told us that its root is in 'Ali's home and its branch is above the residents of Paradise," whereupon he, peace be upon him and his progeny, said: "Aren't my home and 'Ali's the same?"

[53] Thiqatul-Islam al-Kulayni has quoted in an authentic hadith Salim saying that he once asked Abu Ja'far (Imam al-Baqir) (as) about the meaning of the verse: "Then We let those whom We have selected from among Our servants inherit

These verses which demonstrate the Imams' virtues and merits must suffice. Ibn 'Abbas has said: "In praise of 'Ali alone, three hundred verses were revealed."[54] Others say that one fourth of the Holy Qur'an has been revealed in their praise. This comes as no surprise when we consider the fact that they and the Qur'an are twin brothers who do not separate from one another.

Be satisfied for now with what we have stated here of the perfect verses of the Holy Qur'an. Take them easily going and returning, making the advent of morning beams, easily and nicely, forgiving and at ease, from someone very well acquainted therewith, for none can tell you better than one endowed with experience, and peace be with you.

Sincerely,
Sh

---

the Book." The Imam, peace be upon him, explained it as follows: "The one who rushes to do good deeds is the Imam; the one who is moderate is the one who knows the value of the Imam; and the one who does injustice to his own self is the one who is not aware of the significance of the Imam." Something similar to this is cited from Imams Abu 'Abdullah al-Sadiq (as), Abul-Hasan al-Kazim, and Abul-Hasan al-Rida, peace be upon them, who are quoted by al-Saduq and by many others among our narrators. Ibn Mardawayh quotes 'Ali (as) explaining this verse thus: "The ones implied in this verse are we," and the details are available in our book *Tanzil al-Ayat*, as well as in *Ghayat al-Maram*.

[54] This is quoted by Ibn 'Asakir from Ibn 'Abbas, as stated in Section 3, Chapter 9, page 76, of *Al-Sawa'iq al-Muhriqa*.

Letter 13
Dhul-Qi'da 1329

Argument Regarding These Traditions Weak

May Allah bless your hand and pen! How elevated are their pages above the position of that who challenges and opposes! How defensible are their wise writings against the sight of the critic and researcher! Their pages struggle towards one destination, going along an aimed path, in a purposeful way. Their arguments do not come across the hearing of the wise without reverberating in acclamation.

Concerning your latest letter, its torrent has been overflowing, over brimming, supported by perfect verses and worthy proofs, with your own self coming thereby out of the charge put forth against you without committing any shortcoming in whatever entrusted to you. Whoever challenges you is bad in argument, stubborn, arguing about falsehood and acting like the ignorant.

Your opponents, however, may argue that those who narrated these verses supporting your argument are Shi'a, and these cannot be relied upon by the Sunnis. What would your answer, therefore, be? Please kindly provide it, if you will, and please do accept my thanks. Peace be with you.

Sincerely,
S

Letter 14
Dhul-Qi'da 1329

I. Fallacy of Opponent's Argument

Our answer is that the argument of such opponents is wrong. It is baseless because of the fallacy of its minor and major arguments.

As for its minor argument, that is, the claim that "Those who narrated the verses concerning your argument are Shi'a" is obviously false as testified by reliable Sunni authorities who recorded their statements in the meaning which we have stated. Their musnads testify to the fact that they are even more in number than Shi'as, as we explained in our book Tanzilul Ayat al-Bahira, in our chapter titled "Virtues of the Purified 'itra." You may also refer to Ghayatul Maram which is widely circulated throughout the Muslim world.

As for the major one, that is, the claim that Shi'as are not regarded by Sunnis as reliable (in narrating hadith), its fallacy is even more obvious than that of the minor one. Sunni Musndads bear testimony to this fact, and the authorities they relied upon are full of Shi'a names. Take, for example, their six *sahih* books and others which use them as their authorities, the latter being charged by those who attribute to them deviation from the Right Path, stamp them with the stamps of "Rafidis" and "deviators." To them have they attributed extremism, fanaticism, and deviation from the Path.

Among Bukhari's mentors are Shi'a men who have been charged with being "Rafidi" and stamped with hatred; nevertheless, this has never made Bukhari nor others doubt their fairmindedness. The latter relied upon them even in the *sahih* books feeling very comfortable with doing so. So; will the opponents who say that "Shi'as are not relied upon by Sunnis" find a listening ear? Of course not!

II. Opponents do not Know Shi'as

Such opponents, however, are ignorant. Had they known the truth, they would have come to know the fact that Shi'as have followed in the footsteps of and have emulated the Purified 'itra. Their manners are the 'itra's; therefore, everyone they relied upon is unmatchable in truthfulness and trustworthiness. Unmatchable are their reliable heroes in piety and caution. There are no peers for them among their dependable dignitaries in their forsaking the pleasures of this world, in their piety, worship, good manners, self-discipline, self-denial, and self-criticism. Nobody can equal them in ascertaining facts and looking for them with extreme care and moderation.

Had the opponent assessed their value, just as it is in reality, he would have put his confidence in them, entrusting his affairs to them. But his ignorance of them has made him wander at random about them like one riding a blind animal in a dark night. He would charge the trustees of Islam such as Muhammad ibn Ya'qub al-Kulayni, and a truthful among Muslims like Muhammad ibn 'Ali ibn Babawayh al-Qummi, and a mentor of the nation such as Muhammad ibn al-Hasan ibn 'Ali al-Tusi. He would belittle their sacred books which are the custodians of the knowledge of the family of Muhammad, peace and blessings be upon him and them, doubting their mentors who are the pioneers of knowledge and the ones who equal the Holy Qur'an and who have dedicated their lives to promote the teachings of Allah, the Sublime, the Almighty, His book and His Messenger, peace be upon him and his progeny, and the Imams of Muslims and their commoners.

III. Distinction of Emphasizing Illegality of Falsifying Hadith

Both righteous and vicious individuals have equally come to know how these virtuous men judge the case of telling lies. Thousands of their books curse lying, labelling falsification of hadith as sins punishable by Hell-fire. They are distinguished by their judgment of intentional falsification of hadith. They have considered it to break the fast, requiring both compensation and penitence from the person who commits it during the month of Ramadan, and they also require the same for whatever causes the breaking of the fast. Their fiqh and hadith are very clear in this regard; therefore, how can anybody charge their narrators while they are the good, the virtuous, the ones who spend the night praying and the day fasting? Since when have the virtuous among the followers and supporters of Muhammad's family been charged, while the Kharijis, Murji'is and Qadris have not? What other than obvious enmity and ugly ignorance? We seek refuge with Allah against forsaking us, and from Him do we seek help against the bad consequences of injustice and oppression. There is no might nor power except in Allah, the Sublime, the Almighty, and peace be with you.

Sincerely,
Sh

Letter 15

Dhul-Qi'da 1329

I. A Flash of the Truth

Your latest letter has been perfect in organization, clear in expression, sweet, great in benefit, easily accessible, vast in sphere, farsighted, well supported. I have looked into it keenly, and from among its contents indications of your success have flashed, and signs of your victory shone.

II. Requesting Details on Sunnis Relying on Shi'a Authorities

When you stated that Sunnis rely on Shi'as, however, you were very brief. You did not elaborate on your statement in this regard. It would have been better had you mentioned those men by their names and quoted Sunni texts indicating that those men were Shi'as and that they nevertheless relied on them. Could you please provide it so that the flags of truth may be seen and the lights of certainty shine? Peace be with you.

Sincerely,
S

Letter 16
Dhul-Qi'da 1329

A Hundred Shi'a Authorities Relied upon by Sunnis

Yes. I will provide you in a hurry with what you have requested, confining myself to some of those personalities who were visited by people from far and wide, on the condition that I will not be required to elaborate on them, since there is no room for that in this brief exposition. Here are their names and the names of their fathers arranged alphabetically:[1]

1. Aban ibn Taghlib

He was a Kufi reciter of the Holy Qur'an. Al-Dhahabi has recorded his biography in his own *Mizan* saying, "Aban ibn Taghlib of Kufa, is a persistent Shi'a. He, nevertheless, is truthful; so, we will rely on his truthfulness, and let him be punished for his innovation." He has also said that Ahmad ibn Hanbal, Ibn Ma'in and Abu Hatim put their trust in him. Ibn 'Adi quotes him and says that he is "extremist in Shi'ism." Al-Sa'di describes him as "an open deviator." Ibn al-Dhahabi goes on to describe the man's credentials, counting him as an authority relied upon by Muslim and authors of the four Sunan books, namely Abu Dawud, al-Tirmizi, al-Nisa'i and Ibn Majah, marking his name with the latter's initials. Refer to his narration of hadith in Muslim's *Sahih*, in the four Sunan books through al-Hakam and al-A'mash, in addition to Fudayl ibn 'Umar. Sufyan ibn 'Ayinah, Shu'bah, and Idris al-Awdi quote him as recorded in Muslim's book. He died, may Allah have mercy on him, in 141 A.H.

2. Ibrahim ibn Yazid

His name is Ibrahim ibn Yazid ibn 'Umar ibn al-Aswad al-Nakh'i al-Kufi, the faqih. His mother is Malika daughter of Yazid ibn Qays al-Nakh'i and sister of al-Aswad, Ibrahim, and 'Abdul-Rahman, sons of Yazid ibn Qays. Like their uncles 'Alqamah and Ubay, sons of Qays, they were all among the most reliable and authoritative among all Muslims. Authors of the six *sahih* books, as well as others, have all relied upon their authority while keeping in mind their being Shi'as.

---

[1] This Letter has grown quite lengthy because the topic demands it to be as such. Scholars are not bored by its length due to its contents that include precious benefits sought by every researcher and critic. Other than these, let whoever is bored read a portion of it, and let him judge the rest of it accordingly, then let him go directly to Letter No. 17 and the ones that succeed it. For fear of boring you by such a lengthy Letter, we have refrained from including it in lists of books containing valuable and very interesting information.

As regarding our man Ibrahim ibn Yazid, he has been included among Shi'a dignitaries by Ibn Qutaybah] on page 206 of his work *Al-Ma'arif* where he enumerates a few Shi'a dignitaries, taking his reliability for granted. Refer to his hadith in Bukhari's and Muslim's *Sahih* books as quoted by the mother of his uncle 'Alqamah ibn Qays, and by Humam ibn al-Harith, Abu 'Ubaydah ibn 'Abdullah ibn Mas'ud, 'Ubaydah, al-Aswad ibn Yazid, his uncle. Refer also to his hadith in Muslim's *Sahih* through his uncle from his mother's side, 'Abdul-Rahman ibn Yazid, and through Sahm ibn Munjab, Abu Mu'ammar, 'Ubayd ibn Nadlah, and 'Abis. In the two *sahih*s, he is quoted by Fudayl ibn 'Umar, al-Mughirah, Ziyad ibn Kulayb, Wasil, al-Hasan ibn 'Ubaydullah, Hammad ibn Abu Sulayman, and by Sammak. Ibrahim was born in 50 A.H., and he died at the age of either 95 or 96, four months after al-Hajjaj's death.

3. Ahmad ibn al-Mufdil

He is Ahmad ibn al-Mufdil ibn al-Kufi al-Hafri. Abu Zar'ah and Abu Hatim quote him and rely upon him while being fully aware of his status among Shi'as. In Ahmad's biography, as stated in *Al-Mizan*, Abu Hatim highlights this fact by saying: "Ahmad ibn al-Mufdil is one of the Shi'a chiefs, and he is truthful." AlDhahabi mentions him in his book *Al-Mizan*, putting on his name Abu Dawud's and al-Nisa'i's initials, indicating thereby that they consider him an authority. Refer to his hadith in their *sahih* through al-Thawri. He narrates through Asbat ibn Nasir and Isra'i.

4. Isma'il ibn Aban al-Azdi al-Kufi al-Warraq

He is mentor of al-Bukhari, as the latter indicates in his Sahih. Al-Dhahabi mentions him in his *Mizan*. This proves that both al-Bukhari and al-Tirmizi rely on him in their Sahih books. It has also been said that both Yahya and Ahmed cite him, and that al-Bukhari said this about him: "He is truthful," yet others say that the man used to follow the Shi'ite faith. He died in 286 A.H./899 A.D., but al-Qaysarani states that his year of demise was 216 A.H./831 A.D.

Al-Bukhari quotes him directly in more than one place of his Sahih, as al-Qaysarani and others have stated.

5. Isma'il ibn Khalifah al-Malla'i al-Kufi "Abu Isra'il"

He is more famous by his kunya, nickname, "Abu Isra'il" whereby he is identified. Al-Dhahabi mentions him in a chapter about nicknames in his *Mizan* saying, "He was a contemptible Shi'ite, one of the extremists who regard Uthman as *kafir*, apostate." He quotes many of his statements in this sense which we do not have to cite here. Despite all of this, al-Tirmizi quotes him in his Sahih and so do many authors of Sunan books. Abu Hatim considers his hadith as good. Abu Zar'ah says this about him: "He is truthful. There is extremism in his views." Ahmed says, "He used to write down his ahadith."[2] Ibn Ma'een said once about him, "He is trustworthy." Al-Fallas has said, "He is not one of those who tell lies [in narrating hadith, as is the case with Abu Hurayra, for e.g.]. You can refer to his hadith in al-Tirmizi's Sahih and elsewhere which he narrates through the venues of 'Utaybah and Atiyyah al-'Awfi. He is quoted by Isma'il ibn 'Amr al-Bajali and a group of renowned men from their class. Ibn Quraybah has counted him among Shi'ite men in his *Al-Ma'arif* book.

6. Isma'il ibn Zakariyya al-Assadi al-Khalliqani al-Kufi

In his Mizan, al-Dhahabi records his biography. He says, "Isma'il ibn Zakariyya (peace with Prophet Zakariyya) al-Khalliqani al-Kufi is a truthful Shi'ite," regarding him as one of those on whom the authors of the six Sahih books rely, placing on his name a symbol indicative of their consensus in this regard. Refer to his hadith in al-Bukhari's Sahih through the venue of Muhammed ibn Sawqah and 'Ubaydullah ibn Umar[3], and to his

---

[2] This statement is important. Many narrators of hadith did not know how to read and write; they simply memorized hadith, as is the case with the most cited Sunni narrator of all, namely Abu Hurayra. – Tr.

[3] I think this is a typographical error and that the name should be "Abdullah ibn Umar" instead, the famous traditions and son of second caliph Umar ibn al-Khattab. – Tr.

hadith in Muslim's *Sahih* through the venue of Suhayl, Malik ibn Maghul and others. As regarding his hadith about 'Asim al-Ahwal, it exists in both *Sahih* books. He is quoted by both men through the venue of Muhammed ibn al-Sabah and Abu al-Rabee', and through that of Muhammed ibn Bakar by Muslim. He died in Baghdad in 174 A.H./791 A.D. His being a Shi'ite is well known, so much so that this statement was attributed to him: "The servant of Allah who was called upon from the side of the Tur (Mount Sinai) was Ali ibn Abu Talib," and that he used to say, "The first, the last, the manifest and the hidden is Ali ibn Abu Talib." All these statements are lies circulated by liars against this man only because he was a follower of Ali, those who preferred Ali over others. While detailing his biography, al-Dhahabi says the following in his *Mizan* after citing all these lies about him, "Such talk has never been proven with regard to al-Khalliqani; it is the speech only of *zindeeqs*, irreligious folks."

7. Isma'il ibn 'Abbad

His full name is Isma'il ibn 'Abbad ibn al-Abbas al-Taleqani (Abul-Qasim) better known as al-Sahib ibn 'Abbad. Al-Dhahabi has mentioned him in his book *Al-Mizan* putting "DT" on his name to indicate that both Dawud and al-Tirmizi rely on him in their *sahih* books[4]. Then he goes on to describe him as "a talented Shi'a a man of letters". His being Shi'a is a matter which cannot be doubted by anyone. For this reason, he and his father earned high marks of prestige and greatness in the Buwayhid state .He is the first person among their government ministers to be called "sahib" (companion, friend), since he was since his adolescence a companion of Mu'ayyed al-Dawlah ibn Buwayh. This title followed him as he grew up till he was known thereby. Later on it was used for anyone who held the same reins of responsibility in the government. First he was minister to Mu'ayyed al-Dawlah Abu

---

[4] Upon mentioning Isma'il ibn 'Abbad al-Dhahabi departs from his usual approach in his *Al-Mizan* listing him before Isma'il ibn Aban al-Ghanawi and Isma'il ibn Aban al-Azdi. He has indeed greatly wronged his own self discarding all basic rights.

Mansur ibn Rukn al-Dawlah ibn Buwayh. After the latter's demise in Sha'ban of 373 in Jurjan Abul-Hassan Ali better known as Fakhr al-Dawlah brother of Mu'ayyed seized authority and retained Sahib's position. Fakhr al-Dawlah held Sahib in high esteem and fulfilled his wishes in the same way his own father Abu 'Abbad ibn al-Abbas did while he was in the service of Fakhr al-Dawlah's father Rukn al-Dawlah.

When at the age of 59 as-Sahib died on Thursday night 24th of Safar 385 A.H. in Rayy the city of Rayy closed down its shops as a sign of mourning and people gathered in front of his mansion awaiting his coffin. Fakhr al-Dawlah accompanied by government ministers and commanders of the army went there too wearing mourning clothes. When his coffin came out of his house people cried "Allahu Akbar!" in unison kissed the ground in glorification and Fakhr al-Dawlah followed the coffin on foot with the crowd and sat with them during the three days' mourning period. Poets read eulogies and scholars held commemorative ceremonies in his honour and he was praised by all those who could not attend his funeral. Abu Bakr al-Khawarizmi said: "Al-Sahib ibn 'Abbad grew up in the ministry's lap learned how to crawl and walk within its precincts was nursed from the most excellent of its bosoms and inherited it [ministry from his own forefathers." Abu Sa'id al-Rustami composed these verses in his praise:

He inherited ministry: a link in a chain
A great man he was heir of great men.
About the ministry of al-Abbas does 'Abbad narrate
While from 'Abbad does Isma'il Narrate.

In his biography of Sahib al-Tha'alibi says: "I can find no words to fairly describe Sahib's lofty status in knowledge and arts or the prestige he enjoys for being benevolent and generous or his unique virtues and possession of various merits. The best statement I can make on his behalf falls short of doing justice to the least among his virtues and eminence and my best description falls short of being fair to his virtues and characteristics." Sahib has written many precious books including *Al-Muhit* in Language in seven volumes; its chapters are arranged alphabetically. He collected an unmatched library. Nuh ibn al-Mansur one of the kings of Sam'an wrote to him once to invite him to be in charge of running his cabinet of ministers and managing the affairs of his kingdom. He apologized to him saying that he needed four hundred camels just to transport the contents of his library. This much about him should suffice.

8. Isma'il ibn 'Abdul-Rahman ibn Abu Karimah al-Kufi

Better known as al-Suddi he is the renowned interpreter of the Holy Qur'an. Stating his biography al-Dhahabi describes him as "charged with Shi'ism." Hussain ibn Waqid al-Maruzi discusses him claiming that he heard him once cursing Abu Bakr and 'Umar. In spite of all these charges he is quoted by al-Thawri and Abu Bakr ibn 'Ayyash and many in such class of writers. Muslim and authors of the four *sahih* books consider him an authority while Ahmed grants him his full confidence. Ibn 'Adi says that he is truthful. Yahya al-Qattan says there is nothing wrong with the ahadith he narrates. Yahya ibn Sa'id says: "I never heard anyone speaking ill of al-Suddi; none has deserted him." Ibrahim al-Nakh'i once passed by al-Suddi while the latter was interpreting the Holy Qur'an. Ibrahim said that al-Suddi was interpreting the Holy Qur'an according to the commonly used methods. If you read about al-Suddi in *Mizan al-I'tidal* you will find more details about what we have stated above. Refer to al-Suddi's hadith in Muslim's *Sahih* from Anas ibn Malik Sa'd ibn 'Ubaydah and Yahya ibn 'Abbad. Abu 'Awanah al-Thawri Hassan ibn Salih Za'idah and Isra'il have all quoted him being their mentor as stated in the four *sahih* books. He died in 127 A.H./744 A.D.

9. Isma'il ibn Musa al-Fazari al-Kufi

Al-Dhahabi's *Al-Mizan* quotes Ibn 'Uday saying "People despised his extremist Shi'a views." *Al-Mizan* also quotes 'Abdan saying: "Hammad and Ibn Abu Shaybah opposed our visiting him." He asked him once how he fared with "that immoral who curses our ancestors." In spite of all of this both Ibn Khuzaymah and Abu 'Arubah quote him being the instructor of their class. He is in the same category with Abu Dawud and al-Tirmizi who quote him and rely on his authority in their *sahih*s. Abu Hatim mentions him and calls him "trustworthy." Al-Nisa'i says "he is alright." All of this is stated in the man's biography in al-Dhahabi's *Al-Mizan*.

Refer to his hadith in al-Tirmizi's *Sahih* and Abu Dawud's Sunan as narrated by Malik Sharik and 'Umar ibn Shakir a friend of Anas. He died in 245. He was a son of al-Suddi's daughter although he might have denied that and Allah knows best.

10. Talid ibn Sulayman al-Kufi al-A'raj

Ibn Ma'in mentioned him and said: "He used to curse 'Uthman. Some of 'Uthman's followers heard that. They threw a rock at him which broke his leg, hence his nickname "al-A'raj," the lame. Abu Dawud has mentioned him and said he is Rafidi who curses Abu Bakr and 'Uthman. In spite of all of this, Ahmad and Ibn Namir rely on his authority despite their knowledge of his Shi'a beliefs. Ahmad has said, "Talid is a Shi'a, yet we could not find anything wrong with what he narrated." Al-Dhahabi has mentioned him in his book *Al-Mizan*, quoting statements about him made by learned men as stated above. He puts al-Tirmizi's initials on his name to indicate that the latter considers him an authority. Refer to his hadith in al-Tirmizi's *Sahih* through 'Ata ibn al-Sa'ib and 'Abdul Malik ibn 'Umayr.

11. Thabit ibn Dinar

Thabit is better known as Abu Hamzah al-Thumali. His being Shi'a is as clear as the sun. Author of *Al-Mizan* mentions him, stating that the name of 'Uthman was mentioned once in Abu Hamzah's presence. The latter sarcastically asked: "Who is 'Uthman?!" It also states that al-Sulaymani includes Abu Hamzah among the Rafidis. Al-Dhahabi puts al-Tirmizi's initials on Abu Hamzah's name as an indication of his being an authority. Waki' and Abu Na'im quote him and use him as their authority. Refer to his hadith in al-Tirmizi's *sahih* through Anas and al-Sha'bi and others of the same calibre. He died, may Allah have mercy on his soul, in 150 A.H.

12. Thuwayr ibn Abu Fakhita

He is better known as Abu Jahm al-Kufi, a freed slave of Ummu Hani', daughter of Abu Talib. Al-Dhahabi has mentioned him in his *Al-Mizan* and quoted Yunus ibn Abu Ishaq's allegation that he was Rafidi. Nevertheless, both Sufyan and Shu'bah have quoted him, and al-Tirmizi has produced some of his ahadith in his own *Sahih* through the authority of Ibn 'Umar and Zayd ibn Arqam. During the time of Imam al-Baqir (as), he maintained his loyalty to the Imam, and he came to be known as such. In this regard, he made quite a few interesting dialogues with 'Amr ibn Dharr, the judge, his contemporary Ibn Qays, and al-Salt ibn Bahram testifying to this fact.

13. Jabir ibn Yazid ibn al-Harith al-Ju'fi al-Kufi

Al-Dhahabi has narrated his biography in his own *Al-Mizan*, describing him as one of the Shi'a *'ulama*. He has quoted Sufyan saying that he heard Jabir saying that the knowledge with the Prophet (s) was transferred to 'Ali (as), then to al-Hasan (as), and so on till it reached Imam Ja'far al-Sadiq (as), who was one of his contemporaries. Muslim has mentioned him in one of the first chapters of his *Sahih*, quoting al-Jarrah who has heard Jabir saying that he knew seventy thousand ahadith of the Prophet all narrated through the authority of the father of Imam Ja'far al-Sadiq (as) (i.e. Imam Muhammad al-Baqir, peace be upon him). He has also quoted Zuhayr saying, "I know fifty thousand ahadith none of which I have narrated yet."

One day, he quoted one hadith and said, "This is one of the fifty thousand ahadith." According to his biography in al-Dhahabi's *Al-Mizan*, whenever Jabir narrated hadith through al-Baqir (as), he says: "The successor of the successors of the Prophet related to me that..." In his biography in the *Al-Mizan*, Ibn 'Uday says: "Commoners alleged that he [Jabir] used to believe in the return."

Relying on the authority of Za'idah, al-Dhahabi has included his biography in his *Al-Mizan* and said: "Jabir al-Ju'fi is a Rafidi who curses..." In spite of that, both al-Nisa'i and Abu Dawud rely on his authority. Refer to the hadith which he narrates concerning accidental prostrations in both *Sahih*s. Shihab, Abu 'Awanah, and many of their calibre, quote him. Al-Dhahabi, who mentions him in his *Al-Mizan*, has put the initials of both Abu Dawud and al-Tirmizi on his name to indicate their reliance on his authority. He also quotes Sufyan saying that Jabir al-Ju'fi is God-fearing while narrating hadith, and that he has said: "I have never seen anyone more pious than him [Jabir]." He also quotes Shu'bah saying that Jabir is truthful, and "Whenever Jabir narrated hadith, we listened, since he is the most trustworthy of all men." Waki' used to say, "If doubt entertains your mind, you may doubt anyone other than Jabir al-Ju'fi," and that Ibn 'Abd al-Hakam heard al-Shafi'i once saying that Sufyan al-Thawri said once to Shu'bah: "If you ever cast doubt about Jabir, that will signal the end of our friendship." Jabir died in either 127 or 128 A.H., may Allah have mercy on his soul.

14. Jarir ibn 'Abdul-Hamid al-Dabi al-Kufi

In his work *Al-Ma'arif*, Ibn Qutaybah includes him among Shi'a dignitaries, while al-Dhahabi mentions him in *Al-Mizan*, marking his name to denote the consensus of the *sahih*s in relying on his authority. He has praised him saying: "He is the learned man of the Rayy on whose authority many authors rely," testifying to the consensus of opinion regarding his reliability. Refer to his hadith in Bukhari's and Muslim's *Sahih*s narrated through A'mash, Mughirah, Mansur, Isma'il ibn Abu Khalid and Abu Ishaq al-Shaybani. Qutaybah ibn Sa'id, Yahya ibn Yahya and 'Uthman ibn Abu Shaybah have all quoted his ahadith as stated in both *sahih*s. He died, may Allah rest his soul in peace, in Rayy in 187 A.H. at the age of 77.

15. Ja'far ibn Ziyad al-Ahmar al-Kufi

Abu Dawud has mentioned him saying: "He is a truthful Shi'a." Al-Jawzjani has said: "He has deviated from the path," meaning from al-Jawzjani's path to that of the Prophet's Progeny (as). Ibn 'Adi has described him as a pious Shi'a. His grandson al-Husayn ibn 'Ali ibn Ja'far ibn Ziyad has said: "My grandfather Ja'far was one of the chiefs of Shi'as in Khurasan." Abu Ja'far al-

Dawaniqi ordered collars[5] to be put around his neck and the necks of a group of other Shi'as and be pulled like dogs; then he kept all of them in dungeons for quite a long time. Ibn 'Ayinah, Waki', Abu Ghassan al-Mahdi, Yahya ibn Bishr al-Hariri and Ibn Mahdi have all quoted his ahadith, being their mentor. Ibn Ma'in and others have considered him an authority on the Prophet's hadith. Ahmad describes his hadith as "*sahih*," authentic, accurate. Al-Dhahabi has mentioned him in his *Al-Mizan* and narrated what is stated above, putting the initials of both al-Tirmizi and al-Nisa'i on his name as an indication of both men's reliance on him. Refer to his hadith as they quote it in their *sahih*s through Bayan ibn Bishr and 'Ata' ibn al-Sa'ib. He is quoted through other men of the same calibre. He died, may Allah have mercy on his soul, in 167 A.H.

16. Ja'far ibn Sulayman al-Dab'i al-Basri (Abu Sulayman)

On page 206 of his *Ma'arif*, Ibn Qutaybah includes him among Shi'a dignitaries. Ibn Sa'd has mentioned him and emphasized his being a Shi'a and a trustworthy narrator of hadith. Ahmad ibn al-Miqdam has charged him of being "Rafidi." Ibn 'Adi has mentioned him saying: "He is a Shi'a. There is nothing wrong with his narration; his ahadith are by no means refutable, and I consider him as one whose hadith is acceptable." Abu Talib has said: "I have heard Ahmad saying that there is nothing wrong with the ahadith narrated by Ja'far ibn Sulayman al-Dab'i." It was said to Ahmad, "But Sulayman ibn Harb says that he did not write down al-Dab'i's ahadith." Ahmad replied by saying that Ibn Harb did not object that anyone should write down al-Dab'i's ahadith, and that [ibn Harb's prejudice was simply because] al-Dab'i was a Shi'a who quoted ahadith regarding 'Ali [ibn Abu Talib]." Ibn Ma'in has said: "I have heard certain talk from 'Abdul-Razzaq which testified to the man's "sectarian beliefs." I said to him: "Your mentors, such as Mu'ammar, Ibn Jurayh, al-Awza'i, Malik, and Sufyan, are all Sunnis. Where did you learn this [Shi'a] sect from?" He answered: "One day, Ja'far ibn Sulayman al-Dab'i visited us, and I saw him

---

[5] A collar put around the dog's neck; the meaning here is that his time to depart has come when a rope is tightened around his neck.

to be virtuous, pious, and from him did I learn this sect." I guess Muhammad ibn Abu Bakr al-Muqaddami saw contrariwise! He openly used to say that Ja'far learned "Rafidism" from 'Abdul-Razzaq; therefore, he used to curse the latter and say: "Nobody corrupted Ja'far's beliefs other than he ['Abdul-Razzaq]."

Quoting Sahl ibn Abu Khadouthah, al-Aqili has said: "I said to Ja'far ibn Sulayman: 'I have heard that you curse Abu Bakr and 'Umar.' He replied: 'Cursing I do not; but hating, you can say whatever you will.'"

Relying on Jarir ibn Yazid ibn Harun, Ibn Haban has said in his *Thiqat*, "My father sent me once to Abu Ja'far al-Dab'i. I said to the latter: 'I have heard that you curse Abu Bakr and 'Umar.' He replied: 'I do not curse them. But if you want to say that I despise them, feel free;' therefore, I concluded that he was Rafidi."

In his biography of Ja'far in *Al-Mizan*, al-Dhahabi has included all the above and emphasized as well the fact that the man was a pious 'alim "in spite of being a Shi'a." Muslim relies on him in his *Sahih* and quotes some of his unique ahadith which are published nowhere else as al-Dhahabi himself testifies when he narrates Ja'far's biography. Refer to his hadith in the *sahih* narrated through Thabit al-Banani, al-Ja'd ibn 'Uthman, Abu 'Umran al-Jawni, Yazid ibn al-Rashk and Sa'id al-Jariri. Qatan ibn Nasir, Yahya ibn Yahya, Qutaybah, Muhammad ibn 'Ubayd ibn Hasab, Ibn Mahdi and Musaddid have all quoted his ahadith. For example, he has said: "The Messenger of Allah, peace be upon him and his progeny, dispatched a division of the Muslim army under 'Ali's command, etc." Another hadith he has narrated states: "What do you want of 'Ali? 'Ali is of me, and I am of him. He is the *wali* (master) after me of every believer," as quoted in al-Nisa'i's *Sahih* and transmitted through Ibn 'Adi from al-Nisa'i. Al-Dhahabi has stated the above while discussing Ja'far in his *Al-Mizan*. He died in Rajab of 178 A.H.; may Allah be merciful unto him.

17. Jami' ibn 'Umayrah ibn Tha'labah al-Kufi al-Taymi (Taymullah)

Abu Hatim has mentioned his biography in his own *Al-Mizan* at the conclusion of which he states: "Al-Kufi is one of the Shi'a nobility whose hadith is authentically narrated." Ibn Haban has mentioned him and stated, as indicated in *Al-Mizan*, that he is "Rafidi." I say that al-'Ala' ibn Salih, Sadaqah ibn al-Muthanna, and Hakim ibn Jubayr have all derived their knowledge from him, being their mentor.

The Sunan books quote him thrice. Al-Tirmizi has acclaimed his hadith, as al-Dhahabi's *Al-Mizan* testifies. He is one of the *tabi'in*. He learned hadith from Ibn 'Umar and 'Ayesha. One of the ahadith which he learned from Ibn 'Umar states that the latter heard the Messenger of Allah addressing 'Ali thus: "You are my brother in this life and the life hereafter."

18. Al-Harith ibn Hasirah Abul Nu'man al-Azdi al-Kufi

Abu Hatim al-Razi describes him as one of the Shi'a nobility. Abu Ahmad al-Zubayri has attributed to him the belief in the return. Ibn 'Adi mentions him saying: "His hadith is written down in spite of the weakness I have seen therein. He is one of the Kufis who will be burned in the Fire because of their Shi'ism." Thanij has said: "I once asked Jarir: 'Have you met al-Harith ibn Hasirah?' He answered, 'Yes, indeed, I have. I met him as an old man who used to stay silent most of the time, and he insisted on something quite magnanimous.'" Yahya ibn Ma'in has mentioned him and said: "He is trustworthy [though] Khashbi [one of the derogatory names downgrading Shi'as, tr.]." Al-Nisa'i, too, trusts him. Al-Thawri, Malik ibn Maghul, 'Abdullah ibn Namir, and a group of their calibre, have all quoted him, since he was their mentor in whom they put their trust.

Al-Dhahabi has narrated his biography in his *Al-Mizan* stating all the above. Refer to his hadith in the Sunan through Zayd ibn Wahab, 'Ikrimah, and a group of their class. Al-Nisa'i quotes 'Abbad ibn Ya'qub al-Rawajni who quotes a chain of narrators including 'Abdullah ibn 'Abdul-Malik al-Mas'udi that al-Harith ibn Hasirah, according to Zayd ibn Wahab, reported that 'Ali (as) was heard once saying: "I am the servant of Allah and the brother of His Messenger; nobody else can say so except a liar."

Al-Harith ibn Hasirah narrates through Abu Dawud al-Subai'i, through 'Umran ibn Hasin, saying: "I was sitting once in the presence of the Messenger of Allah, peace be upon him and his progeny, with 'Ali sitting beside him. The Messenger of Allah, peace be upon him and his progeny, recited 'Or who else [other than Allah] that would respond to the one in dire need for help, remove his distress, and make ye vicegerents on earth?' 'Ali was shaken and moved a great deal; thereupon, the Messenger of Allah, peace be upon him and his progeny, patted 'Ali's shoulder and said: 'Nobody loves you except a true believer [a *mu'min*], and nobody hates you except a hypocrite till the Day of Judgment.'"

Traditionists such as Muhammad ibn Kuthayyir and others have quoted the hadith cited above from Al-Harith ibn Hasirah. Al-Dhahabi has transmitted it while stating the biography of Nafi' ibn al-Harith through the same chain of narrators. When he comes to Al-Harith ibn Hasirah, he comments saying, "He is truthful; but he is also Rafidi."

19. Al-Harith ibn 'Abdullah al-Hamadani

He was one of the close friends of the Commander of the Faithful (as) and one of the best *tabi'in*. His being a Shi'a needs no proof. He is the first of those counted by Ibn Qutaybah in his *Ma'arif* as Shi'a dignitaries. Al-Dhahabi has mentioned him in his *Al-Mizan*, admitting that he was one of the most highly recognized *'ulama* among the *tabi'in*; then he quotes Ibn Haban's statement saying that he was "extremist" in his Shi'a beliefs. After that, he states a great deal about some people's anger with him because of his Shi'a beliefs. In spite of all this, he also records their consensus that the man is the most knowledgeable, pious, and best informed about rituals. He has also admitted that the ahadith narrated by al-Harith are in existence in the four books of *sunan*. He declares the fact that Nisa'i, in spite of his prejudice, has strongly relied on the authority of al-Harith, admitting that the public, in spite of belittling the man, kept quoting his ahadith in all religious matters, and that al-Sha'bi called him a liar, then he turned around and quoted him!

Al-Dhahabi states the following in his *Al-Mizan*: "Obviously, al-Nisa'i falsifies him when it comes to the latter's tone and tale; but when the man narrates hadith, he does not disbelieve in him." *Al-Mizan* quotes Muhammad ibn Sirin saying: "There were five well-known companions of Ibn Mas'ud. I came to know four of them, but I missed al-Harith whom I never saw. He was the best among them."

A great deal of controversy exists regarding which of the other three, namely Alqamah, Masruq, or 'Ubaydah, is the best. I say that Allah has enabled trustworthy traditionists to do justice to al-Sha'bi and prove him a liar. This has been pointed out by Ibn 'Abd al-Birr in his book *Jami'' Bayanul 'Ilm* which quotes the frank statement made by Ibrahim al-Nakh'i belying al-Sha'bi, adding verbatim: "I think that al-Sha'bi has received his fair punishment for saying the following about al-Harith al-Hamadani: 'Al-Harith, one of the liars, informed me that..., etc.'"[6] Ibn 'Abd al-Birr has said: "Al-Harith has shown no indication of being a liar; some people have borne grudge against him simply because he loved 'Ali so much and preferred him over others. This is the reason why al-Sha'bi has called him a liar, since al-Sha'bi favours Abu Bakr, stating that the latter was the first to embrace Islam, and he favours 'Umar, too."

Among those who bore grudge against al-Harith was Muhammad Ibn Sa'd who included al-Harith's biography in Volume 6 of his *Tabaqat*, saying that al-Harith speaks "maliciously." He does not do al-Harith, nor any other Shi'a notable, any justice even when it comes to knowledge or feats. The "malicious" talk Ibn Sa'd is referring to is nothing other than allegiance to Muhammad's progeny and his taking them for guides in all matters, as Ibn 'Abd al-Birr has admitted in his above-quoted

---

[6] See page 196 of the abridged version of *Al-Jami' Baynal 'Ilmi wa Fad'ilih* by the contemporary scholar Shaykh Ahmad ibn 'Umar al-Muhammasani al-Beiruti.

statement. Al-Harith's demise took place in 65 A.H.; may Allah have mercy on his soul.

20. Habib ibn Abu Thabit al-Asadi al-Kahili al-Kufi

He was one of the *tabi'in*. Qutaybah, in his *Ma'arif*, and Shahristani, in his *Al-Milal wal Nihal*, have both included him among Shi'a dignitaries. Al-Dhahabi has mentioned him in his *Al-Mizan*, marking his name with the indication that authors of the six *sahih*s rely on his authority without any hesitation. Yahya Ibn Ma'in and a group of other scholars have all trusted him.

Al-Dawalibi, however, has spoken ill of him and classified his traditions as "weak" just because of his being a Shi'a. What truly amazes me is the attitude of Ibn 'Awn who was unable to find any pretext to cast doubt about Habib's traditions, in spite of his ardent desire to do so; therefore, he had to look down at him and call him "a'war," one-eyed. One's real handicap is sinning and speaking ill of others, not in losing an eye.

Refer to Habib's traditions in Bukhari's and Muslim's *Sahih*s as narrated through Sa'id ibn Jubayr and Abu Wa'il. His hadith narrated through Zayd ibn Wahab is recorded only in Bukhari's *Sahih*. In Muslim's *Sahih*, his hadith is narrated through Muhammad ibn 'Ali ibn 'Abdullah ibn 'Abbas, and through Tawus, al-Dahhak al-Mashriqi, Abu 'Abbas ibn al-Sha'ir, Abu al-Minhal 'Abdul-Rahman, 'Ata' ibn Yasin, Ibrahim ibn Sa'd ibn Abu Waqqas, and through Mujahid. In both *sahih*s, Misar, al-Thawri, and Shu'bah have quoted his traditions. In Muslim's *Sahih*, his ahadith are quoted by Sulayman al-A'mash, Hasin, 'Abdul-'Aziz ibn Sayah and Abu Ishaq al-Shaybani. He died, may Allah have mercy on his soul, in 119 A.H.

21. Al-Hasan ibn Hayy

Hayy's full name is Salih ibn Salih al-Hamadani, brother of 'Ali ibn Salih. Both men, who were born twins, are on the top of the list of Shi'a nobility. 'Ali was born only one hour earlier. Nobody has ever heard his brother calling him by his first name; instead, he used to always refer to him as "Abu Muhammad." This has been mentioned in Vol. 6 of Ibn Sa'd's *Tabaqat*, in the chapter dealing with al-Hasan. The author states: "Al-Hasan was one of the dignitaries, but he is inflicted with Shi'ism. He did not participate in the Jum'a prayers, and he preached denunciation of unjust rulers." He also mentions the fact that the man never invoked Allah's mercy on 'Uthman.

Ibn Sa'd has mentioned him in Vol. 6 of his *Tabaqat*, saying, "He is trustworthy; he narrates many ahadith, and he is a Shi'a." Imam Ibn Qutaybah has included his name among other narrators of hadith in his *Ma'arif*, highlighting his being a Shi'a. At the conclusion of his book, he lists al-Hasan among such narrators. Muslim and authors of the *sunan* books have all relied on his authority. Refer to his hadith in Muslim's *Sahih* as narrated by Sammak ibn Harb, Isma'il al-Sadi, 'Asim al-Ahwal, and Harun ibn Sa'd. 'Ubaydullah ibn Musa al-'Abasi, Yahya ibn Adam, Hamid ibn 'Abdul-Rahman al-Rawasi, 'Ali ibn al-Ja'd, Ahmad ibn Yunus and all renowned men of their intellectual calibre have learned hadith from him.

In his biography in *Al-Mizan*, al-Dhahabi indicates that Ibn Ma'in and others have trusted his [al-Hasan's] hadith. He adds saying that 'Abdullah ibn Ahmad has quoted his father saying that al-Hasan is more authentic than Sharik. Al-Dhahabi also states that Abu Hatim has said: "He is a trust; he has a sound and authentic memory," and that Abu Zar'ah has said: "He has combined in him accomplishment, *fiqh*, piety, and asceticism," and that Nisa'i has trusted him. He also quotes Abu Na'im saying: "I have quoted eight hundred traditionists; I have found none better than al-Hasan ibn Salih," and that he has also said: "I have come across nobody who did not err other than al-Hasan ibn Salih." He quotes 'Ubaydah ibn Sulayman saying: "Allah is too shy to harm al-Hasan ibn Salih." He quotes Yahya ibn 'Ali Bakir asking al-Hasan ibn Salih: "Describe to us how to conduct the ceremonial bathing of the deceased;" he could not do so because of being overcome by tears. He quotes 'Ubaydullah ibn Musa saying: "I used to recite the holy Qur'an in the presence of 'Ali ibn Salih. Having finished reciting 'Exercise patience [O Muhammad]!; We have granted them a respite only for an appointed time,' his brother fell down snorting like a wounded bull; so, 'Ali lifted him up, wiped and washed his face then supported him against falling again," and that Waki' has said: "Al-Hasan and 'Ali sons of Salih and their mother divided night-time among them into three parts: each alternates in his portion thereof in keeping vigil, spending it in prayers and adoration. When their mother died, they split it into equal halves. Then 'Ali died; therefore, al-Hasan used to stay all night long worshipping."

Abu Sulayman al-Darani has said: "I have never seen anyone more awe-stricken than al-Hasan son of Salih who stood up one night to recite Chapter 78 of the Holy Qur'an and fainted yet continued reciting till dawn." He was born, may Allah have mercy upon him, in 100 A.H. and he died in 169 A.H.

22. Al-Hakam ibn 'Utaybah al-Kufi

Ibn Qutaybah has indicated the fact that al-Hakam ibn 'Utaybah was a Shi'a in his *Ma'arif* and included him among Shi'a nobility. Both Bukhari and Muslim rely on his authority. Refer to his hadith in their *sahih*s as narrated by Abu Jahifah, Ibrahim al-Nakh'i, Mujahid, and Sa'id ibn Jubayr. In Muslim's *Sahih*, it is narrated by 'Abdul-Rahman ibn Abu Layla, al-Qasim ibn Mukhaymarah, Abu Salih, Dharr ibn 'Abdullah, Sa'id ibn 'Abdul-Rahman ibn 'Abzi, Yahya al-Jazzar, Nafi (a slave of Ibn 'Umar), 'Ata' ibn Abu Rabah, 'Imarah ibn 'Umayr, 'Arrak ibn Malik, al-Sha'bi, Maymun ibn Mahran, al-Hasan al-'Arni, Mus'ab ibn Sa'd and 'Ali ibn al-Husayn.

In both *sahih*s, his ahadith are quoted by Mansur, Misar and Shu'bah. Particularly in Bukhari's *Sahih*, his ahadith are narrated by 'Abdul-Malik ibn Abu Ghaniya. In Muslim's *Sahih*, his ahadith are narrated by al-A'mash, 'Amr ibn Qays, Zayd ibn Abu Anisa, Malik ibn al-Maghul; Aban ibn Taghlib, Hamzah al-Zayyat, Muhammad ibn Jehada, Mutraf and Abu 'Awanah. He died in 115 A.H. at the age of 65.

23. Hammad ibn 'Isa al-Jehni

He drowned at Juhfa. Abu 'Ali has mentioned him in his book *Muntahal Maqal*. Al-Hasan ibn 'Ali ibn Dawud abridged the said article in his own concise *Mukhtasar*, in a chapter dealing with biographies of notables, a group of Shi'a *'ulama* and authors of biographies and dictionaries who regard him as most trustworthy, a follower of the rightly-guided Imams, peace be upon them. He learned from Imam al-Sadiq, peace be upon him, seventy ahadith by the holy Prophet, peace be upon him and his progeny, but he did not relate more than twenty of them. He has authored a few books with which followers of our faith are familiar.

Once he entered in the presence of Imam Abul-Hasan al-Kazim, peace be upon him, and said: "May my life be sacrificed for you! Please pray Allah to bless me with a house, a wife, a son, a servant, and a pilgrimage every year." The Imam said: "Lord! I invoke Thee to send blessings unto Muhammad and the progeny of Muhammad, and to bless this man with a house, a wife, a son, a servant, and a pilgrimage for fifty years each." Hammad said: "When he prayed for my performing the pilgrimage fifty times, I became sure I would never live beyond that. I have performed the annual pilgrimage forty-eight times; this is my house with which Allah has blessed me; yonder there is my wife behind the curtain listening to me; this is my son, and this is my servant; I have been blessed with all of these."

Two years later, and having performed the pilgrimage fifty times, he accompanied Abul 'Abbas al-Nawfali al-Qasir on his fifty-first pilgrimage. When he reached the place where pilgrims put on the *ihram* garb, he entered the Johfa river for a bath, but the torrent overwhelmed him, and he drowned before being able to perform his 51st pilgrimage. His death, may Allah have mercy on his soul, took place in 209 A.H. His birth-place is Kufa, but he resided in Basrah. He lived over seventy years. We have conducted a thorough research of his biography in our book *Mukhtasar al-Kalam fi Mu'allifi al-Shi'a min Sadr al-Islam* [A Brief Discourse of Shi'a Authors of Early Islam].

Al-Dhahabi has mentioned him and put "TQ" on his name as a reference to those among the authors of the Sunan who have quoted him [Tirmizi] and Dar Qutni, and mentioned the fact that he drowned in 208 A.H., and that he narrated hadith through Imam al-Sadiq (as). The author has shown his grudge towards this man, calling his hadith "weak" for no reason other than his beliefs being Shi'a. Strange enough, Dar Qutni calls his hadith "weak" on one hand, while on the other he uses him as an authority in his own Sunan - thus indeed do some people behave!

24. Hamran ibn 'Ayinah

He is brother of Zurarah. Both men were among the most reliable Shi'as, custodians of the *shari'a*, oceans of the knowledge about Muhammad's progeny (as). They were lanterns that shone in the dark and pillars of guidance. They frequented Imams al-Baqir and al-Sadiq (as) and enjoyed a lofty status in the eyes of the Imams among the Prophet's descendants. Al-Dhahabi mentions Hamran in his *Al-Mizan*, marking his name with Q to indicate who among the compilers of the sunan relies upon his authority [i.e. Dar Qutni. Then al-Dhahabi adds: "He has narrated hadith from Abul Tufayl and others. Hamzah has recited the holy Qur'an to him, and he himself is used to recite it with perfect accuracy." Ibn Ma'in considers his hadith "negligible," while Abu Hatim hails him as a mentor. Yet Abu Dawud labels him "Rafidi."

25. Khalid ibn Mukhlid al-Qatwani

Also known as Abul-Haytham al-Kufi, he is one of Bukhari's mentors, as the latter states in his *Sahih*. Ibn Sa'd mentions him on page 283, Vol. 6, of his *Tabaqat*, saying, "He was a staunch Shi'a. He died in Kufa in mid-Muharram of 213 A.H. during the reign of al-Ma'mun. He was extremist in his Shi'a beliefs, and writers have documented this fact."

Abu Dawud mentions him saying: "He is truthful; but he follows Shi'ism." Al-Jawzjani says the following about him: "He never ceases denouncing [certain persons], publicly propagating his corrupt sect." Al-Dhahabi narrates his biography in his own *Al-Mizan*, quoting the views of both Abu Dawud and Jawzjani stated above. Yet both Bukhari and Muslim have relied upon his authority in several chapters of their respective *sahih*s. Refer to his hadith as in Bukhari's *Sahih* as narrated from al-Mughirah ibn 'Abdul-Rahman, and in Muslim's *Sahih* by Muhammad ibn Ja'far ibn Abul Kathir, Malik ibn Anas, and Muhammad ibn Musa. Both *sahih*s quote his *Al-Mizan* from Sulayman ibn Bilal and 'Ali ibn Mushir. Al-Bukhari quotes his hadith in several places of his *Sahih*, without referring to any chain of narrators, quoting two of his ahadith from Muhammad ibn 'Uthman ibn Karamah. Muslim narrates his hadith as transmitted by Abu Karib, Ahmad ibn 'Uthman al-'Awdi, al-Qasim ibn Zakariyyah, 'Abd ibn Hamid, Ibn Abu Shaybah, and Muhammad ibn 'Abdullah ibn Namir. Authors of the sunan have all relied on the authority of his hadith, while being aware of his sect.

26. Dawud ibn Abu 'Awf (Abul-Hijab)

Ibn 'Adi has mentioned him saying, "I cannot rely upon his authority due to his being a Shi'a. The majority of the ahadith he narrates are related to the virtues of Ahl al-Bayt."

Consider with amazement such a statement! No harm, indeed, can reach Dawud from these Nasibis since both Sufyans quote his ahadith, in addition to 'Ali ibn 'Abis and others belonging to the elite among their peers. Both Abu Dawud and al-Nisa'i have relied upon his authority, and so have Ahmad and Yahya. Al-Nisa'i has said the following about him: "There is nothing wrong with his ahadith." Abu Hatim has said: "His hadith is sound." Al-Dhahabi has quoted such testimonies in his *Sahih*. Refer to his hadith in Abu Dawud's *Sunan*, in al-Nisa'i's through Abu Hazim al-Ashja'i, 'Ikrimah, and others.

27. Zubayd ibn al-Harith ibn 'Abdul-Karim al-Yami al-Kufi

Also known as Abu 'Abdul-Rahman, he is mentioned in al-Dhahabi's *Al-Mizan* where the author says: "He is a trustworthy *tabi'i* who inclines towards Shi'ism." Then he quotes statements to prove that Zubayd's hadith has been verified by al-Qattan, and that there are other renowned critics and verifiers who regard him trustworthy. Abu Ishaq al-Jawzjani has included a crude statement about him which is typical of his attitude and that of other Nasibis, stating:

> "Among the residents of Kufa, there is a faction whose faith is not appreciated [by Nasibis], yet they happen to be masters of hadith. Among them are: Abu Ishaq, Mansur, Zubayd al-Yami, al-A'mash and other peers. People have tolerated them for no reason other than their truth in narrating hadith, and their narrations testify to the authenticity of one another,"

Up to the conclusion of his statement which truth has dictated to him to reveal. Often, truth is spoken by the fair minded just as it is by the stubborn and obstinate. What harm can reach these lofty pillars of knowledge, the masters of hadith in Islam, if such a critic does not appreciate their holding in high esteem the holy Prophet's kin who are the gates of salvation, the protectors of all humans on earth after the Prophet (s) himself, his nation's ark of salvation? What harm can befall them from the critic who has no choice except to pursue his quest till reaching their door steps, and no option but to beg their own favours?

> If dignitaries of my tribe are pleased with me Then let its villains chafe and be angry.

These authorities do not pay any attention to al-Jawzjani or others like him, having been held trustworthy by the authors of the *sahih* books and by those of all sunan as well. Refer to Zubayd's hadith in both Bukhari's and Muslim's *Sahih*s as transmitted by Abu Wa'il, al-Sha'bi, Ibrahim al-Nakh'i, and Sa'd ibn 'Ubaydullah. Only Bukhari quotes his hadith through Mujahid. In Muslim's *Sahih*, his hadith is narrated by Murrah al-Hamadani, Muharib ibn Dithar, Ammarah ibn 'Umayr, and Ibrahim al-Taymi. His hadith is quoted in both *sahih*s as transmitted by Shu'bah, al-Thawri, and Muhammad ibn Talhah. In Muslim's *Sahih*, his hadith is narrated by Zuhayr ibn Mu'awiyah, Fadil ibn Ghazwan, and

Husayn ibn al-Nakh'i. He died, may Allah have mercy on his soul, in 124 A.H.

28. Zayd ibn al-Habab Abul-Hasan al-Kufi al-Tamimi

Ibn Qutaybah has included his biography among those whose biographies he has included among Shi'a dignitaries in his work *Al-Ma'arif*. Al-Dhahabi has mentioned him in his *Al-Mizan*, describing him as "pious, trustworthy, truthful." He indicates his being vouched as trustworthy by Ibn Ma'in and Ibn al-Madini. He has quoted Abu Hatim and Ahmad describing him as truthful, adding that 'Adi has said: "He is one of the reliable Kufi traditionists whose trustworthiness is never doubted." Muslim has relied on his authority. Refer to the latter's *sahih* containing his hadith as narrated by Mu'awiyah ibn Salih, al-Dahhak ibn 'Uthman, Qurrah ibn Khalid, Ibrahim ibn Nafi', Yahya ibn Ayyub, Saif ibn Sulayman, Hasan ibn Waqid, 'Ikrimah ibn 'Ammar, 'Abdul-'Aziz ibn Abu Salma, and 'Aflah ibn Sa'id. His hadith is quoted by Ibn Abu Shaybah, Muhammad ibn Hatim, Hasan al-Hulwani, Ahmad ibn al-Munthir, Ibn Namir, Ibn Karib, Muhammad ibn Rafi', Zuhair ibn Harb, and Muhammad ibn al-Faraj.

29. Salim ibn Abul Ja'd al-Ashja'i al-Kufi

He is brother of 'Ubayd, Ziyad, 'Umran, and Muslim, sons of Abul-Ja'd.

In Volume 6 of *Al-Tabaqat*, Sa'd mentions all of them on page 2303 and the succeeding pages. When he comes to Muslim, he says, "Abul-Ja'd begot six sons. Two of them followed Shi'ism. These are Salim and 'Ubayd. Two others are Murji'is, while the remaining two agree with the Kharijites. Their father used to say: 'What is the matter with you? I wonder why Allah has made your views vary so much.'" Ibn Qutaybah has discussed them on page 156 of his *Ma'arif* in a chapter dealing with Shi'a *tabi'in* and their successors.

A group of learned scholars has testified to the Shi'a views of Salim ibn Abul-Ja'd. Qutaybah, on page 206 of his *Ma'arif*, has included him among Shi'a dignitaries, and so has al-Shahristani in his work *Al-Milal wal Nihal* on page 27, Vol. 2, in the footnote of his chapter on Ibn Hazm. Al-Dhahabi has mentioned him in his *Al-Mizan*, calling him a trustworthy *tabi'i*. He has also stated that his hadith from al-Nu'man ibn Bashir and Jabir is included in both *sahih*s. In fact, his hadith, from Anas ibn Malik and Karib, is included in both *sahih*s as scholars of hadith already know. Al-Dhahabi says that his hadith from 'Abdullah ibn 'Umar, and from Ibn 'Umar, exists in Bukhari's *Sahih*. The latter also contains his hadith from Ma'dan ibn Abu Talha and the latter's father. His hadith is quoted in both *sahih*s by al-A'mash, Qatadah, 'Amr ibn Murrah, Mansur, and Hasin ibn 'Abdul-Rahman. He also knows hadith quoted by al-Nisa'i and Abu Dawud in their respective Sunan. He died in either 87 or 97 A.H. during the reign of Sulayman ibn 'Abdul-Malik, or, as some say, during that of 'Umar ibn 'Abdul-'Aziz, and Allah knows best.

30. Salim ibn Abu Hafsah al-'Ijli al-Kufi

Al-Shahristani includes him in his book *Al-Milal wal-Nihal* among Shi'a nobility. Al-Fallas says: "He is a weak traditionist who is extremist in his Shi'a beliefs." Ibn 'Adi says: "People criticize his extremism; but I hope there is nothing wrong with his hadith." Muhammad ibn Bashir al-'Abdi says: "I have seen Salim ibn Abu Hafsah as a fool with a long beard - what a beard! He says: 'I wish I had been a partner of 'Ali in everything he possessed.'"

Al-Husayn ibn 'Ali al-Ju'fi has said: "I have seen Salim ibn Abu Hafsah as a fool with a long beard who used to often say, 'Here I come, O killer of Na'thal, annihilator of Banu Umayyah!'" 'Amr ibn al-Salim ibn Abu Hafsah asked him once: "Did you kill 'Uthman?" He answered: "Did I?!" 'Amr said: "Yes, you did. You do not condemn his murder." Abu ibn al-Madini has said: "I have heard Jarir saying, 'I broke my friendship with Salim ibn Abu Hafsah because he used to always defend the Shi'as.'" Al-Dhahabi has detailed his biography, mentioning all the above. On page 234 of Vol. 6 of his *Tabaqat*, Ibn Sa'd mentions him and says: "He was very staunch in his Shi'a beliefs. He entered Mecca during the reign of the 'Abbasides crying, 'Here I come, here I come, O killer of the Umayyads!' His voice was quite loud, so much so that his call was heard by Dawud ibn 'Ali who inquired: 'Who is this man?' People informed him that it was Salim ibn Abu Hafsah, and they explained his story and views."

Al-Dhahabi has included his biography in his *Al-Mizan* commenting, "He was chief of those who belittled Abu Bakr and 'Umar." In spite of this, however, both Sufyans quote his hadith, and so does Muhammad ibn Fudayl, while al-Tirmizi has relied on his authority, and Ibn Ma'in has held him trustworthy. He died in 137 A.H.

31. Sa'd ibn Tarif al-Iskafi al-Hanzali al-Kufi

Al-Dhahabi mentions him, marking his name with TQ as a reference to the authors of *sunan* who quote him (i.e. al-Tirmizi and Dar Qutni). Al-Dhahabi also quotes al-Fallas saying that Sa'd is "weak, extremist in his Shi'a beliefs." In spite of his being a "Shi'a extremist," al-Tirmizi and others quote him. Refer to his hadith in al-Tirmizi's *Sahih* as narrated by 'Ikrimah and Abul-Wa'il. He also narrates hadith as transmitted by al-Asbagh ibn Nabatah, 'Uman ibn Talhah and 'Umayr ibn Ma'mun. Isra'il, Haban and Abu Mu'awiyah all quote him.

32. Sa'id ibn Ashwa'

He is mentioned in al-Dhahabi's *Al-Mizan* where the author says: "Sa'id ibn Ashwa' is a famous and truthful Kufi judge. Al-Nisa'i says that there is nothing wrong with his hadith, and that he is a friend of al-Sha'bi. Al-Jawzjani describes him as extremist, heretic, and a Shi'a zealot."

Both al-Bukhari and al-Muslim rely on his authority in their respective *sahih*s. His hadith from al-Sha'bi is regarded as authentic by authors of both *sahih* books. In both Bukhari's and Muslim's *Sahih*s, his hadith is quoted by Zakariyyah ibn Abu Za'idah and Khalid al-Haththa'. He died during the reign of Khalid ibn 'Abdullah.

33. Sa'id ibn Khaytham al-Hilali

Ibrahim ibn 'Abdullah ibn al-Junayd was asked once: "Sa'id ibn Khaytham is a Shi'a. What do you think of him?" He answered: "Let's say that he is a Shi'a, but he also is trustworthy."

Al-Dhahabi mentions him in his *Al-Mizan*, quoting Ibn Ma'in narrating the gist of what has just been stated above. He has also marked his name with the initials of both al-Tirmizi and al-Nisa'i to indicate that both authors quote his hadith in their *sahih*s. He also mentions the fact that Sa'id narrates hadith from Yazid ibn Abu Ziyad and Muslim al-Malla'i. His nephew, Ahmad ibn Rashid, too, narrates his hadith.

34. Selamah ibn al-Fudayl al-Abrash

He was a Rayy judge and a reporter of traditions related to the battles in which the holy Prophet (s) participated as transmitted by Ibn Ishaq. His *kunyat* (surname) is Abu 'Abdullah. In his biography in the *Al-Mizan*, Ibn Ma'in says: "Selamah al-Abrash al-Razi is a believer in Shi'ism and a man whose hadith is [often] quoted, and there is no fault in the latter." Abu Zar'ah has also said in the *Al-Mizan* that the natives of Rayy do not like him because of his (religious) views. Actually, their attitude is due to their own views regarding all followers of the household of the Prophet (s).

Al-Dhahabi has mentioned him in his *Al-Mizan*, marking his name with the initials of Abu Dawud and al-Tirmizi and saying: "He is well remembered for his prayers and supplications." He died in 191 A.H. Ibn Ma'in testifies to the fact that the hadith related to the Prophet's military expeditions as narrated by Selamah is more reliable than anyone else's. Zanih is quoted as having said that he had heard Selamah al-Abrash saying that he had heard hadith related to the expeditions from Ishaq twice, and that he had also written down his ahadith as he had done with those of the expeditions.

35. Selamah ibn Kahil ibn Hasin ibn Kadih ibn Asad al-Hadrami Abu Yahya

A group of scholars following the faith of the majority of Muslims, such as Ibn Qutaybah in his *Ma'arif*, who mentions on page 206 his distinction, and al-Shahristani in his *Al-Milal wal-Nihal*, on page 27, Vol. 2, have included him among Shi'a nobility. Authors of the six *sahih*s have all relied on his authority, and so have others. He has learned hadith from men like Abu Jahifah, Suwayd ibn Ghaflah, al-Sha'bi, 'Ata' ibn Abu Rabah, all cited in Bukhari and Muslim. In Muslim, he quotes hadith from Karib, Dharr ibn 'Abdullah, Bakir ibn al-Ashaj, Zayd ibn Ka'b, Sa'id ibn Jubayr, Mujahid, 'Abdullah ibn 'Abdul-Rahman ibn Yazid, Abu Selamah ibn 'Abdul-Rahman, Mu'awiyah ibn al-Suwayd, Habib ibn 'Abdullah, and Muslim al-Batin. Al-Thawri and Shu'bah have both cited his hadith in these two works, while in Bukhari, his hadith is cited by Isma'il ibn Abu Khalid. In Muslim, he is quoted by Sa'id ibn Masruq, Aqil ibn Khalid, 'Abdul-Malik ibn Abu Sulayman, 'Ali ibn Salih, Zayd ibn 'Abu Anisah, Hammad ibn Selamah, and al-Walid ibn Harb.

Selamah ibn Kahil died on 'Ashura of 121 A.H.

36. Sulayman ibn Sa'id al-Khuza'i al-Kufi

He used to be the supreme head of the Shi'as of Iraq, the arbitrator among them, their custodian and advisor. They had all met in his house when they swore the oath of allegiance to Imam Husayn (as). He is the herald of the *tawwabin* (the penitents) among the Shi'as, those who rose to avenge the murder of Imam Husayn (as). They were four thousand strong who camped at Nakhila early in Rabi' al-Thani, 65 A.H., then marched towards 'Ubaydullah ibn Ziyad and engaged his army at Jazira. They fought fiercely till each and every one of them died. Sulayman, too, was martyred at a place called 'Ayn al-Warda after Hasin shot him with a deadly arrow. He was 93 years old then. His head and that of al-Musayyab ibn Najba were carried as trophies to Marwan ibn al-Hakam.

His biography is recorded in Vol. 6, Part One, of Ibn Sa'd's *Tabaqat*, and in the *Isti'ab* of Ibn 'Abd al-Birr. All those who wrote the stories of the ancestors have recorded his biography and praised his virtues, faith and piety. He enjoyed a lofty status, a position of honour and dignity among his folks, and his word weighed heavily.

He is the one who killed Hawshab, the notorious enemy of the Commander of the Faithful, in a duel at Siffin. Sulayman was keen to notice that the enemies of Ahl al-Bayt had gone astray. Traditionists have sought his audience. The ahadith he narrates about the Prophet (s), the ones which he directly reported or those transmitted by Jubayr ibn Mut'im relying on his authority, are recorded in both Bukhari's and Muslim's *Sahih*s. In the latter, he is cited by Abu Ishaq al-Subay'i and 'Adi ibn Thabit. Sulayman has narrated ahadith which are not included in either *sahih*s. These include ahadith from the Commander of the Faithful, his son Imam al-Hasan al-Mujtaba (as), and Abiy. In works other than these *sahih*s, his hadith is transmitted by Yahya ibn Ya'mur, 'Abdullah ibn Yasar, and by others.

37. Sulayman ibn Tarkhan al-Taymi al-Basri

A slave of Qays, the *imam*, he is one of the most reliable authorities on hadith. Ibn Qutaybah has included him among Shi'a dignitaries in his book Al-Ma'arif. Authors of the six *sahih*s, as well as others, have relied on his authority. Refer to his hadith in both *sahih*s through Anas ibn Malik, Abu Majaz, Bakr ibn 'Abdullah, Qatadah, and Abu 'Uthman al-Nahdi. Muslim's *Sahih* quotes his hadith through others. In both *sahih*s, his hadith is cited by his son Mu'tamir, and by Shu'bah and al-Thawri. Another party cites his hadith in Muslim's *Sahih*. He died in 143 A.H.

38. Sulayman ibn Qarm ibn Ma'adh

He is also known as Abu Dawud al-Dabi al-Kufi. Ibn Haban mentions him within the text of Sulayman's biography in *Al-Mizan*. Ibh Haban has said, "He is a Rafidi - very much so." Nevertheless, Ahmad ibn Hanbal has trusted him. At the conclusion of Sulayman's biography as recorded in *Al-Mizan*, Ibn 'Adi says, "The ahadith narrated by Sulayman ibn Qarm are authentic. Moreover, his are by far more reliable than those related by Sulayman ibn Arqam."

Muslim, al-Nisa'i, al-Tirmizi, and Abu Dawud have all cited his ahadith. When al-Dhahabi mentions him, he puts the initials of these traditionists on his name. Refer to Muslim's *Sahih* where Abul-Jawab's hadith is narrated by Sulayman ibn Qarm from al-A'mash, up to the Prophet (s). The said hadith states that the Prophet (s) has said that a man keeps company with those whom he loves.

In the *sunan*, his ahadith quote Thabit through Anas successively saying that the Prophet (s) has said: "Seeking knowledge is a religious obligation upon every Muslim." He quotes al-A'mash from 'Amr ibn Murrah, from 'Abdullah ibn al-Harith, from Zuhair ibn al-Aqmar, from 'Abdullah ibn 'Umar who says that al-Hakam ibn Abul 'As used to keep company with the Prophet (s) and then would go and narrate it [in a twisted manner] to Quraysh; therefore, the Prophet (s) denounced his behaviour and all his descendants as well till the Day of Judgment.

39. Sulayman ibn Mahran al-Kahili al-Kufi al-Asla'

He is one of the Shi'a nobility and a most trusted traditionist. Many a genius among Sunni men of knowledge, such as Ibn Qutaybah in his *Ma'arif* and al-Shahristani in his *Al-Milal wal-Nihal*, as well as many others, have all included him among Shi'a dignitaries.

In his biography of Zubayd, al-Jawzjani says the following in his book *Al-Mizan*: "Among the people of Kufa, there are some folks whose sect is not appreciated, yet they are the masters of hadith among Kufi traditionists. Among them are: Abu Ishaq, Mansur, Zubayd al-Yami, al-A'mash, and other peers. People tolerate them only because they are truthful in narrating hadith," up to the end of his statement which clearly exposes his stupidity and prejudice. What harm can reach these dignitaries if the Nasibis do not appreciate their commitment to discharge the Divine commandment of seeking the Pleasure of Allah through remaining faithful to His Prophet's kin and kith? These Nasibis, as a matter of fact, tolerate these men not only because they are truthful in narrating hadith, but rather because they are indispensable. Had they rejected these men's hadith, the majority of the Prophet's ahadith would have then been abandoned, as al-Dhahabi himself admits in his *Al-Mizan* while discussing the biography of Aban ibn Taghlib. I think that al-Mughirah's statement: "Abu Ishaq and your A'mash have rendered Kufa to destruction" is said due only to these men's Shi'a beliefs. Other than that, both Abu Ishaq and al-A'mash are oceans of knowledge and custodians of the prophetic legacy.

Al-A'mash has left us many interesting incidents which vividly portray his greatness. One of them, for example, is included by Ibn Khallikan in al-A'mash's biograpy in *Wafayat al-A'yan* where the author states:

> "Hisham ibn 'Abdul-Malik once wrote to al-A'mash saying: 'Recount for me 'Uthman's virtues and 'Ali's vices.' Al-A'mash took the letter and tossed it into his she-camel's mouth. Then he turned to the messenger and said: 'This is my answer.' The messenger, however, pleaded to al-A'mash saying that his master had vowed to kill him if he did not return with an answer. He also pleaded to al-A'mash's brothers to pressure their brother to write something. Finally, he wrote: 'In the Name of Allah, Most Gracious, Most Merciful. Had 'Uthman had all the virtues of the people of the world, they would not have availed you aught, and had 'Ali had in him all the vices of the people of the world, they would not have harmed you in the least; therefore, worry about your own soul, and peace be with you.'"

Another anecdote is narrated by Ibn 'Abd al-Birr in his chapter on the *'ulama*'s statements evaluating each other's work in his book *Jami' Bayanul 'Ilm wa Fada'ilih*.[7] The author quotes 'Ali ibn Khashram saying, "I have heard Abul-Fadl ibn Musa say, 'I entered the house of al-A'mash once accompanied by Abu Hanifah to visit him during his sickness. Abu Hanifah said: 'O Abu Muhammad! Had I not feared my visits would be a nuisance to you, I would have visited you more often'. Al-A'mash answered,

---

[7] Refer to page 199 of its summary in the book written by the scholar Shaykh Ahmad ibn 'Umar al-Muhammasani al-Beiruti.

'You are a nuisance to me even at your own home; so, imagine how I feel when I have to look at your face.'" Abul-Fadl continues to say that having left the house of al-A'mash, Abu Hanifah said, 'Al-A'mash never observed the fast of the month of Ramadan.' Ibn al-Khashram then asked al-Fadl what Abu Hanifah meant. Al-Fadl answered, 'Al-A'mash used to observe the *suhur* during the month of Ramadan according to the Prophet's hadith as narrated by Huzayfah al-Yemani.'" In fact, he used to observe the Holy Qur'anic verse: "Therefore, eat and drink till you can distinguish the white thread from the black one, from the dawn, and complete the fast till night-time." (2:187)

Authors of *Al-Wajiza* and *Bihar Al-Anwar* have both quoted Hasan ibn Sa'id al-Nakh'i who quotes Sharik ibn 'Abdullah, the judge, saying, "I visited al-A'mash when he was sick prior to his demise. While I was there, Ibn Shabramah, Ibn Layla and Abu Hanifah entered and inquired about his health. He told them that he was suffering from an acute feebleness, that he feared God for his sins, and he almost broke in tears. Abu Hanifah then said to him: 'O Father of Muhammad! Fear Allah! Look now after yourself. You used to narrate certain ahadith about 'Ali which, if you denounce, would be better for you.' Al-A'mash answered: 'Do you dare to say this to a man like me?' He even denounced him, and there is no need here to go into that. He was, may Allah have mercy on his soul, as al-Dhahabi describes him in his *Al-Mizan*, a trusted Imam. He was exactly what Ibn Khallikan had described while discussing his biography in his own *Wafiyyat al-A'yan*, a trustworthy and virtuous man of knowledge. Scholars have all conceded his truthfulness, equity and piety. Authors of the six *sahih* books, as well as many others besides them, have all relied on his authority. Refer to his hadith in Bukhari's and Muslim's *Sahih* books from Zayd ibn Wahab, Sa'id ibn Jubayr, Muslim al-Batin, al-Sha'bi, Mujahid, Abu Wa'il, Ibrahim al-Nakh'i and Abu Salih Thakwan. He is cited in these works by Shu'bah, al-Thawri, Ibn 'Ainah, Abu Mua'awiyah Muhammad, Abu 'Awanah, Jarir, and Hafs ibn Ghiyath. Al-A'mash was born in 61 A.H. and he died in 148 A.H., may Allah be merciful unto him.

40. Sharik ibn 'Abdullah ibn Sinan al-Nakh'i al-Kufi the judge

Imam Abu Qutaybah, in his *Ma'arif*, has unreservedly included him among Shi'a nobility. At the conclusion of Sharik's biography as recorded in *Al-Mizan*, 'Abdullah ibn Idris swears that Sharik is a Shi'a. Abu Dawud al-Rahawi is quoted in *Al-Mizan*, too, to have heard Sharik saying, "'Ali is the best of creation; whoever denies this fact is *kafir* (apostate)."[8] What he meant, of course, is that 'Ali is the best of all men excluding the Prophet (s), as all Shi'as believe. For this reason, al-Jawzjani, as quoted in *Al-Mizan*, describes him as "biased," meaning biased towards the faith of Ahl al-Bayt and preferring it to Jawzjani's sect. *Al-Mizan* also quotes Sharik's ahadith regarding the Commander of the Faithful. He cites Abu Rabi'ah from Ibn Buraydah from his father upto the Prophet who said: "For every Prophet there is a vicegerent and heir."

He was very zealous about disseminating the knowledge pertaining to the virtues of the Commander of the Faithful, and to pressure the Umayyads to recognize and publicize his merits, peace be upon him. In his work *Durrat al-Ghawwas*, al-Hariri, as in Sharik's biography in Ibn Khallikan's *Wafayyat al-A'yan*, says, "Sharik had an Umayyad friend of his. One day, Sharik recounted the attributes of 'Ali ibn Abu Talib (as). His Umayyad friend said that 'Ali was 'a fine man.' This enraged Sharik who said, 'Is this all that can be said about 'Ali, that he was a fine man, no more?'"[9]

---

[8] Ibn 'Adi quotes a chain of narrators including al-Husayn ibn 'Ali al-Sukuni al-Kufi, Muhammad ibn al-Hasan al-Sukuni, Salih ibn al-Aswad, al-A'mash, and 'Atiyyah, stating that Jarir was asked once: "How was 'Ali's status among your folks?" Jarir answered: "He was the best of mankind." This has been quoted by Muhammad Ahmad al-Dhahabi in his biography of Salih ibn Abul-Aswad in *Al-Mizan*. In spite of al-Dhahabi's extreme fanaticism, all he had to say in his comment about this hadith is his statement: "He probably meant during his ['Ali's] lifetime."

[9] His statement "What a great man 'Ali was," though flattering, does not do justice to the status of the Imam, peace be upon him, even coming from one of his adversaries. Sharik's rejection of such a feeble compliment and his anger thereat are, according to the norms of tradition, justified. There is quite a difference between the statement of this Omayyad vagabond who infers "What a great man 'Ali was," having heard 'Ali's outstanding virtues, as well as the

At the conclusion of Sharik's biography as stated in *Al-Mizan*, Ibn Abu Shaybah has quoted 'Ali ibn Hakim ibn Qadim citing 'Ali saying that once a complaint was brought with a man to Sharik's attention. The man said: "People claim that your mind is doubtful." Sharik answered: "You fool! How can I ever be doubtful?! I wish I had been present in the company of 'Ali to let my sword be drenched with the blood of his enemies."

Anyone who studies Sharik's life-style will be convinced that the man was a very loyal follower of the path of Ahl al-Bayt (as). He transmitted a great deal of traditions narrated by the most learned followers of Ahl al-Bayt. His son 'Abdul-Rahman has said, "My father has learned queries from Ja'far al-Ju'fi, in addition to ten thousand rare traditions." 'Abdullah ibn al-Mubarak is quoted in *Al-Mizan* saying, "Sharik is more knowledgeable about the Kufians' hadith than Sufyan. He was an avowed enemy of 'Ali's foes, one who spoke ill of them." 'Abdul-Salam ibn Harb once asked him: "Why don't you visit a sick brother of yours?" He inquired: "And who is that?" The man answered: "Malik ibn Maghul." Sharik, as stated in the latter's biography in *Al-Mizan*, then said: "Anyone who speaks ill of 'Ali and 'Ammar is surely no brother of mine."

Once the name of Mu'awiyah was mentioned in his presence and was described as "clement." Sharik, as stated in his biography in *Al-Mizan* as well as in Ibn Khallikan's *Wafiyyat al-A'yan*, said: "Whoever discards equity and fights 'Ali can never be clement." He narrated one hadith from Asim, Dharr, 'Abdullah ibn Mas'ud successively indicating that the Prophet (s) had said: "If you see Mu'awiyah on my pulpit, kill him." This is quoted by al-Tabari, and al-Tabari in turn is quoted by al-Dhahabi while the latter discusses the biography of Abbad ibn Ya'qub.

---

verses of the Exalted and Almighty stating: "We have decreed, and the most capable of decreeing are We..." The comparison between the statement of that Omayyad man and those of Allah is indeed quite manifest; yet Allah Almighty did not content Himself with just saying "What a great servant of Allah he is," but also added: "He is oft-returning;" so, *Wafiyyat al-A'yan* does not provide any answer to such a question.

Ibn Khallikan's *Wafiyyat* includes a biography of Sharik where the author quotes a dialogue between Sharik and Mis'ab ibn 'Abdullah al-Zubairi, in the presence of the 'Abbaside ruler al-Mahdi. Mis'ab asked Sharik: "Do you really belittle Abu Bakr and 'Umar?" up to the conclusion of the incident.

In spite of all of this, al-Dhahabi has described him as a "truthful *imam*." He also quotes Ibn Ma'in saying that Sharik is "truthful, trustworthy." At the conclusion of the biography, the author states: "Sharik was a bastian of knowledge. Ishaq al-Azraq learned from him nine thousand ahadith." He also quotes Tawbah al-Halabi saying, "We were at Ramla once, and someone wondered who the nation's man was. Some people said it was Lahi'ah, while others said it was Malik. We asked 'Isa ibn Yunus to state his view. He said: 'The nation's man is Sharik,' who was then still alive."

Muslim and authors of the four books of sunan have all relied on Sharik's authority. Refer to his hadith as they quote it transmitted by Ziyad ibn Alaqah, 'Ammar al-Thihni, Hisham ibn 'Urwah, Ya'li ibn 'Ata', 'Abdul-Malik ibn 'Umayr, 'Ammarah ibn al-Qa'qa' and 'Abdullah ibn Shabramah. These reporters have cited Sharik's hadith from Ibn Shaybah, 'Ali ibn Hakim, Yunus ibn Muhammad, al-Fadl ibn Musa, Muhammad ibn al-Sabah, and 'Ali ibn Hajar. He was born in either Khurasan or Bukhara in 95 A.H., and he died in Kufa on a Saturday early in Thul-Qi'dah, 177 or 178.

41. Shu'bah ibn al-Hajjaj Abul-Ward al-'Atki al-Wasiti (Abu Bastam)

Born in Wasit but lived in Basra, Abu Bastam is the first to inquire in Iraq about traditionists, and he is credited with helping the weak and the abandoned. He is considered among Shi'a nobility by many highly intellectual Sunni scholars such as Qutaybah in his *Al-Ma'arif*, and al-Shahristani in his *Al-Milal wal-Nihal*. Authors of the six *sahih* books and others have all relied on his authority. His hadith is ascertained in Bukhari's and Muslim's *sahih* books as transmitted by Abu Ishaq al-Subai'i, Isma'il ibn

Abu Khalid, Mansur, al-A'mash and others. In both Bukhari's and Muslim's books, his hadith is cited by Muhammad ibn Ja'far, Yahya ibn Sa'id al-Qattan, 'Uthman ibn Jabalah and others. He was born in 83 and he died in 160 A.H., may Allah be merciful on him.

42. Sa'sa'ah ibn Sawhan ibn Hajar ibn al-Harith al-'Abdi

Imam Ibn Qutaybah describes him on page 206 of his *Ma'arif* as one of the famous Shi'a dignitaries. Ibn Sa'd states on page 154, Vol. 6, of his *Tabaqat*: "[Sa'sa'ah] is very well known all over Kufa as an orator and a companion of 'Ali with whom he has witnesed the Battle of the Camel together with his brothers Zayd and Sihan sons of Sawhan. Sihan is known as an orator before Sa'sa'ah, and he was the standard-bearer during the Battle of the Camel.[10] Having been killed, Sihan was succeeded in bearing the standard by Sa'sa'ah. Sa'sa'ah has narrated hadith from Imam 'Ali (as), and also from 'Abdullah ibn 'Abbas. He is a trusted traditionist although the ahadith he has narrated are not many." Ibn 'Abd al-Birr mentions him in his Isti'ab saying: "He accepted Islam during the life-time of Prophet Muhammad (s) although he never met him in person due to his being very young then."

He is chief among his tribesmen, descendants of 'Abd al-Qays. He is quite an eloquent orator, a man of wisdom who has acquired a total command over the language. He is, indeed, a man of piety, virtues, and wisdom. He is counted among the companions of 'Ali, peace be upon him. Yahya ibn Ma'in is quoted saying that Sa'sa'ah, Zayd and Sihan sons of Sawhan are all orators, and that Zayd and Sihan were killed during the Battle of the Camel. He also cites a critical problem which 'Umar, then caliph, could not solve; therefore, the caliph delivered a sermon in which he asked people for their suggestions. Sa'sa'ah, then a youth, stood and clarified its complexity and put forth a suggestion to it which was unanimously accepted. This should not surprise the

---

[10] He was also one of those who were put in charge of fighting the renegades as Ibn Hajar indicates as he discusses Sihan ibn Sawhan in Part One of his *Al-Isabah*.

reader since the descendants of Sawhan were among the most prominent masters of Arabia, pillars in virtue and descent. Ibn Qutaybah mentions them on page 138 of his chapter on renowned dignitaries and men of influence in his *Ma'arif*. The author says: "Sawhan's descendants were Zayd ibn Sawhan, Sa'sa'ah ibn Sawhan, Sihan ibn Sawhan, of Banu 'Abd al-Qays." He adds: "Zayd was among the best of men. He narrated saying that the Prophet (s) had said: 'Zayd is indeed a good man, and Jandab - what a man he is!' People inquired: 'Why do you mention these men alone?' The Prophet answered: 'The arm of one of them will precede in thirty years the rest of his body in entering Paradise, while the other will deal heavy blows so that right is distinguished from wrong.' The first, as it came to pass, participated in Jalawla' Battle where his arm was chopped off. He also participated in the Battle of the Camel on the side of 'Ali (as). He asked the Imam: 'O Commander of the Faithful! It looks like I am going to meet my fate.' The Imam (as) asked him, 'How do you know that, O father of Sulayman?' He answered: 'I have seen in a vision my arm stretching from heaven to pull me away from this world.' He was killed by 'Amr ibn Yathribi, while his brother Sihan was killed during the Battle of the Camel."

It is no secret that the Prophet's prophecy regarding Zayd's arm preceding the rest of his body in entering Paradise is regarded by all Muslims as a testimony for his prophethood, a sign of the truth of the religion of Islam, and a recognition of the men of truth. All biographies of Zayd have mentioned it. Refer to his biography in *Al-Isti'ab*, *Al-Isabah*, and others. Traditionists have recorded the above, each in his own way of wording it, adding that [in "spite" of his being Shi'a] he was promised Paradise; so, praise be to the Lord of the Worlds.

Al-'Asqalani mentions Sa'sa'ah ibn Sawhan in Part Three of his *Isaba*, saying: "He narrates traditions about 'Uthman and 'Ali (as). He has participated in the Battle of Siffin on 'Ali's side. He is an eloquent orator who has encounters with Mu'awiyah." Al-Sha'bi has said: "I used to learn how to deliver sermons from him."[11] Abu Ishaq al-Subai'i, al-Minhal ibn 'Amr ibn Baridah, and others have all cited his hadith. Al-'Ala'i, narrating Ziyad's encounters, says that once al-Mughirah banished Sa'sa'ah, in accordance to an edict which he had received from Mu'awiyah, from Kufa to Jazirah, or to Bahrain (some historians say to the island of Ibn Fakkan), where he died in banishment just as Abu Dharr al-Ghifari had died before him in the Rabatha desert (southern Iraq). Al-Dhahabi mentions Sa'sa'ah and describes him as "a well-known and trusted traditionist," citing testimonies to his trustworthiness from Ibn Sa'd and Nisa'i, and marking his name to indicate that al-Nisa'i relies on his authority. Whoever does not rely on his authority does not in fact harm anyone but his own self, as the holy Qur'an says: "We have not done them any harm; they have only harmed their own selves."(2:57)

43. Tawus ibn Kisan al-Khawlani al-Hamadani al-Yamani

He is 'Abdul-Rahman's father. His mother is Persian, and his father is Ibn Qasit, a Namri slave of Bajir ibn Raysan al-Himyari. Sunni intellectuals regard him a Shi'a without any question. Among their dignitaries, al-Shahristani mentions him in his *Al-Milal wal-Nihal*, and Ibn Qutaybah in his *Al-Ma'arif*. Authors of the six *sahih* books, as well as others, have all relied on his authority. Refer to his hadith in both *sahih* books where he cites Ibn 'Abbas, Ibn 'Umar and Abu Hurayrah, and in Muslim's *Sahih* where he cites 'Ayesha, Zayd ibn Thabit, and 'Abdullah ibn 'Umar. His hadith is recorded in Bukhari alone as transmitted by al-Zuhri, and in Muslim by many renowned traditionists. He died in Mecca while performing the rite of pilgrimage one day before the day of Tarwiya (i.e. on the 7th of Dhul-Hijjah), in either 104 or 106 A.H. His funeral was quite eventful. His coffin was carried by

---

[11] It was said to al-Sha'bi, as mentioned in the biography of Rashid al-Hijri in al-Dhahabi's *Al-Mizan*, "What is the matter with you? Why do you find fault with 'Ali's companions? Haven't you learned what you have learned from any of them?" He asked: "From whom?" They answered: "From al-Harith and Sa'sa'ah." He said: "As regarding Sa'sa'ah, he was, indeed, an eloquent orator, and I learned from him how to deliver sermons, and truly al-Harith was an expert in mathematics, and from him did I learn the same."

'Abdullah son of al-Hasan son of the Commander of the Faithful (as). He was vying with others to carry it, so much so that his headwear dropped, and his clothes were torn from the back side by the stampede, as narrated by Ibn Khallikan in his biography of Tawus in *Wafayyat al-A'yan*.

44. Zalim ibn 'Amr ibn Sufyan Abul-Aswad al-Du'ali

His being a Shi'a and a faithful adherent to the faith during the *wilayat* of Imams 'Ali, al-Hasan and al-Husayn, as well as other members of the Ahl al-Bayt, peace be upon all of them, is more visible than the sun, and it requires no reiteration.[12] We have dealt with it in detail in our work *Mukhtasar al-Kalam fi Muallifi al-Shi'a min Sadr al-Islam*. His being a Shi'a is a matter which nobody disputes. In spite of this fact, authors of the six *sahih* books have relied on his authority. Refer to his hadith about 'Umar ibn al-Khattab in Bukhari's *Sahih*. In Muslim's, his hadith is cited by Abu Musa and 'Umran ibn Hasin. In both *sahih* books, his hadith is cited by Yahya ibn Ya'mur. In Bukhari's, 'Abdullah ibn Buraydah quotes him, and in Muslim's, his hadith is narrated by his son Abu Harb. He died, may Allah Almighty have mercy on him, at the age of 85 in Basrah in 99 A.H. by the plague which devastated the city. He is the one who laid down the foundations of Arabic grammar according to rules which he learned from the Commander of the Faithful (as), as we have expounded in our book *Al-Mukhtasar*.

45. 'Amr ibn Wa'ilah ibn 'Abdullah ibn 'Umar al-Laithi al-Makki

Also known as Abul-Tufayl, he was born in the same year when the Battle of Uhud took place, i.e. 3 A.H. He was for eight years contemporary of the Prophet (s). Ibn Qutaybah has included him among so-called "extremist Rafidis," stating that he was al-Mukhtar's standard-bearer and the last of the *sahabah* to die. Ibn 'Abd al-Birr has mentioned him in his chapter on *kunayat* in his

---

[12] Suffices you for proof testifying to this fact what is mentioned by Ibn Hajar in his biography in Part Three of his *Isabah*, Vol. 2, page 241.

Isti'ab saying, "He resided in Kufa, and he accompanied 'Ali (as) in all his battles. When 'Ali (as) was killed, he left for Mecca." He concludes by saying, "He was a virtuous and wise man, swift in providing an accurate answer, eloquent. He was also one of the Shi'as of 'Ali, peace be upon him." He also indicates that "Once, Abul-Tufayl approached Mu'awiyah and the latter asked him: 'For how long have you mourned the death of your friend Father of al-Hasan (as)?' He answered: 'I have grieved as much as the mother of Moses grieved when she parted with her son, and I complain unto Allah for my shortcomings.' Mu'awiyah asked him: 'Were you among those who enforced a siege around 'Uthman's house?' He answered: 'No; but I used to visit him.' Then Mu'awiyah asked him: 'What stopped you from rescuing him?' He retorted: 'What about you? What stopped you from doing so when sure death surrounded him, while you were in Syria a master among his subjects?!' Mu'awiyah replied: 'Can't you see that avenging his murder is an indication of my support?' 'Amir then told Mu'awiyah that he acted exactly like the one implied in the verses composed by the brother of Ju'f the poet in which the latter says: 'You mourn my death, yet while I was alive, you did not even sustain me against starvation.'"

Al-Zuhri, Abul-Zubair, al-Jariri, Ibn Abul-Hasin, 'Abdul-Malik ibn Abjar, Qatadah, Ma'ruf, al-Walid ibn Jami', Mansur ibn Hayyan, al-Qasim ibn Abu Bardah, 'Amr ibn Dinar, 'Ikramah ibn Khalid, Kulthum ibn Habib, Furat al-Qazzaz, and 'Abdul-Aziz ibn Rafi' have all narrated his hadith as it exists in Muslim's and Bukhari's *Sahih* books. Bukhari's work contains traditions of the Prophet (s) regarding the pilgrimage which are narrated by Abul-Tufayl. He describes the Prophet's characteristics, and he narrates about the prayers and signs of prophethood from Ma'adh ibn Jabal, and he narrates about fate from 'Abdullah ibn Mas'ud. He narrates from 'Ali (as), Huzayfah ibn al-Yemani, 'Abdullah ibn 'Abbas and 'Umar ibn al-Khattab, as is well-known by all researchers of Muslim's hadith besides that of the authors of his *musnad*s. Abul-Tufayl, may Allah Ta'ala encompass his soul with His mercy, died in Mecca in 100 A.H. (some say in 102, while still others say 120), and Allah knows best.

46. 'Abbad ibn Ya'qub al-Asadi al-Ruwajni al-Kufi

He is mentioned by Dar Qutni who says, "'Abbad ibn Ya'qub is a truthful Shi'a." Ibn Hayyan mentions him and says, "'Abbad ibn Ya'qub used to invite people to Rafidism." Ibn Khuzaymah says, "'Abbad ibn Ya'qub is a man whose traditions are never doubted, though his faith is questioned, etc." 'Abbad narrates from al-Fadl ibn al-Qasim, Sufyan al-Thawri, Zubayd, Murrah, that Ibn Mas'ud used to interpret the verse "Allah has spared the Believers from fighting" (Qur'an, 25:33) to imply that they were spared from fighting 'Ali. He quotes Sharik, 'Asim, Dharr, from 'Abdullah who has stated that the Messenger of Allah (s) has said: "When you see Mu'awiyah on my pulpit, kill him." This hadith is recorded by Tabari and others. 'Abbad says that anyone who does not mention in his daily prayers that he dissociates himself from the enemies of the Prophet's progeny (as) shall be resurrected in their company. He also says, "Allah Almighty is too fair to let Talhah and al-Zubayr enter Paradise; they fought 'Ali after swearing allegiance to him." Salih al-Jazrah has said: "'Abbad ibn Ya'qub used to denounce 'Uthman." 'Abbad al-Ahwazi quotes his trusted authorities saying that 'Abbad ibn Ya'qub used to denounce "their" ancestors. In spite of all this, Sunni Imams like al-Bukhari, al-Tirmizi, Ibn Majah, Ibn Khuzaymah, and Ibn Abu Dawud rely on his authority, their mentor, in whom they all place their trust.

In spite of his intolerance and prejudice, Abu Hatim has mentioned him and said that he is a trusted *shaykh*. Al-Dhahabi mentions him in his *Al-Mizan* and says, "He is one of the extremist Shi'as, leaders of innovators; yet he is truthful when narrating hadith." He goes on to mention what has already been stated above regarding 'Abbad's views. Al-Bukhari quotes him directly while discussing *tawhid* in his own *sahih*. He died, may Allah be merciful unto him, in Shawwal of 150 A.H. Al-Qasim ibn Zakariyyah al-Mutarraz has intentionally misquoted 'Abbad's statements regarding the digging the sea and the flow of its water, and we seek refuge with Allah against telling lies about the Believers; He is surely the One Who foils their schemes.

47. 'Abdullah ibn Dawud

He is father of 'Abdul-Rahman al-Hamadani al-Kufi. He resided in Al-Harbiyya, a Basrah suburb. Qutaybah has included him among renowned Shi'a personalities in his own *Al-Ma'arif*, and al-Bukhari has relied on his authority in his own *Sahih*. Refer to his hadith from al-A'mash, Hisham ibn 'Urwah and Ibn Jurayh. His hadith is narrated in Bukhari's *Sahih* by Musaddid, 'Amr ibn 'Ali, and, in some places, by Nasr ibn 'Ali. He died in 212 A.H.

48. 'Abdullah ibn Shaddad ibn al-Had

Al-Had's full name is Usamah ibn 'Abdullah ibn Jabir ibn al-Bashir ibn 'Atwarah ibn 'Amir ibn Malik ibn Laith al-Laithi al-Kufi Abul-Walid, a companion of the Commander of the Faithful (as). His mother is Salma daughter of 'Amis al-Khayth'ami, sister of Asma'. He is nephew, from the mother's side, of 'Abdullah ibn Ja'far and Muhammad ibn Abu Ja'far, and brother of 'Amara daughter of Hamzah ibn 'Abdul Muttalib from the mother's side. Ibn Sa'd includes him among residents of Kufa who were distinguished for their *fiqh* and knowledge and who belong to the *tabi'in*. At the conclusion of his biography, the author states on page 86 of Vol. 6 of his *Tabaqat*: "During the reign of 'Abdul-Rahman ibn Muhammad ibn al-Ash'ath, 'Abdullah ibn Shaddad was among those who recite the Holy Qur'an and know it by heart and who fought al-Hajjaj, and he was killed during the Dujail Battle." He also says, "He was a trustworthy *faqih* who narrated a great deal of hadith, and he was a Shi'a."

The battle referred to above took place in 81 A.H. All authors of the *sahih* books have relied on the authority of 'Abdullah ibn Shaddad. His hadith is quoted by Ishaq al-Shaybani, Ma'bid ibn Khalid and Sa'd ibn Ibrahim. Their ahadith from 'Abdullah ibn Shaddad exist in both *sahih* books as well as in others, in addition to all *musnad*s. Al-Bukhari and Muslim quote his hadith as transmitted from 'Ali (as), Maymuna and 'Ayesha.

49. 'Abdullah ibn 'Umar ibn Muhammad ibn Aban ibn Salih ibn 'Umayr al-Qarashi al-Kufi

Also known as Mishkadanah, he is mentor of Muslim, Abu Dawud, al-Baghwi, and many other peers who all learned hadith from him. Abu Hatim has mentioned him testifying to his truthfulness. He quotes his hadith and states that he is a Shi'a. Salih ibn Muhammad ibn Jazrah has mentioned him and said that he is a Shi'a "extremist." In spite of this, 'Abdullah ibn Ahmad has narrated hadith from his father. Abu Hatim states that Mishkadanah is trustworthy. Al-Dhahabi has mentioned him in his *Al-Mizan*, describing him as "a truthful man who has learned a great deal of hadith from Ibn al-Mubarak, al-Dar Wardi, and their group of scholars. Muslim, Abu Dawud, al-Baghwi and many others have recorded a great deal of his ahadith." He has marked his name with the initials of Muslim and Abu Dawud indicating thereby their reliance on his hadith, and quoting what the learned scholars named above have said about him. He has also stated that he died in 239 A.H. Refer to his hadith in Muslim's *Sahih* as transmitted through 'Abdah ibn Sulayman, 'Abdullah ibn al-Mubarak, 'Abdul-Rahman ibn Sulayman, 'Ali ibn Hashim, Abul-Ahwas, Husayn ibn 'Ali al-Ju'fi and Muhammad ibn Fudayl. In his chapter dealing with causes of dissension, Muslim quotes his hadith directly. Abul-'Abbas al-Sarraj has said that he died either in 238 or 237 A.H.

50. 'Abdullah ibn Lahi'ah ibn 'Uqbah al-Hadrami Egypt's judge and scholar

In his *Ma'arif*, Ibn Qutaybah has included him among famous *shaykhs*. In his biography of 'Abdullah ibn Lahi'ah in his *Al-Mizan*, Ibn 'Adi has described him as an "extremist Shi'a." Quoting Talhah, Abu Ya'li states: "Abu Lahi'ah has said: 'Hay ibn 'Abdullah al-Ghafari has narrated through the authority of Abu 'Abdullah Rahman al-Hibli from 'Abdullah ibn 'Umar that during his sickness (which preceded his demise), the Messenger of Allah (s) told us to fetch his brother. We brought him Abu Bakr, but he turned away from him and said: 'I had asked for my brother'. We then brought 'Uthman, but again the Messenger of Allah (s) turned away from him. 'Ali (as) was then brought in his presence. He covered him with his own mantle and inclined his head on his shoulder for a while (as if he was whispering something in his ear). When 'Ali left, people asked him: 'What has the Prophet (s) said to you?' He answered: 'He has taught me a thousand chapters each of which leads to a thousand sections.'"

Al-Dhahabi mentions him in his *Al-Mizan*, marking his name with DTQ to denote who among the authors of the *sahih* books quotes him [i.e. Abu Dawud, al-Tirmizi, and Dar Qutni. Refer to his hadith in al-Tirmizi's *Sahih*, Abu Dawud and all *musnad*s. Ibn Khallikan has greatly praised him in his *Wafiyyat al-A'yan*. Refer to his hadith in Muslim's *sahih* as transmitted by Yazid ibn Abu Habib. In his book *Al-Jam' Bayna Kitabay Abu Nasr al-Kalabathi wa Abu Bakr al-Asbahani* [Compilation of Both Books of Abu Nasr al-Kalabathi and Abul-Faraj al-Asbahani, al-Qaysarani includes him among Bukhari's and Muslim's reliable authorities. Ibn Lahi'ah died on Sunday, mid-Rabi'ul Akhir, 174 A.H.

51. 'Abdullah ibn Maymun al-Qaddah al-Makki

A friend of Imam Ja'far ibn Muhammad al-Sadiq (as), he is relied upon by al-Tirmizi. Al-Dhahabi mentions him and marks his name with al-Tirmizi's initials as an indication that the latter cites his hadith. He adds saying that he narrates hadith through the authority of Imam Ja'far ibn Muhammad al-Sadiq (as), and of Talhah ibn 'Umar.

52. 'Abdul-Rahman ibn Salih al-Azdi

His name is Abu Muhammad al-Kufi. His friend and student 'Abbas al-Duri says that he was a Shi'a. Ibn 'Adi mentions him and says, "He is burnt in the fire of Shi'ism." Salih Jazrah says that 'Abdul-Rahman used to oppose 'Uthman. Abu Dawud says that 'Abdul-Rahman has compiled a book containing the vices of some of the companions of the Prophet (s), and that he is a bad person. In spite of all this, both 'Abbas al-Duri and Imam al-Baghwi narrate his hadith. Al-Nisa'i has quoted him. Al-Dhahabi has referred to him in his *Al-Mizan* and marked his name with al-Nisa'i's initials as an indication of the latter's reliance on him. He also quotes what the Imams (among the Sunnis) have said about him as stated above. He indicates that Ma'in trusts him, and that he died in 235 A.H. Refer to his hadith in the Sunan books as transmitted through Sharik and a group of his peers.

53. 'Abdul-Razzaq ibn Humam ibn Nafi' al-Himyari al-San'ani

One of the Shi'a nobility and honourable ancestry, he is included by Ibn Qutaybah among renowned Shi'as in his *Ma'arif*. Ibn al-Athir, on page 137, Vol. 6, of his *Al-Tarikh Al-Kamil*, mentions 'Abdul-Razzaq's death in the end of the events of 211 A.H. thus: "In that year, the traditionist 'Abdul-Razzaq ibn Humam al-San'ani, one of Ahmad's Shi'a mentors, died." Al-Muttaqi al-Hindi mentions him while discussing hadith number 5994 in his *Kanz al-'Ummal*, on page 391, Vol. 6, stating that he is a Shi'a. Al-Dhahabi, in his *Al-Mizan*, says, "'Abdul-Razzaq ibn Humam ibn Nafi', Abu Bakr al-Himyari's mentor, is a Shi'a dignitary of San'a, was one of the most trusted traditionists among all scholars." He narrates his biography and adds: "He has written a great deal, authoring [in particular] *Al-Jami' Al-Kabir*. He is a custodian of knowledge sought by many people such as Ahmad, Ishaq, Yahya, al-Dhahabi, al-Ramadi, and 'Abd." He discusses his character and quotes al-'Abbas ibn 'Abdul-'Azim, accusing him of being a liar. He states that al-Dhahabi has denounced such an accusation. He says, "Not only Muslim, but all those who have memorized hadith have agreed with al-'Abbas, while the Imams of knowledge rely on his authority." He goes on to narrate his biography, quoting al-Tayalisi saying: "I have heard Ibn Ma'in say something from which I became convinced that 'Abdul-Razzaq was a Shi'a. Ibn Ma'in asked him: 'Your instructors, such as Mu'ammar, Malik, Ibn Jurayh, Sufyan, al-Awza'i, are all Sunnis. Where did you learn the sect of Shi'ism from?' He answered: 'Ja'far ibn Sulayman al-

Zab'i once paid us a visit, and I found him to be virtuous and rightly guided, and I learned Shi'ism from him.'"

'Abdul-Razzaq, as quoted above, statement in which he says that he is a Shi'a indicates that he has learned Shi'ism from Ja'far al-Zab'i, but Muhammad ibn Abu Bakr al-Muqaddimi thinks that Ja'far al-Zab'i himself has learned Shi'ism from 'Abdul-Razzaq. He even denounces 'Abdul-Razzaq for this reason. In *Al-Mizan*, he is quoted as saying, "I wish I had lost 'Abdul-Razzaq for good. Nobody has corrupted Ja'far's beliefs other than he." The "corruption" to which he refers is Shi'ism!

Ibn Ma'in has heavily relied on 'Abdul-Razzaq's authority, in spite of his "admission" that he is a Shi'a as stated above. Ahmad ibn Abu Khayth'amah, as in 'Abdul-Razzaq's biography in *Al-Mizan*, has said, "It has been said to Ibn Ma'in that Ahmad says that 'Ubaydullah ibn Musa rejects 'Abdul-Razzaq's hadith because of his Shi'a beliefs. Ibn Ma'in has responded thus: 'I swear by Allah, Who is the only GOD, that 'Abdul-Razzaq is a hundred times superior to 'Ubaydullah, and I have heard 'Abdul-Razzaq's hadith and found it to be many times more in volume than 'Ubaydullah's.'" Also in 'Abdul-Razzaq's biography in *Al-Mizan*, Abu Salih Muhammad ibn Isma'il al-Dirari is quoted saying, "While we were in San'a guests of 'Abdul-Razzaq, we heard that Ahmad and Ibn Ma'in, joined by others, had rejected 'Abdul-Razzaq's hadith, or say disliked it, because of the traditionist being a Shi'a. The news deeply depressed us. We thought that we had spent our resources and taken the trouble to make the trip there all in vain. Then I joined the pilgrims for Mecca where I met Yahya and asked him about this issue. He, as stated in 'Abdul-Razzaq's biography in *Al-Mizan*, said: 'O Abu Salih! Even if 'Abdul-Razzaq abandons Islam altogether, we shall never reject his hadith.'"

Ibn 'Adi has mentioned him and said: "'Abdul-Razzaq has reported ahadith dealing with virtues, but nobody has endorsed them.[13] He also counts the vices of certain people, which views are rejected by others;[14] above all, he is believed to be a Shi'a."

In spite of all this, Ahmad ibn Hanbal was asked once, as indicated in 'Abdul-Razzaq's biography in *Al-Mizan*, whether he knew of any hadith better than that reported by 'Abdul-Razzaq, and his answer was negative. Ibn al-Qaysarani states at the conclusion of 'Abdul-Razzaq's biography in his own book *Al-Jami' Bayna Rijalul Sahihain*, quoting Imam Ahmad ibn Hanbal saying, 'If people dispute Mu'ammar's hadith, then the final arbitrator is 'Abdul-Razzaq.' Mukhlid al-Shu'ayri says that he was once in the company of 'Abdul-Razzaq when a man mentioned Mu'awiyah. 'Abdul-Razzaq, as stated in his biography in *Al-Mizan*, then said: 'Do not spoil our meeting by mentioning the descendants of Abu Sufyan.'" Zayd ibn al-Mubarak has said: "We were in the company of 'Abdul-Razzaq once when we recounted

---

[13] Yes, he was agreed upon by those who are fair, and they included it in their sahihs with satisfaction. Those who opposed it are the Nasibis and Kharijites. It includes what is narrated by Ahmad ibn al-Azhar, who is unanimously considered as an authority, saying: "'Abdel-Razzaq has taught me a few exclusive ahadith which he knows through a chain of narrators that includes Mu'ammar, al-Zuhri, and 'Ubaydullah and ends with Ibn 'Abbas who says that the Messenger of Allah (s) looked once at 'Ali and said: 'You are a chief in this life, and a chief in the life to come; whoever loves you loves me, and whoever hates you hates me; the one you love is loved by Allah, and the one you dislike is disliked by Allah; woe unto those who despise you.'" This is quoted by al-Hakim on page 128, Vol. 3, of his *Al-Mustadrak*, followed by the author's comment thus: "This is an authentic hadith according to the authority of both Shaykhs." Among others is what 'Abdel-Razzaq has narrated from Mu'ammar, from Ibn Najih, from Mujahid, from Ibn 'Abbas who says that Fatima (as) once said: "O Messenger of Allah! You have married me to a provider who has no money." He said: "Are you not pleased that Allah cast a look at the inhabitants of the earth and chose from among them two men, and He made one of them your father and the other your husband?" This hadith is quoted by al-Hakim on page 129, Vol. 3, of his *Al-Mustadrak* through Sarih ibn Younus, Abu Hafs, al-A'mash, Abu Salih, up to Abu Hurayrah.

[14] Allah forbid that they have abominations only Mu'awiyah and his oppressive gang are more likely to have. Among such abominations is narrated by 'Abdel-Razzaq through a chain of narrators that includes: Ibn 'Ayinah, 'Ali ibn Zayd ibn Jath'an, Abu Nadrah, up to Abu Sa'd who quotes the Prophet (s) saying: "If you see Mu'awiyah sitting on my pulpit, kill him."

ibn al-Hadthan's hadith. When 'Umar's address to 'Ali and al-'Abbas: 'You (i.e. 'Abbas) have come to demand your inheritance of your nephew (the Prophet, peace be upon him and his progeny), while this man (i.e. 'Ali) has come to demand his wife's inheritance of her father' was read, 'Abdul-Razzaq, as stated in his biography in *Al-Mizan*, said: 'Behold this shameless, impertinent man using 'nephew' and 'father' instead of 'the Messenger of Allah (s)'!"

In spite of all this, all compilers of hadith have recorded his traditions and relied on his authority. It has even been said, as Ibn Khallikan states in his *Wafiyyat al-A'yan*, that people did not travel to anyone after the demise of the Prophet (s) as often as they did to 'Abdul-Razzaq's. He is quoted by the Imams of contemporary Muslims such as Sufyan ibn 'Ayinah, among whose mentors 'Abdul-Razzaq himself was one, Ahmad ibn Hanbal, Yahya ibn Ma'in, and others.

Refer to his hadith in all the *sahih* books, as well as all *musnad*s, which all contain quite a few of his ahadith. He was born, may Allah have mercy on his soul, in 211 A.H. He was contemporary to Abu 'Abdullah Imam al-Sadiq (as) for twenty-two years.[15] He died during the first days of the Imamate of Imam Abu Ja'far al-Jawad (as), nine years before the Imam's demise;[16] may Allah resurrect him in the company of these Imams to whose service, seeking of the Pleasure of Allah, he sincerely dedicated his life.

54. 'Abdul-Malik ibn 'Ayan

He is brother of Zararah, Hamran, Bakir, 'Abdul-Rahman, Malik, Musa, Daris, and Umm al-Aswad, all descendants of 'Ayan, and all are notable Shi'as. They have won the sublime cup for

---

[15] The reason for this is the fact that he, peace be upon him and his progeny, died in 148 A.H. at the age of 65.

[16] The demise of Imam al-Jawad, peace be upon him, took place in 220 A.H.; he was 25 years old. They have committed a mistake those who say that 'Abdul-Razzaq narrated hadith from al-Baqir, for al-Baqir, peace be upon him, died in 114 at the age of 57, twelve years prior to 'Abdul-Razzaq's birth.

serving the Islamic Shari'a, and they have produced a blessed and righteous progeny that adheres to their sect and views.

Al-Dhahabi mentions 'Abdul-Malik in his *Al-Mizan*, citing Abu Wa'il and others quoting Abu Hatim saying that he has reported authentic ahadith, and that Ma'in has said that there is nothing wrong with his hadith, while another authority testifies thus: "He is truthful, yet he is Rafidi, too." Ibn Ayinah has said: "'Abdul-Malik, a Rafidi, has reported hadith to us." Abu Hatim says that he is among the earliest to embrace Shi'a Islam, and that his hadith is authentic. Both Sufyans have transmitted his hadith and reported it well-documented by others.

In his book *Al-Jami' Bayna Rijalul Sahihain*, Ibn al-Qaysarani, as quoted in both works by Sufyan ibn A'yinah, has this to say about him: "'Abdul-Malik ibn 'Ayan, brother of Hamran al-Kufi, was a Shi'a whose hadith about *tawhid* is recorded by Bukhari as transmitted by Abu Wa'il, and about *iman* as recorded in Muslim's."

He died during the life-time of Imam al-Sadiq (as) who earnestly invoked the Almighty's mercy upon him. Abu Ja'far ibn Babawayh has reported that Imam al-Sadiq (as), accompanied by his disciples, visited 'Abdul-Malik's gravesite in Medina. May he receive the good rewards and live eternally in peace.

55. 'Ubaydullah ibn Musa al-'Abasi al-Kufi

He is al-Bukhari's mentor, as the latter acknowledges on page 177 of his *Sahih*. Ibn Qutaybah has included him among traditionists in his work *Al-Ma'arif*, stating that the man is a Shi'a. When he recounts a roll call of notable Shi'as in his chapter on sects on page 206 of his book *al-Ma'arif*, he includes 'Ubaydullah among them. On page 279, Vol. 6, of his *Tabaqat*, Ibn Sa'd narrates 'Ubaydullah's biography without forgetting to indicate that he is a Shi'a, and that he narrates hadith supportive of Shi'ism, thus, according to Ibn Sa'd, weakening his hadith in the eyes of many people. He also adds saying that 'Ubaydullah is also very well familiar with the Holy Qur'an. He records on page 139, Vol. 6, of his *Al-Kamil* the date of his death at the conclusion of events that took place in 213 A.H., stating: "'Ubaydullah ibn Musa al-'Abasi, the jurist, was a Shi'a who taught al-Bukhari as the latter himself acknowledges in his *Sahih*." Al-Dhahabi mentions him in his *Al-Mizan* saying, "Ubaydullah ibn Musa al-'Abasi al-Kufi, al-Bukhari's mentor, is no question trustworthy, but he also is a deviated Shi'a." Yet the author admits that both Abu Hatim and Ma'in have trusted his hadith. He says, "Abu Hatim has said that the hadith narrated by Abu Na'im is more authentic, yet 'Ubaydullah's is more authentic than all of them when it comes to the ahadith transmitted by Isra'il."

Ahmad ibn 'Abdullah al-Ajli has said, "'Ubaydullah ibn Musa is very knowledgeable of the Holy Qur'an, a major authority therein. I have never seen him arrogant or conceited, and he was never seen laughing boisterously." Abu Dawud says, "'Ubaydullah ibn al-'Abasi was a Shi'a heretic." At the conclusion of the biography of Matar ibn Maymun in *Al-Mizan*, al-Dhahabi states: "'Ubaydullah, a Shi'a, is trustworthy." Ibn Ma'in used to learn hadith from 'Ubaydullah ibn Musa and 'Abdul-Razzaq knowing that they were both Shi'as. In Thahbi's *Al-Mizan*, while documenting 'Abdul-Razzaq's biography, the author quotes Ahmad ibn 'Ali Khaythamah saying, "I inquired of Ibn Ma'in once regarding what I heard about Ahmad's alleged rejection of 'Ubaydullah ibn Musa's hadith because of his being a Shi'a. Ibn Ma'in answered: 'I swear by Allah Who has no associate that 'Abdul-Razzaq is superior to 'Ubaydullah a hundred times, and I have heard from 'Abdul-Razzaq many times more ahadith than I heard from 'Ubaydullah.'"

Sunnis, like all others, rely on 'Ubaydullah's hadith in their respective *sahih* books. Refer to his hadith in both *sahih* books transmitted by Shayban ibn 'Abdul-Rahman. Bukhari's *Sahih* quotes his hadith as reported by al-A'mash ibn 'Urwah and Isma'il ibn Abu Khalid. His hadith as recorded in Muslim's *Sahih* is reported from Isra'il, al-Hasan ibn Salih, and Usamah ibn Zayd. Al-Bukhari quotes him directly. He is also quoted directly by Ishaq ibn Ibrahim, Abu Bakr ibn Abu Shaybah, Ahmad ibn Ishaq al-Bukhari, Mahmud ibn Ghaylan, Ahmad ibn Abu Sarij, Muhammad ibn al-Hasan ibn Ashkab, Muhammad ibn Khalid al-Dhahabi, and Yusuf ibn Musa al-Qattan. Muslim quotes his hadith as reported by al-Hajjaj ibn al-Sha'ir, al-Qasim ibn Zakariyyah, 'Abdullah al-Darmi, Ishaq ibn al-Mansur, Ibn Abu Shaybah, 'Abd ibn Hamid, Ibrahim ibn Dinar, and Ibn Namir. Al-Dhahabi states in his *Al-Mizan* that 'Ubaydullah died in 213 A.H. adding, "He was well known for his asceticism, adoration, and piety." His death took place in early Dhul-Qi'da; may Allah Almighty sanctify his resting place.

56. 'Uthman ibn 'Umayr 'Abdul-Yaqzan al-Thaqafi al-Kufi al-Bijli

He is also known as 'Uthman ibn Abu Zar'ah, 'Uthman ibn Qays, and 'Uthman ibn Abu Hamid. Abu Ahmad al-Zubayri says that 'Uthman believes in the return. Ahmad ibn Hanbal says, "Abu Yaqzan was joined in dissenting by Ibrahim ibn 'Abdullah ibn Hasan." Ibn 'Adi says the following about him: "He has embraced the bad sect, and he believes in the return, although trusted authorities have quoted him knowing that he was weak." The fact of the matter is that whenever some people desire to belittle a Shi'a traditionist and undermine his scholarly ability, they charge him with preaching the concept of the return. Thus have they done to 'Uthman ibn 'Umayr, so much so that Ibn Ma'in has said: "There is really nothing wrong with 'Uthman's hadith."

In spite of all attacks on him, al-A'mash, Sufyan, Shu'bah, Sharik and other peers have not in the least hesitated to quote him. Abu Dawud, al-Tirmizi and others have all quoted him in their sunan and relied on his authority. Refer to his hadith as they record it through Anas and others. Al-Dhahabi has documented his biography and quoted the statements by notable scholars as cited above, putting DTQ on his name to indicate who among the authors of the sunan quote him.

57. 'Adi ibn Thabit al-Kufi

Ibn Ma'in has described him as a "Shi'a extremist," while Dar Qutni calls him "Rafidi, extremist, but also reliable." Al-Jawzjani says that the man has "deviated." Al-Mas'udi says, "We have never seen anyone who is so outspoken in preaching his Shi'a views like 'Adi ibn Thabit." In his *Al-Mizan*, al-Dhahabi describes him as "the learned scholar of Shi'as, the most truthful among them, the judge and Imam of their mosques. Had all the Shi'as been like him, their harm would have been minimized." Then he goes on to document his biography and quote the views of the scholars cited above. He recounts the scholars who describe him as trustworthy such as Dar Qutni, Ahmad ibn Hanbal, Ahmad al-'Ajli, Ahmad al-Nisa'i, placing on his name the initials of authors of all the six *sahih* books who quote him.

Refer to his hadith in both Bukhari's and Muslim's *Sahih* books as transmitted by al-Bara' ibn 'Azib, 'Abdullah ibn Yazid (his maternal grand-father), 'Abdullah ibn Abu Awfah, Sulayman ibn Sard, and Sa'id ibn Jubayr. His hadith reported by Zarr ibn Habish and Abu Hazim al-Ashja'i is recorded in Muslim's *Sahih*. His hadith is quoted by al-A'mash, Mis'ar, Sa'id, Yahya ibn Sa'id al-Ansari, Zayd ibn Abu Anisa, and Fudayl ibn Ghazwan.

58. 'Atiyyah ibn Sa'd ibn Janadah al-'Awfi

He is Abul-Hasan al-Kufi, the renowned *tabi'i*. Al-Dhahabi has mentioned him in his *Al-Mizan*, quoting Salim al-Muradi saying that 'Atiyyah adhered to Shi'ism. Imam Ibn Qutaybah has included him among traditionists in his *Ma'arif* following his grandson al-'Awfi, al-Husayn ibn 'Atiyyah, the judge, adding, "'Atiyyah, a follower of Shi'ism, has been a jurist since the reign of al-Hajjaj." Ibn Qutaybah has mentioned a few renowned Shi'as in his chapter on sects in his *Ma'arif*, listing 'Atiyyah al-'Awfi among them. Ibn Sa'd mentions him on page 212, Vol. 6, of his *Tabaqat* indicating his firm belief in Shi'ism. His father, Sa'd ibn Janadah, was a companion of 'Ali (as). Once he visited the Imam in Kufa and said: "O Commander of the Faithful! I have been blessed with a newly born son; would you mind choosing a name for him?" The Imam answered: "This is a gift (*'atiyyah*) from Allah; therefore, do name him 'Atiyyah."

Ibn Sa'd has said: "'Atiyyah ibn al-Ash'ath went out in an army to fight al-Hajjaj. When al-Ash'ath's army fled, 'Atiyyah fled to Persia. Al-Hajjaj wrote an edict to Muhammad ibn al-Qasim ordering him to call him to his presence and give him the option to either denounce 'Ali or be whipped four hundred lashes, and his beard and head be shaven. So, he called him and read al-Hajjaj's letter to him, but 'Atiyyah refused to succumb; therefore, he had him whipped four hundred lashes and his head and beard were shaven. When Qutaybah became governor of Khurasan, 'Atiyyah rebelled against him and remained there till 'Umar ibn Habirah became ruler of Iraq. It was then that he wrote to him asking permission to go there. Granted permission, he came to Kufa where he stayed till he died in 11 A.H." The author adds, "He was, indeed, a trusted authority, and he reported many authentic ahadith."

All his descendants were sincere followers of Muhammad's progeny (as). Among them were noblemen, highly distinguished personalities like al-Husayn ibn al-Hasan ibn 'Atiyyah who was appointed governor of the district of Al-Sharqiyya succeeding Hafs ibn Ghiyath, as stated on page 58 of the same reference, then he was transferred to al-Mahdi's troops. He died in 201 A.H. Another is Sa'd ibn Muhammad ibn al-Hasan ibn 'Atiyyah, also a traditionist, who became governor of Baghdad.[17] He used to quote his father Sa'd from his uncle al-Husayn ibn al-Hasan ibn 'Atiyyah.

Back to the story of 'Atiyyah al-'Awfi. He is considered a reliable authority by Dawud and al-Tirmizi. Refer to his hadith in their *sahih* books from Ibn 'Abbas, Abu Sa'id and Ibn 'Umar. He has also learned hadith from 'Abdullah ibn al-Hasan who quotes his father who quotes his grand-mother al-Zahra', Mistress of the women of Paradise. His son al-Hasan ibn 'Atiyyah has learned hadith from him, and so have al-Hajjaj ibn Arta'ah, Mis'ar, al-Hasan ibn Adwan and others.

59. Al'ala' ibn Salih al-Taymi al-Kufi

---

[17] This can be extracted from the biography of his grandfather Sa'd ibn Janadah in Part One of the *Al-Isabah*.

In his biography of Al'ala' in *Al-Mizan*, Abu Hatim says the following about him: "He is one of the seniors of the Shi'as." In spite of this, Abu Dawud and al-Tirmizi have relied on his authority. Ma'in trusts him. Both Abu Hatim and Abu Zar'ah say that there is nothing wrong with his hadith. Refer to his hadith in both al-Tirmizi's and Abu Dawud's *sahih* books from Yazid ibn Abu Maryam and al-Hakam ibn 'Utaybah, in addition to all Sunni *musnad*s. Abu Na'im and Yahya ibn Bakir quote him, and so do many of their peers. He must be distinguished from Al'ala' ibn Abul-'Abbas, the Meccan poet. The latter is a Sufyani shaykh.

His hadith is reported by Abul-Tufayl. He is in a higher rank than Abul-'ala' ibn Salih; the latter is a Kufian, while the poet is Meccan. Both are mentioned in al-Dhahabi's *Al-Mizan*, where the author inaccurately quotes a statement pertaining to their being Shi'a seniors. Al'ala' the poet has composed poetry in praise of the Commander of the Faithful (as) which serves as irrefutable proof of his dedication and also highlights the truth about the Imam. He has also several poetic eulogies appreciated by Allah, His Messenger, and the believers.

60. 'Alqamah ibn Qays ibn 'Abdullah al-Nakh'i Abu Shibil

He is uncle of al-Aswad and Ibrahim, sons of Yazid. He is also a follower of the Progeny of Muhammad (s). Al-Shahristani, in his *Al-Milal wal-Nihal*, has included him among Shi'a nobility. He is master among the traditionists mentioned by Abu Ishaq al-Jawzjani who spitefully says, "There has been a group of people among the residents of Kufa whose sect [of Shi'ism is not appreciated; they are the masters among Kufi traditionists." 'Alqamah and his brother 'Ali have been companions of 'Ali (as). They have both participated in Siffin where 'Ali was martyred. The latter used to be called "Abul-Salat" (man of the prayers) due to his quite frequent prayers. 'Alqamah drenched his sword with the blood of the oppressive gang. His foot slid, yet he continued to wage *jihad* in the way of Allah, remaining an enemy of Mu'awiyah till his death. Abu Bardah included 'Alqamah's name among the emissary to Mu'awiyah during the latter's reign, but 'Alqamah objected and even wrote to Abu Bardah saying: "Please remove my name (from the list); please do remove it." This is recorded by Ibn Sa'd in his biography of 'Alqamah on page 57, Vol. 6, of his *Tabaqat*.

'Alqamah's fair mindedness and prestige among Sunnis is undisputed in spite of their knowledge of his Shi'a beliefs. Authors of the six *sahih* books, as well as others, have all relied on his authority. Refer to his hadith in Muslim and Bukhari from Ibn Mas'ud, Abul-Darda'ah and 'Ayesha. His hadith about 'Uthman and Abu Mas'ud is recorded in Muslim's *Sahih*. In both *sahih* books, his hadith is narrated by his nephew Ibrahim al-Nakh'i. In Muslim's *Sahih*, his hadith is transmitted by 'Abdul-Rahman ibn Yazid, Ibrahim ibn Yazid, and al-Sha'bi. He died, may Allah have mercy on his soul, in 62 A.H. in Kufa.

61. 'Ali ibn Badimah

Al-Dhahabi mentions him in his *Al-Mizan* quoting Ahmad ibn Hanbal saying, "He has reported authentic ahadith," that he is a pioneer of Shi'ism, that Ibn Ma'in has trusted him, that he narrates hadith from Makrimah and others, and that both Shu'bah and Mu'ammar have learned hadith from him. He marks his name to indicate that the authors of sunan have all quoted his hadith.

62. 'Ali ibn al-Ja'd

He is Abul-Hasan al-Jawhari al-Baghdadi, a slave of Banu Hashim. One of al-Bukhari's mentors, he is included by Qutaybah among notable Shi'as in his book *Al-Ma'arif*. His biography in *Al-Mizan* indicates that for sixty years, 'Ali used to fast every other day. Al-Qaysarani mentions him in his book *Al-Jami' Bayna Rijalul Sahihain*, stating that al-Bukhari alone has narrated twelve thousand ahadith reported by 'Ali ibn al-Ja'd. He died in 203 A.H. at the age of 96.

63. 'Ali ibn Zaid

His full name is 'Ali ibn Zaid ibn 'Abdullah ibn Zuhayr ibn Abu Malika ibn Jad'an Abul-Hasan al-Qarashi al-Taymi al-Basri. Ahmad al-'Ajli has mentioned him saying that the man follows the Shi'a School of Muslim Law. Yazid ibn Zari' has said that 'Ali ibn Yazid has been a Rafidi. In spite of all this, the learned scholars among the *tabi'in*, such as Shu'bah, 'Abdul-Warith, and many of their peers, have all quoted his hadith. He is one of the three jurists for whom Basrah has acquired fame, the others are Qatadah and 'Ash'ath al-Hadani. They were all blind. When al-Hasan al-Basri died, they suggested to 'Ali to take his place due to his accomplishments. He was so prestigious that only renowned dignitaries were his companions, something not too many Shi'as could enjoy during those days.

Al-Dhahabi has mentioned him in his *Al-Mizan* stating the above facts about him. In his book *Al-Jami' Bayna Rijalul Sahihain*, al-Qaysarani states his biography and says that Muslim has quoted his hadith as reported by Thabit al-Banani, and that he has learned about *jihad* from Anas ibn Malik. He died, may Allah have mercy on him, in 131 A.H.

64. 'Ali ibn Salih

He is brother of al-Hasan ibn Salih. We have already said a word about his virtues when we recounted the biography of his brother al-Hasan. He is one of the early Shi'a scholars, just like his brother. In his chapter on sales, Muslim relies on his authority.

'Ali ibn Salih has reported hadith from Salameh ibn Kahil, while Waki' has quoted him; they, too, are both Shi'as. He was born, may Allah be merciful unto his soul, and his twin brother al-Hasan, in 100 A.H., and he died in 151 A.H.

65. 'Ali ibn Ghurab Abu Yahya al-Fazari al-Kufi

Ibn Hayyan has described him as "an extremist Shi'a." Probably for this reason, al-Jawzjani drops him completely. Abu Dawud has said that 'Ali's hadith has been rejected, while both Ibn Ma'in and Dar Qutni trust him. Abu Hatim has said that there is nothing wrong with his hadith. Abu Zar'ah says he considers him truthful. Ahmad ibn Hanbal says, "I find him quite truthful." Ibn Ma'in describes him as "the poor man, the man of the truth," while al-Dhahabi mentions him in his *Al-Mizan* quoting both pros and cons regarding his hadith as mentioned above, and marking his name with SQ to identify which authors of the sunan rely on his authority. He reports hadith from Hisham ibn 'Urwah and 'Ubaydullah ibn 'Umar.

On page 273, Vol. 6, of his *Tabaqat*, Ibn Sa'd says the following about him: "Isma'il ibn Raja' quotes his hadith regarding what al-A'mash had said about 'Uthman." He died, may Allah have mercy on his soul, in Kufa in early Rabi'ul-Awwal 184 A.H., during Harun's regime.

66. 'Ali ibn Qadim Abul-Hasan al-Khuza'i al-Kufi

He is mentor of Ahmad ibn al-Furat, Ya'qub al-Faswi and a group of their peers who have all learned hadith from him and relied on his authority. Ibn Sa'd mentions him on page 282, Vol. 6, of his *Tabaqat* and describes him as an "extremist Shi'a." Probably for this reason alone that Yahya regards his hadith as "weak." Abu Hatim says that he is truthful. Al-Dhahabi mentions him in his *Al-Mizan*, quoting the above stated views about him, and marking his name to indicate that Abu Dawud and al-Tirmizi have both quoted his hadith. His hadith is recorded in their books from Sa'id ibn Abu 'Urwah and Qatar. He died, may Allah be merciful unto his soul, in 213 A.H. during al-Ma'mun's regime.

67. 'Ali ibn al-Munthir al-Tara'ifi

He is professor of al-Tirmizi, al-Nisa'i, Ibn Sa'id, 'Abdul-Rahman ibn Abu Hatim, and other peers who have all learned hadith from him and relied on his authority. Al-Dhahabi mentions him in his *Al-Mizan*, marking his name with TSQ as an indication of which authors of the sunan quote his hadith. He quotes the following from al-Nisa'i: "'Ali ibn al-Munthir is a staunch Shi'a, very trustworthy." He states that Ibn Hatim has said that the man is truthful and trustworthy, and that he reports hadith from Fudayl, Ibn 'Ayinah and al-Walid ibn Muslim. Al-Nisa'i testifies to the fact that he is "a staunch Shi'a," and that he relies on his hadith which is recorded in both *sahih* books. This, indeed, provides food for thought for those who cast doubt about his reliability. Al-Munthir, may Allah be merciful unto his soul, died in 256 A.H.

68. 'Ali ibn al-Hashim ibn al-Barid Abul-Hasan al-Kufi al-Khazzaz al-'Aithi

He is one of Imam Ahmad's mentors. Abu Dawud mentions him and describes him as a "well-ascertained Shi'a." Ibn Haban says that he is an "Shi'a extremist." Ja'far ibn Aban says, "I have heard Ibn Namir say that 'Ali ibn Hashim is extremist in his Shi'a beliefs." Al-Bukhari has said that both 'Ali ibn Hashim and his father are over-zealous in their Shi'a beliefs. Probably for this reason, al-Bukhari has rejected his hadith, but all other five authors of the *sahih* books have relied on his authority. Ibn Ma'in and others have trusted him, while Abu Dawud has included him among the most reliable traditionists. Abu Zar'ah has said that he is truthful, and al-Nisa'i has stated that there is nothing wrong with his hadith. Al-Dhahabi mentions him in his *Al-Mizan*, quoting what we have already cited above.

Al-Khatib al-Baghdadi, in a chapter dealing with 'Ali's character in his own *Tarikh* (history), Vol. 12, page 116, quotes Muhammad ibn Sulayman al-Baghindi saying that 'Ali ibn Hashim ibn al-Barid is truthful, a man who used to follow Shi'ism. He also quotes Muhammad ibn 'Ali al-Ajiri saying: "Once I asked Abu Dawud about 'Ali ibn Hashim ibn al-Barid. He suggested that I should ask 'Isa ibn Yunus. The latter has said: 'He belongs to those who call for Shi'ism.'" All of this is true. He also quotes al-Jawzjani saying that Hisham ibn al-Barid and his son 'Ali ibn Hashim are extremist in their "corrupt sect."

In spite of all this, authors of five *sahih* books rely on 'Ali ibn Hashim. Refer to his hadith about marriage in Muslim's *Sahih* as reported by Hisham ibn 'Urwah, and in his chapter dealing with seeking permission as transmitted from Talha ibn Yahya. His hadith in Muslim's *Sahih* is transmitted by Abu Mu'ammar Isma'il ibn Ibrahim and 'Abdullah ibn Aban. Ahmad ibn Hanbal, too, has reported his hadith, in addition to both sons of Shaybah, and a group of their class of reporters whose mentor was none other than 'Ali ibn Hashim. Al-Dhahabi says, "He died, may Allah have mercy on his soul, in 181 A.H.," adding, "His death is probably the earliest of those of Imam Ahmad's mentors."

69. 'Ammar ibn Zurayq al-Kufi

Al-Sulaymani calls him "Rafidi," as al-Dhahabi states while discussing 'Ammar in his *Al-Mizan*. In spite of this allegation, Muslim, Abu Dawud and al-Nisa'i rely on his authority. Refer to his hadith in Muslim's *Sahih* as transmitted by al-A'mash, Abu Ishaq al-Subai'i, Mansur, and 'Abdullah ibn 'Isa. His hadith is reported in Muslim's *Sahih* by Abul-Jawab, Abul-Hawas Salam, Ibn Ahmad al-Zubayri, and Yahya ibn Adam.

70. 'Ammar ibn Mu'awiyah or Ibn Abu Mu'awiyah

He is also called Khabab, or Ibn Salih al-Dihni al-Bijli al-Kufi, Abu Mu'awiyah. He is one of the Shi'a heroes who suffered a great deal of persecution while defending Muhammad's Progeny (as), so much so that Bishr ibn Marwan cut off his hamstrings only because he was a Shi'a. He is mentor of both Sufyans, in addition to Shu'bah, Sharik, and al-'Abar, who have all learned hadith from him and relied on his authority. Ahmad, Ibn Ma'in, Abu Hatim and other people have also relied on his authority. Muslim and four authors of sunan have quoted his hadith. Al-Dhahabi has included his biography in his own *Al-Mizan* and quoted the views stated above regarding his being a Shi'a and a trustworthy traditionist, adding that nobody had spoken ill of him except al-'Aqili, and that there was no fault in him other than his being a Shi'a. Refer to his hadith about the pilgrimage in Muslim's *Sahih* from Abul-Zubayr. He died in 133 A.H.; may Allah have mercy on his soul.

71. 'Amr ibn 'Abdullah Abu Issaq al-Subai'i al-Hamadani al-Kufi

He is Shi'a according to Ibn Qutaybah's *Ma'arif*, and Shahristani's *Al-Milal wal Nihal*. He was one of the masters of traditionists whose sect, in its roots and branches, the Nasibis do not appreciate due to the fact that Shi'as have followed in the footsteps of Ahl al-Bayt, deriving their method of worship from their own leadership in all religious matters. For this reason, al-Jawzjani has said in his biography of Zubayd in *Al-Mizan*: "Among the residents of Kufa, there is a group whose sect is not appreciated; they are the chiefs of Kufi traditionists such as Abu Ishaq, Mansur, Zubayd al-Yami, al-A'mash and other peers. People have tolerated them because of being truthful in narrating hadith, without adding aught of their own thereto."

Among what the Nasibis have rejected of Abu Ishaq's hadith is this one:

"'As the author of *Al-Mizan* indicates, Amr ibn Isma'il has quoted Abu Ishaq saying that the Messenger of Allah (s) has said, 'Ali is like a tree whose root I am, and whose branches are 'Ali, whose fruit are al-Hasan and al-Husayn, whose leaves are the Shi'as.'"

In fact, al-Mughirah's statement "nobody caused the Kufis to perish except Abu Ishaq and al-A'mash" is uncalled for except for the fact that these men are Shi'as and are loyal to Muhammad's progeny (as). They have become custodians of all ahadith pertaining to the attributes of the latter, peace be upon them. They were oceans of knowledge, and they followed Allah's commandments. They are relied upon by the authors of all six *sahih* books and by others. Refer to Abu Ishaq's hadith in both *sahih* books from al-Bara' ibn 'Azib, Yazid ibn Arqam, Harithah ibn Wahab, Sulayman ibn Sard, al-Nu'man ibn Bashir, 'Abdullah ibn Yazid al-Khadmi, and 'Amr ibn Maymun.

He is quoted in both *sahih* books by Shu'bah, al-Thawri, Zuhayr, and by his grandson Yusuf ibn Ishaq ibn Abu Ishaq. Ibn Khallikan says in 'Amr's biography in *Al-Wafiyyat* that 'Amr was born three years before 'Uthman took charge of ruling the Muslims, and that he died either in 127 A.H. or in 128 A.H., or in 129 A.H., whereas both Yahya ibn Ma'in and al-Mada'ini say that he died in 132 A.H., and Allah knows best.

72. 'Awf ibn Abu Jamila al-Basri Abu Sahl

He is well known as "al-A'rabi" [the bedouin], although his origin is really not from the desert. Al-Dhahabi mentions him in his *Al-Mizan* and says that "He is also called 'Awf the Truthful, while some say that he follows Shi'ism; *despite that*, a group of scholars has trusted him." He also quotes Ja'far ibn Sulayman describing him as Shi'a and quotes Bandar calling him "Rafidi." Ibn Qutaybah has included him in his own *Al-Ma'arif* among Shi'a dignitaries. He has taught hadith to Ruh, Hawdah, Shu'bah, al-Nadr ibn Shamil, 'Uthman ibn al-Haytham and many others of their calibre. Authors of the six *sahih* books as well as others have all relied on his authority. Refer to his hadith in Bukhari's *Sahih* from al-Hasan and Sa'id, sons of al-Hasan al-Basri, Muhammad ibn Sirin and Siyar ibn Salamah. His hadith in Muslim's *Sahih* is transmitted by Al-Nadr ibn Shamil. His hadith from Abu Raji' al-'Ataridi exists in both *sahih*s. He died, may Allah have mercy on him, in 146 A.H.

73. Al-Fadl ibn Dakin

His real name is 'Amr ibn Hammad ibn Zuhayr al-Malla'i al-Kufi, and he is well known by Abu Na'im. He is al-Bukhari's mentor, as the latter admits in his own *Sahih*. A group of elite scholars, like Ibn Qutaybah in his *Al-Ma'arif*, has included him among Shi'a dignitaries. Al-Dhahabi mentions him in his *Al-Mizan* and says: "I have heard ibn Ma'in saying: 'If a man's name is mentioned in the presence of Abu Na'im and he calls him a good person and praises him, then rest assured that that person is a Shi'a; whereas if he labels someone as Murji', then rest assured that he is a good Sunni.'" Al-Dhahabi says that this statement proves that Yahya ibn Ma'in inclines towards believing in the Return. It also proves that the man considers al-Fadl as a very staunch Shi'a.

In his biography of Khalid ibn Mukhlid in his *Al-Mizan*, al-Dhahabi quotes al-Jawzjani saying that Abu Na'im follows the Kufi sect, i.e. Shi'ism. To sum up, the fact that al-Fadl ibn Dakin is a Shi'a has never been disputed. Nevertheless, all authors of the six *sahih* books rely on him. Refer to his hadith in Bukhari's *Sahih* from Humam ibn Yahya, 'Abdul-'Aziz ibn Abu Salamah, Zakariyyah ibn Abu Za'idah, Hisham al-Distwa'i, al-A'mash, Misar, al-Thawri, Malik, Ibn 'Ayinah, Shaybah, and Zuhayr. His hadith in Muslim is transmitted by Saif ibn Abu Sulayman, Isma'il ibn Muslim, Abu 'Asim Muhammad ibn Ayyub al-Thaqafi, Abul Amis, Musa ibn 'Ali, Abu Shihab Musa ibn Nafi', Sufyan, Hisham ibn Sa'd, 'Abdul-Wahid ibn Ayman, and Isra'il. Al-Bukhari quotes him directly, while Muslim quotes his hadith as transmitted by Hajjaj ibn al-Sha'ir, 'Abd ibn Hamid, Ibn Abu Shaybah, Abu Sa'd al-Ashajj, Ibn Namir, 'Abdullah al-Darmi, Issaq al-Hanzali, and Zuhayr ibn Harb.

He was born in 133 A.H., and he died in Kufa on a Thursday night on the last day of Sha'ban, 210 A.H., during al-Mu'tasim's reign. Ibn Sa'd mentions him on page 279 A.H., Vol. 6, of his *Tabaqat*, describing him as "trustworthy, reliable, a man who has narrated a great deal of hadith, and an authority therein."

74. Fadil ibn Marzuq al-Aghar al-Ruwasi al-Kufi Abu 'Abdul-Rahman

Al-Dhahabi mentions him in his *Mizan* and describes him as a well-known Shi'a, quoting Sufyan ibn 'Ayinah and Ibn Ma'in testifying to this fact. He quotes Ibn 'Adi saying that he hopes there is nothing wrong with the hadith he narrates, then he quotes al-Haytham ibn Jamil saying that the latter once mentioned Fadl ibn Marzuq once and described him as "one of the Imams of guidance."

In his *Sahih*, Muslim relies on the authority of Fadil's ahadith which deals with prayers as transmitted by Shaqiq ibn 'Uqbah, and with *zakat* by 'Adi ibn Thabit. His hadith dealing with *zakat* as recorded by Muslim is transmitted by Yahya ibn Adam and Abu Usamah. In the *sunan*, his hadith is quoted by Waki', Yazid, Abu Na'im, 'Ali ibn al-Ja'd and many peers. Zayd ibn al-Habab has in fact lied regarding what he attributed to him of hadith dealing with the appointment of 'Ali (as) as Amr by the Prophet (s). He died, may Allah have mercy on him, in 158 A.H.

75. Fitr ibn Khalifah al-Hannat al-Kufi

'Abdullah ibn Ahmad once asked his father about Fitr ibn Khalifah. He answered, "He is a reporter of authentic hadith. His hadith reflects an attitude of a responsible person, but he also is a follower of Shi'ism." 'Abbas has quoted Ibn Ma'in saying that Fitr ibn Khalifah is a trusted Shi'a. Ahmad has said: "Fitr ibn Khalifah is trusted by Yahya, but he is an extremist Khashbi." Probably for this reason alone, Abu Bakr ibn 'Ayyash has said, "I have not abandoned the traditions reported by Fitr ibn Khalifah except because of his bad sect," i.e. for no fault in him other than his being a Shi'a.

Al-Jawzjani says: "Fitr ibn Khalifah has deviated from the path." During his sickness, he was heard by Ja'far al-Ahmar saying: "Nothing pleases me more than knowing that for each hair in my body there is an angel praising Allah Almighty on my behalf because of my love for Ahl al-Bayt, peace be upon them." Fitr ibn Khalifah narrates hadith from Abul-Tufayl, Abu Wa'il, and Mujahid. His hadith is quoted by Usamah, Yahya ibn Adam, Qabisah and others of the same calibre. Ahmad and others have trusted him. Murrah has said the following about him, "He is a responsible narrator of hadith who has memorized what he narrates by heart." Ibn Sa'd says, "He is, Insha-Allah, trustworthy." Al-Dhahabi discusses him in his *Mizan*, stating the learned scholars' views, which have already been stated above, concerning his character. Ibn Sa'd has quoted the same on page 253, Vol. 6, of his *Tabaqat*.

When Qutaybah mentions renowned Shi'as in his *Ma'arif*, he includes Fitr ibn Khalifah among them. Al-Bukhari has quoted Fitr's hadith as narrated by Mujahid. Al-Thawri has quoted Fitr's hadith dealing with etiquette as recorded in al-Bukhari's work. Authors of the four *sunan* books, as well as others, have all quoted Fitr's hadith. He died, may Allah have mercy on him, in 153 A.H.

76. Malik ibn Isma'il ibn Ziyad ibn Dirham Abu Hasan al-Kufi al-Hindi

He is one of Bukhari's mentors as stated in the latter's *Sahih*. Ibn Sa'd mentions him on page 282, Vol. 6, of his *Tabaqat*. He concludes by saying that "Abu Ghassan is trustworthy, truthful, a very staunch Shi'a." Al-Dhahabi mentions him in his *Mizan*, which proves his reliability and prestige, stating that the man has learned the teachings of the sect of Shi'ism from his mentor al-Hasan ibn Salih, that Ibn Ma'in has said that nobody in Kufa is more accurate in reporting hadith than Abu Ghassan, and that Abu Satim has said: "Whenever I look at him, he seems as though he has just left his grave, with two marks of prostration stamped on his forehead."

Al-Bukhari has quoted him directly in many chapters of his *Sahih*. Muslim has quoted his hadith on criminal penalties in his own *Sahih* as transmitted by Harun ibn 'Abdullah. Those who narrate his hadith in Bukhari are: Ibn 'Ayinah, 'Abdul-Aziz ibn Abu Salamah, and Isra'il. Both al-Bukhari and Muslim quote his hadith from Zuhayr ibn Mu'awiyah. He died, may Allah have mercy on him, in Kufa in 219 A.H.

77. Muhammad ibn Khazim

He is very well known as Abu Mu'awiyah al-Darir al-Tamimi al-Kufi. Al-Dhahabi mentions him saying, "Muhammad ibn Khazim al-Darir is confirmed, truthful; nowhere at all have I seen his hadith as weak; I shall discuss him in my chapter on *kunayat*." When the author mentions him in his said chapter, he states: "Abu Mu'awiyah al-Darir is one of the most renowned and trustworthy Imams of hadith," and he goes on to say: "Al-Hakim has said that both Shaykhs rely on his authority, and he is famous for being an extremist Shi'a."

All authors of the six *sahih*s have relied on his authority. Al-Dhahabi has marked his name with "A" to indicate that all traditionists rely on his authority. Refer to his hadith in Bukhari's and Muslim's *Sahih*s from al-A'mash and Hisham ibn 'Urwah. Muslim's *Sahih* contains other ahadith he has narrated through other trusted reporters. In Bukhari's *Sahih*, his hadith is reported by 'Ali ibn al-Madini, Muhammad ibn Salam, Yusuf ibn 'Isa, Qutaybah, and Musaddad. In Muslim's *Sahih*, he is quoted by Sa'd al-Wasiti, Sa'd ibn Mansur, 'Amr al-Naqid, Ahmad ibn Sinan, Ibn Namir, Issaq al-Hanzali, Abu Bakr ibn Abu Shaybah, Abu Karib,

Yahya ibn Yahya, and Zuhayr. Musa al-Zaman has reported his hadith in both *sahih*s. Muhammad ibn Khazim was born in 113 A.H., and he died in 195 A.H.; may Allah be merciful unto him.

78. Muhammad ibn 'Abdullah al-Dabi al-Tahani al-Nishapuri Abu 'Abdullah al-Hakim

He is an Imam of *huffaz*, those who memorize the entirety of the holy Qur'an and hadith by heart, and author of about one thousand books. He toured the lands seeking knowledge and learning hadith from about two thousand mentors. He may be compared with the most renowned scholars of his time such as al-Sa'luki. Imam ibn Furk and all other Imams consider his status to be superior even to their own. They appreciate him and his contributions; they cherish his name and reputation, without doubting his mastership at all. All learned Sunni scholars who could not achieve as much as he did envy him. He is one of the Shi'a heroes, a protector of the Islamic Shari'a.

The author of *Al-Mizan* narrates his biography and describes him as "a truthful Imam, a very renowned Shi'a." He quotes Ibn Tahir saying: "I once asked Abu Isma'il 'Abdullah al-Ansari about al-Hakim Abu Abdullah. He said: 'He is an Imam in hadith, a wretched Rafidi.'" Al-Dhahabi has recounted a few of his interesting statements such as his saying that the Chosen One (s) came to the world circumcised, with a smile on his face, and that 'Ali (as) is a *wasi*. The author adds the following: "His being truthful and knowledgeable of what he reports is a unanimously accepted fact." He was born in Rabi' al-Awwal of 321 A.H., and he died in Safar of 405 A.H., may Allah have mercy on his soul.

79. Muhammad ibn 'Ubaydullah ibn Abu Rafi' al-Madani

He, Abu 'Ubaydullah, his brothers al-Fadl and 'Abdullah sons of 'Ubaydullah, his grandfather Abu Rafi', his uncles Rafi', al-Hasan, al-Mughirah, 'Ali, and their sons as well as grandsons, are all among good Shi'a ancestors. The books they have authored testify to the depth of their Shi'a conviction, as we have mentioned in Section 2, Chapter 12, of our book *Al-Fusul al-Muhimmah*.

Ibn 'Uday mentions Muhammad ibn 'Ubaydullah ibn Abu Rafi' al-Madani, adding, at the conclusion of his biography in the *Mizan*, that the man is among Kufi Shi'as. When al-Dhahabi states his biography in his own *Mizan*, he marks it with TQ as an indication of which authors of the *sunan* books quote his hadith (i.e. Tirmizi and Dar Qutni). He also mentions that he quotes his father and grandfather, and that Mandil and 'Ali ibn Hashim quote his hadith. His hadith is also quoted by Haban ibn 'Ali, Yahya ibn Ya'li and others. Muhammad ibn 'Ubaydullah ibn Abu Rafi' al-Madani may have also reported hadith from his brother 'Abdullah ibn 'Ubaydullah who is well known as a traditionist by researchers of hadith. Al-Tabarani in his *Al-Mu'jam al-Kabir* has relied on the authority of Muhammad ibn 'Ubaydullah ibn Abu Rafi' al-Madani who quotes his father and grandfather saying that the Messenger of Allah (s) has said to 'Ali (as), "The first to enter Paradise will be I and you, then al-Hasan and al-Husayn, with our progeny behind us, and our Shi'as on our right and left."

80. Muhammad ibn Fudayl ibn Ghazwan Abu 'Abdul-Rahman al-Kufi

Ibn Qutaybah has included him among Shi'a dignitaries in his work *Al-Ma'arif*, and Ibn Sa'd has mentioned him on page 271, Vol. 6, of his *Tabaqat*, saying, "He is a trustworthy and reliable traditionist who as reported a great deal of hadith; he also is a Shi'a, and some scholars [for this reason] do not rely on his authority." Al-Dhahabi has mentioned him in his chapter containing those well-known because of their fathers' reputation at the conclusion of his *Mizan*, describing him as a truthful Shi'a. He also mentions him in his chapter containing those whose first name is Muhammad, describing him as "a man of truth and fame," adding that Ahmad has described him as a Shi'a whose hadith is authentic, and that Abu Dawud has described him as a "Shi'a by profession" (!), adding that he was a man of hadith and knowledge, that he learned the Qur'an from Hamzah, that he has written numerous books, and that Ibn Ma'in has trusted him and Ahmad spoken well of him. Al-Nisa'i has said that there is nothing wrong with his hadith.

Authors of the six *sahih* books, as well as many others, have relied on his authority. Refer to his hadith in Bukhari as transmitted by Muhammad ibn Namir, Ishaq al-Hanzali, Ibn Abu Shaybah, Muhammad ibn Salam, Qutaybah, 'Umran ibn Maysarah, and 'Amr ibn 'Ali. His hadith is transmitted in Bukhari by 'Abdullah ibn 'Amir, Abu Karib, Muhammad ibn Tarf, Wasil ibn 'Abd al-A'la, Zuhayr, Abu Sa'd al-Ashajj, Muhammad ibn Yazid, Muhammad ibn al-Muthanna, Ahmad al-Wak'i, and 'Abdul-'Aziz ibn 'Umar ibn Aban. He died, may Allah have mercy on him, in Kufa in 194 or 195 A.H.

81. Muhammad ibn Muslim ibn al-Ta'ifi

He was one of the most distinguished companions of Imam Abu 'Abdullah al-Sadiq, peace be upon him. Shaykh al-Ta'ifa Abu Ja'far al-Tusi has mentioned him in his book *Rijal al-Shi'a*, and al-Hasan ibn 'Ali ibn Dawud has included him in his chapter on the most trustworthy traditionists in his book *Al-Mukhtasar*. Al-Dhahabi includes his biography and quotes Yahya ibn Ma'in and others who say that the man is truthful. He adds saying that al-Qa'nabi, Yahya ibn Yahya, and Qutaybah have all transmitted his traditions, and that 'Abdul-Rahman ibn Mahdi once mentioned Muhammad ibn Muslim ibn al-Ta'ifi and said: "His books [of traditions] are all authentic," and that Ma'ruf ibn Wasil said: "I saw Sufyan al-Thawri once accompanied by Muhammad ibn Muslim ibn al-Ta'ifi who was writing down his hadith." Yet those who have labelled his hadith as "weak" have done so only on the grounds of his being a Shi'a, although their prejudice has not at all harmed him. His hadith from 'Amr ibn Dinar about ablution exists in Muslim's *Sahih*. According to Ibn Sa'd's *Tabaqat*, as stated on page 381, Vol. 5, his hadith is quoted by Waki' ibn al-Jarrah and one hundred others. In that year, his name-sake Muhammad ibn Muslim ibn Jummaz died in Medina. Ibn Sa'd has included both of their biographies in Vol. 5 of his *Tabaqat*.

82. Muhammad ibn Musa ibn 'Abdullah al-Qatari al-Madani

Al-Dhahabi has mentioned him in his *Mizan* quoting Abu Hatim testifying to his being a Shi'a. He also quotes al-Tirmizi saying that the man is trustworthy, and he even marks his name with the initials of Muslim and the authors of *sunan* as an indication of their reliance on his authority. Refer to his hadith about foods in Muslim's *Sahih* transmitted from 'Abdullah ibn 'Abdullah ibn Abu Talha. He is also quoted by al-Maqbari and a group of his peers. Others who have quoted his hadith are: Ibn Abu Fadik, Ibn Mahdi, Qutaybah, and others of their intellectual calibre.

83. Mu'awiyah ibn 'Ammar al-Dihni al-Bajli al-Kufi

He is among our highly respected and revered Shi'as, prestigious and trustworthy. His father 'Ammar is a good example for perseverance and persistence in adhering to the principles of justice, a model Allah has brought forth for those who are patient while suffering for His Cause. A few tyrants cut off his hamstrings because of being a Shi'a, as we have indicated above, without succeeding in swaying him, till he left this world to receive his rewards. His son Mu'awiyah was meted the same treatment, and the father is but a model for the son. He has accompanied Imams al-Sadiq and al-Kazim, peace be upon them, and learned from them a great deal. He has authored many books - as indicated above - and he is quoted by Shi'a reporters such as Ibn Abu 'Umayr and others. Muslim and al-Nisa'i have relied on his authority. His hadith about *hajj* is quoted in Muslim's *Sahih* by al-Zubayr. In Muslim, he is quoted by both Yahya ibn Yahya and Qutaybah. He has also narrated hadith from his father 'Ammar, and from a group of his peers, and such ahadith exist in Sunni *musnads*. He died, may Allah have mercy on him, in 175 A.H.

84. Ma'ruf ibn Kharbuth al-Karkhi

Al-Dhahabi describes him[18] in his *Mizan* as "a truthful Shi'a," marking his name with the initials of al-Bukhari, Muslim, and Abu

---

[18] Some say "Ibn Fayruz," others say "Ibn Fayruzan," while still others call him "Ibn 'Ali."

Dawud to indicate that they all quote his hadith. He also quotes Abul Tufayl saying that Ma'ruf narrates a few ahadith. His hadith is narrated by Abu 'Asim, Abu Dawud, 'Ubaydullah ibn Musa and others. He also quotes Abu Hatim saying that the latter writes down his hadith.

Ibn Khallikan mentions him in his *Wafiyyat* and describes him as one of the servants of 'Ali ibn Musa al-Rida, peace be upon him. He goes on to praise him, quoting a statement of his in which he says, "I have come unto the Almighty Allah, leaving everything behind me, with the exception of serving my master 'Ali ibn Musa al-Rida, peace be upon him." When Ibn Qutaybah discusses a few Shi'a notables in his work *Al-Ma'arif*, he includes Ma'ruf ibn Kharbuth among them. Muslim has relied on the authority of Ma'ruf ibn Kharbuth; refer to his hadith about *hajj* in his *sahih* from Abul Tufayl. He died in Baghdad in 200 A.H.;[19] his gravesite is now a mausoleum. Sirri al-Saqti was one of his students.

85. Mansur ibn al-Mu'tamir ibn 'Abdullah ibn Rabi'ah al-Salami al-Kufi

He is one of the companions of Imams al-Baqir and al-Sadiq (as), and he has narrated hadith from them, as the author of *Muntahal Maqal fi Ahwal al-Rijal* states. Ibn Qutaybah includes him among Shi'a nobility in his book *Al-Ma'arif*. Al-Jawzjani has included him among the narrators "whose sect is not appreciated by [certain] people" in the roots and branches of religion, due to their adherence to what they have learned from Muhammad's progeny (as). Says he: "Among the people of Kufa there is a group whose sect is not appreciated; these are chiefs of Kufa's traditionists such as Abu Ishaq, Mansur, Zubayd al-Yami, al-A'mash and other peers. People have tolerated them just because they are truthful in narrating hadith."[20] Why do they bear so much grudge against these truthful men? Is it because of their upholding

---

[19] Some say in the year 201 A.H., while others say it was the year 204 A.H.

[20] As in Zubayd al-Yami's biography in *Al-Mizan*. We have quoted this statement from al-Jawzjani while discussing the biographies of Zubayd, al-A'mash, and Abu Ishaq, and we included noteworthy comments on them.

the Two Weighty Things? Or their embarking upon the Ark of Salvation? Or their entering into the city of the Prophet's knowledge through its Gate, the Gate of Repentance? Or is it their seeking refuge with the "Refuge of all the world"? Or is it their obedience to the Prophet's will to be kind unto his descendants? Or is it their heart's submission to Allah and their weeping for fear of Him, as is well known about them?

Stating the biography of Mansur ibn al-Mu'tamir ibn 'Abdullah ibn Rabi'ah, Ibn Sa'd says the following about Mansur on page 235 of Vol. 6 of his *Tabaqat*: "He has lost his eye-sight because of excessive weeping for fear of Allah. He used to carry a handkerchief for the purpose of drying his tears. Some allege that he fasted and prayed for sixty years." Can a man of such qualities be a burden on people? No, indeed, but we have been inflicted by some people who do not know what fairness is; so, we are Allah's, and unto Him is our return.

In his biography of Mansur ibn al-Mu'tamir ibn 'Abdullah ibn Rabi'ah, Ibn Sa'd also quotes Hammad ibn Zayd saying, "I have seen Mansur in Mecca, and I think he belongs to those Khashbis, yet I do not think that he tells a lie when he quotes hadith." Behold the underestimation, grudge, contempt and manifest enmity this statement bears. How surprised I am when I consider his statement: "I do not think that he tells lies..." As if telling lies is one of the practices of those who are sincere to Muhammad's progeny. As if Mansur alone is truthful, rather than all other Shi'a traditionists. Name-calling... As if the Nasibis could not find a name whereby they can call the Shi'as other than misnomers such as Khashbis, Turabis, Rafidis, etc. As if they have never heard the Almighty's Commandment: "And do not exchange bad names; what an evil it is to use a bad name after having accepted faith (Qur'an, 49:11)."Ibn Qutaybah has mentioned the "Khashbis" in his book *Al-Ma'arif* and said: "These are Rafidis. Ibrahim al-Ashtar met 'Ubaydullah ibn Ziyad in the battle-field. Most of Ibrahim's men had guaiacum wood panels; therefore, they were labelled 'khashbis,' men associated with panelling, out of scorn." In fact, they called them so just to humiliate them and look down upon them and their wooden weapons with which they were able to beat Ibn Marjanah, predecessor of the Nasibis, thus annihilating those heretics, murderers of Muhammad's progeny. "Allah has cut off the tail of those who committed injustice; all praise be to Allah, Lord of the Worlds (Qur'an, 6:45)."There is no harm, therefore, in this noble name, nor is there any harm in its synonyms like Turabis, after Abu Turab (Imam 'Ali, as); we are proud of it.

We have digressed. Let us go back to our main topic and state that it is the consensus of traditionists to rely on Mansur. For this reason, all authors of the six *sahih* books, as well as others, rely on his authority, knowing that he is Shi'a. Refer to his hadith in Bukhari's and Muslim's *Sahih*s from Abu Wa'il, Abul Duha, Ibrahim al-Nakh'i and other peers. He quotes Shu'bah, al-Thawri, Ibn 'Ayinah, Hammad ibn Zayd and others who are the most distinguished of that class of reporters of hadith. Ibn Sa'd has said that Mansur's death took place at the end of the year 132 A.H., adding, "He is a trusted authority who has reported a great deal of hadith; he is a man of sublime prestige; may Allah have mercy on him."

86. Al-Minhal ibn 'Amr al-Kufi the *tabi'i*

He is one of the renowned Shi'as of Kufa. For this reason, al-Jawzjani has categorized his hadith as "weak," describing him as a "follower of the bad sect." Ibn Hazm has spoken ill of him in the same manner, and Yahya ibn Sa'd, too, chews his name. Ahmad ibn Hanbal states contrariwise. He says: "Abu Bishr is more dear to me than a sweet cool fountain, and he is more reliable than others."

In spite of being a staunch Shi'a, stating so in public even during the time of al-Mukhtar, he is not doubted by scholars regarding the accuracy of his hadith. He is quoted by Shu'bah, al-Mas'udi, al-Hajjaj ibn Arta'ah, and many peers of their intellectual calibre. He is trusted by Ibn Ma'in, Ahmad al-'Ijli and others. In his *Mizan*, al-Dhahabi quotes their assessment of the man as we have stated above, marking his name with the initials of Bukhari and Muslim as an indication that they both consider his hadith reliable. Refer to his hadith in Bukhari's *Sahih* from Sa'id ibn Jubayr. In Bukhari's *Sahih*, in the author's section on Tafsir, his hadith is transmitted by Zayd ibn Abu Anisa. Al-Mansur ibn al-Mu'tamir has quoted him in a chapter on prophets.

87. Musa ibn Qays al-Hadrami Abu Muhammad

Al-'Aqili describes him as an "extremist Rafidi." Once, Sufyan asked him about Abu Bakr. He answered: "'Ali is more dear to me." Musa ibn Qays reports hadith from Salamah ibn Kahil, Iyad ibn Iyad, ending with Malik ibn Ja'na reporting that "I heard Umm Salamah saying that 'Ali is with the truth; whoever follows him is a follower of the truth, and whoever abandons him certainly abandons the truth; this is decreed." This has been narrated by Abu Na'im al-Fadl ibn Dakin from Musa ibn Qays. Musa ibn Qays has reported hadith praising Ahl al-Bayt in volumes which angered al-'Aqili who said to him what he said. Ibn Ma'in has trusted and relied on him. Abu Dawud and Sa'd ibn Mansur have both relied on his authority in their respective *sunan*. Al-Dhahabi has included his biography in his own *Mizan*, stating about him what we have already stated above. Refer to his hadith in the *sunan* from Salamah ibn Kahil and Hajar ibn 'Anbasah. His hadith is transmitted by Dakin, 'Ubaydullah ibn Musa and other reliable authorities. He died, may Allah have mercy on him, during the reign of al-Mansur.

88. Naif' ibn al-Harith Abu Dawud al-Nakh'i al-Kufi al-Hamadani al-Subay'i

Al-'Aqili described him as being an "extremist Rafidi." Al-Bukhari says: "People speak ill of him [because of being a Shi'a]." Sufyan, Hamam, Sharik and a group of the most renowned scholars of such calibre have all quoted him. Al-Tirmizi relies on him in his own *sahih*. Authors of *musnads* have all recorded his hadith. Refer to his hadith in Tirmizi and others from Anas ibn Malik, Ibn 'Abbas, 'Umran ibn Hasin and Zayd ibn Arqam. Al-Dhahabi has included his biography and stated what we have already said above.

89. Nuh ibn Qays ibn Rabah al-Hadani

He is also known as al-Tahi al-Basri. Al-Dhahabi mentions him in his *Mizan*, describing his hadith as authentic, adding that Ahmad and Ibn Ma'in trust him. He also quotes Abu Dawud saying that the man is a Shi'a. Al-Nisa'i has said that there is nothing wrong with his hadith, putting on his name the initials of Muslim and authors of the *sunan* as an indication that they all quote his hadith. In Muslim's *Sahih*, his ahadith about beverages are quoted by Ibn 'Awn. His ahadith on the dress codes exist in Muslim's *Sahih*, too, as narrated by his brother Khalid ibn Qays. In Muslim, he is quoted by Nasr ibn 'Ali. In works other than Muslim's, his hadith is quoted by al-Ash'ath and by many others of his calibre. Nuh ibn Qays ibn Rabah reports from Ayyub, 'Amr ibn Malik and a group of other men.

90. Harun ibn Sa'd al-'Ijli al-Kufi

Al-Dhahabi mentions him and puts Muslim's initial on his name as an indication that the latter quotes him, then he describes him as "truthful in his own right," but he also calls him "a hated Rafidi" who narrates from 'Abbas from Ibn Ma'in that he is an extremist Shi'a. He has learned hadith from 'Abdul-Rahman ibn Abu Sa'id al-Khudri, who in turn quotes Muhammad ibn Abu Hafs al-'Attar, al-Mas'udi, and Hasan ibn Hayy. Abu Hatim says that there is nothing wrong with his hadith. I remember one of his ahadith which describes Hell-fire; it is recorded in Muslim's *Sahih* as narrated by al-Hasan ibn Salih from Harun ibn Sa'd al-'Ijli, from Salman.

91. Hashim ibn al-Barid ibn Zayd Abu 'Ali al-Kufi

Al-Dhahabi mentions him and puts the initials of Abu Dawud and al-Nisa'i on his name to indicate that he is one of their authorities, quoting Ibn Ma'in and others testifying to his being trustworthy, in addition to his own testimony to being a "Rafidi." He quotes Ahmad saying that there is nothing wrong with his hadith. Hashim narrates hadith from Zayd ibn 'Ali and Muslim al-Batin, and he is quoted by al-Kharibi and his son 'Ali ibn Hashim, to whom we referred above, in addition to a group of other renowned scholars. Hashim adhered to Shi'ism, and this has been made clear when we discussed 'Ali ibn Hashim.

92. Hubayrah ibn Maryam al-Himyari

He is one of the companions of Imam 'Ali (as), equal only to al-Harith in his sincerity as well as companionship. Al-Dhahabi mentions him and puts on his name the initials of the authors of *sunan* books as a reference to his being one of the authorities of their *musnads*, then he quotes Ahmad saying, "There is nothing wrong with his hadith, and he is more dear to us than al-Harith." Al-Dhahabi quotes Ibn Kharash describing Hubayrah as "weak; he used to assault the wounded in Siffin." Al-Jawzjani says the following about him: "He is a follower of al-Mukhtar who used to put an end to the life of those wounded in the Khazir Battle."

Al-Shahristani, in his book *Al-Milal wal Nihal*, has included him among Shi'a notables, a fact taken for granted by everyone. His hadith from 'Ali (as) is unquestioned in the *sunan*, and he is quoted by both Abu Ishaq and Au Fakhita."

93. Hisham ibn Ziyad Abul Miqdam al-Basri

Al-Shahristani has included him in his *Al-Milal wal Nihal* among Shi'a notables. Al-Dhahabi mentions him twice: once under his alphabetical index, and once in his chapter on *kunayat*, placing a Q on his name to indicate that Dar Qutni of the *sunan* relies on his authority. Refer to his hadith in Tirmizi's *Sahih* and other works as transmitted from al-Hasan and al-Qardi. He is quoted by Shayban ibn Farukh, al-Qawariri and others.

94. Hisham ibn 'Ammar ibn Nasr ibn Maysarah Abu al-Walid

He is also called al-Zafri al-Dimashqi. He is one of Bukhari's mentors as the latter states in his *Sahih*. Ibn Qutaybah includes him among Shi'a notables when he mentions quite a few of them in his chapter on sects in *Al-Ma'arif*. Al-Dhahabi mentions him in his *Mizan*, describing him as "the Imam, orator, and reciter of the Holy Qur'an of Damascus, its traditionist and scholar, a man of truth who has narrated a great deal of hadith, though he has a few [ideological] defects, etc."

Al-Bukhari quotes him directly in his chapter on "those who voluntarily grant extensions for repayment of debt" in his chapter on sales in his *sahih* and in other chapters with which researchers are familiar. Some of such chapters, I believe, are his books *Al-Maghazi*, his book on beverages, and his chapter on the attributes of the companions of the Prophet (s). Hisham ibn 'Ammar narrates hadith from Yahya ibn Hamzah, Sadaqah ibn Khalid, 'Abdul-Hamid ibn Abul 'Ishrin and others. The author of *Al-Mizan* says: "Many quote his hadith; they travel to his place to learn from him how to recite the Holy Qur'an and the narration of hadith. His hadith is quoted by al-Walid ibn Muslim, one of his mentors, while he himself narrates from Abu Lahi'ah. 'Abdan has said that there is no traditionist like him in the world, while someone else has said that Hisham is outspoken, wise, easy to comprehend, and he has acquired a great deal of knowledge."

Like other Shi'as, Hisham ibn 'Ammar believes that the Qur'anic diction is created only by Allah Almighty. When Ahmad [ibn Hanbal] heard about this, as the author of *Al-Mizan* states in his biography of Hisham ibn 'Ammar, he responded by saying, "I have known him to be wreckless; may Allah annihilate him." Ahmad has also come across a book written by Hisham in which one of the latter's sermons says: "Praise be to Allah Who has manifested Himself unto his creatures through what He has created." This caused Ahmad to be extremely furious, so much so that he required all those who used to pray behind Hisham to repeat their prayers. Ahmad could not see that Hisham's statement is very clear in stating that Allah is superior to being seen, glorified above those who inquire about Him with "how" or "where," appreciative of His norm of creation. His statement may be compared with one saying: "He has manifested His miracles in everything He has created," or it may even be more pertinent and fitting than the latter; but scholars of the same calibre speak of each other in the light of their own likes and dislikes, each according to his own degree of knowledge. Hisham ibn 'Ammar was born in 153 A.H., and he died at the commencement of Muharram of 245 A.H.; may Allah have mercy on him.

95. Hashim ibn Bashir ibn al-Qasim ibn Dinar al-Wasiti Abu Mu'awiyah

His birth-place is Balkh. His grandfather al-Qasim had moved to Wasit to engage in trade. Ibn Qutaybah includes him in his *Al-Ma'arif* among Shi'a nobility. He is mentor of Imam Ahmad ibn Hanbal and all those of his calibre. Al-Dhahabi has mentioned him in his book *Al-Mizan*, marking his name with an indication that all authors of the six *sahih* books rely on his authority, and describing him as one who knows the Holy Qur'an by heart. Says al-Dhahabi: "He is one of the most renowned scholars. He learned hadith from al-Zuhri and Hasan ibn 'Abdul-Rahman. His hadith is quoted in turn by al-Qattan, Ahmad, Ya'qub al-Dawraqi, and by many others."

Refer to his hadith in Bukhari's and Muslim's *Sahih* books as transmitted by Hamid al-Tawil, Isma'il ibn Abu Khalid, Abu Ihaq al-Shaybani, and by others. He is quoted in both books by 'Umar, al-Naqid, 'Amr ibn Zararah, and Sa'id ibn Sulayman. In Bukhari, his hadith is quoted by 'Amr ibn 'Awf, Sa'd ibn al-Nadir, Muhammad ibn Nabahan, 'Ali ibn al-Madini, and Qutaybah. In Muslim, he is quoted by Ahmad ibn Hanbal, Shurayh, Ya'qub al-Dawraqi, 'Abdullah ibn Mu'it', Yahya ibn Yahya, Sa'id ibn Mansur, Ibn Abu Shaybah, Isma'il ibn Salim, Muhammad ibn al-Sabah, Dawud ibn Rashid, Ahmad ibn Mani', Yahya ibn Ayyub, Zuhayr ibn Harb, 'Uthman ibn Abu Shaybah, 'Ali ibn Hajar, and Yazid ibn Harun. He died, may Allah have mercy on him, in Baghdad in 183 A.H. at the age of 79.

96. Waki' ibn al-Jarrah ibn Malih ibn 'Adi

His *kunyat* is "Abu Sufyan," after his son Sufyan al-Ruwasi al-Kufi. He belongs to the tribe of Qays Ghilan. In his *Ma'arif*, Ibn Qutaybah includes him among Shi'a notables. In his book titled *Tahthib*, Ibn al-Madani has said that Waki' adheres to Shi'ism. Marwan ibn Mu'awiyah never doubted that Waki' was "Rafidi."

Once, Yahya ibn Ma'in visited Marwan and found him with a tablet containing statements about this person and that. Among its contents was a statement describing Waki' as Rafidi. Ibn Ma'in said to Marwan: "Waki' is better than you." "Better than me?!" exclaimed Marwan. Ibn Ma'in answered: "Yes, better than you." Ibn Ma'in indicates that Waki' came to know about this dialogue and he responded by saying, "Yahya is a friend of ours." Ahmad ibn Hanbal was asked once, "If there is a discrepancy in narrating hadith between Waki' and Abdul-Rahman ibn Mahdi, whose hadith shall we accept?" Ahmad answered that he personally preferred 'Abdul-Rahman's hadith for reasons which he stated. Among them was this one: "'Abdul-Rahman never speaks in a derogatory manner about our ancestors, unlike Waki' ibn al-Jarrah." This is supported by a statement recorded by al-Dhahabi at the conclusion of his biography of al-Hasan ibn Salih wherein he says that Waki' used to say: "Al-Hasan ibn Salih, in my view, is an Imam of hadith." Some people said to him, "But he does not invoke Allah's mercy on 'Uthman." He said, "Do you invoke Allah's mercy upon al-Hajjaj's soul?" thus equating 'Uthman with al-Hajjaj.

Al-Dhahabi has mentioned him in his book *Al-Mizan* stating the above views about him. All authors of the six *sahih* books as well as others rely on his authority. Refer to his hadith in Bukhari's and Muslim's *Sahih* books as transmitted by al-A'mash, al-Thawri, Shu'bah, Isma'il ibn Abu Khalid, and 'Ali ibn al-Mubarak. He is quoted in both books by Ishaq al-Hanzali and Muhammad ibn Namir. Al-Bukhari quotes his hadith as transmitted by 'Abdullah al-Hamidi, Muhammad ibn Salam, Yahya ibn Ja'far ibn A'yan, Yahya ibn Musa, and Muhammad ibn Muqatil. In Muslim's book, he is quoted by Zuhayr, Ibn Abu Shaybah, Abu Karib, Abu Sa'd al-Ashajj, Nasr ibn 'Ali, Sa'd ibn Azhar, Ibn Abu 'Umar, 'Ali ibn Kashram, 'Uthman ibn Abu Shaybah, and Qutaybah ibn Sa'd. He died, may Allah have mercy on his soul, in Fid when he was in the company of a caravan returning from the pilgrimage, in Muharram of 197 A.H. at the age of 68.

97. Yahya ibn al-Jazzar al-'Arni al-Kufi

He is one of the companions of the Commander of the Faithful, peace be upon him. Al-Dhahabi mentions him in his book *Al-Mizan* and marks his name to indicate that Muslim and authors of the *sunan* rely on his authority, describing him as "truthful" and "trustworthy," and quoting al-Hakam ibn Atbah saying that Yahya ibn al-Jazzar is "extremist" in his Shi'a views. Ibn Sa'd has mentioned him on page 206, Vol. 6, of his *Tabaqat* saying: "Yahya ibn al-Jazzar adheres to Shi'ism, and he goes to extremes in doing so; yet many have said that he is trustworthy, and that he narrates many ahadith."

I have seen how Muslim's *Sahih* contains one hadith about prayers which he narrates from 'Ali, and another about faith transmitted from 'Abdul-Rahman ibn Abu Layla. Al-Hakam ibn 'Utayba and al-Hasan al-'Urfi quote his hadith in Muslim and others.

98. Yahya ibn Sa'id al-Qattan

His *kunyat* is "Abu Sa'id." He is a slave of Banu Tamim al-Basri, and he is the most renowned traditionist of his time. Qutaybah has included him in his *Ma'arif* among Shi'a notables. Authors of the six *sahih* books and others have relied on his authority. His hadith from Hisham ibn 'Urwah, Hamid al-Tawil, Yahya ibn Sa'id al-Ansari and others stands on solid grounds in Bukhari, Musaddad, 'Ali ibn al-Madini and Bayan ibn 'Amr. In Muslim's book, his hadith is transmitted by Muhammad ibn Hatim, Muhammad ibn Khalad al-Bahili, Abu Kamil Fadl ibn Husayn al-Jahdari, Muhammad al-Muqaddimi, 'Abdullah ibn Hashim, Abu Bakr ibn Abu Shaybah, 'Abdullah ibn Sa'd, Ahmad ibn Hanbal, Ya'qub al-Dawraqi, Ahmad ibn 'Abdah, 'Amr ibn 'Ali, and 'Abdul-Rahman ibn Bishr. He died, may Allah Almighty have mercy on him, in 198 A.H. at the age of 78.

99. Yazid ibn Ziyad al-Kufi Abu 'Abdullah

He is a slave of Banu Hashim. Al-Dhahabi mentions him in his book *Al-Mizan*, placing on his name the initials of Muslim and four authors of *sunan* to indicate that they quote him. He cites Abu Fadl saying: "Yazid ibn Ziyad is one of the foremost Shi'a Imams." Al-Dhahabi has admitted that he is one of the renowned Kufi scholars. In spite of all this, many have assaulted him, preparing against him all means of belittling and charging due to the fact that, relying on Abu Barzah or maybe Abu Bardah, he has narrated one hadith stating the following: "We were in the company of the Prophet (s) when some singing was heard. Then 'Amr ibn al-'Aas and Mu'aiyah came singing. The Prophet (s) said: 'O Mighty Lord! Involve both of these men in dissension, and hurl them in Hellfire.'" Refer to his hadith on beverages in Muslim's *Sahih* from 'Abdul-Rahman ibn Abu Layla as reported from him by Sufyan ibn 'Ayinah. He died, may Allah Almighty have mercy on him, in 136 A.H. at the age of about ninety.

100. Abu 'Abdullah al-Jadali

Al-Dhahabi has mentioned him in his chapter on *kunayat*, placing on his name "DT" to indicate that he is among those relied upon by both Dawud and Tirmizi in their *sahih* books, then he describes him as an "abhorred Shi'a." He quotes al-Jawzjani saying that the man is the standard-bearer of al-Mukhtar. He also quotes Ahmad describing him as "trustworthy." Al-Shahristani has included him among Shi'a dignitaries in his book *Al-Milal wal Nihal*. Ibn Qutaybah has included him among the most zealous of "Rafidis" in his book *Al-Ma'arif*. Refer to his hadith in both Tirmizi's and Abu Dawud's *sahih* books as well as all Sunni *musnads*.

Ibn Sa'd mentions him on page 159, Vol. 6, of his *Tabaqat* where he says that, "Abu 'Abdullah al-Jadali is a very zealous Shi'a. Some allege that he headed al-Mukhtar's police force, and that he was sent once to 'Abdullah ibn al-Zubayr accompanied by eight hundred men to annihilate them and support Muhammad ibn al-Hanafiyyah against Ibn al-Zubayr's scheme." Ibn al-Zubayr, in fact, had enforced a siege around the houses of Ibn al-Hanafiyyah and Banu Hashim, surrounding them with fire wood in preparation for burning them alive because of refusing to swear the oath of allegiance to him, but Abu 'Abdullah al-Jadali saved them from a certain death; therefore, may Allah reward him for what he did for His Prophet's household (as).

This much concludes what we liked to count in a hurry a hundred Shi'a heroes who are authorities relied upon by the Sunnis. They are custodians of the nation's knowledge. Through them, the prophetic legacy is preserved, and they are sought by the authors of the *sahih* and *musnad* books. We have mentioned them by their names and quoted Sunni texts testifying to their being Shi'as while still remaining authorities, as you had requested. I think those who raise objections will see their error in claiming that the Sunnis do not rely on the authority of Shi'as. They will come to know that their criterion is truthfulness and accuracy, regardless of the school of thought, Sunni or Shi'a. If the hadith narrated by the Shi'as is all rejected, then the vast majority of the prophetic legacy will be lost, as al-Dhahabi himself admits while narrating the biography of Aban ibn Taghlib in his book *Al-Mizan*. There can be no better testimony than that.

You, may Allah render the truth victorious through your person, know that there have been quite a few ancestors of the Shi'as, other than the ones we have counted here, whose full count is many times more than this hundred, upon whose authority the Sunnis rely. These "others" are even of a higher calibre; they are narrators of even more authentic hadith, having acquired more knowledge. And they were closer to the Prophet's time, with a seniority in embracing the Shi'a beliefs. They are Shi'a companions [*sahabah*] of the Prophet (s), may Allah be pleased with all of them. We have dealt with their blessed names at the conclusion of our work *Al-Fusul al-Muhimmah*. They are also among the trustworthy *tabi'in* whose authority is relied upon. Each one of them is a trustworthy man who has memorized the entire text of the Holy Qur'an by heart, and his argument is irrefutable. Among such men are those who were martyred while supporting the lesser and the greater Camel Battles, Siffin, Al-Nahrawan, in Hijaz as well as in Yemen, when Bisr ibn Arta'ah invaded them, during the dissension of al-Hadrami who was sent to Basrah by

Mu'awiyah. They include those who were martyred on the Taff Battle with the Master of the Youths of Paradise [Imam Husayn ibn 'Ali, as], and those who were martyred with his grandson Zayd, and many others who had to face a great deal of injustice and persecution, avenging the massacre of the Prophet's progeny. Among them were those who were murdered just because of being very strong in their beliefs. Others were unfairly exiled from their homes, and those who had to resort to *taqiyya*, fearing for their lives or due to their physical weakness, such as al-Ahnaf ibn Qays, al-Asbagh ibn Nabatah, Yahya ibn Ya'mur, the latter being the first to apply dots to the Arabic alphabet, al-Khalil ibn Ahmad al-Farahidi, who founded the rules of Arabic grammar and scansion, Ma'adh ibn Muslim al-Harra, who laid the foundations of the science of conjugation in the Arabic language, and many others whose complete biographies would require huge volumes.

Overlook the hatred of the Nasibis towards these men through their use of attacking; they call them "weak" traditionists, and they chew their names, thus depriving themselves of their knowledge. There are hundreds of reliable Shi'as who have learned hadith by heart, who are light-houses of guidance, ignored by Sunnis. For these men, Shi'as have dedicated indices and bibliographies containing their biographies and stories. These works prove the extent of service these men have rendered to the tolerant Shari'a. Whoever researches them will find them to be models of truthfulness and trustworthiness, piety, asceticism, worship, and sincerity in bringing people closer to Allah Almighty and to His Messenger (s), to His Book, and to the Imams of Muslims as well as to their commoners. We pray Allah to enable us and your own self to benefit from their blessings; He is the Most Merciful.

Sincerely,
Sh

Letter 17
Dhul-Hijjah 3, 1329 A.H.

I. Appreciating the debater's sentiments

I swear by your eyes that I have never seen anyone more good-hearted, faster in dealing with the topic, more attentive, deeper in vision, stronger in argument, clearer in proof, than you. Your letters have come like a flowing waterfall, and your arguments have taken control over all my senses and sentiments. Your latest letter twists the necks of men, smashes the head of falsehood.

II. Admitting There is no Objection if Ahl ul-Sunnah Rely on Shi'a Authorities

The Sunni no longer has any excuse for not relying on his Shi'a brother if the latter is trustworthy. Your view in this regard is the clear truth, and that of your opponents is nothing more than fanaticism and intolerance. Their argument that it is wrong to rely on the Shi'as contradicts their actual deeds, and their deeds in fact contradict their arguments. Their arguments and deeds do not race with each other in the arena, nor do they pursue the same goal, due to the clash between them which causes them to clash. For this reason, their argument has been proven faulty, while yours remains invincible. During such a short time, you have produced what I would consider a dissertation for which a title like "Shi'a Authorities in Support of Sunni Authorities" may be appropriate. The objective is not to defend this sect or that or win an argument; rather, I hope it will, if Allah so wills, bring a glorious reform to the Islamic world.

III. His belief in the Miracles of Ahl al-Bayt

We believe in all Allah's miracles, in those of our Master the Commander of the Faithful, and in those of Ahl al-Bayt, peace be upon them, more than what you indicate.

IV. Dilemma at Compromising the Above with what Ahl Al-Qibla do

The question now is why have the people of the qibla turned away from following the path of the Imams of Ahl al-Bayt (as)? Why didn't they worship Allah through their own concepts of usul and furu'? Why have they not taken their word as the final word in the matter in which they differed? Why have the nation's scholars not been researching their views? Why have they instead opposed them ideologically? The nation's scholars have always been, from sons to fathers, referring to those besides Ahl al-Bayt without denying doing so. If the Book's verses and the Sunnah's texts are as you indicate, Ahl al-Qibla would not have turned away from the Imams of Ahl al-Bayt, nor would they have accepted any alternative to them. But they did not understand of the Book and the Sunnah other than the praise of Ahl al-Bayt, and the necessity of loving and respecting them. The ancestors are closer to the truth and more familiar with the meanings of the Sunnah and the Book ("and follow their own guidance (Qur'an, 6:90)," Wassalam.

Sincerely,
S

Letter 18
Dhul-Hijjah 4, 1329

I. Sentiments Reciprocated

Thank you for thinking so highly of me, the unworthy that I am, and I appreciate your compliments as well as the contents of my letters; therefore, I look humbly to such gracefulness, and I bow down before such kindness to honor its greatness and prestige.

II. Debater's Error in Generalizing Regarding Ahl al-Qibla

But I request you to reconsider what you have stated regarding those who turned away from Ahl al-Bayt, generalizing them about all Ahl al-Qibla. I remind you that half of Ahl al-Qibla are the Shi'as of Muhammad (s) who have not turned away nor shall ever turn away from the Imams of Ahl al-Bayt in as far as the origins and branches of the faith are concerned. It is their view that following their sect, peace be upon them, is one of the strict commandments of the Book and the Sunnah; therefore, they worship Allah Almighty thus in every time and place. This is the way of their good ancestors as well as that of their posterity since the Messenger of Allah (s) passed away.

III. The Nation's Politicians are the Ones Who Turned Away from Ahl al-Bayt

Those who have turned away from the beliefs of Ahl al-Bayt in as far as the roots and branches of the creed are concerned are the nation's politicians, the ones who control its destiny, due to their turning away from the succession (to the Prophet), affecting such a succession by elections, although they knew for sure that it was assigned for the Commander of the Faithful 'Ali ibn Abu Talib (as). They saw that the Arabs would not tolerate such a succession if restricted to one dynasty; therefore, they started interpreting its texts, assuming power through elections so that every suburb of theirs may enjoy it sooner or later. So, it was here and it was there. They sacrificed their means and might to keep it that way and support that principle, eradicating all contrary views and trends. Necessity forced them to turn away from the school of thought of Ahl al-Bayt. They started interpreting the texts of the Book or the Sunnah to mean the necessity of following such a concept. Had they yielded to the clear proofs, and referred the elite and the commoners to them in matters relevant to the roots and branches of religion, they would have found no alternative to adhering to their principle. They would have then become among the greatest callers to Ahl al-Bayt. But this did not agree with their ambition, scheme and politics. Whoever looks carefully in these matters will find out that turning away from the imams of Ahl al-Bayt in his sect is but turning away from their leadership, which was next only to that of the Messenger of Allah (s), and that interpreting the arguments regarding their special leadership was adopted after interpreting the arguments regarding their general leadership; otherwise, nobody would have turned away from them.

IV. The Imams of Ahl al-Bayt (without any argument) are not Inferior to others

Leave their texts and arguments alone, and look at them while overlooking the former; do you then find them, in their knowledge, deeds, or worship, less than Imam al-Ash'ari, or the other four Imams, or any others at all? And if the answer is No, then why should others be followed then? Leadership should be given to the most qualified.

V. Which Fair Court Judges Calling Their Followers "Strayers"?

Which just arbitrator decides that those who uphold their rope and follow into their footsteps are strayers? Sunnis are above passing such a judgment, and peace be with you.

Sincerely,
Sh

Letter 19
Dhul-Hijjah 5, 1329

I. No Fair Arbitrator Would Call Followers of Ahl al-Bayt Strayers

No; any fair arbitrator would never label those who have upheld the rope of Ahl al-Bayt, who follow in their footsteps, as "strayers," nor are they, by any means, inferior to other Imams.

II. Following Their Sects is Carrying out the Responsibility

Adherence to their sect obligates them and clears their conscience, just like adhering to any of the four sects; there is no doubt about that.

III. It Could be Said that They Have the Priority to Lead

It may be said that your Twelve Imams are even more worthy of being followed than the four Imams or any others, since all of them follow one sect which they have scrutinized and agreed upon by consensus. Contrariwise, the four Imams' disagreements among themselves exist in all departments of jurisdiction, leaving its sources exclusive, unchecked. It is well known that if one person verifies something, his effort cannot equate that of twelve Imams. This is clear to any fair minded person, ant it leaves no argument for any unjust person. Yes, the Nasibis may dispute referring your sect to the Imams of Ahl al-Bayt, and I may, at a later time, ask you to prove their error.

IV. Requesting Texts Relevant to the Khilafate

For the time being, I request you to go ahead and indicate what you claim to be statements nominating Imam 'Ali ibn Abu Talib (as) as the successor to the Prophet (s). Derive your arguments from Sunni references, and peace be with you.

Sincerely,
S

Letter 20
Dhul-Hijjah 9, 1239

I. A General Reference to the Texts

Anyone who is acquainted with the biography of the holy Prophet (s), especially researching his conduct while laying the foundations of the Islamic State and its legislative system, the establishment of its bases, the issuing of its codes and the organizing of its affairs on behalf of the Almighty Allah..., will find 'Ali (as) the vizier of the Messenger of Allah (s), his supporter against his foes, the custodian of his knowledge, the heir of his government, his vicegerent, and the one in charge after him. Whoever studies the statements and actions of the Prophet (s), while at home or on a journey, will find his statements, peace and blessings of Allah Almighty be upon him and his progeny, sequential in this regard from the beginning of his Call till his demise.

II. A Reference to the House on the Day of Warning

Refer to such statements at the dawn of the Call, before Islam was preached in Mecca publicly, when the Almighty revealed unto him the verse "And warn thy nearest tribe (Qur'an, 26:214)."

He invited them to the house of his uncle Abu Talib. They were forty men, more or less. Among them were his uncles Abu Talib, al-Hamzah, al-'Abbas, and Abu Lahab. The hadith in this regard is sequentially reported by Sunnis. At the conclusion of his statement to them, the Messenger of Allah, peace be upon him and his progeny, said:

> "O descendants of 'Abdul Muttlib! I swear by God that I know no youth among the Arabs who has brought his people something better than what I have brought you. I have brought you the best of this life and the life to come, and God has commanded me to call you towards Him. Therefore, who

among you shall support me in this matter and be my brother, the executor of my will, and my successor?"

All the listeners, with the exception of 'Ali, who was the youngest among them, kept silent. 'Ali responded by saying: "I, O Messenger of Allah, am willing to be your vizier in this matter." The Messenger of Allah (s) then took 'Ali by the neck and said: "This is my brother, executor of my will and vizier; therefore, listen to him and obey him." Those present laughed and kept saying to Abu Talib: "Allah has commanded you to listen to your son, and to obey him!"

III. Sunni Reporters of this Hadith

Many of those who have learned the prophetic legacy by heart have reported the hadith above verbatim as such. Among them are: Ibn Ishaq, Ibn Jarir, Ibn Abu Hatim, Ibn Mardawayh, Abu Na'im, al-Bayhaqi in his book *Al-Dala'il*, both al-Tha'labi and al-Tabari in their exegeses of Surah al Shu'ara' in their book *Al-Tafsir al-Kabir*, in Vol. 2 of al-Tabari's *Tarikh al-Umam wal Muluk*. Ibn al-Athir has reported it as an undisputed fact in Vol. 2 of his *Al-Kamil* when he mentioned how the Almighty commanded His Messenger to declare his call to the public, Abul-Fida in Vol. of his *Tarikh* while discussing who was the first to embrace Islam, Imam Abu Ja'far al-Iskafi al-Mu'tazili in his book *Naqd al-Uthmaniyyah* declaring its accuracy,[1] al-Halabi in his chapter on the Prophet's hideout at the house of Arqam in his well-known *Sirah*.[2]

---

[1] As on page 263, Vol. 3, of *Sharh Nahjul Balaghah* by Ibn Abul Hadid, Egyptian edition. As regarding his book *Naqd al-'Uthmaniyya*, it is a unique book worthy of the attention of any seeker of the truth. It is on page 257 and its succeeding pages up to page 281, Vol. 3, of the *Sharh*, at the end the commentary at the conclusion of the "*qasi'a*" sermon.

[2] Refer to the fourth page of that chapter, or to page 381 of the first volume of *Al-Sira al-Halabiyya*. Ibn Taymiyyah's wrecklessness is unfair, and his judgment is due to his well-known fanaticism. This hadith is quoted by the Egyptian sociologist Muhammad Hasanayn Haykal; refer to the second column on page five of the supplement to issue 2751 of his newspaper *Al-Siyasa* dated Dhul-Qi'da 12, 1350, and you will find it there explained in detail. If you refer to the fourth column on page six of the supplement to issue 2785 of the same newspaper, you will find the author quoting this hadith from Muslim's, Ahmad's

In this same context, with almost identical wording, has this hadith been reported by many masters of hadith and most reliable Sunni authorities such as al-Tahawi, Diya' al-Maqdisi in his *Mukhtara*, and Sa'id ibn Mansur in his *Sunan*. Refer to what Ibn Hanbal has recorded of 'Ali's hadith on pages 111 and 159 of Vol. 1 of his *Musnad*. He also pointed out at the beginning of page 331 of Vol. 1 of his *Musnad*, to a very significant hadith from Ibn 'Abbas] containing ten characteristics in which 'Ali has distinguished himself from everyone else. That hadith is published in Nisa'i, too, from Ibn 'Abbas, on page 6 of his *Khasa'is al 'Alawiyyah*, and on page 132, Vol. 3, of Hakim's *Mustadrak*. Al-Dhahabi has narrated it in his *Talkhis*], vouching for its authenticity. Refer to Vol. 6 of *Kanz al-'Ummal* which contains all the details.[3] Refer also to *Muntakhabul Kanz* which is cited in the footnote of Imam Ahmad's *Musnad*; refer to the footnote on pages

---

musnad, 'Abdullah ibn Ahmad's *Ziyadat al-Musnad*, Ibn Hajar al-Haithami's *Jami'ul Fara'id*, Ibn Qutaybah's *'Uyun al-Akhbar*, Ahmad ibn 'Abd Rabbih's *Al-'Iqd al-Farid*, 'Amr ibn Bahr al-Jahiz in his dissertation on the descendants of Hashim, and Imam Abu Ishaq al-Tha'labi's *Tafsir*. This hadith is also quoted by the British author Georges in his well-known book *A Treatise on Islam*, translated into the Arabic by an atheist from a Protestant descent calling himself Hashim al-'Arabi. You can also find this hadith on page 79 of the treatise's Arabic version, 6th edition. Due to the fame this hadith enjoys, a few non-Arab writers have included it in their books, especially in French, English and German. In his book *Heroes and Hero Worship*, Thomas Carlyle quotes it briefly.

[3] Refer to hadith 6008 on page 392, and you will find it quoted from Ibn Jarir, while hadith 1045 on page 396 is quoted from Ahmad's *Musnad* and from al-Dia al-Maqdisi's *Al-Mukhtara*, and from al-Tahawi. Ibn Jarir has verified it. Also refer to hadith 6056 on page 397 and you will find it quoted from Ibn Ishaq, Ibn Jarir, Ibn Abu Hatim, Ibn Mardawayh, Abu Na'im, al-Bayhaqi on the branches of faith, and in the *Dala'il*, and hadith 6102 on page 401 and you will find it quoted from Ibn Mardawayh, and hadith 6155 on page 408 and you will find it quoted from Ahmad's *Musnad* and from Ibn Jarir from *Al-Diya fil Mukhtara*. Whoever researches *Kanz al-'Ummal* will find this hadith in various places throughout the book. If you look into page 255, Vol. 3, of *Sharh Nahjul Balaghah* by the Mu'tazilite Imam Ibn Abul-Hadid, or at the end of the explanation of the "*qasi'a* sermon" in it, you will find this hadith in its entirety.

41 and 43 of Vol. 5 of the book to find all details. This, we believe, suffices to serve as glorious proof, and peace be with you.

Sincerely,
Sh

Letter 21

Raising Doubts about the Hadith's Authenticity
Dhul-Hijjah 10, 1329

Your debater strongly doubts the credibility of this hadith. For one thing, both Shaykhs have not included it in their *sahih* books, nor have the authors of other *sahih* books. I do not think that this hadith has been narrated by any reliable Sunni traditionist, and I do not think that you yourself consider it authentic, and peace be with you.

Sincerely,
S

Letter 22
Dhul-Hijjah 1329

I. Proving the Text's Authenticity

Have I not ascertained its reliability by Sunnis, I would not have mentioned it to you. Yet Ibn Jarir and Imam Abu Ja'far al-Iskafi have taken its authenticity for granted.[1] Several other critics have also considered it authentic. It is sufficient proof for its authenticity the fact that it is reported by the reliable authorities upon whose accuracy the authors of *sahih* books rely unhesitatingly. Refer to page 111, Vol. 1, of Ahmad's *Musnad*,

---

[1] Refer to hadith 6045 of the hadith included in *Kanz al-'Ummal*, page 396, Vol. 6, where you will find reference made to Ibn Jarir's verification of this hadith. If you refer to *Muntakhab al-Kanz*, the beginning of the footnote on page 44, Vol. 5, of Ahmad's *Musnad*, you will find reference to Ibn Jarir's verification of this hadith. As regarding Abu Ja'far al-Iskafi, he has emphatically judged its accuracy in his book *Naqd al-'Uthmaniyya*; so, refer to the text of page 263, Vol. 3 of *Sharh Nahjul Balaghah* by al-Hadid, Egyptian edition.

where you will read this hadith as narrated by Aswad ibn 'Amir[2] from Sharik,[3] al-A'mash,[4] Minhal,[5] 'Abbad ibn 'Abdullah al-Asadi,[6] from 'Ali (as) chronologically. Each one of these men in the chain of narrators is an authority in his own right, and they all are reliable traditionists according to the testimony of the authors of the *sahih* books without any dispute. Al-Qaysarani has mentioned them in his book *Al-Jami' Bayna Rijal al-Sahihain*. There is no doubt that this hadith is authentic, and the narrators report it from various ways each one of which supports the other.

II. Why the Shaykhs Have Not Reported it

The reason why both shaykhs [Bukhari and Muslim], and their likes, have not quoted this hadith is due to the fact that it did not agree with their own personal views regarding the issue of succession. This is why they have rejected a great deal of authentic texts for fear the Shi'as may use them as pretexts; therefore, they hid the truth knowingly. There are many Sunni shaykhs, may Allah forgive them, who have likewise hidden such texts, and they have in their method of hiding a well-known history written down by al-Hafiz ibn Hajar in his *Fath Al-Bari*. Al-Bukhari has assigned a special chapter for this theme at the conclusion of his chapter on

---

[2] Both al-Bukhari and al-Muslim have relied on him in their *sahihs*. They have both learned hadith from Shu'bah, and Bukhari has learned it from 'Abdul-'Aziz ibn Abu Salamah, while Muslim has learned hadith from Zuhayr ibn Mu'awiyah and Hammad ibn Salamah. His hadith is narrated in Bukhari by Muhammad ibn Hatim ibn Bazi'. In Muslim's *Sahih* he is quoted by Harun ibn 'Abdullah the critic, and by Abu Shaybah and Zuhayr.

[3] Muslim has relied on his authority in his *Sahih*, as we explained when we discussed him in Letter No. 16.

[4] Both Bukhari and Muslim rely on his authority in their respective *sahihs*, as we have stated while discussing him in Letter No. 16.

[5] Al-Bukhari has relied on him, as we explained when we mentioned him in Letter No. 16.

[6] His full name is 'Abbad ibn 'Abdullah ibn al-Zubayr ibn al-Awwam al-Qarashi al-Asadi. Al-Bukhari and Muslim rely on his authority in their respective *sahihs*. He has heard hadith from Asma' and 'Ayesha daughters of Abu Bakr. He is quoted in both *sahih*s by Ibn Abu Malka, Muhammad ibn Ja'far ibn al-Zubayr, and Hisham ibn 'Umar.

"Al-'Ilm," in Vol. 1, page 25, of his *Sahih*, subtitled "A Chapter on Those Who Recognized the Knowledge of some People Rather than that of Others."

III. Whoever Knows These Shaykhs Knows Why

Whoever knows the way al-Bukhari thought, his own attitudes towards the Commander of the Faithful (as), and towards all Ahl al-Bayt (as), will come to know that Bukhari's pen falls short of narrating texts regarding them, and his ink dries up before recounting their attributes. He will not be surprised to see him rejecting this particular hadith as well as others similar to it; therefore, we seek refuge with Allah, the Almighty, the Sublime, and peace be with you.

Sincerely,
Sh

Letter 23
Dhul-Hijjah 14, 1329

I. Convinced of the Authenticity of this Hadith
I have, indeed, read this hadith on page 111 of Volume One of Ahmad's *Musnad* and ascertained the reliability of his sources and found them to be the most reliable authorities. Then I researched his avenues in narrating this hadith, and I found them to be sequential: each one of them supports the other; therefore, I have contented myself to believe in its contents.

II. Unreliability Based on Non-Sequential Narration
But you do not rely on an authentic hadith that deals with the issue of succession unless it is sequentially narrated [*mutawatir*], for succession, according to your Shi'a philosophy, is one of the roots of religion, and this hadith cannot be considered as "*mutawatir*" (consecutively reported) and, therefore, it cannot be relied upon.

III. Its Reference to Restricted Succession
It may be said that 'Ali is the successor of the Prophet (s) in his own Household alone; so, where is the text that testifies to his succession among the general public?

IV. Its Rebuttal
This hadith may even be revoked, since the Prophet has refrained from publicly supporting the gist thereof. Because of this, the companions found no reason why they should not swear the oath of allegiance to the three righteous caliphs, may Allah be pleased with them.

Sincerely,
S

Letter 24
Dhul-Hijjah 15, 1329

I. Why Relying on this Hadith

Sunnis rely on every correct hadith to confirm their concept of succession, be it *mutawatir* or not. We rely on the authenticity of this hadith in our argument against theirs simply because they themselves testify to its authenticity, thus binding themselves to what they have considered to be binding. Our own proof regarding succession from our viewpoint depends on its *tawatur* from our own sources, as is obvious to everyone.

II. Restricted Succession is Unanimously Rejected

The claim that 'Ali is the successor of the Messenger of Allah (s) only in his household is rejected due to the fact that whoever believes that 'Ali is the successor of the Messenger of Allah in his household also believes that he is his successor among the public as well, and whoever denies his succession over the public also denies his succession among his family. There is no way to separate one from the other; so, why bring up a philosophy which runs contrary to the consensus of all Muslims?

III. Revocation is Impossible

I cannot overlook your statement that this hadith is revoked, which contradicts both reason and Shari'a, since in order to abrogate, a statement has to be made before the effect of its precedent becomes manifest, as is clear to everyone. The only pretext for abrogation here is the allegation that the Prophet (s) supposedly refrained from [publicly] expounding on the gist of this hadith. The hadith itself proves that he, peace and blessings of Allah be upon him and his progeny, did not refrain from doing so; rather, texts in this meaning are consecutive, supporting one another. If we suppose that there is no text in the same meaning after this one, then how can it be proven that the Prophet (s) had changed his mind or refrained from its enforcement? "They follow nothing other than their own whims and desires, after guidance from their Lord has already come unto them (Qur'an, 53:23)" and peace be with you.

Sincerely
Sh

Letter 25
Dhul-Hijjah 16, 1329

I. His Belief in the Text
I have believed in the One Who has caused you to dissipate the darkness [of ignorance], clarify what is ambiguous, and made you one of His signs and a facet of His own manifestations.

II. Requesting More Texts
May Allah bless your father, provide me with more such texts, and peace be with you.

Sincerely,
S

Letter 26
Dhul-Hijjah 17, 1329

I. Clear Texts Recounting Ten of 'Ali's Exclusive Merits

Suffices you, besides the hadith of the Household, what Imam Ahmad has indicated in Vol. 1 of his book *Al-Mustadrak*, and al-Dhahabi in his Concise, who both admit its authenticity, as well as other authors of the *sunan* from generally accepted avenues. They all quote 'Umar ibn Maymun saying: "I was sitting once in the company of Ibn 'Abbas when nine men came to him and said 'O Ibn 'Abbas! Either come to debate with us, or tell these folks that you prefer a private debate.' He had not lost his eye-sight yet. He said: 'I rather debate with you.' So they started talking, but I was not sure exactly what they were talking about. Then he stood up and angrily said: 'They are debating about a man who has ten merits nobody else ever had. They are arguing about a man whom the holy Prophet (s) has said, 'I shall dispatch a man whom Allah shall never humiliate, one who loves Allah and His Messenger (s) and who is loved by both,' so each one of them thought to him such an honour belonged. The holy Prophet (s) inquired about 'Ali. When the latter came unto him, with his eyes swelling in ailment, he (s) blew in his eyes, shook the standard thrice and gave it to him. 'Ali came back victorious with Safiyya bint Huyay [al-Akhtab] among his captives.'" Ibn 'Abbas proceeded to say, "Then the Messenger of Allah (s) sent someone with Surah al-Tawbah, but he had to send 'Ali after him to discharge the responsibility, saying: 'Nobody can discharge it except a man who is of me, and I am of him.'" Ibn 'Abbas also said, "The Messenger of Allah (s), with 'Ali sitting beside him, asked his cousins once: 'Who among you elects to be my *wali* in this life and the life hereafter?' They all declined, but 'Ali said: 'I would like to be your *wali* in this life and the life to come,' whereupon he (s) responded by saying: 'You are, indeed, my *wali* in this life and the life hereafter.'" Ibn 'Abbas continues to say that 'Ali was the first person to accept Islam after d, and that the Messenger of Allah (s) took his own robe and put it over 'Ali, Fatima, Hasan and Husayn, then recited the verse saying: "Allah wishes to remove all abomination from you, O Ahl al-Bayt [people of my household] and purify you with a perfect purification (Qur'an, 33:33)." He has also said: "'Ali bought his own soul. He put on the Prophet's garment and slept in his bed when the infidels sought to murder him," till he says: "The Messenger of Allah (s) went on Tabuk expedition accompanied by many people. 'Ali asked him: 'May I join you?' The Messenger of Allah (s) refused, whereupon 'Ali wept. The Prophet (s) then asked him: 'Does it not please you that your status to me is similar to that of Aaron's to Moses, except there is no Prophet after me? It is not proper for me to leave this place before assigning you as my vicegerent.' The Messenger of Allah (s) has also said the following to him: 'You are the *wali* of every believing man and woman.'"

Ibn 'Abbas has said: "The Messenger of Allah closed down all doors leading to his mosque except that of 'Ali who used to enter the mosque on his way out even while in the state of *janaba*. The Messenger of Allah (s) has also said: 'Whoever accepts me as the *wali*, let him/her take 'Ali as the *wali*, too.'" As a matter of fact, al-Hakim, having counted the sources from which he quoted this hadith, comments by saying, "This is an authentic hadith according to *isnad*, yet both shaykhs did not narrate it this way." Al-Dhahabi has quoted it in his *Talkhis* and described it as an authentic hadith.

II. Why Rely Upon it

Clear and irrefutable proofs highlight the fact that 'Ali was the Prophet's vicegerent. Have you noticed how the Prophet (s) has named him *wali* in this life and the life to come, thus favouring him over all his kin, and how he regarded his status to himself as similar to that of Aaron to Moses, without any exception other than Prophethood, and exception which reflects generality?

You also know that what distinguished Aaron from Moses was mostly his being the vizier of his brother, his *de facto* participation in his brother's Message, his vicegerency, and the enforcement by Moses of people's obedience to Aaron as his statement, to which references is included in the Holy Qur'an (20:29-32), and which clearly says: "And let my brother Aaron, from among my household, be my vizier, to support me and take part in my affair," and his statement: "Be my own representative among my people; reform them, and do not follow the path of corrupters (Qur'an 7:142)," and the Almighty's response: "O Moses! Granted is your prayer (Qur'an 20:36)." According to this text, 'Ali is the Prophet's vicegerent among his people, his vizier among his kin, his partner in his undertaking - not in Prophethood - his successor, the best among his people, and the worthiest of their leadership alive or dead. They owed him obedience during the Prophet's lifetime as the Prophet's vizier, just as Aaron's people had to obey Aaron during the lifetime of Moses.

Whoever becomes familiar with the status hadith will immediately consider its deep implications without casting any doubt at the gist of its context. The Messenger of Allah (s) has made this very clear when he said: "It is not proper for me to leave this place before assigning you as my vicegerent." It is a clear text regarding his succession; nay, it even suggests that had the Prophet (s) left without doing so, he would have done something he was not supposed to have done. This is so only because he was commanded by the Almighty to assign him as his own successor according to the meaning of the verse saying "O Messenger! Convey that which has been revealed unto you from your Lord, and if you do not do it, then you have not conveyed His Message at all (Qur'an 5:67)." Anyone who examines the phrase "then you have not conveyed His Message at all," then examines the Prophet's statement: "It is not proper for me to leave this place before assigning you as my vicegerent," will find them both aiming at the same conclusion, as is quite obvious. We should also not forget the Prophet's hadith saying: "You are the *wali* of every believer after me." It is a clear reference to the fact that he is the Prophet's *wali* and the one who takes his place, as al-Kumait, may Allah have mercy on his soul, has implied when he said: "A great Vicegerent, a fountain-head of piety, an educator!" And peace be with you.

Sincerely,
Sh

Letter 27
Dhul-Hijjah 18, 1329

Raising Doubts About the Status Hadith

The "status hadith" is authentic and well-known, but al-Amidi, who verified and ascertained hadith, and who is considered the master of the science of *usul*, has doubted its sources and suspected its narrators. Your debater may uphold al-Amidi's view; so, how can you prove him wrong? And peace be with you.

Sincerely,
S

Letter 28
Dhul-Hijjah 19, 1329

I. The Status Hadith Stands on Most Solid Grounds

Al-Amidi has done nobody injustice except his own self by casting doubt about the authenticity of this hadith which is one of the most accurate *sunan* and a most solid legacy.

II. Binding Proofs

Nobody else has doubted its accuracy, nor did anyone else dare to argue about its grounds. Even al-Dhahabi, who is a most prejudiced narrator, has admitted its accuracy in his *Talkhis Al-Mustadrak*[1]. Ibn Hajar al-Haithami, in spite of his antagonistic views embedded in his *Al-Sawa'iq al-Muhriqa*, has quoted this hadith in his chapter on "Al-Shubuhat," citing statements by the foremost narrators of hadith testifying to its accuracy; so, refer to that book. Had this hadith not been accurate, al-Bukhari would not have included it in his book, in spite of his prejudice when it comes to counting 'Ali's merits and those of Ahl al-Bayt (as).

---

[1] Letter No. 26 contains his admission of its authenticity.

Mu'awiyah was the leader of the oppressive gang. He stood in enmity against the Commander of the Faithful (as), fought him, cursed him from Muslims' pulpits and ordered people to do likewise. Yet, in spite of his insolent hostility, he never doubted the status hadith. Nor has Sa'd ibn Abu Waqqas exaggerated when he, according to Muslim, was asked by Mu'awiyah why he hesitated to denounce "Abu Turab;" he answered him by saying:[2] "I remember three ahadith of the Messenger of Allah which I have personally heard, because of which I shall never curse him. Had I had just one of his exclusive merits, it would have been more precious for me than a herd of the choicest red camels. I have heard the Messenger of Allah (s), who was then accompanied by a few people participating in some of his campaigns, saying to 'Ali: 'Are you not pleased that your status to me is similar to that of Aaron to Moses except that there will be no Prophet after me?'"[3] Mu'awiyah was dumbfounded, and he could not utter a word or pressure Sa'd.

In addition to all of this, Mu'awiyah himself has narrated the same hadith. Ibn Hajar says in his book *Al-Sawa'iq al-Muhriqa*:[4] "Ahmad has said that a man once asked Mu'awiyah a question and his answer was: 'Forward your question to 'Ali because he is more knowledgeable.' Yet the man said: 'Your own answer to this matter is dearer to me than that of 'Ali.' Mu'awiyah was angry, and he said: 'What a bad statement you have uttered! You hate a man whom the Messenger of Allah used to gorge with knowledge? He even told him that his status to him was like that of Aaron to Moses except that there would be no Prophet after him? Whenever 'Umar was confused about a matter, he sought 'Ali's advice....'"[5] In short,

---

[2] This occurs in his section dealing with 'Ali's virtues at the beginning of page 324, Vol. 2, of his *Sahih*.

[3] Al-Hakim, too, quotes it at the beginning of page 109, Vol. 3, of his *Al-Mustadrak*, admitting its authenticity due to its being endorsed by Muslim.

[4] This occurs in the fifth *maqsad* of *Al-Maqasid* when the author discusses verse 14 in Section 11, page 107, of *Al-Sawa'iq al-Muhriqa*.

[5] He says that others have quoted it, and that some added to it "Get up; may Allah never allow you to stand up," and his name is omitted from the *diwan*, to the end of his quotation on page 107 of his *Al-Sawa'iq al-Muhriqa*. This proves

the status hadith is considered, according to the consensus of all Muslims, regardless of their sects and inclinations, to be authentic.

III. Its Sunni Narrators

Authors of both *Al-Jami' Baynal Sihah Al-Sitta* and *Al-Jami' Bayna Rijal al-Sahihain* have quoted it, and it is included in Bukhari's chapter on the Battle of Tabuk in his *Sahih*, in Muslim's chapter on 'Ali's merits in his *Sahih*, in a chapter on the attributes of the Prophet's companions in Ibn Majah's *sunan*, and in a chapter on 'Ali's merits in Hakim's *Al-Mustadrak*. Imam Ahmad Ibn Hanbal has quoted it in his *Musnad* from several different reporters. Ibn 'Abbas, Asma' bint 'Amis, Abu Sa'd al-Khudri, Mu'awiyah ibn Abu Sufyan,[6] and many other companions have all narrated it as recorded in the *musnad*. Al-Tabrani has quoted it as narrated by Asma' bint 'Amis, Umm Salamah, Habis ibn Janadah, Ibn 'Umar, 'Ali ibn Abu Talib (as),[7] and many others. Al-Bazzaz has included it in his *Musnad*,[8] and so has al-Tirmizi in his *Sahih*[9] depending on the authority of Abu Sa'id al-Khudri. In *Al-Isti'ab*, in a chapter dealing with 'Ali, the author quotes Ibn 'Abdul Birr narrating it, then he comments thus: "This is one of the most reliable and accurate ahadith narrated about the Prophet by Sa'd ibn Abu Waqqas." Sa'd's references are numerous and are enumerated by Ibn Abu Khayth'amah and others. Ibn 'Abbas, Abu Sa'id al-Khudri, Umm Salamah, Asma' bint Amis, Jabir ibn

---

that a group of late traditionists besides Ahmad has quoted the status hadith from Mu'awiyah.

[6] As we mentioned in the beginning of this Letter, quoting the fifth *maqsad* of the *Maqasid* of verse 14 of the verses discussed in Chapter 11, *Al-Sawa'iq al-Muhriqa*, page 107.

[7] As Ibn Hajar describes in the first hadith of the forty ones which he discusses in the second section of chapter 9, page 72, of his *Al-Sawa'iq al-Muhriqa*. Al-Sayyuti has stated the following while discussing 'Ali (as) in his chapter on the righteous caliphs: "Al-Tabrani has quoted this hadith from all these men, adding to them Asma' bint Qays."

[8] Al-Sayyuti indicates so while discussing 'Ali (as) in his chapter on the caliphs on page 65.

[9] As attested to by hadith 2504 of the hadith of *Kanz al-'Ummal*, page 152, Volume 6.

'Abdullah, and quite a few other traditionists have all narrated it." As a matter of fact, whoever researches the Battle of Tabuk and refers to books of traditions and biographies will find them mentioning this hadith. Those who have written biographies of 'Ali, among authors of glossaries of ancient as well as modern times, regardless of their inclinations and sectarian preferences, have all quoted this hadith. It is also quoted by anyone who writes about the merits of Ahl al-Bayt, those of the Imams among the companions of the Prophet (s) such as Ahmad ibn Hanbal, and by others before or after his time. It is a hadith taken for granted by all past Muslim generations.

IV. Why al-Amidi Suspects It

There is no lesson to learn about the doubt cast by al-Amidi regarding this hadith in his *Musnad*, since the man knows nothing about the science of traditions, and his knowledge about *musnad*s and narrators is the knowledge of illiterate commoners who do not know the meaning of hadith. In fact, his own extensive knowledge in the science of usul is the reason why he has fallen in such a dilemma. According to the requirements of usul, he saw it to be a correct hadith which he could not get rid of except by suspecting its isnad, thinking that that would be possible. Indeed, that was only his unattainable desire, and peace be with you.

Sincerely,
Sh

Letter 29

Dhul-Hijjah 20, 1329

I. Believing in Our Arguments Regarding the Hadith's Sanad

All what you have mentioned regarding the authenticity of the status hadith is indeed beyond any doubt. Al-Amidi has stumbled in a way which has proven his distance from the science of hadith, and from traditionists. I have bothered you with mentioning his views in clarifying what is already clear. This is my mistake for which I invoke your forgiveness, since you are apt to forgive.

II. Doubting its General Application

I have come to know that there are others besides al-Amidi from among your arbitrators who claim that there is no proof that the status hadith has a general application, and that it is restricted to its own context. They support their view by the hadith's text itself, saying that the Prophet's statement is due only to its time context, that is, when he left him in Medina during the Battle of Tabuk. The Imam, peace be upon him, asked him: "Why do you leave me with women and children?" His answer, peace be upon him and his progeny, was: "Aren't you pleased that your status to me is similar to that of Aaron to Moses, except there will be no Prophet after me?" as if he (s) explained that his position to him is like that of Aaron to Moses when the latter left him to represent him among his people when he left for the Tur Mountain [Mount Sinai]. The gist of the Prophet's statement would be something like: "You are to me, during this Battle of Tabuk, like Aaron to Moses who had to depart to communicate with his Lord."

III. Doubting its being Binding

Your arbitrators may even say that this hadith is not a binding proof, even if its implication is general, and a restricted hadith cannot be applied in its general sense, and peace be with you.

Sincerely,
S

Letter 30
Dhul-Hijjah 22, 1329

I. Arabs Regard it General

We refer their argument that the hadith lacks a general application to Arabs who are very well familiar with their language and grammar. You are the Arabs' authority whose view is invincible and undisputed. Do you see your nation doubting the generality of this status hadith? I do not think so. You are above that. Persons of your prestige do not doubt the generality of the additive gender and its inclusion of all implications. If you, for example, say: "I have granted you my judicial power," will your power be restricted to a few matters rather than others? Or will your statement be general and inclusive of all implications? Allah be Praised! You do not see it other than general, and its meaning as inclusive! If the Muslims' ruler says to one of his subjects: "I have appointed you my own vicegerent over people," or "granted you my own status, or position, over them, or granted you my own wealth," will it come to mind anything other than the general meaning of such a statement? Or will the speaker wish to select some matters rather than others? If he said to one of his ministers: "You may enjoy during my lifetime the same position 'Umar enjoyed during the lifetime of Abu Bakr, but you are not my friend," would this statement be seen, according to common rules, as implying a few situations rather than all? I do not see you saying accepting anything other than its general application, and I do not doubt at all that you interpret the statement of the holy Prophet: "Your status to me is like that of Aaron to Moses" except as indicative of generality of application, following the guidelines of its similar texts in the Arabic language and its norms of speech, especially when he excluded Prophethood, thus making its generality inclusive of everything else quite clear. You are surrounded by Arabs; so, ask them if you wish.

II. Disproving Claim of Restriction

As regarding the debater's statement claiming that this hadith is restricted to its context, this claim is rejected on two grounds:

First, the hadith itself is generalizing, as you know. The assumption "If we presume that it is specific" does not exclude it from its general meaning, because whoever makes an assumption does not confine his assumption to only one single possibility. Say, if one person in the state of *najasa* (impurification) touches Surah al-Kursi [verse of the Throne] for example, and you tell him: "Nobody in the state of *najasa* should touch the holy Qur'an," will your statement be confined to Surah al-Kursi only, or will it be general regarding the entire text of the holy Qur'an? I cannot imagine that anyone will understand that it is restricted to Surah al-Kursi in particular. If a physician sees his patient eating dates and forbids him from eating anything sweet, will the prohibition be taken to imply only dates, or will it be general to include everything sweet? I do not consider the one who claims its meaning to be restricted as one adhering to the common concepts of the basics of language; rather, he will then be distant from its grammar, far from common sense, a foreigner to our world. So is the one who claims that the status hadith is applied specifically to the Battle of Tabuk alone; there is no difference between both cases.

Second, this hadith was not articulated by the Prophet (s) upon leaving 'Ali (as) as his representative in Medina during the Battle of Tabuk; otherwise, the debater will have had the right to claim its restricted application. Our *sahih* books are sequential through the Imams among the Prophet's purified progeny (as) proving that it was said on other occasions to which the researcher may refer. Sunni *sunan* bear witness to this fact, as researchers know. We say that the wording of this hadith testifies to the fact that the claim that it was said only during the Battle of Tabuk is groundless, as is already obvious.

III. Disproving its Non-Binding Application

Their claim that the specified generalization cannot be binding over the rest is an obvious mistake and a serious error. Nobody would say so except one who approaches matters like someone riding a blind animal in a dark night. We seek refuge with Allah against ignorance, and we thank Him for our sound health. Specifying the general does not exclude it from being applied as a testimony against the rest as long as the specified matter is not general, especially if it is related to this hadith. If a master tells his servant: "Be generous to everyone who is visiting me today save Zayd." If the servant surrounds only Zayd with generosity, he will not only be disobeying his master and become liable for his error, according to the judgment of all the wise, he will also deserve to be punished a punishment commensurate with his mistake. No wise man would listen to his excuse if he produces one; nay, even his excuse will seem to them to be even worse than his guilt. This is so only because of its obvious general implication, having been specified, regarding the rest, as is obvious.

You very well know that Muslims have always been accustomed to use as proof the specified generalizations without any exception. The ancestors among the companions and the tabi'in, as well as those who followed the latter, and so on till today, especially the Imams among the progeny of the Prophet (s) and all other Imams among the Muslims, do just that. This is a matter which does not need raising any doubts. Suffices you for proof what the four Imams and other Mujtahids have said in their chapters on being aware of the branches of legislative rules as proofs of their explanations. The wheel of knowledge has been spinning on acting upon generally accepted facts. There is nothing general that does not have room for a specification. If these generalities are dropped, the door of knowledge will be shaken. We seek refuge with Allah, and peace be with you.

Sincerely,
Sh

Letter 31
Dhul-Hijjah 22, 1329

Requesting Sources of this Hadith

You have not provided any proof testifying to this hadith as being said on any occasion besides that of Tabuk. I am very eager to be acquainted with its pristine sources; so, please take me to its fountain-heads, and peace be with you.

Sincerely,
S

Letter 32
Dhul-Hijjah 24, 1329

I. Among Its Sources: the Prophet's Visit to Umm Salim

One of its sources is the discourse of the Prophet (s) with Umm Salim,[1] a woman of lengthy achievements, a woman of

---

[1] She is daughter of Milhan Ibn Khalid al-Ansari and sister of Haram ibn Milhan. Her father and brother were martyred in the company of the Prophet (s). She possessed a great deal of accomplishment and wisdom. She narrated a few ahadith of the Prophet (s), and she is quoted by her son Anas, in addition to Ibn 'Abbas, Zayd ibn Thabit, Abu Salamah ibn 'Abdul-Rahman, and by others. She is considered to be in the first row of those who accepted and supported the Islamic faith, and she herself was a caller to Islam. During the pre-Islamic period of *jahiliyya*, she was in love with Malik ibn al-Nadar from whom she conceived her son Anas ibn Malik. At the dawn of Islam, she was among the foremost to embrace it, and she invited her husband Malik to believe in Allah and His Messenger, but he refused; so, she deserted him, and he in his rage moved to Syria where he died as a *kafir*. She advised her son, who was then ten years old, to serve the Prophet (s), and the Prophet (s) accepted his service in order to please her. Many Arab men of prestige sought her hand, but she always used to say: "I shall not get married except when Anas reaches manhood;" so, Anas always used to say: "May Allah reward my mother, for she took very good care of me." Due to her own influence, Abu Talhah al-Ansari became Muslim. He

wisdom who enjoyed a special prestigious status with the Messenger of Allah (s) due to being among the foremost in accepting Islam, and because of her sincerity, contributions, and sacrifices in the cause of Islam. The Prophet (s) used to visit her and talk to her at her own house. One day, he said to her: "O Umm Salim (mother of Salim)! 'Ali's flesh is of mine, and his blood is of my own; he is to me like Aaron to Moses."[2] It is obvious that this hadith is only an excerpt of his lengthy hadith which is stated for the purpose of conveying the truth and providing advice for the sake of Allah in order to highlight the status of his vicegerent, the one who would take his own place (of responsibility) once he is gone, and it cannot be confined to the Battle of Tabuk.

II. The Case of Hamzah's Daughter

---

sought her hand when he was still *kafir*, but she refused to marry him unless he embraced Islam; so, he accepted her invitation to embrace the new faith, and his dowery to her was his own acceptance of Islam. She conceived a son by him, but the baby fell sick and died; so, she said: "Nobody should mention his death to his father before me." When her husband came home and inquired about his son, she said: "He is in most content;" so he thought that she meant their son was asleep. She served him his dinner, then she put on her best clothes and perfume, and he went to bed with her. The next day she said to him: "Pray for your son's soul." Abu Talha narrated this story to the Messenger of Allah (s) who said to him: "Allah blessed you last night." She continues to say that he (s) invoked Allah to provide me with what I wanted and even more. In that same night, she conceived 'Abdullah ibn Abu Talha upon whom Allah showered His blessings. He is the father of Ishaq ibn 'Abdullah ibn Abu Talha, the *faqih*, and his brothers were ten; each one of them was a man of knowledge. Umm Salim used to participate in the Prophet's military campaigns. On the Day of Uhud, she had a dagger to stab any infidel who would come near her. She rendered Islam a great service, and I do not know any woman besides her whom the Prophet (s) used to visit in her own house and she would offer him a present. She was aware of the status of his progeny, knowledgeable of their rights... May Allah shower His choicest mercy on her.

[2] This hadith, I mean Umm Salim's, is number 2554 of the ones numbered in *Kanz al-'Ummal* as narrated on page 154 of its sixth volume. It also exists in *Muntakhab al-Kanz*; so, refer to the last line of the footnote on page 31 of Volume 5 of Ahmad's *Musnad*, where you will find it verbatim.

A similar hadith was made in the case of Hamzah's daughter in whose regard 'Ali, Ja'far and Zayd disputed. The Messenger of Allah (s) said then: "O 'Ali! You are to me like Aaron to Moses, etc."

III. Leaning on 'Ali

Another incident occurred when Abu Bakr, 'Umar, and Abu 'Ubaydah ibn al-Jarrah were in the company of the Prophet (s) who was leaning on 'Ali. The Prophet (s) patted 'Ali's shoulder and said: "O 'Ali! You are the strongest among the believers in faith, the first (man) to embrace Islam, and your status to me is similar to that of Aaron to Moses."[3]

IV. The First Fraternity

The ahadith narrated during the First Fraternity also include this text. These were made in Mecca prior to the migration, when the Messenger of Allah (s) consummated brotherhood among the emigrants in particular.

V. The Second Fraternity

On the occasion of the Second Fraternity, while in Medina, five months after the migration, the Prophet (s) made fraternity between the emigrants (Muhajirun) and the supporters (Ansar). In both events, he (s) chose 'Ali as his brother,[4] thus preferring him

---

[3] This is quoted by al-Hasan ibn Badr, al-Hakim in his chapter on *kunyat*, al-Shirazi in his chapter on surnames, volume six, and by Ibn al-Najjar. It is hadith 6029 and also 6032 of the ones numbered in *Kanz al-'Ummal*, page 395.

[4] Discussing the biography of 'Ali (as) in his *Isti'ab*, Ibn 'Abd al-Birr describes him thus: "He made brotherhood with the Messenger of Allah, peace be upon him and his progeny, among the immigrants, then between the immigrants and the supporters. In each of these instances, he (s) said to 'Ali (as): 'You are my brother in this life and the life hereafter,' then he made brotherhood between himself and 'Ali (as)." The details are in the books of traditions and history. For the details of the first brotherhood, refer to page 26, Vol. 2, of *Al-Sira al-Halabiyya*, and in the second brotherhood on page 120, Vol. 2, also of *Al-Sira al-Halabiyya*, where you will find how the Prophet (s) favoured 'Ali (as) in both occasions over everyone else. In *Al-Sira al-Dahlaniyya*, the details of the

over all others, saying to him: "You are to me like Aaron to Moses except there will be no Prophet after me." Narrations in this regard are consecutively reported. Refer to what others state about the First Fraternity such as the hadith narrated by Zayd ibn Abu 'Awfah. Imam Ahmad ibn Hanbal has included it in his book *Manaqib 'Ali*, Ibn 'Asakir in his *Tarikh*,[5] al-Baghwi and al-Tabrani in their *Mujma's*, al-Barudi in his *Al-Ma'rifa*, by Ibn 'Adi[6] and others.

The hadith under discussion is quite lengthy, and it contains guidelines about how to establish brotherhood. It ends with: "'Ali said: 'O Messenger of Allah! My soul has expired, and my spine has been broken, having seen what you have done for your companions while leaving me alone. If this is a sign of your anger with me, then I complain only to you and beg your pardon.' The Messenger of Allah said: 'I swear by the One Who sent me to convey the truth about Him, I have not spared you except for my own self. You are to me like Aaron to Moses, except there will be no Prophet after me. You are my Brother, heir and companion.' 'Ali (as) asked him: 'What shall I inherit from you?' He (s) answered: 'Whatever Prophets before me left for those who inherited them: the Book of their Lord, and the Sunnah of their Prophet. You will be my companion in my house in Paradise together with my daughter Fatima. You are my Brother and Companion.' Then he, peace be upon him and his progeny, recited the verse: 'They are brethren seated conveniently facing each other,'" referring to the brethren whose hearts Allah has joined in affection who look at each other with sincere compassion.

---

circumstances of the first brotherhood and those of the second are similar to what is published in *Al-Sira al-Halabiyya*. The author also stated that the second brotherhood took place five months after the migration.

[5] This is quoted from Ahmad and Ibn 'Asakir by a group of trusted authorities such as al-Muttaqi al-Hindi; so, refer to hadith 918 of his *Kanz al-'Ummal* at the beginning of page 40 of its fifth volume. It is also quoted on page 390, Vol. 6, from Ahmad's book *Manaqib 'Ali*, numbering it hadith 4972.

[6] This is quoted from these Imams by a group of trusted authorities such as al-Muttaqi al-Hindi at the beginning of page 41, Vol. 5, of of his *Kanz al-'Ummal*, numbering it hadith 919.

Refer also to the events of the Second Fraternity. Al-Tabrani, in his *Al-Tafsir Al-Kabir*, quotes Ibn 'Abbas reporting one hadith stating that the Messenger of Allah (s) said to 'Ali (as): "Are you angry because I have established brotherhood between the Ansar and the Muhajirun and have not selected a brother for you from among them? Are you not pleased that your status to me is like that of Aaron to Moses, except there will be no Prophet after me?"[7]

VI. Closing the Doors

The same hadith was also said when the companions' doors overlooking the Prophet's mosque in Medina were ordered closed except that of 'Ali. Jabir ibn 'Abdullah quotes the Messenger of Allah, peace be upon him and his progeny, saying: "O 'Ali! It is permissible for you to do at this mosque whatever is permissible for me, and you are to me like Aaron to Moses, except there will be no Prophet after me." Huzayfah ibn 'Asid al-Ghifari has said

---

[7] This is quoted by al-Muttaqi al-Hindi in his *Kanz al-'Ummal* and *Al-Muntakhab*; so, refer to the *Muntakhab*'s footnote on page 31 of its fifth volume regarding Ahmad's *Musnad*, and you will find it verbatim just as we have quoted it here. It is not difficult to sift the gist of the phrase "You have angered 'Ali (as)" and comprehend the meanings of companionship, compassion, and the love of a compassionate and kind father to his son. If you wonder how 'Ali had some doubts in the second time he was left behind, although in the first time he had some doubt, too, then he found out that the Prophet, peace be upon him and his progeny, had kept him there just for himself, and why he did not consider the second incident in the light of the first. The answer is that the second incident could not be compared with the first one, for the first was regarding the immigrants in particular; so, the comparison did not forbid the prophet (s) from creating brotherhood with 'Ali (as), contrary to the second which was between the immigrants and the supporters. One immigrant in the second instance may be joined in brotherhood to a supporter, and vice versa. Since the prophet and the wasi were both immigrants, the assumption in the second instance was that they should not be brothers; so, 'Ali thought that his brother would be a supporter, just like others by way of comparison. When the Messenger of Allah (s) did not create brotherhood between him and any of the supporters, some doubt entertained his mind, but Allah and His Messenger insisted on favouring him, and so it was: he and the Messenger of Allah (s) became brothers, contrary to the common norm of practice among all the immigrants and supporters at that time and place.

that the Prophet, peace be upon him and his progeny, once delivered a *khutba* on the occasion of closing those doors in which he said: "There are some men who have disliked that I got them out of the mosque while keeping 'Ali. Allah, the Dear and Mighty, inspired to Moses and his brother to reside with their people in Egypt and make their homes a *qibla* and say their prayers," till he said: "'Ali to me is like Aaron to Moses. He is my Brother, and none of you is allowed to cohabit therein other than he."

The sources of this hadith are numerous, and they cannot all be counted in a brief letter like this, yet I hope that what I have stated here suffices to falsify the claim that the status hadith is confined only to the Battle of Tabuk. How much can such a claim weigh in the light of abundance of sources of this hadith?

VII. The Prophet Comparing 'Ali and Aaron to the Two Stars

Anyone who is familiar with the biography of the Prophet (s) will find him, peace be upon him and his progeny, describing 'Ali and Aaron as the two bright stars arranged alike, neither one differing from the other. This by itself is a testimony to the generality of status of this hadith, yet the generality of the status is what comes to mind regardless of any pretext, as we have explained above, and peace be with you.

Sincerely,
Sh

Letter 33
Dhul-Hijjah 25, 1329

When was 'Ali and Aaron Described as the Two Stars?

It has not been clarified yet what you claim that he, peace be upon him and his progeny, used to describe 'Ali and Aaron as the two stars which are alike; when did he do that?

Sincerely,
S

Letter 34
Dhul-Hijjah 27, 1329

Research the biography of the Prophet, peace be upon him and his progeny, and you will find him describing 'Ali and Aaron as two bright stars in the heart of the skies, the eyes positioned in the face, neither of them is distinguished in his nation from the other.

I. The Occasion of Shabar, Shubayr and Mushbir

Have you noticed how he, peace be upon him and his progeny, had insisted that 'Ali should name his sons just like Aaron did, calling them Hasan, Husayn, and Muhsin? He (as) has said: "I have named them after Aaron's sons, Shabar, Shubayr, and Mushbir,"[1] intending thereby to emphasize the similarity between

---

[1] This is quoted by the traditionists according to their own authentic sources of the traditions of the Messenger of Allah, peace be upon him and his progeny. Refer to pages 265 and 168, Vol. 3, of *Al-Mustadrak*, and you will find the text of this hadith described as authentic according to the endorsement of both Shaykhs. Imam Ahmad has also quoted it from 'Ali's hadith on page 98, Vol. 1, of his *Musnad*. Ibn 'Abdul-Birr, too, quotes the biography of the grandson of the Prophet al-Hasan (as) from *Isti'ab*, and even al-Dhahabi quotes it in his *Talkhis*, taking its authenticity for granted, in spite of his fanaticism and deviation from this nation's Aaron, and from its Shabar and Shubayr. It is also

himself and Aaron, and generalizing such a similarity in all areas and aspects.

II. The Occasion of Fraternity

For the same reason, 'Ali has cherished his brother and favoured him over all others, thus achieving the goal of generalizing the similarity of both Aarons to their respective brothers, making sure that there must be no difference between them. He, peace be upon him and his progeny, created brotherhood among his companions, as stated above, making, in the first incident, Abu Bakr brother of 'Umar, and 'Uthman brother of 'Abdul-Rahman ibn 'Awf. In the Second Fraternity, Abu Bakr became brother of Kharijah ibn Zayd, and 'Umar was made brother of 'Atban ibn Malik. Yet on both occasions, 'Ali was made brother of the Messenger of Allah, peace be upon him and his progeny, as you have come to know.

There is no room here to quote all verified texts citing Ibn 'Abbas, Ibn 'Umar, Zayd ibn Arqam, Zayd ibn Abu 'Awfah, Anas ibn Malik, Huzayfah ibn al-Yemani, Makhduj ibn Yazid, 'Umar ibn al-Khattab, al-Bara' ibn 'Azib, 'Ali ibn Abu Talib, and others narrating this hadith as such. The Messenger of Allah (s) has also said to 'Ali: "You are my Brother in this life and the life hereafter."[2] In Letter No. 20, we stated how he (s) took 'Ali by the neck, saying: "This is my Brother, vicegerent and successor among you; therefore, listen to him and obey him." He, peace be upon him and his progeny, came out to meet his companions with a broad

---

quoted by al-Baghwi in his *Mu'jam*, and 'Abdul-Ghani from his *Idah*, as is recorded on page 115 of *Al-Sawaiq al-Muhriqa*, from Salman whose text is almost similar, and also from Ibn 'Asakir.

[2] Al-Hakim has quoted it on page 14, Vol. 3, of his *Al-Mustadrak* as narrated by Ibn 'Umar from two authentic sources and endorsed by both Shaykhs. Al-Dhahabi has also quoted it in his *Talkhis*, taking its authenticity for granted. Al-Tirmizi, too, quotes it as cited by Ibn Hajar on page 72 of his *Al-Sawa'iq al-Muhriqa*; so, refer to the seventh hadith of the ones included in Section 2 of Chapter 9 of *Al-Sawa'iq al-Muhriqa*. All those who have discussed the brotherhood hadith among writers of traditions and chronicles have accepted it without any argument.

smile on his face. 'Abdul-Rahman ibn 'Awf asked him what pleased him so much. He answered: "It is due to a piece of good news which I have just received from my Lord regarding my brother and cousin, and also regarding my daughter. The Almighty has chosen 'Ali a husband for Fatima." When the Mistress of all women of the world was wed to the master of the Prophet's progeny (as), the Prophet, peace be upon him and his progeny, said: "O Umm Ayman! Bring me my brother." Umm Ayman asked: "He is your brother, and you still marry him to your daughter?!" He said: "Yes, indeed, Umm Ayman." She called 'Ali in.[3]

Quite often, the Prophet (as) used to point to 'Ali and say: "This is my brother, cousin, son-in-law, and father of my descendants."[4] Once he spoke to him and said: "You are my brother and companion." In another occasion, he said to him: "You are my brother, friend, and companion in Paradise." He once addressed him in a matter that was between him, his brother Ja'far, and Zayd ibn Harithah, saying: "O 'Ali! You are, indeed, my brother and the father of my descendants. You are of me and for me."[5] He made a covenant with him once saying: "You are my brother and vizier; you complete my religion, fulfil my promise, pay my debts on my behalf, and clear my conscience."[6] When death approached him, may both my parents be sacrificed for him, he said: "Fetch me my

---

[3] This is quoted by al-Hakim on page 159, Vol. 3, of his *Al-Mustadrak*. Al-Dhahabi, too, has quoted it in his *Talkhis*, admitting its authenticity. Ibn Hajar copies it in Chapter 11 of his *Al-Sawa'iq al-Muhriqa*. All those who wrote about the wedding of al-Zahra' (as) have, without any exception, mentioned it.
[4] This is included by al-Shirazi in his chapter on surnames, and by Ibn al-Najjar who quotes Ibn 'Umar. Al-Muttaqi al-Hindi has transmitted it in his *Kanz al-'Ummal* and *Al-Muntakhab* which he attaches to the footnote of his *Musnad*; so, refer to the second line of the footnote on page 32 of its fifth volume.
[5] Al-Hakim quotes it on page 217, Vol. 3, of his *Mustadrak*, the authenticity of whose narrators is endorsed by Muslim. Al-Dhahabi has admitted the same in his own *Talkhis*.
[6] Al-Tabrani has quoted it in his *Al-Kabir* from Ibn 'Umar, and it is transmitted by al-Muttaqi al-Hindi in his *Kanz al-'Ummal* as well as *Al-Muntakhab*; so, refer to *Al-Muntakhab* to see the inclusion of the footnote on page 32, Vol. 5, of the *Musnad*.

brother." They called 'Ali in. He said to him: "Come close to me." 'Ali (as) did. He kept whispering in his ears till his pure soul departed from his body. 'Ali even caught some of the Prophet's saliva.[7]

The Messenger of Allah, peace be upon him and his progeny, has also said: "It is written on the gate of Paradise: 'There is no god but Allah, Muhammad is the Messenger of Allah, 'Ali is the Brother of the Messenger of Allah.'"[8] The Almighty, when the Prophet left 'Ali sleeping in his bed while the enemies were outside plotting to murder him, addressed Gabriel and Michael thus: "I have created brotherhood between both of you and let the life-span of one of you be longer than that of the other. Which one of you wishes to have the life of the other be longer than his own?" Each held his own life dearer. The Almighty said: "Why can't you be like 'Ali ibn Abu Talib between whom and Muhammad (s) I have created brotherhood, and he has chosen to sleep in Muhammad's bed, offering to sacrifice his own life for his brother? Go down to earth and protect him from his foes." They both came down. Gabriel stood at 'Ali's head while Michael stood at his feet. Gabriel cried: "Congratulations! Congratulations! Who can be like you, O son of Abu Talib? Even Allah brags about you to His angels!" Regarding that incident, the verse "And there are among men those who trade their own lives for the Pleasure of Allah (Qur'an, 2:207)" was revealed.[9]

'Ali himself is quoted saying: "I am the servant of Allah and the Brother of His Messenger. I am the strongest in believing in the

---

[7] This is quoted by Ibn Sa'd on page 51, Part Two, Vol. 2, of his *Tabaqat*, and also on page 55, Vol. 4, of *Kanz al-'Ummal*.

[8] This is quoted by al-Tabrani in his *Al-Awsat*, by al-Khatib in his *Al-Muttafaq wal-Muftaraq*, and it is transmitted by the author of *Kanz al-'Ummal*; so, refer to *Al-Muntakhab* and see the inclusion of a footnote on page 35, Vol. 5, of Ahmad's *Musnad*. It is also transmitted by Ibn 'Asakir in his footnote on page 46.

[9] This is quoted by authors of books of traditions in their respective works, and it is briefly referred to by Imam Fakhrul-Din al-Razi as he interprets this verse of Surahal-Baqara, on page 189, Vol. 2, of his *Al-Tafsir al-Kabir*.

Prophet. Nobody else can say so except a liar."[10] He has also said: "By Allah! I am his Brother and *wali*, his cousin and the inheritor of his knowledge; who else is more worthy of it than me?"[11] On the Day of Shura, he said to 'Uthman, 'Abdul-Rahman, Sa'd, and al-Zubayr: "Do you know of anyone among the Muslims other than myself with whom the Messenger of Allah established Brotherhood?" They answered: "We bear witness, no."[12] When 'Ali stood to duel with al-Walid during the Battle of Badr, the latter asked him: "Who are you?" 'Ali answered: "I am the servant of Allah and the brother of His Messenger."[13] When 'Umar was caliph, 'Ali asked him:[14] "Suppose some Israelites come to you and one of them told you that he was cousin of Moses, would he receive a preferred treatment than the others?" 'Umar answered: "Yes, indeed." 'Ali said: "I, by Allah, am the brother of the Messenger of Allah and his cousin." 'Umar took off his mantle and spread it for 'Ali to sit on, saying: "By Allah, you will sit nowhere else other than on my own mantle till each one of us goes his way." 'Ali did so while 'Umar was pleased by that gesture of respect for the brother and cousin of the Messenger of Allah as long as he was in his company.

III. The Occasion of Closing the Doors

---

[10] This is quoted by al-Nisa'i in *Al-Khasa'is al-'Alawiyya*, and by al-Hakim at the beginning of page 112, Vol. 3, of his *Al-Mustadrak*, by Abu Shaybah and Ibn Abu 'Asim in *Al-Sunnah*, and by Abu Na'im in *Al-Ma'rifa*. It is also transmitted by al-Muttaqi al-Hindi in *Kanz al-'Ummal* and *Muntakhab al-Kanz*. Refer to *Al-Muntakhab* and read what Ahmad has included in the footnote on page 40, Vol. 5, of his *Musnad*.

[11] Refer to page 126, Vol. 3, of the *Al-Mustadrak*. It is quoted by al-Dhahabi in his *Talkhis*, where the author does not dispute its authenticity at all.

[12] This is quoted by Ibn 'Abdl al-Birr in 'Ali's biography in the *Isti'ab*, in addition to many other trusted authorities.

[13] This is quoted by Ibn Sa'd while discussing Badr's military campaign in his *Tabaqat*, page 15, part One, Vol. 2.

[14] As Dar Qutni quotes in the fifth *maqsad* of the *Maqasid* of the verse enjoining kindness to the Prophet's kin, and it is verse 14 of the ones counted by Ibn Hajar in Part 11 of his *Al-Sawa'iq al-Muhriqa*; so, refer to page 107 of *Al-Sawa'iq al-Muhriqa*.

'Well, I seem to have lost control over my pen. The Prophet, peace be upon him and his progeny, ordered the doors of his companions' houses overlooking the mosque to be closed for good, as a measure to protect the mosque's sanctity against *janaba* or *najasa*, but he allowed 'Ali's door to remain open, permitting him to cross the mosque's courtyard even while being in the state of *janaba*, just as Aaron was permitted to do, thus providing another proof for the similarity of positions of both men, peace be upon them, in their respective creeds and nations. Ibn 'Abbas has said: "The Messenger of Allah, peace be upon him and his progeny, ordered all the doors of his companions closed except that of 'Ali who used to enter even while in the state of *janaba*, having no other way out."[15] 'Umar ibn al-Khattab has narrated an authentic hadith which has been reproduced in both *sahih* books wherein he says:[16] " 'Ali ibn Abu Talib was granted three tokens of prestige; had I had one of them, it would have been dearer to me than all red camels [of Arabia]: his wife Fatima daughter of the Messenger of Allah, his residence at the mosque neighbouring the Messenger of Allah and feeling at home therein, and the standard during the Battle of Khaybar."

Sa'id ibn Malik, as quoted in an authentic hadith, once mentioned a few unique merits of 'Ali and said: "The Messenger of Allah turned out everyone from the mosque, including his uncle al-'Abbas and others. Al-'Abbas asked him: 'Why do you turn us out and keep 'Ali?' He, peace be upon him and his progeny, answered: 'It is not I who has turned you out and kept 'Ali. It is Allah who has turned you out while keeping him.'"[17] Zayd ibn

---

[15] This hadith is quite lengthy, and it contains ten exclusive merits of 'Ali, and we have quoted it Letter No. 26.

[16] It exists on page 125, Vol. 3, of *Al-Mustadrak*. It is quoted by Abu Ya'li, as stated in Part 3, Chapter 9, of *Al-Sawa'iq al-Muhriqa*; so, refer to page 76 of this book. It is also quoted in this meaning in almost similar wording by Ahmad ibn Hanbal while quoting ahadith by 'Umar and his son 'Abdullah, and by many other trusted traditionists through various avenues.

[17] As stated at the beginning of page 17, Vol. 3, of *Al-Mustadrak*. This hadith is included in Sunni books of traditions, and it is quoted by many trusted Sunni authorities.

Arqam has said: "A few companions of the Messenger of Allah (s) used to have the doors of their houses overlooking the mosque. The Messenger of Allah, peace be upon him and his progeny, then said: 'Close down all these doors except 'Ali's.' Some people did not like it, and they talked about it. So, the Messenger of Allah, peace be upon him and his progeny, stood one day, praised the Almighty then said: 'I have ordered these doors to be closed save 'Ali's, and some of you have disliked that. I have not closed down a door nor opened it, nor gave any order, except after being commanded by my Lord to do so.'"[18]

Quoting Ibn 'Abbas, Al-Tabrani has said that the Messenger of Allah, peace be upon him and his progeny, stood up once and said: "I have not turned you out acting on my own personal desire, nor have I left a door open out of my own personal preference. I only follow whatever inspiration I receive from my Lord."[19] And the Messenger of Allah said once to Ali (as): "O 'Ali! It is not permissible for anybody other than your own self to be present [in the mosque] while being in the state of *janaba*."[20] Sa'd ibn Abu Waqqas, al-Bara' ibn 'Azib, Ibn 'Abbas, Ibn 'Umar, and Huzayfah ibn al-Yemani, have all said: "The Messenger of Allah, peace be upon him and his progeny, came out to the mosque once and said: 'Allah inspired to his Prophet Moses to build Him a pure mosque in which nobody other than Moses and Aaron would live. Allah has inspired to me to build a sanctified mosque wherein only I and my brother 'Ali are permitted to sleep.'"[21]

---

[18] As quoted about him by Ahmad on page 369, Vol. 4, of the *Musnad*. It is also quoted by al-Diya as stated in *Kanz al-'Ummal* and its *Muntakhab*; so, refer to *Al-Muntakhab* to see what is included in the footnote for page 29 of the fifth volume of the *Musnad*.

[19] As he is quoted by al-Muttaqi al-Hindi at the end of the footnote on the page referred to above.

[20] As quoted by al-Tirmizi in his *Sahih* and quoted from him by al-Muttaqi al-Hindi as we have stated when referring to his *Muntakhab*. It is also quoted by al-Bazzaz from Sa'd, as stated in hadith 13 of the ahadith which Ibn Hajar quotes in Section 2, Chapter 9, of his *Al-Sawa'iq al-Muhriqa*; so, refer to page 73 of the same.

[21] As they are quoted by 'Ali ibn Muhammad al-Khatib, the Shafi'i *faqih* who is better known as Ibn al-Maghazli, in his book *Al-Manaqib* from various sources,

There is no room here to state all the ascertained texts narrated by Ibn 'Abbas, Abu Sa'id al-Khudri, Zayd ibn Arqam, a companion from the tribe of Khath'am, Asma' bint 'Amis, Umm Salamah, Huzayfah ibn Asid, Sa'd ibn Abu Waqqas, al-Bara' ibn 'Azib, 'Ali ibn Abu Talib, 'Umar, 'Abdullah ibn 'Umar, Abu Dharr al-Ghifari, Abul Tufail, Buraydah al-Aslami, Abu Rafi', freed slave of the Messenger of Allah, Jabir ibn 'Abdullah al-Ansari, and others have all narrated the same hadith. It is also well known that the Messenger of Allah, peace be upon him and his progeny, invoked the Almighty once saying: "O Lord! The my brother Moses had prayed you saying: 'Lord! Remove depression from my chest, untie my tongue's knot so that people may understand my speech, and let my brother Aaron be my vizier from among my household to support me in my undertaking and participate therein,' and you, Lord, responded with: 'We shall support you through your brother and bestow upon you a great authority (Qur'an, 28:35).' Lord! I am your servant Muhammad; therefore, I invoke you to remove depression from my chest, to make my undertaking easier to carry out, and to let 'Ali be my brother from among my household."[22]

Al-Bazzaz has likewise indicated that the Messenger of Allah, peace be upon him and his progeny, took 'Ali's hand and said: "Moses had prayed his Lord to purify His mosque through Aaron, and I have prayed my Lord to purify mine through you." He then sent a messenger to Abu Bakr ordering him to close down his door which overlooked the mosque, and Abu Bakr responded expressing his desire to honour the Prophet's command. Then he sent another messenger to 'Umar to do likewise, and another to al-'Abbas for the same purpose. Then he, peace be upon him and his progeny, said: "It is not I who has closed down your doors, nor

---

and transmitted by the trusted researcher al-Balkhi in Chapter 17 of his *Yanabi' al-Mawaddah*.

[22] This is quoted by Imam Abu Ishaq al-Tha'labi from Abu Dharr al-Ghifari in his interpretation of the following verse of Surahal-Ma'ida: "Verily, your *wali* are: Allah, His Messenger, and the Believers," in his *Al-Tafsir al-Kabir*, similar to which is transmitted from Imam Ahmad's *Musnad* by the Balkhi researcher.

have I kept 'Ali's door open out of my own accord; rather, it is Allah Who has opened his door and closed yours."

This much suffices to prove the similarity between 'Ali and Aaron in all circumstances and conditions, and peace be with you.

Sincerely,
Sh

Letter 35
Dhul-Hijjah 27, 1329

Requesting Other Texts

May Allah reward your father! How eloquent your arguments and how convincing! Please oblige and go ahead to state the rest of the clear consecutively reported (*mutawatir*) texts, Wassalamo Alaikum.

Sincerely,
S

Letter 36
Dhul-Hijjah 29, 1329

I. Hadith by Ibn 'Abbas

Refer to what Abu Dawud al-Tayalisi has reported, as stated in a chapter discussing 'Ali in *Isti'ab* through the authority of Ibn 'Abbas who is quoted saying: "The Messenger of Allah, peace be upon him and his progeny, has said to 'Ali ibn Abu Talib: 'You are next to me alone as the *wali* of every believer.'"[1]

II. 'Umran's Hadith

Another authentic hadith is narrated by 'Umran ibn Hasin who says: "The Messenger of Allah, peace be upon him and his

---

[1] This is quoted by Abu Dawud and other authors of books of traditions from Abu 'Awanah al-Waddah ibn 'Abdullah al-Yashkuri through a chain of narrators: Abu Balj Yahya ibn Salim al-Fizari, 'Amr ibn Maymun al-'Awdi, ending with Ibn 'Abbas. The men who have quoted this tradition are all authorities in their own right, and they are relied upon by both Shaykhs in their respective *sahih*s with the exception of Yahya ibn Salim whom they do not quote, yet even the pioneers of criticism and verification have all declared his trustworthiness, and that he used to mention the name of Allah most frequently. Al-Dhahabi, while stating his biography in his *Al-Mizan*, quotes Ibn Ma'in, al-Nisa'i, Dar Qutni, Muhammad ibn Sa'id, Abu Hatim, and many others all testifying to the fact that the man is a trusted authority.

progeny, deployed an army division under the command of 'Ali ibn Abu Talib who chose, as his share of the *khums*, a slave-girl for himself, and people criticized him. Four men vowed to complain against him to the Messenger of Allah, peace be upon him and his progeny. When they came to the Prophet, one of them stood up and said: 'O Messenger of Allah! Have you seen how 'Ali has done such and such?' The Prophet (s) turned his face away from him. The second stood up and spoke likewise, and the Prophet (s) ignored him, too. The third stood up and repeated what his fellows had previously stated, and he, too, was ignored. The fourth one stood up and stated exactly as had been stated by his fellows. It was then that the Messenger of Allah, peace be upon him and his progeny, turned to them with anger in his eyes and said: 'What do you want of 'Ali? 'Ali is of me and I am of him, and only after me is he the *mawla* of all believers.'"[2]

III. Buraydah's Hadith

Also refer to Buraydah's hadith quoted verbatim on page 356 of Vol. 5 of Ahmad's *Musnad*. He says: "The Messenger of Allah sent two armies to Yemen. One of them was led by 'Ali ibn Abu Talib (as), and the other by Khalid ibn al-Walid. He instructed them thus: 'When you combine your forces, let 'Ali be the overall leader.[3] But if you disperse, then each one of you is the leader over

---

[2] This is quoted by many authors of books of traditions such as Imam al-Nisa'i in his *Al-Khasa'is al-'Alawiyya*, Ahmad ibn Hanbal (when quoting 'Umran's hadith at the beginning of page 438, Vol. 4, of his *Musnad*), al-Hakim on page 111, Vol. 3, of his *Al-Mustadrak*, al-Dhahabi in his *Talkhis al-Mustadrak*, admitting its authenticity due to its endorsement by Muslim. It is quoted by Ibn Abu Shaybah and Ibn Jarir, and the hadith both men quote from him has been verified by al-Muttaqi al-Hindi at the beginning of page 400, Vol. 6, of *Kanz al-'Ummal*. It is also quoted by al-Tirmizi from reliable sources as mentioned by al-'Asqalani while discussing 'Ali's biography in his *Al-Isabah*. The Mu'tazilite scholar has quoted it on page 450, Vol. 2, of *Sharh Nahjul Balaghah*, commenting: "This is narrated by Abu 'Abdullah Ahmad [ibn Hanbal] in his *Musnad* in more than one place." He also narrates it in his book *Fada'il 'Ali* ['Ali's virtues], and it is narrated by most traditionists.
[3] The Messenger of Allah, peace be upon him and his progeny, as long as he lived, never required anyone to issue orders to 'Ali; on the contrary, he vested

his own troops.' We then battled Banu Zubayda, and 'Ali selected one of the captives, a slave-girl, for himself; so, Khalid and I wrote to the Messenger of Allah, peace be upon him and his progeny, to inform him of the incident. When I came to the Messenger of Allah, peace be upon him and his progeny, and the letter was read for him, I noticed anger in his eyes; therefore, I pleaded to him by saying: 'This is the place for those who seek refuge; you have sent me with a commander and ordered me to obey him, and I have done just that.' The Messenger of Allah, peace be upon him and his progeny, said: 'Do not ever plot against 'Ali, for he is of me and I am of him, and he is your *wali* after me.'"[4]

---

upon him the responsibility of issuing orders to others. He was his standard-bearer in every campaign, unlike many others. Abu Bakr and 'Umar were both ordinary soldiers in Usamah's troops, serving under the standard tied for him by the Messenger of Allah (s) who ordered him to take charge of the Mu'ta expedition. He personally enlisted both men, according to the consensus of chroniclers, and he also made them soldiers of Ibn al-'As. These facts are stated by al-Hakim on page 43, Vol. 3, of his *Al-Mustadrak*, and they are cited by al-Dhahabi in his *Talkhis al-Mustadrak*, admitting the authenticity of the hadith. As regarding 'Ali himself, he was never to receive orders, nor to be the subject of anyone other than the Prophet himself since the inception of his mission and till his demise, peace be upon him and his progeny.

[4] This is quoted by Ahmad on page 356 from 'Abdullah ibn Buraydah who quotes his father. On page 347, Vol. 5, of his *Musnad*, relying on a chain of narrators including Sa'id ibn Jubayr and Ibn 'Abbas, he quotes Buraydah saying: "I participated in 'Ali's campaign against Yemen, and I felt that his attitude towards me was cool. When I came to the Messenger of Allah and mentioned 'Ali, I belittled him. Having done so, I saw the face of the Messenger of Allah (s) change colour, and he said to me: 'O Buraydah! Do I not have more authority over the believers than the believers have over their own selves?' I answered: 'Yes, indeed, O Messenger of Allah.' He said: 'To whomsoever I am a *mawla*, 'Ali is his *mawla*.'" This is quoted by al-Hakim on page 110, Vol. 3, of his *Al-Mustadrak*, in addition to many traditionists. It is, as you see, quite clear in its gist, for when he starts with the question "Do I not have more authority over the believers than the believers have over their own selves?" he bears testimony to the meaning of "mawla" in this hadith to be "the one who is *awla*, i.e. most worthy of ruling" them, as is quite obvious. Similar to this hadith is what has been quoted by many traditionists such as Imam Ahmad at the end of page 483, Vol. 3, of his *Musnad*, from 'Amr ibn Shas al-Aslami, one of those who were present at Hudaybiya, who quotes the same adding: "I accompanied 'Ali to

Al-Nisa'i has quoted the following words of the Prophet (s) *verbatim* on page 17 of his *Al-Khasa'is al-'Alawiyyah*: "O Buraydah! Do not try to make me dislike 'Ali, for 'Ali is of me, and I am of him, and he is your *wali* after me." Jarir, too, quotes Buraydah's statement *verbatim* thus: "The Prophet's face became red with anger, and he said: 'To whomsoever I have been *mawla*, 'Ali is his *mawla*;' therefore, I forgot my own anger against 'Ali and said that I would never speak ill of 'Ali again."[5] Al-Tabrani, too, has quoted this hadith in detail. Among what he narrates is that when Buraydah came from Yemen and entered the mosque, he found a crowd standing by the room of the Prophet (s). Upon seeing him, they stood up to greet him and ask him what news he had brought them. He said: "Good news. Allah has rendered victory upon the Muslims." They asked him: "Then what brought you here?" He answered: "An incident regarding a slave-girl whom 'Ali chose as his share of the *khums*, and I have come here to inform the Prophet about it." They said: "Inform him of it, do inform him, so that he may change his heart about 'Ali," while the Prophet, peace be upon him and his progeny, was standing overhearing their conversation from within. He, thereupon, came out angrily and said: "What is the matter with those who bear grudge against 'Ali? Whoever hates 'Ali hates me, too, and whoever abandons 'Ali abandons me. 'Ali is of me and I am of him; he has been created of my own mould, and my own mould is

---

Yemen, and he was cool to me during the trip, so much so that I concealed some feelings against him. When I came back, I complained about him at the mosque till the news reached the Messenger of Allah (s). I entered the mosque one afternoon, and the Messenger of Allah, peace be upon him and his progeny, was present there accompanied by many of his companions. As soon as he saw me, he stared at me till I sat down. He said to me: 'O 'Amr! By Allah you have hurt me.' I said: 'I seek refuge with Allah against hurting you, O Messenger of Allah!' He said: 'Yes; whoever hurts 'Ali hurts me, too.'"

[5] As he is quoted by al-Muttaqi al-Hindi on page 398, Vol. 6, of *Kanz al-'Ummal*. He is also quoted in *Muntakhab al-Kanz*.

Ibrahim's (Abraham's), and I am even superior to Ibrahim,[6] one progeny descending from another, and Allah is all-Hearing, all-Knowing. O Buraydah! Have you not come to know that 'Ali's share is a lot more than the slave-girl he took, and that he is your *wali* after me?"[7] - There is no doubt about the authenticity of this hadith, and its narrators are quite numerous, and they are all reliable.

IV. Hadith Recounting Ten Exclusive Attributes [of 'Ali]

Similar to this narration is what al-Hakim has narrated from Ibn 'Abbas who cites a particular hadith of weight and significance. In it he counts ten exclusive attributes of 'Ali, and he quotes the Messenger of Allah, peace be upon him and his progeny, addressing 'Ali thus: "You are the *wali* of every believer after me."[8]

V. 'Ali's Hadith

Likewise, in another hadith, he, peace be upon him and his progeny, has said, "O 'Ali! I have prayed Allah to grant me five wishes concerning you, and He granted me four and denied the

---

[6] When he was told that 'Ali was created of his own mould, peace be upon him and his progeny, thus by necessity becoming superior to this man, he said: "And I am created of Ibrahim's mould," mistakingly thinking that Ibrahim (Abraham) is superior to him, peace be upon him and his progeny, which contradicts the truth of the matter.

[7] Ibn Jarir has quoted this hadith from al-Tabrani who includes it on page 103 of his book *Al-Sawa'iq al-Muhriqa* while discussing the second *maqsad* of verse 14 of the ones which he discusses in Chapter 11 of *Al-Sawa'iq al-Muhriqa*. But when he comes to the statement "Have you not come to know that 'Ali's share is more than a slave-girl?" his pen halts, and he cannot finish the hadith in its entirety! This is not strange, coming from him and his likes; and praise be to Allah for our good health.

[8] This is quoted by al-Hakim at the beginning of page 134, Vol. 3, of *Al-Mustadrak*, al-Dhahabi in his *Talkhis al-Mustadrak*, admitting its authenticity, al-Nisa'i on page 6 of his *Al-Khasa'is al-'Alawiyya*, and Imam Ahmad on page 331, Vol. 1, of his *Musnad*. We have quoted it verbatim at the beginning of Letter No. 26.

fifth." He continues to say: "He has granted me that you are the *wali* of the believers after me."⁹

VI. Wahab's Hadith

A similar hadith is transmitted by Ibn al-Sakan from Wahab ibn Hamzah and is quoted in Wahab's biography in *Isti'ab* thus: "I travelled once with 'Ali and found him to be cold towards me; therefore, I decided to complain about him to the Prophet upon returning. So I mentioned him to the Messenger of Allah and I spoke ill of him, whereupon he (s) said: 'Do not say so about 'Ali, for he is your *wali* after me.'" Al-Tabrani, in his book *Al-Mujma' al-Kabir*, cites Wahab's statement with a minor alteration in its wording thus: "Do not say this about 'Ali, for he is the most worthy of being your leader after me."¹⁰

VII. Ibn Abu 'Asim's Hadith

Ibn Abu 'Asim has quoted 'Ali's hadith from the Prophet through a chain of narrators thus: "Do I not have more authority over the believers than they themselves have?" People answered in the affirmative. The Prophet (s) then said: "To whomsoever I have been *wali*, 'Ali is his *wali*;"¹¹ and our *sahih* books in this regard are *mutawatir* from the Imams of the Purified Progeny (as).

This much should suffice to prove our point, although *ayat al-wilayat* alone suffices to support our claim, and praise be to Allah, Lord of the Worlds, Wassalamo Alaikum.

Sincerely,
Sh

---

⁹ This hadith is number 6048 among the ones cited in *Kanz al-'Ummal*, page 396, Vol. 6.

¹⁰ This hadith is numbered 2579 among the ones cited in *Kanz al-'Ummal*, page 155, Vol. 6.

¹¹ This is transmitted by al-Muttaqi al-Hindi from Ibn Abu 'Asim on page 397, Vol. 6, of *Kanz al-'Ummal*.

Letter 37
Dhul-Hijjah 29, 1329

"Wali" is a Linguistic Denominator; so Where is the Text?

The word "wali" is a common denominator between the supporter and the friend, the loved one and the brother-in-law, the follower, the ally, and the neighbour. Whoever takes charge of a matter is its "wali." The ahadith you have quoted may simply mean: 'Ali is your supporter, or friend, or loved one, after the Prophet; so, where is the text which you claim?

Sincerely,
S

Letter 38
Dhul-Hijjah 29, 1329

I. Explaining the Implications of "Wali"

You have indicated, while explicating the meanings of "wali," that whoever takes charge of anyone becomes the latter's *wali*. This, indeed, is the connotation of "wali" in as far as those ahadith are concerned. It is the same that comes to mind. Its meaning is similar to saying "The minor has had for his *wali* both his father and his paternal grandfather, then he was put in the custody of either of them, then in the custody of the legal administrator." This implies that these persons are the ones who are in charge of looking after him and administer his affairs on his own behalf.

II. Proving its Connotation

The proofs testifying to the meaning connoted in the word concealed from the discreet. His statement, peace be upon him and his progeny, "And he is your *wali* after me" clearly restricts "wilayat" to him and only him. This mandates that we should underscore the meaning which we have just attached to this word, a meaning which does not agree with that of any other interpretation. Support, love, friendship, and the like are not confined to one single person, and the believers, men and women, are *walis* of one another. What merit, other than what we have just indicated, could the Prophet (s) have emphasized in this hadith regarding his brother and *wali* if we say that the meaning of the word *wali* is something else that differs from what we have indicated above? What a hidden matter has the Prophet (s) decided to unveil through the medium of such ahadith had the meaning of "wali" been the supporter, the loved one, or the like? The Messenger of Allah, peace be upon him and his progeny, is above clarifying what is already clear, or pointing out what is already taken for granted. His wisdom is vast, his infallibility is incumbent, his Message is conclusive and is more than what some people think. Yet these ahadith are quite clear in stating that *wilayat* is assigned for 'Ali after the Messenger of Allah, peace be upon him and his progeny. This, too, requires applying the same meaning which we have suggested. It simply is not conducive to the meanings of supporter, loved one, etc., since there is no doubt that 'Ali is known to have been supported, loved, and befriended by Muslims due to his being raised in the lap of prophethood, to his contributions to the promotion of its message, till he, peace be upon him, passed away. Supporting, loving and befriending the Muslims, therefore, are not confined to 'Ali alone after the Messenger of Allah, peace be upon him and his progeny, as is quite obvious.

Suffices you for a testimony to this meaning what Imam Ahmad has stated on page 347 of Vol. 5 of his *Musnad* through the correct path of narrators who cite Sa'id ibn Jubayr quoting Ibn 'Abbas citing Buraydah saying: "I participated in 'Ali's invasion of Yemen, and I found him to be cool to me; so, when I came to the Messenger of Allah, peace be upon him and his progeny, I mentioned 'Ali and belittled him; thereupon, I saw the Messenger's face changing colour, and he asked me: 'O Buraydah! Do I not have more authority over the believers than the believers have over their own selves?' I answered: 'Yes, indeed, O Messenger of Allah'. He (s) then said: 'To whomsoever I have been *mawla*, 'Ali, too, is his *mawla*." This hadith is also quoted by al-Hakim on page 110, Vol. 3, of his *Mustadrak*, where he considers it authentic relying on the authority of Muslim. Al-Dhahabi has quoted it in his *Talkhis*, taking its authenticity for granted for the same reason that be Muslim, too, considers it authentic. You yourself know the implication the introductory question "Do I not have more authority over the believers than they themselves have?" carries, a meaning that supports what we have suggested. Anyone who scrutinizes these ahadith, as well as all matters relevant to them, will have no doubt in what we have stated, and praise be to Allah.

Sincerely,
Sh

Letter 39
Dhul-Hijjah 30, 1329

Requesting the Wilayat Verse

I testify that you are firm in your beliefs, sincere in your campaign, forceful and unmatched in facing your debater, invincible in the field. I am a believer in the ahadith according to the way which you have suggested. Had I not been obliged to believe in the *sahabah*, I would have accepted your judgement, but taking the word's meaning in the way those *sahabah* have taken it is a must, following in the footsteps of the good ancestors, may Allah be pleased with all of them.

But you have not acquainted us with the terse verse which you claim, at the conclusion of Letter No. 36, that supports your view regarding the interpretation of these ahadith. Recite it for us so that we may comprehend its meaning by the Will of Allah Almighty, Wassalam.

Sincerely,
S

Letter 40
Muharram 2, 1320

I. The Verse of Wilayat and its Revelation in 'Ali's Honour

Yes, indeed, I would like to recite unto you one of the perfect verses of Allah, the Exalted, the Almighty, in His great Book which distinguishes right from wrong. It is one of the verses of Surah al Ma'ida (Table cloth for food):[1]

---

[1] This is why people in Syria call a Shi'ah "mutawali," due to his taking for *mawla* Allah, His Messenger, and those who have truly believed, that is, those in whose honour the same verse was revealed. Linguistically, the "mutawali" is singular, and the "mutawla" are the Shi'ahs. They are so-called because they accepted the *wilayat* of 'Ali and Ahl al-Bayt (as).

Only Allah is your wali and His Messenger and those who believe, those who say their prayers and offer zakat (even) while prostrating (in prayers). And whoever takes for wali Allah, His Messenger, and the believers, they, indeed, are the party of Allah; they are the ones who shall achieve victory. (Qur'an, 5:55-56)

Nobody doubts the fact that these verses were revealed in honour of 'Ali who offered his own ring in the way of Allah while engaged in performing the prayers.

II. Why it was Revealed

The *sahih* books consecutively report, through the authority of the Imams from among the Purified Progeny, stating that it was revealed in honour of 'Ali when he, out of charity, offered his ring while prostrating in prayers. Refer to what has been said in this regard by others such as Ibn Salam who quotes hadith from the Prophet, peace be upon him and his progeny. Refer to it as published in Nisa'i's *Sahih*, or in *Al-Jami Bayna al-Sihah al-Sittah*, in a chapter dealing with the interpretation of Surah al Ma'ida. Likewise, refer to the hadith of Ibn 'Abbas who explains the meanings of these verses in imam al-Wahidi's book *Asbab al-Nuzul*. Al-Khatib has included it in *Al-Muttafaq*.[2] Also refer to 'Ali's hadith in the *musnads* of Ibn Mardawayh and Abul-Shaykh. If you wish, refer to it in *Kanz al-'Ummal*.

Its revelation to honour 'Ali is a matter of consensus among scholars of the exegesis of the Holy Qur'an. Such consensus is attested to by many Sunni scholars like Imam al-Qawshaji in his chapter on imamate in *Sharh al Tajrid*. Chapter 18 of *Ghayat al-Maram* includes one hadith narrated through the Sunnis testifying to our claim. Had I not aspired to be brief, in addition to the fact that this issue is as clear as the sun in midday, I would have quoted for you many comments thereupon in authentic chronicles, but,

---

[2] It is hadith number 5991 of the ones cited in *Kanz al-'Ummal* on page 391, Vol. 6.

praise to Allah, it is a matter which does not entertain any doubt. Despite that, we do not like to let this letter be without a few ahadith narrated by the majority of Muslims.

Suffices us what Imam Abu Ishaq Ahmad ibn Ibrahim al-Nishapuri al-Tha'labi[3] has stated in his *Al-Tafsir al-Kabir*. When the writer comes to this verse, he quotes Abu Dharr al-Ghifari saying:

"I have heard the Messenger of Allah, peace be upon him and his progeny, with these ears - may I be deaf if I tell a lie - and saw him with these eyes - may I be blinded if I lie - saying: 'Ali is the leader of the pious, the annihilator of infidels; whoever supports him is supported by Allah, and whoever abandons him is abandoned by Allah.' I have, indeed, said my prayers once in the company of the Messenger of Allah, peace be upon him and his progeny, when a beggar came to the mosque and nobody gave him anything. 'Ali was in the state of ceremonial prostration when he beckoned to him to take his ring. The beggar came and took it from 'Ali's finger, whereupon the Messenger of Allah, peace be upon him and his progeny, invoked Allah, the Almighty, the Omniscient, and prayed Him on behalf of 'Ali saying: 'Lord! My Brother Moses had prayed to you saying: Lord! Remove the distress from my bosom, render my mission easy for me, and untie my tongue's knot so that people may understand me, and let me have a vizier from my own kin, my brother Aaron, to support my endeavour and participate in my undertaking, so that we may both praise you a great deal and mention your Name a great deal; You have been most Kind unto us (Qur'an, 20:25-35)Thereupon, You inspired to him: Verily, your prayer has been granted, O Moses! (Qur'an, 20:36).

---

[3] He died in 337. Ibn Khallikan mentions him in his *Wafiyyat al-A'yan* saying: "He was the unique authority of his time in the science of exegesis; he wrote *Al-Tafsir al-Kabir*, which surpassed all other books of *tafsir*," and he goes on to say: "He is mentioned by 'Abdul-Ghafir ibn Isma'il al-Farsi in his book *Siyaq Nishapur*, where the author lauds him and describes him as 'accurate in transmitting, trustworthy.'"

Lord! I am Your servant and Prophet; therefore, remove my distress, render my mission easy for me, and grant me a vizier from my kin, 'Ali, to support my endeavour'. By Allah, the Messenger of Allah, peace be upon him and his progeny, had hardly finished his supplication before Gabriel, the trusted one, brought him this verse: 'Only Allah is your wali and His Messenger and those who believe, those who say their prayers and offer zakat (even) while prostrating (in prayers). And whoever takes for wali Allah, His Messenger, and the believers, they, indeed, are the party of Allah; they are the ones who shall achieve victory (Qur'an, 5:55-56).'"

III. Why Using it as a Testimonial

You, may Allah support righteousness through your own person, know that the meaning of the word "wali" in such a context is "one who has the top priority in faring with one's affairs." We say "Such and such is the minor's *wali*." Lexicographers have made it clear that whoever takes charge of someone's affairs is the latter's *wali*. The meaning of the verse, therefore, is as though Allah says that "the ones who take charge of your affairs and have priority even over your own lives in faring with the latter are: Allah, the Almighty and Omniscient, His Messenger, and 'Ali," for in 'Ali alone have all these qualities been combined: faith, saying the prayers, and offering *zakat* even while prostrating in prayers, and for whom these verses were thus revealed. The Almighty has in these verses reserved *wilayat* for Himself and for both His Messenger and *wasi* in the same manner. The *wilayat* of Allah, the Almighty and Omniscient, is general and inclusive. So is the *wilayat* of the Prophet as well as his *wali*; it carries the same meaning. It is not possible to apply to it in this context the meanings of "supporter, loved one, etc.," since such a restriction [of application] is groundless, as is quite obvious. I believe this is a quite clear matter, and praise to Allah, Lord of the Worlds.

Sincerely,
Sh

Letter 41
Muharram 3, 1330

"Mumins" is Plural; Why Apply it to the Singular?

It may be said in rebutting your objection that the phrase "the Mu'mins who say their prayers and offer *zakat* (even) while prostrating (in prayers)" is applied to the plural; so, why should it be applied to the Imam, may Allah glorify his countenance, who is singular? What is your answer if you are asked thus?

Sincerely,
S

Letter 42
Muharram 4, 1330

I. Arabs Address the Singular Using the Plural Form

1) The answer to your question is that Arabs apply the plural expression while addressing an individual due to the nice effect it produces [i.e. respect].

II. Testimonials

A testimony to this fact is what the Almighty says in Surah Al-i-'Imran:

> Those to whom some people said: "A large army has been raised against you; so, fear them," yet it only increased their faith, and they said: "Allah suffices us, and He is the One upon Whom we depend most." (Qur'an, 3:173)

The person implied in these verses of Al-i-'Imran is none other than Na'im ibn Mas'ud al-Ashja'i, according to the consensus of scholars of exegesis, traditionists, and chroniclers. Yet Allah Almighty has applied to him, the singular person that he is, the plural form just to express respect for those who did not listen to his statements nor heeded his dissuading calls. Abu Sufyan had given him ten camels in order to demoralize and frighten the Muslims regarding the strength of the polytheists, and he did just that. Among his statements then was: "People have gathered a mighty force to attack you; so, fear for your own lives." Many Muslims disliked the idea of fighting that force just because of his statement, but the Messenger of Allah, peace be upon him and his progeny, came out accompanied by seventy cavaliers to meet them, and they all returned from the battle-field safely, whereupon this verse was revealed praising the seventy believers who came out with the Messenger of Allah, peace be upon him and his progeny, heedless to the dissuasion of those who wished to demoralize them.

In applying the word "people" for just one individual, a nice and divine point is made which is complimenting the seventy men who came out with the Prophet. This surely sounds more eloquent when used as such; it is better than saying: "Those to whom a man said that a large army had been raised..., etc.," as is obvious. There are numerous verses in the Holy Qur'an similar to this one, as well as in the Arabic language as a whole. The Almighty Allah says: "O you who believe! Remember Allah's blessing unto you when some folks intended to lay their (evil) hands upon you, and He protected you against their harm." In fact, the person who intended to lay his evil hands upon them and hurt them was a man from the tribe of Muharib named Ghawrath - others say it was 'Amr ibn Jahsh of Banu al Nadir - who unsheathed his sword and shook it intending to strike the Holy Prophet (s), but Allah, the Almighty and the Glorified, foiled his attempt, according to the narration of the incident as recorded by traditionists, authors of chronicles, and scholars of exegesis, and as transmitted by Ibn Hisham in the campaign of That al Riqa' in Vol. 3 of his book titled *Sirah*. Allah has applied the collective plural "people" for this lone man just to express His blessings, the Dear One, the Omnipotent, upon the Muslim masses manifested in the safety of the Prophet, peace be upon him and his progeny. In the Mubahala verse, He has applied both the singular and the plural forms to the "sons," "women," and "selves" to both the Hasanain, Fatima, and 'Ali in particular, just to honour to their lofty status, may Allah be pleased with them. Examples for the application of the plural form for the individual wherever necessary are innumerable and beyond recounting, and they all prove the license to use the plural form while talking about one individual whenever there is a nice eloquent effect thereto.

III. Quoting Imam al-Tibrisi

In his interpretation of this verse, in *Mujma'ul Bayan fi Tafsir al-Qur'an*, Imam al-Tibrisi comments on the usage of the plural form to refer to the Commander of the Faithful as a token of respect and veneration, stating that lexicographers describe the singular using the plural form to show respect and veneration. He says: "Such an application is too well known in their language to require proofs."

IV. Quoting al-Zamakhshari

In his *Kashshaf*, al-Zamakhshari mentions another nice point when he says: "If you wonder how it can be accurate to use the plural with 'Ali, may Allah be pleased with him, I will tell you that he is addressed in the plural form, although he is only one man, so that people may follow his example and earn rewards like his, and so that Allah may point out the fact that a believer's attitude should be like 'Ali's, that is, being eager to do deeds of righteousness and goodwill by looking after the poor, so much so that even the performance of something which does not permit any delay, such as saying the prayers, should not make them postpone it till they are through."

V. What I have Stated

I personally have a nice and more precise point. When the Almighty applied the plural rather than the singular form, as many do, then those who hated 'Ali as well as all those who were envious of and in competition with Banu Hashim would not be able to tolerate hearing it in the singular form, for they would then be unable to hide the truth or water it down. Because of their desperation, they might even do something quite harmful to Islam. It is quite possible that it was for this reason that the verse was revealed in the plural form though applied to the singular: in order to avoid the harm resulting from disgracing those folks. The verses after that particular one vary in form and status, gradually preparing them for *wilayat*, till Allah perfected His religion and completed His blessing, as was his usual habit, peace be upon him and his progeny, and that of the wise in attaining what otherwise is quite difficult to attain. Had the verse come in the singular form, those folks would have then put their fingers in their ears, covered themselves with their own clothes and become stubborn, arrogant, and naughty. This is a sublime wisdom manifested in all the verses of the Holy Qur'an which were revealed to highlight the attributes of the Commander of the Faithful and those among his purified household, as is quite obvious. We have explained these statements and brought irrefutable proofs and obvious testimonies in our books *Sabil al-Muminin* and *Tanzil al-Ayat*, and praise be to Allah for His Guidance and Support, Wassalam.

Sincerely,
Sh

Letter 43
Muharram 4, 1330

Context Denotes "the Loved one" or the Like

May Allah bless your father! You have, indeed, dispelled my doubts and thus overcome my suspicion, so much so that truth has become manifest. Nothing remains to say other than the fact that the context of the said verse denotes the prohibition of taking the infidels for *walis*. The verses which precede and succeed it testify to this fact, and this supports the claim that the connotation of the word "wali" in this verse is the supporter, loved one, friend, or the like; so, what would your answer be? Kindly state it, Wassalam.

Sincerely,
S

Letter 44
Muharram 5, 1330

I. Context is not Indicative of "Supporter" or the Like

Here is my answer: This verse, if one were to scrutinize it, overlooking the verses which precede it and which prohibit taking the infidels for *walis*, does not connote praising the Commander of the Faithful or recommending him for leadership and imamate by threatening dissidents with his might or by warning them against being punished by him. This is so because in the preceding verse, if and when scrutinized independently, Allah Almighty states: "O ye who believe! If anyone of you relinquishes his religion, then Allah will raise a people whom He loves and who love Him, softhearted with the believers, mighty against the unbelievers, struggling in His Path, not fearing anyone while doing so. This, indeed, is Allah's favour; He grants it to whomsoever He pleases, and Allah is vast in knowledge (Qur'an, 5:54)."[1] This verse is

---

[1] This is similar in meaning to the hadith of the Messenger of Allah, peace be upon him and his progeny, saying: "You, folks of Quraysh, shall never cease

revealed on behalf of the Commander of the Faithful (as), warning others of his might and that of his followers, as the Commander of the Faithful has himself stated on the Battle of the Camel and is stated by Imams al-Baqir and al-Sadiq (as).

The same meaning is applied by al-Tha'labi in his *Tafsir al-Qur'an*. It is also narrated by the author of *Muj'maul Bayan fi Tafsir al-Qur'an* from 'Ammar, Huzayfah, and Ibn 'Abbas. It is interpreted in this way according to the consensus of Shi'as who narrate it consecutively from the Imams of the Purified Progeny (as). The verse of the *wilayat* will thus come after hinting to his *wilayat* and referring to the necessity of accepting his imamate. Its context would then be an explanation of that hint, and an elaboration on the hint that preceded it which suggests his government; so, how can it be said that this verse was revealed in the context of prohibiting taking the infidels for *walis*?

II. Context does not Outweigh the Proofs

The Messenger of Allah, peace be upon him and his progeny, has himself equated the status of the Imams among his descendants to

---

feuding till Allah sends you a man the sincerity of whose faith He has tested to strike your necks with his sword, while you run away in fear like frightened cattle." Abu Bakr asked: "Is it I, O Messenger of Allah?" He answered: "No." 'Umar asked: "Is it I, O Messenger of Allah?" He answered: "No; but it is he that mends the sandal." The narrator continues to say: "'Ali then had in his hand the Prophet's sandal which he was mending for the Messenger of Allah, peace be upon him and his progeny." This hadith has been recorded by many authors of books of traditions, and it is hadith number 610 at the beginning of page 393, Vol. 6, of *Kanz al-'Ummal*. Also similar to it is his saying, peace be upon him and his progeny, "Among you is a man who shall fight for the implementation of the Qur'an just as I have fought for its revelation." Abu Bakr asked: "Am I the one?" He answered: "No." 'Umar asked likewise, and the Prophet (s) answered: "No, but it is the man who is inside mending the sandal," whereupon 'Ali came out of the room carrying the Prophet's sandal after having finished mending it. This hadith is quoted by Imam Ahmad ibn Hanbal in his *Musnad* as transmitted by Abu Sa'id, and it is narrated by al-Hakim in his *Al-Mustadrak*, Abu Ya'li in his *Musnad*, and by many authors of books of traditions. Al-Muttaqi al-Hindi quotes it from them on page 155 of the sixth volume of his book.

that of the Holy Qur'an, indicating that they both shall never separate from each other, and that they are equal in significance to the Book (Qur'an) itself; through them can right be distinguished from wrong. To them, taking this verse as a proof is consecutively reported. The meaning they have always applied to the word "wali" in such a context is identical to the one which I have applied above; therefore, context does not bear any weight if you take it to contradict their texts,[2] for all Muslims are in consensus regarding the application of context as a proper argument. When context and proof collide with one another, they abandon the connotation of the context and yield to the judgement of the proof. This is so due to the fact that the connotation of this verse's context is not relied upon, since the Glorious Book itself is not arranged in the order of its compilation, according to the consensus of all Muslim scholars, but according to the sequence of the revelation of its verses. As such, there are quite a few verses which give a meaning that contradicts their context. Take, for example, the Verse of Purification. The fact that the chapter where it exists deals with women is quite clear in restricting its connotation to the five individuals [men and women] who were covered with the mantle. Generally speaking, to interpret a verse in a way which contradicts its context does not in any way violate its miraculous aspect, it does not harm its eloquence, and it does not hurt to resort to it whenever irrefutable proofs demand it, Wassalamo Alaikum.

Sincerely,
Sh

---

[2] What weight can a superficial interpretation have if it contradicts the spirit of the entire text?

Letter 45
Muharram 6, 1330

Resorting to Interpretation Following in the Footsteps of the Predecessors is Unavoidable

Had it not been for the caliphate of the Righteous Caliphs, which is correct beyond any doubt, we would not have had any choice other than accepting your view and interpreting this verse and others according to your own judgement, but to cast doubts about the soundness of their caliphate, may Allah be pleased with them, is out of the question. Resorting to interpretation, then, is unavoidable, since we have believed in them as well as in those who swore the oath of allegiance to them, Wassalam.

Sincerely,
S

Letter 46
Muharram 6, 1330

The three righteous caliphs, may Allah be pleased with them, are, indeed, the subject of the study and debate; to use such caliphate, however, to rebut our arguments is totally rejected.

I. Believing in the Ancestors does not Require Interpretation

To believe in those caliphs, as well as in those who swore allegiance to them, does not require interpreting the arguments. In justifying their caliphate, you yourselves resort to interpretation, as we will clarify if necessary.

II. Interpretation is Impossible

Interpreting the texts which we have stated to you is impossible; so is the case with what we have *not* stated yet, such as the Ghadir's hadith and that of the Will, particularly when backed by irrefutable traditions which support one another, the latter being sufficient by themselves to require reference to manifest texts. Whoever acquaints himself with the latter will find them irrefutable testimonials and unequivocable verdicts, Wassalam.

Sincerely,
Sh

Letter 47
Muharram 7, 1320

Requesting Testimonial Traditions

I wish you had stated those traditions supporting such texts and thereby complemented your research, Wassalam.

Sincerely,
S

Letter 48
Muharram 8, 1330

Forty Ahadith Supporting the Texts

Consider forty such supporting ahadith:

1) Consider the statement of the Messenger of Allah, peace be upon him and his progeny, while holding 'Ali's neck, "This is the Imam of the righteous, the slayer of the debauchees; victorious is whoever supports him, forsaken (by Allah) is whoever abandons him." He (s) raised his voice while saying the last phrase. This is included by al-Hakim as narrated by Jabir on page 129, Vol. 3, of *Al-Mustadrak*,[1] where the author comments saying: "This is one hadith the authenticity of which is attested to by its own chain of narrators, though both authors (of *sahih* books) did not record it."

2) Consider his statement, peace be upon him and his progeny, "It has been revealed to me that 'Ali has three exclusive merits: that he is the chief of the Muslims, the Imam of the righteous, and the leader of those whose foreheads radiate with the mark of faith." It is included by al-Hakim at the beginning of page

---

[1] This is hadith number 2527 of the ones cited in *Kanz al-'Ummal*, page 153, Vol. 6, and it is quoted by al-Tha'labi from Abu Tharr when the author attempts to interpret the verse of *wilayat* in his book *Al-Tafsir al-Kabir*.

138, Vol. 3, of his *Mustadrak*[2] where the author comments: "This is one hadith the accuracy of which is attested to by its own chain of narrators, though both authors (of the sahih books) did not record it."

3) Consider his statement, peace be upon him and his progeny, "It has been revealed to me that 'Ali is the chief of the Muslims, the *wali* of the pious, and the leader of those whose foreheads radiate with the mark of faith." It is recorded by Ibn al-Najjar][3] and many other authors of books of traditions.

4) Consider his statement, peace be upon him and his progeny, to 'Ali: "Welcome, chief of the Muslims, Imam of the pious!" It is included by Abu Na'im in *Hilyat al-Awliya'*.[4]

5) Consider his statement, peace be upon him and his progeny, "The first to enter through this door is the Imam of the pious, the chief of Muslims, the head of the religion, the seal of the *wasis*, and the leader of those whose foreheads radiate with the mark of faith," whereupon 'Ali entered and he, peace be upon him and his progeny, stood up happily excited, hugged him and wiped his sweat saying: "You shall fulfil my covenant, convey my message, and after me clarify whatever seems to be ambiguous."[5]

6) Consider his statement, peace be upon him and his progeny, "Allah has promised me that 'Ali is the standard of guidance, the Imam of whoever accepts my *wilayat*, the light for whoever obeys me, and the word which I have mandated unto the

---

[2] It is also quoted by al-Barudi, Ibn Qani', Abu Na'im, and al-Bazzar. It is hadith 2628 of the ones cited in *Kanz al-'Ummal*, page 157, Vol. 6.

[3] It is hadith 2630 of the ones cited in *Kanz al-'Ummal*, page 157, Vol. 6.

[4] It is news item number 11 of the ones Ibn Abul Hadid states on page 450, Vol. 2, of *Sharh Nahjul Balaghah*, and it is hadith number 2627 of the ones cited in *Kanz al-'Ummal*, page 157, Vol. 6.

[5] This is quoted by Abu Na'im in his *Hilyat al-Awliya'* from Anas and transmitted in detail by Ibn Abul Hadid on page 450, Vol. 2, of his *Sharh Nahjul Balaghah*; so, refer to news item 9 on that page.

pious."⁶ As you see, these six ahadith contain obvious texts regarding his imamate and the obligation to obey him, peace be upon him.

7) Consider his statement, peace be upon him and his progeny, pointing to 'Ali, "This is the first to have believed in me, the first to shake hands with me on the Day of Resurrection; he is the foremost friend, and he is the *faruq* of this nation who distinguishes between right and wrong; he is the chief of the believers."⁷

8) Consider his statement, peace be upon him and his progeny, "O you group of the Ansars! Shall I lead you to that which, as long as you adhere to it, you shall never go astray? It is 'Ali; love him as you love me, and respect him as you respect me, for Gabriel has commanded me to say so to you on behalf of Allah, the Almighty, the Omniscient."⁸

---

⁶ This is quoted by Abu Na'im in his *Hilyat al-Awliya'* from one hadith narrated by Abu Barzah al-Aslami and Anas ibn Malik, and it is transmitted by the Mu'tazilite scholar on page 449, Vol. 2, of his *Sharh Nahjul Balaghah*; so, refer to the third news item on that page.

⁷ This is quoted by al-Tabrani in his *Kabir* from the ahadith narrated by Salman and Abu Tharr. It is quoted by al-Bayhaqi in his *Sunan*, and by Ibn 'Uday in his *Al-Kamil*; it also is hadith number 2608 of the ones included in *Kanz al-'Ummal*, Vol. 6, page 156.

⁸ This is quoted by al-Tabrani in his *Kabir*, and it is hadith number 2625 of the ones included in *Kanz al-'Ummal*, Vol. 6, page 157, and the tenth on page 450, Vol. 2, of *Sharh Nahjul Balaghah* by Ibn Abul Hadid; so, look and see how he has made their right guidance conditional upon upholding 'Ali; thus, those who do not do so would certainly stray. See how he has commanded them to love him just as they love the Prophet (s), and to respect him in the same way they respect the Prophet (s). This is so only because of his being his successor, the one to take charge after him. If you consider the verse "Gabriel has commanded me to tell you so," then truth becomes manifest to you.

9) Consider his statement, peace be upon him and his progeny, "I am the city of knowledge, and 'Ali is its gate; whoever aspires to attain knowledge, let him approach through the gate."[9]

10) Consider his statement, peace be upon him and his progeny, "I am the house of wisdom and 'Ali is its gate."[10]

11) Consider his statement, peace be upon him and his progeny, "'Ali is the gateway of my knowledge, the one who is to explain to my nation after me what I have been sent with; loving him is a mark of genuine faith, and hating him is hypocrisy."[11]

---

[9] This is quoted by al-Tabrani in his *Kabir* from Ibn 'Abbas as stated on page 107 of *Al-Jami' al-Saghir* by Sayyuti. It is also quoted by al-Hakim in *Manaqib 'Ali*, page 226, Vol. 3 of his authentic *Mustadrak* from two sources: one of them is Ibn 'Abbas from yet two authentic sources, and the other from Jabir ibn 'Abdullah al-Ansari. He has brought forth irrefutable proofs for its authenticity. Imam Ahmad ibn Hanbal ibn al-Siddiq al-Magharibi, of Cairo, has dedicated an entire book only to prove the authenticity of this hadith, and he has crammed it with information and titled it *Fath al-Malak al-'Ali Bisihhati Hadith Babul 'Ilm 'Ali*, printed in Egypt at the Islamic Press.

It is worthy of the attention of researchers, for it contains invaluable information. Views of the Nasibis and their likes are worthless *vis-a-vis* this hadith that is as commonly used as a popular proverb by both the elite and the common residents of the urban districts and the countryside. We have even considered their criticism, and we have found it to be sheer submission to sentiment, lacking in proof, full of extreme fanaticism, as declared by al-Hafiz Salahud-Din al-'Ala'i when he quoted the false allegation of al-Dhahabi and others who charge that it is incorrect. He comments saying: "These have not produced any proof for their claim except its being a fabrication so that it may not indict them."

[10] This is quoted by al-Tirmizi in his *Sahih*, in addition to Ibn Jarir, and from them it is quoted by several authorities such as al-Muttaqi al-Hindi on page 401, Vol. 6, of his *Kanz al-'Ummal*, where he quotes Ibn Jarir saying: "This is a tradition of whose authenticity we are quite sure." It is also quoted from al-Tirmizi by Jalal ud-Din al-Sayyuti while discussing the "hamza" in language in his *Jami' al-Jawami'* and *Al-Jami' al-Saghir*; so, refer to page 170, Vol. 1, of *Al-Jami' al-Saghir*.

[11] This is quoted by al-Daylami from Abu Tharr's hadith as stated on page 156, Vol. 6, of *Kanz al-'Ummal*

12) Consider his statement, peace be upon him and his progeny, to 'Ali: "You shall clarify to my nation all matters wherein they differ." This is recorded by al-Hakim on page 122, Vol. 3, of his *Mustadrak*[12] as reported by Anas. The author then comments: "This is an authentic hadith according to the endorsement of both Shaykhs [Bukhari and Muslim], although they did not quote it themselves." In fact, whoever scrutinizes this hadith and others similar to it will come to know that 'Ali's status with relevance to the Messenger of Allah is similar to that of the Messenger of Allah to the Almighty Himself, for Allah says to His Messenger: "We have sent you Our revelations only so that you may clarify for them all the matters in which they dispute, and as guidance and mercy unto those who believe;" while in this hadith the Messenger of Allah (s) tells 'Ali: "You shall clarify to my nation all matters wherein they differ after me."

13) Consider his statement, peace be upon him and his progeny, as recorded by Ibn al-Sammak from Abu Bakr, "'Ali's status to me is similar unto that of mine to my Lord."[13]

14) Consider his statement, peace be upon him and his progeny, as recorded by al-Dar al-Qutni in *Al-Afrad* where the author quotes Ibn 'Abbas citing the Prophet saying: "'Ali ibn Abu Talib is (like) the gate of salvation to the Israelites; whoever enters through it becomes a true believer [*mu'min*], and whoever gets out of it becomes infidel."[14]

15) Consider his statement, peace be upon him and his progeny, on the day of 'Arafat during Hijjatul Wada' [the farewell

---

[12] *Ibid*.
[13] This is quoted by Ibn Hajar in the fifth *maqsad* of the *maqasid* of chapter 14 of the ones discussed in Chapter 11 of his *Al-Sawa'iq al-Muhriqa*; so, refer to page 106 of the same.
[14] This hadith is number 2528 among the ones cited in *Kanz al-'Ummal*, page 153, Vol. 6.

pilgrimage]: "'Ali is of me, and I am of 'Ali, and nobody pays my debts other than I or 'Ali."[15]

"It is the statement of a glorious Messenger empowered by the One Who manifests the Throne, Able, Obeyed: how trustworthy He is! Nay! Your fellow is not possessed at all." (Qur'an, 81:19-22)

"He does not speak out of his own personal inclination; it is but a revealed inspiration." (Qur'an, 53:3-4)

---

[15] This is quoted by Ibn Majah in his chapter on the virtues of the Prophet's companions on page 92, Vol. 1, of his *Sunan*, by al-Tirmizi and al-Nisa'i in their respective *sahih*s, and it is hadith number 2531 among the ones cited in *Kanz al-'Ummal*, page 153, Vol. 6. It is also quoted by Imam Ahmad on page 164, Vol. 4, of his *Musnad* from hadith narrated from various authentic sources by Janadah.

Suffices you the fact that it is quoted from a chain of narrators which includes: Yahya ibn Adam, Isra'il ibn Younus and his grandfather Abu Ishaq al-Subay'i who quotes Habashi. All of these men are authorities relied upon by both Shaykhs in their respective *sahih*s. Whoever studies this hadith in Ahmad's *Musnad* will come to know that it was said during the Farewell Pilgrimage which shortly preceded the departure of the Prophet, peace be upon him and his progeny, from this vanishing world. Prior to that, he, peace be upon him and his progeny, had sent Abu Bakr to recite ten verses of SurahBara'a to the residents of Mecca, then he, according to Imam Ahmad on page 151, Vol. 1, of his *Musnad*, said to him: "Go see Abu Bakr before he discharges his mission, and as soon as you meet him, take the message from him, then carry it yourself to the people of Mecca and read it to them."

'Ali met Abu Bakr at the Juhfa and took the tablets from him. Abu Bakr went back to the Prophet, peace be upon him and his progeny, and asked him: "O Messenger of Allah! Have you received any message from Allah against me?" He answered: "No, but Gabriel has come to me and told me that nobody conveys Allah's Message except I or a man of my own family." Another narration, recorded by Ahmad on page 510, Vol. 1, of his *Musnad* from 'Ali (as), says that when the Prophet dispatched him with SurahBara'a, he said to him: "Either I should carry it, or you." 'Ali said: "If it cannot be avoided at all, then I will go." He (s) said: "Then proceed, for Allah will make your tongue firm, and He will guide your heart."

So, whither are you going? And what shall you say about these clear arguments and explicit texts?

If you carefully scrutinize this much, examine the wisdom behind making such an announcement during the supreme pilgrimage in front of the witnesses, truth will then appear to you most manifestly. And if you examine his words how few, and their meaning how encompassing, you will then have a great reverence for him, for he has learned a great deal and digested and researched what he has learned. None other than 'Ali remains to be worthy of discharging any responsibility. No wonder, then, that he, and only he, executes the Prophet's own will, taking his own position of leadership as vicegerent and vizier; praise be to Allah Who has guided us to all this, for without Allah's guidance, we would not have been thus guided.

16) Consider his statement, peace be upon him and his progeny, "Whoever obeys me obeys Allah, and whoever disobeys me disobeys Him; and whoever obeys 'Ali obeys me, too; and whoever disobeys 'Ali also disobeys me." This is recorded by al-Hakim on page 121, Vol. 3, of his *Mustadrak*, and by al-Dhahabi in his *Talkhis*. Both authors have relied on the authority of both Shaykhs to endorse this hadith.

17) Consider his statement, peace be upon him and his progeny, "O 'Ali! Whoever abandons me abandons Allah; and whoever abandons you abandons me, too." This is recorded by al-Hakim on page 124, Vol. 3, of his *Sahih*, where he comments saying: "This hadith is authentic through *isnad*, though the Shaykhs did not record it."

18) Consider his statement, peace be upon him and his progeny, as quoted by Umm Salamah, "Whoever denounces 'Ali denounces me, too," which is recorded by al-Hakim at the beginning of page 121, Vol. 3, of *Al-Mustadrak* as ascertained by both Shaykhs, and it is narrated by al-Dhahabi in his *Talkhis* where the author testifies to its authenticity.

It is recorded by Ahmad among the *ahadith* narrated by Umm Salamah on page 323, Vol. 6, of his *Musnad*, and by al-Nisa'i on page 17 of *Al-Khasa'is al-Alawiyya*, in addition to many other traditionists. So is the statement of the Messenger of Allah, peace be upon him and his progeny, as included among the ahadith narrated by 'Amr ibn Shash thus: "Whoever harms 'Ali harms me, too."[16]

19) Consider his statement, peace be upon him and his progeny, "Whoever loves 'Ali loves me, too; and whoever despises 'Ali despises me, too." This hadith is recorded by al-Hakim who describes it as authentic on page 130, Vol. 3, of *Al-Mustadrak*, and it is narrated by al-Dhahabi in his *Talkhis* where he admits reference to its authenticity for the same reason. Such is the case of 'Ali's statement:[17] "I swear by the One Who has cleft the seed [so that a plant may grow therefrom] and created the breeze from nothing, the Ummi Prophet (s) has promised me that nobody loves me except a true believer (*mu'min*), and nobody hates me except a hypocrite."[18]

---

[16] You have come to know by now the hadith narrated by 'Amr ibn Shash with our commentary in Letter 36.

[17] As quoted by Muslim in his chapter on *iman*, page 46, Vol. 1, of his *Sahih*. Ibn 'Abd al-Birr explains its gist while narrating 'Ali's biography in the *Isti'ab* from a group of companions. Buraydah's hadith has been quoted in Letter No. 36 above. His hadith, peace be upon him and his progeny, "O Allah! Befriend whoever befriends 'Ali, and be the enemy of whoever sets himself as the enemy of 'Ali" is consecutively reported (*mutawatir*), as admitted by the author of *Al-Fatawa al-Hamidiyya* in his treatise entitled "*Al-Salat al-Fakhira fil Ahadith al-Mutawatira.*"

[18] Narrated, through al-Azhar, by 'Abdul-Razzaq, Mu'ammar, al-Zuhri, 'Ubaydullah, and Ibn 'Abbas, each from the other, and all are reliable authorities. For this reason, al-Hakim, having labelled the hadith as "*sahih*" because of its endorsement by both Shaykhs, says: "Abul-Azhar, according to their consensus view, is trustworthy, and if authorities unanimously agree on the authenticity of one hadith, then it has to be held authentic," then he continues to say: "I have heard Abu 'Abdullah al-Qarashi saying that he heard Ahmad ibn Yahya al-Halwani saying: 'When Abul-Azhar came from San'a and started narrating this hadith to the people in Baghdad, Yahya ibn Ma'in rejected it. When he opened his place to the public, as usual, he inquired about the Nisaburi

20) Consider his statement, peace be upon him and his progeny, "O 'Ali! You are a leader in this life and the life hereafter; whoever loves you loves me, too, and whoever loves me is loved by Allah; your foe is my foe, and my foe is Allah's foe; woe unto whoever despises you after me."[19] This is recorded by al-Hakim at the beginning of page 128, Vol. 3, of *Al-Mustadrak*, and its authenticity is ascertained by both Shaykhs.[20]

21) Consider his statement, peace be upon him and his progeny, "O 'Ali! Glad tidings to whoever loves and believes in you, and woe unto whoever hates you and tells lies about you." This is recorded by al-Hakim on page 135, Vol. 3, of his *Al-Mustadrak*, where he comments saying: "This hadith is authentic by way of its being consecutively reported (through *isnad*, consecutive reporting). Neither shaykh records it."

22) Consider his statement, peace be upon him and his progeny, "Whoever wishes to live the way that I have lived and die the way that I shall die and reside in the Eternal Garden, which is promised to me by my Lord, let him accept 'Ali as his/her *wali*, for surely he never gets you out of guidance, nor will he ever hurl you into misguidance."

23) Consider his statement, peace be upon him and his progeny, "I enjoin whoever believes and trusts in me to be mindful

---

writer who quotes 'Abdul-Razzaq stating such ahadith, Abul-Azhar stood up and said that it was he. Yahya ibn Ma'in laughed at his statement, stood up, and brought him to sit closer to him and inquired of him about how I personally came to be the only one who heard such hadith from 'Abdul-Razzaq. I told him that I had just come from San'a, and when I bade him farewell, he told me that he owed me a unique hadith which nobody else had ever heard, and by Allah it was this hadith verbatim. Yahya ibn Ma'in then believed him and apologized to him.'"

[19] We have quoted this hadith in Letter No. 10 above.
[20] We have quoted this hadith, too, in Letter No. 10; so, refer to our commentary about it and about the one that precedes it.

of the *wilayat* of 'Ali ibn Abu Talib, for whoever accepts him as the *wali* accepts me as such, and whoever accepts me as the *wali* has indeed accepted Allah as such; and whoever loves him loves me, and whoever loves me loves Allah; and whoever hates him hates me, too, and whoever hates me hates Allah, the Almighty, the Omniscient."

24) Consider his statement, peace be upon him and his progeny, "Whoever is pleased to live my life and die my death, and then reside in the Garden of Eden, planted for me by my Lord, then let him take 'Ali as the *wali* after me, and let him accept the authority of whoever 'Ali places in charge, and let him follow the examples of my progeny after me, for they are my offspring: they are created out of my own mould and blessed with my understanding and knowledge; therefore, woe unto those who deny their favours from among my nation, who cut their ties with them; may Allah never grant them my intercession."

25) Consider his statement, peace be upon him and his progeny, "Whoever loves to live my life and die my death and enter the Garden my Lord has promised me, the Garden of Eternity, then let him take 'Ali and his descendants after him as his *walis*, for they shall never take you out of guidance, nor shall they ever drag you into misguidance."[21]

26) At the beginning of page 156, Vol. 6, of *Kanz al-'Ummal*, al-Daylami quotes Ammar citing the Messenger of Allah (s) telling 'Ammar the following: "O 'Ammar! If you see 'Ali walking on one path while other people walk on another, walk with 'Ali and leave the people, for he shall never lead you to destruction, nor shall he ever take you out of right guidance."

27) Consider his statement, peace be upon him and his progeny, according to one hadith narrated by Abu Bakr, "My hand

---

[21] Refer to our comment on this hadith and the one that precedes it in our Letter No. 10.

and 'Ali's are equal when it comes to justice." This is hadith 2539 recorded on page 153, Vol. 6, of *Kanz al-'Ummal*.

28) Consider his statement, peace be upon him and his progeny, "O Fatima! Are you not pleased that Allah, the Unique, the Sublime, has looked unto the inhabitants of the earth and chose from among them two men: one of them is your father and the other is your husband?"[22]

29) Consider his statement, peace be upon him and his progeny, "I am the Warner, and 'Ali is the Guide; through you, O 'Ali, shall guidance be attained after me." This is recorded by al-Daylami who quotes Ibn 'Abbas, and it is hadith 2631 on page 157, Vol. 6, of *Kanz al-'Ummal*.

30) Consider his statement, peace be upon him and his progeny, "O 'Ali! Nobody is permitted to remain in the state of *janaba* other than I and you."[23] Likewise is the hadith recorded by al-Tabrani as quoted by Ibn Hajar in his *Al-Sawa'iq al-Muhriqa* as narrated by Umm Salamah, al-Bazzar, and Sa'd; so, refer to hadith 13 of *Al-Arba'in al-Nawawiyya* which he quotes in Chapter 9. The latter quotes the Messenger of Allah, peace be upon him and his progeny, saying: "Nobody is permitted to be in the state of *janaba* in this mosque except I and 'Ali."

31) Consider his statement, peace be upon him and his progeny, "I and this (meaning 'Ali) are the Proofs unto my nation on the Day of Judgement." This is recorded by al-Khatib as narrated by Anas. How could the father of al-Hassan (as) be Proof just like the Prophet (s) was, had he not been his vicegerent and successor?

---

[22] This is quoted by al-Hakim on page 129, Vol. 3, of his authentic *Al-Mustadrak*, and it is narrated by quite a few authors of books and traditions, all testifying to its authenticity.

[23] Refer to our comment on this hadith in Letter No. 34, and also scrutinize the books of traditions to which we have referred.

32) Consider his statement, peace be upon him and his progeny, "It is written on the gate of Paradise: 'There is no god but Allah, Muhammad is the Messenger of Allah, 'Ali is the Brother of the Messenger of Allah.'"[24]

33) Consider his statement, peace be upon him and his progeny, "It is written on the Throne's leg: 'There is no god but Allah, Muhammad is the Messenger of Allah, I (God) have supported him (Muhammad) through 'Ali, and I have aided him through 'Ali."

34) Consider his statement, peace be upon him and his progeny, "Whoever wishes to discern Noah's determination, Adam's knowledge, Ibrahim's clemency, Moses' discretion, Christ's asceticism, then let him look unto 'Ali." This is recorded by al-Bayhaqi in his *Sahih* and by Imam Ahmad ibn Hanbal in his *Musnad*.[25]

35) Consider his statement, peace be upon him and his progeny, "O 'Ali! There is a resemblance in you to Jesus (as) who was hated by the Jews to the extent that the latter even cast doubts

---

[24] This is quoted by al-Tabrani in his *Awsat*, and by al-Khatib in his *Al-Muttafaq wal-Muftaraq*, as stated at the beginning of page 159, Vol. 6, of *Kanz al-'Ummal*. We have quoted it in Letter No. 34 and commented on it in a way which hopefully benefits the researcher.

[25] This is transmitted from both of them by Abul-Hadid in the fourth news item of his news to which he has referred on page 449, Vol. 2, of *Sharh Nahjul Balaghah*. It is also quoted by Imam al-Razi while discussing the meaning of the verse of Mubahala in his *Al-Tafsir al-Kabir*, p. 288, Vol. 2, taking for granted the authenticity of this hadith according to the views of those who act upon it as well as those who do not. This hadith is also quoted by Ibn Battah from Ibn 'Abbas's hadith, as stated on page 34 of *Fath al-Malik al-'Ali Bisihhati Babil 'Ilm 'Ali* by Imam Ahmad ibn al-Sadiq al-Hasani al-Magharibi of Cairo. Among those who have admitted that 'Ali is the one who is acquainted with the secrets of all prophets combined is the Shaykh of all men of knowledge, namely Muhiy ud-Din ibn al-'Arabi, as quoted by the learned al-Sha'rani in Section 32 of his book *Al-Yawaqit wal-Jawahir*, page 172.

about his mother's honour, and loved by the Christians to the extent that they attributed to him a status which is not his."

36) Consider his statement, peace be upon him and his progeny, "The foremost (among believers) are three: Joshua son of Nuh [of the tribe of Ephraim - tr.] who was the foremost to believe in Moses, the believer implied in Surah Yasin [Chapter 36 of the Holy Qur'an] who was the foremost to believe in Jesus, and 'Ali ibn Abu Talib who was the foremost in believing in Muhammad (s)."[26]

37) Consider his statement, peace be upon him and his progeny, "The foremost in testifying (to the Prophets' truth) are three: Habib al-Najjar, the believer implied in Surah Yasin, who said: 'O my people! Follow the Messengers (of God);' Izekiel [whose name means "Strength of God" - tr.], the believer from the family of Pharaoh, who said: 'Do you intend to kill a man just for saying that his Lord is Allah?,' and 'Ali ibn Abu Talib, who is superior to all of them."[27]

38) Consider his statement, peace be upon him and his progeny, to 'Ali: "The nation will turn treacherous to you; you shall live adhering to my faith and will be murdered for safeguarding it; whoever loves you loves me, too, and whoever hates you hates me, too, and this ('Ali's beard) will be drenched with blood from this ('Ali's head)."[28] 'Ali (as) himself has said: "One of the Prophet's predictions is that the nation will be treacherous to me after his

---

[26] This is quoted by al-Tabrani and Ibn Mardawayh who rely on the authority of Ibn 'Abbas. It is also quoted by al-Daylami from 'Ayesha, and it is one of the lengthy traditions.

[27] This is quoted by Abu Na'im and Ibn 'Asakir from Abu Layla, and quoted also by al-Najjar from Ibn 'Abbas; so, refer to ahadith 30 and 31 of the forty ahadith cited by Ibn Hajar in Part Two, Section 9, of his *Al-Sawa'iq al-Muhriqa*, at the conclusion of page 74 and the page following it.

[28] This is quoted by al-Hakim on page 122, Vol. 3, of his *Al-Mustadrak* where the author admits its authenticity. Al-Dhahabi quotes it in his own *Talkhis*, admitting its authenticity.

demise." Ibn Abbas has quoted the Messenger of Allah, peace be upon him and his progeny, telling 'Ali, "You will certainly encounter a great deal of hardship after me;"[29] 'Ali inquired: "Shall I be able to keep my faith intact?" and the Messenger of Allah, peace be upon him and his progeny, answered him in the affirmative.

39) Consider his statement, peace be upon him and his progeny, "Among you is one who will fight for its (Qur'an's) interpretation just as I fought for its revelation." The audience was very excited. Among them were Abu Bakr and 'Umar. Abu Bakr asked: "Am I the one?" and the Prophet's answer was negative. 'Umar inquired: "Is it I?" and the Prophet (s) answered: "No; but it is the one who is mending the shoes," meaning thereby 'Ali; therefore, we visited 'Ali to convey the good news to him, but he did not even raise his head, as if he had already heard it from the Messenger of Allah, peace be upon him and his progeny."[30] Similar narrative is the hadith narrated by Abu Ayyub al-Ansari during 'Umar's caliphate. According to al-Hakim, who relies on two references which he indicates on page 139 and the page that follows it, Vol. 3, of his *Mustadrak*, 'Umar has said that the Messenger of Allah, peace be upon him and his progeny, ordered those who reneged from their faith, and who dissented, to be fought. Ibn 'Asakir, as indicated in hadith 2588 on page 155, Vol.

---

[29] This hadith and the one succeeding it, i.e. Ibn 'Abbas's hadith, are quoted by al-Hakim on page 140, Vol. 3, of his *Mustadrak*, and al-Dhahabi quotes him in his *Talkhis al-Mustadrak*. Both authors admit the authenticity of this hadith due to its endorsement by both Shaykhs.

[30] This is quoted by al-Hakim on page 122, Vol. 3, of *Al-Mustadrak*, saying that it is an authentic hadith according to its endorsement by both Shaykhs who have not included it in their books. Al-Dhahabi has admitted its authenticity for the same reason when he quoted it in his *Talkhis al-Mustadrak*. Imam Ahmad has produced it from Abu Sa'id on pages 82 and 33, Vol. 3, of his *Musnad*, and al-Bayhaqi has quoted it in *Shu'ab al-Iman*. Imam Ahmad has included Abu Sa'id's hadith on pages 82 and 33, Vol. 3, of his *Musnad*, and al-Bayhaqi quotes it in his *Shu'ab al-Iman*, Sa'id ibn Mansur in his *Sunan*, Abu Na'im in his *Hilyat al-Awliya'*, and Abu Ya'li in his Sunan numbering it 2585, page 155, Vol. 6, of *Kanz al-'Ummal*.

6 of *Kanz al-'Ummal*, states that 'Ammar ibn Yasir has said that the Messenger of Allah, peace be upon him and his progeny, has said, "O 'Ali! The oppressive gang will fight you; but you are on the right track; whoever refrains from supporting you is not of me." Abu Dharr al-Ghifari, as al-Daylami is quoted at the close of page 155, Vol. 6, of *Kanz al-'Ummal*, has quoted the Messenger of Allah, peace be upon him and his progeny, saying: "I swear by the One in whose hands my life is placed that among you is a man who shall fight after me for the interpretation of the Qur'an just as I fought the polytheists for its revelation." Muhammad ibn 'Ubaydullah ibn Abu Rafi', as indicated by al-Tabrani in his *Mujma' al-Kabir* and indicated on page 155, Vol. 6, of *Kanz al-'Ummal*, has quoted his father and grandfather Abu Rafi' saying that the Messenger of Allah, peace be upon him and his progeny, has addressed him thus: "O Abu Rafi'! A group of people shall fight 'Ali after me; Allah has made mandated that they should be fought. Whoever is unable to fight them with his hands, let him fight them with his tongue; if he still is unable to do so, then by his heart." Al-Akhdar al-Ansari[31] has quoted the Messenger of Allah, peace be upon him and his progeny, saying: "I fight for the revelation of the Qur'an, while 'Ali fights for its interpretation."

40) He, peace be upon him and his progeny, has said: "O 'Ali! I am superior to you due to my being a Prophet, while you are superior to all other people due to seven merits: You are the foremost among them to believe in Allah, the most just in fulfilling Allah's Promise, the most obedient to the Commandments of Allah, the most equitable, the most fair in dealing with the public, the most far-sighted in all issues, and the one who enjoys the

---

[31] His name is Ibn Abul-Akhdar. Ibn al-Sakan mentions him and quotes this hadith in his regard from al-Harith ibn Hasirah from Jabir al-Ju'fi from Imam al-Baqir from his father Zaynul-'Abidin, peace be upon them, from al-Akhdar from the Prophet (s). Ibn al-Sakan says: "He is not quite famous among the Prophet's companions, and his traditions ought to be verified." This is quoted by al-Asqalani in his biography of al-Akhdar in *Al-Isabah*. Al-Dar Qutni has produced this hadith in his *Ifrad*, saying: "This hadith is narrated only by Jabir al-Ju'fi, who is a Rafizi."

highest status in the sight of Allah." Abu Sa'id al-Khudri quotes the Messenger of Allah, peace be upon him and his progeny, saying: "O 'Ali! You possess seven qualities about which nobody can dispute with you: You are the first to truly believe in Allah, the most just in fulfilling Allah's Promise, the most obedient to Allah's Commandments, the most compassionate to the public, the most informed of all issues, and the highest among them in status."[32]

There is no room here to quote all such traditions which, as a whole, support one another and are all indicative of one meaning, and that is: 'Ali is second only to the Messenger of Allah, peace be upon him and his progeny, in faring with this nation, and that he is next only to the Messenger of Allah, peace be upon him and his progeny, in leading it. These traditions convey such a meaning, even if their texts are not consecutively reported, and this much should suffice as an irrefutable proof, Wassalam.

Sincerely,
Sh

---

[32] Abu Na'im has quoted it among the traditions reported by Ma'ath, as well as the hadith succeeding it, that is, that of Abu Sa'id, in his *Hilyat al-Awliya'*, and they are on page 156, Vol. 6, of *Kanz al-'Ummal*.

Letter 49

Muharram 11, 1330

I. Admitting 'Ali's Merits

Imam Abu 'Abdullah Ahmad ibn Hanbal has said: "Nobody among the companions of the Messenger of Allah (s) has possessed as many virtues as 'Ali ibn Abu Talib has."[1] Ibn 'Abbas has said, "No verses of the Book of Allah have descended in honour of any man [besides the Prophet] as much as they have in honour of 'Ali."[2] On another occasion, he has said, "As many as three hundred verses of the Glorious Book of Allah, the Sublime, have been revealed in praise of 'Ali;" and yet in another instance he has said,[3] "Whenever Allah reveals 'O ye who believe...,' 'Ali is implied as their prince and dignitary; and Allah even rebuked the followers of the Messenger of Allah, peace be upon him and his progeny, on several occasions, in His precious Book while always speaking well of 'Ali." 'Abdullah ibn Ayyash ibn Abu Rabi'ah has said, "'Ali possessed a very sharp edge in knowledge; he has the seniority in embracing Islam; he is the son-in-law of the Messenger of Allah, peace be upon him and his progeny, and he is the *faqih* of his Sunnah, the hope for victory during wartime, and the most generous in giving."[4] Imam Ahmad ibn Hanbal was asked once about 'Ali and Mu'awiyah; he said:[5] "'Ali used to have quite a few

---

[1] Al-Hakim has quoted it on page 107 of his *Sahih* from *Al-Mustadrak*. Al-Dhahabi did not comment on it in his book *Talkhis al-Mustadrak*.
[2] Ibn 'Asakir, as well as many other authors of books of traditions, have all quoted it.
[3] From one hadith quoted by al-Tabrani, Ibn Abu Hatim, and many other authors of books of tradition. It is transmitted by Ibn Hajar who also quotes the three ahadith that precede it in Section 3, Chapter 9, page 76, of his *Al-Sawa'iq al-Muhriqa*.
[4] This is quoted from Ibn 'Ayyash by chroniclers and authors of sunan, and it exists where *Al-Sawa'iq al-Muhriqa* has already referred.
[5] As quoted by al-Salafi in his *Tayyuriyyat*, and it is transmitted by Ibn Hajar where we have indicated a short while ago while referring to *Al-Sawa'iq al-Muhriqa*.

enemies. His enemies looked for something whereby they could find fault with him. Having found none, they came to a man [Mu'awiyah] who had fought and killed him, and they praised that man only out of their spite of 'Ali." Isma'il the judge, al-Nisa'i, Abu 'Ali al-Nishapuri and many others have said that nobody, among all the companions of the Prophet (s), was praised as much as 'Ali was.[6]

II. Such Merits do not Necessitate his Caliphate

There is no argument about your point, yet an argument is raised if you claim that the Prophet (s), during his lifetime, had promised him the caliphate. All these texts are not bound proofs to support such a claim; they simply enumerated the imam's attributes and virtues, and the number of such texts is indeed high. We believe that he, may Allah glorify his countenance, was worthy of all of them and of even more, and I am sure you have come across several times as many such texts suggesting his nomination for the caliphate. Yet a nomination is not akin to a binding pledge for caliphate, as you know, Wassalam.

Sincerely,
S

Letter 50
Muharram 13, 1330

Why Interpret Texts on His Behalf as Indicative of His Imamate

Anyone like you, who is deep in thinking, gifted with a far insight, an authority on linguistic sources and derivatives, aware of its meanings and connotations, deriving guidance from the Messenger of Allah, peace be upon him and his progeny, believing

---

[6] This is well-known about them. Ibn Hajar has copied it at the beginning of Section 2, Chapter 9, page 72, of his *Al-Sawa'iq al-Muhriqa*

in his wisdom and conclusive prophethood, appreciative of his deeds and statements ("He does not speak of his own inclinations (Qur'an, 53:3), " certainly cannot miss the gist of such texts, nor do their conclusions, which are derived from logic and common sense, remain secret to him. It is not possible that you, the recognized authority on Arabic (i.e. *athbat*[7]) that you are, fail to perceive that these texts have all granted 'Ali a very sublime status, one which Allah Almighty and His Prophets do not grant except to the successors of such Prophets, to the ones they trust most to take charge of their religion, to the custodians of such religion. If they do not explicitly indicate the caliphate for 'Ali, they undoubtedly hint to it, leading to such conclusion by necessity. Such an obligation is quite obvious from their precise meaning. The Master of Prophets (s) is above granting such a lofty status to anyone other than his successor, his vicegerent. Yet whoever deeply scrutinizes the texts concerning 'Ali (as) and very carefully and fairly digests their implications will find their vast majority aiming at endorsing his imamate, indicative of it either through explicit announcements, such as the previously quoted ones, and such as the Covenant of al-Ghadir, or by virtue of necessity, such as the ones stated in Letter No. 48. Take, for example, his statement, peace be upon him and his progeny, "'Ali is with the Qur'an and the Qur'an is with 'Ali; they both shall never separate from each other till they meet me by the Pool [of Kawthar],"[8] and his statement, peace be upon him and his progeny, "'Ali to me is like

---

[7] "Athbat" is the plural of "thabat," and "asnad" is he plural of "sanad," and the latter means "hujjah," i.e. proof or authority.

[8] This is quoted by al-Hakim on page 124, Vol. 3, of his *Al-Mustadrak*, as well as by al-Dhahabi in his *Talkhis al-Mustadrak*. Both authors testify to its authenticity. It is one of the few elaborate ahadith. Anyone who is ignorant of the fact that 'Ali is with the Qur'an and the Qur'an is with 'Ali, after having studied the authentic traditions dealing with the Two Weighty Things, i.e. the Book and the 'Itrat (Progeny), he should be referred to what we have quoted in this regard in our Letter No. 8 above, and let him recognize the rights of the Imam of the Prophet's Progeny, and their undisputed and undoubted chief.

the head to the body,"[9] and his statement, peace be upon him and his progeny, according to a tradition narrated by 'Abdul Rahman ibn 'Awf,[10] "I swear by the One in Who hold my life, you will have to uphold the prayers, pay the zakat, or else I shall send you a man of my own self, or like my own self," then the Prophet (s) took 'Ali's hand and said: "This is he;" up to the end of countless such texts. This is an obvious benefit to which I attract the attention of all seekers of the truth, one which unveils what is ambiguous, delves deeply in independent research. He (s) has only followed what he himself comprehends of the moral obligations of such sacred texts, without being overtaken by his own personal emotions or inclinations, Wassalam.

Sincerely,
Sh

---

[9] This is quoted by al-Khatib in the ahadith narrated by al-Bara', and by al-Daylami in those narrated by Ibn 'Abbas. It is transmitted by Ibn Hajar on page 75 of his *Al-Sawa'iq al-Muhriqa*; so, refer to hadith number 35 of the forty ahadith which he quotes in Section Two, Chapter 9, of *Al-Sawa'iq al-Muhriqa*.
[10] It is hadith number 6133, page 405, Vol. 6, in *Kanz al-'Ummal*. Suffices you for a proof that 'Ali's soul is akin to that of the Prophet (s) to study the verse of Mubahala according to the explanations stated by al-Razi in his *tafsir* titled *Mafatih al-Ghayb*, page 488, Vol. 2, and refer also to what we have mentioned while dealing with this verse.

Letter 51
Muharram 14, 1330

Rebutting the Arguments Through Similar Ones

Their debaters may refute your claim by citing texts which enumerated the virtues of the three righteous caliphs, and by citing other texts praising the posterity from the Muhajirun (Meccan Immigrants) and the Ansar (Medenite Supporters); so, what would you say to that?

Sincerely,
S

Letter 52
Muharram 15, 1330

Rejecting the Rebuttal's Premises

We believe in the virtues of all posterity since the time of the Muhajirun and the Ansar, may Allah be pleased with them and they with Him, and these are beyond count or reckoning. Certain verses of the Book (Qur'an), in addition to a few Sunni *sahih* books, must suffice you for a testimony in this regard. We have scrutinized these, too. We have not found them at all, and Allah knows best, to be in contradiction to the texts that praise 'Ali (as), or even in any way eligible to disqualify him [from caliphate]. Yes, our opponents may stand alone in narrating the *ahadith* which are not authentic according to our sources. Their use of such *ahadith* to disprove our views is rejected and is not expected from any unbiased arbitrator. We by no means can take them into serious consideration. Do you not see how we do not argue by quoting the texts narrated only by our own sources? On the contrary, we base our arguments on their own narrations regarding events such as the Ghadir incident or the like. But we have scrutinized the texts pertaining to these virtues recorded by their sources, and we could not find any clues in them opposing such caliphate, nor do they contain anything suggesting it; therefore, they have not been relied upon by anyone to prove the legitimacy of the caliphate of the three righteous caliphs, Wassalam.

Sincerely,
Sh

Letter 53
Muharram 16, 1330

Requesting the Hadith Pertaining to the Ghadir Incident

You have repeatedly referred to the Ghadir incident. Please narrate its story from Sunni sources so that we may look into it, Wassalam.

Sincerely,
S

Letter 54
Muharram 18, 1330

Glitters of Ahadith Relevant to the Ghadir Incident

Relying on the consensus of narrators of hadith, al-Tabrani and many others[1] have quoted Zayd ibn Arqam saying:

> "The Messenger of Allah, peace be upon him and his progeny, once delivered a sermon at Ghadir Khumm under the shade of a few trees saying, 'O people! It seems to me that soon I will be called upon and will respond to the call.[2]

---

[1] Many renowned authorities have admitted its authenticity, so much so that even Ibn Hajar stated the same, quoting al-Tabrani and others, in the *shubha* (allegation) number 11 of the ones which he enUmarates on page 25, Section 5, Chapter One, of his book *Al-Sawa'iq al-Muhriqa*.

[2] He has eulogized his own pure soul simply to attract their attention to the fact that time had come to bring his mission to perfection, necessitating the appointment of his successor, and that he is unable to postpone doing so for fear he might be called upon [i.e. die] before discharging such mission which he is to bring to perfection, a mission that is indispensable to his nation.

I have my responsibility³ and you have yours;⁴ so, what do you say?' They said: 'We bear witness that you have conveyed the Message, struggled and advised [the nation]; therefore, may Allah reward you with the best of His rewards.' He asked them: 'Do not you also bear witness that there is no god but Allah and that Muhammad is His Servant and Messenger, that His Paradise is just and that His Fire is just, that death is just, that the life after death is just, that the Hour will undoubtedly approach, and that Allah shall bring the dead to life from their graves?' They said: 'Yes, indeed, we do bear witness to all of that.' He said: 'O Mighty Lord! Bear witness that they have.' Then he said: 'O people! Allah is my Master, and I am the *mawla* (master) of the believers. I have more authority over their lives then they themselves have;⁵ therefore, to whomsoever I have been a *mawla*, this

---

[3] Since the appointment of his brother weighs heavily against those who compete, envy, create dissension and hypocrisy, he, peace be upon him and his progeny, desired, before making such an announcement, to first apologize to them in the hope that that might touch and unify their hearts and in apprehension of their speeches and deeds; he said: "And I am responsible," so that they might come to know that he receives orders, and that he is responsible to discharge them; therefore, he simply has to do so. Imam al-Wahidi, in his book *Asbabul Nuzul*, quotes Abu Sa'id al-Khudri saying: "The verse 'O Messenger! Convey that which has been revealed unto you from your Lord' was revealed on Ghadir Khumm day in reference to 'Ali ibn Abu Talib (as)."

[4] By saying "You, too, are responsible," he, peace be upon him and his progeny, may have implied, as quoted by al-Daylami and others and stated in *Al-Sawa'iq al-Muhriqa* and other books from Ibn Sa'id, that they should follow in their footsteps, since they are responsible regarding 'Ali's *wilayat*. Imam al-Wahidi has said: "They are responsible regarding the *wilayat* of 'Ali and Ahl al-Bayt." Thus, the purpose of his saying "and you, too, are responsible" is to threaten those who would dispute the authority of his *wali* and *wasi*.

[5] Many have contemplated upon this sermon, giving it due attention, and they have come to know that its gist is nothing other than a reference to the fact that 'Ali's *wilayat* is as much a root of the faith as his own responsibility as the Imam, for the Prophet (s) first put the question: "Do not you bear witness that there is no god but Allah, and that Muhammad is His Servant and Messenger?" Then he said: "The Hour is approaching; there is no doubt about it, and Allah shall certainly bring to life those who are in the graves," following that with a statement in which he mentioned the *wilayat* so that it would be understood that

('Ali) is his *mawla*;⁶ O Lord! Befriend whoever befriends him, and be an enemy of whoever sets himself as his enemy.' Then he said: 'O people! I am to precede you, and you shall join me, at the Pool [of Kawthar] which is wider than the distance from Basra to San'a; it contains as many silver cups as the stars; and I shall ask you when you join me about the Two Weighty Things, how you shall succeed me in faring with them; the Greatest Weighty Thing is the Book of Allah, the Omniscient, the Sublime, one end of which is in Allah's hand and the other in yours; so, uphold it so that you may not go astray, and your faith shall not suffer any alteration; and the other are my Ahl al-Bayt, for the most Gracious and Knowing has informed me that they both shall never part from each other till they join me at the Pool.'"⁷

In a section dealing with 'Ali's virtues in *Al-Mustadrak*, the author indicates that Zayd ibn Arqam⁸ is quoted through two sources both of which are held reliable by both Shaykhs: al-Hakim [one of such sources] says that when the Messenger of Allah, peace be upon him and his progeny, returned from his Farewell Pilgrimage, he camped at Ghadir Khumm and ordered the believers to sweep the area under a few huge trees where a pulpit of camel litters was made for him. He stood and said: "It seems as if I have been called upon and responded to the call, and I enjoin

---

the latter bears the same significance like the matters about which he has asked them and to which they have agreed. This is obvious to all the discreet who are familiar with the methods and objectives of speech.

⁶ His statement: "I am the mawla" is an outspoken testimony to a significant fact. The meaning of "mawla" is: one who is "awla," foremost in status, superior. Thus, the meaning of his statement is: "Allah is superior to me, and I am superior to the believers, and whoever considers me to be superior to him must also consider 'Ali as such."

⁷ This wording of the hadith is quoted by al-Tabrani, Ibn Jarir, al-Hakim al-Tirmizi, from Zayd ibn Arqam. It is transmitted by Ibn Hajar from al-Tabrani and others in this exact wording, without questioning its authenticity; so, refer to page 25 of *Al-Sawa'iq al-Muhriqa*.

⁸ Refer to page 21 of *Al-Khasa'is al-'Alawiyya*, where the Prophet (s) is quoted saying: "To whomsoever I have been the *wali*, this ('Ali) is his *wali*.

you to look after both the Book of Allah and my Progeny; see how you fare with them after me, for they shall never part from each other till they join me at the Pool." Then he added: "Allah, the Dear and Mighty, is my Master, and I am the master of every believer," then he took 'Ali by the hand and said: "To whomsoever I have been a master, this 'Ali is [henceforth] his master; O Lord! Befriend whoever befriends him, and be the enemy to whoever antagonizes him." The author quotes this lengthy *hadith* in its entirety. In his *Talkhis*, al-Dhahabi quotes it without commenting on it. Al-Hakim, too, quotes it as narrated by Zayd ibn Arqam in his *Al-Mustadrak*, admitting its authenticity. In spite of his intolerance, al-Dhahabi admits the same in his *Talkhis*, to which you may refer.

Imam Ahmad ibn Hanbal has quoted the same hadith as narrated by Zayd ibn Arqam thus:

> "We were in the company of the Messenger of Allah, peace be upon him and his progeny, when he camped in a valley called Wadi Khumm, and he ordered everyone to gather for prayers in midday heat. He then delivered a sermon to us under the shade of a robe over a rush tree [*Juncus spinosus*] to protect him from the heat of the sun. He said: 'Do you know - or do you bear witness - that I have more authority over a believer's life than the believer himself has?' They answered: 'Yes, indeed, you do.' He said: 'Whosoever accepts me as his *mawla*, 'Ali is his *mawla*; O Lord! Befriend whosoever befriends 'Ali and be the enemy of whomsoever opposes 'Ali.'"

Al-Nisa'i quotes Zayd ibn Arqam saying that when the Prophet (s) returned from the Farewell Pilgrimage, and having reached Ghadir Khumm, he ordered the ground under a few huge trees to be swept clean. He announced: "It looks like I have been invited [to my Lord's presence] and I have accepted the invitation, and I am leaving with you the Two Weighty Things, one of them is bigger than the other: the Book of Allah and my Progeny, my Household; so, see how you succeed me in faring with both of them, for they shall never part from each other till they join me at the Pool." Then he added: "Allah is my Master, and I am the master (*mawla*) of every believer." Taking 'Ali's hand, he added saying, "To whomsoever I have been a master, this 'Ali is his master; O Lord! Befriend those who befriend him, and be the enemy of all those who antagonize him." Abul-Tufail says: "I asked Zayd: 'Have you heard these words of the Messenger of Allah, peace be upon him and his progeny, yourself?'"[9] He answered that all those who were there under the huge trees had seen the Prophet with their own eyes and heard him with their own ears. This hadith is recorded by Muslim in a chapter on the attributes of 'Ali in his *Sahih* from several different narrators ending with Zayd ibn Arqam, but he abridged it and cut it short - and so do some people behave.

Imam Ahmad has recorded this hadith from al-Bara' ibn 'Azib[10] from two avenues saying; it reads: "We were in the

---

[9] Abul-Tufayl's question is obviously indicative of his amazement at this nation's overlooking this matter regarding 'Ali in spite of the hadith it narrates from its Prophet (s) in his honor on the day of the Ghadir. As if suspicious of the accuracy of the narrated hadith, he went ahead and inquired of Zayd, having heard him narrate the same, "Did you hear it from the Messenger of Allah?!" His tone is that of someone amazed, bewildered, and skeptical. Zayd answered him that all individuals present under those trees had, indeed, seen the Prophet with their eyes and heard him with their ears; so, Abul-Tufayl then knew that the matter was just as al-Kumait, may Allah be merciful unto his soul, says:

On the day of the *dawh*, the *dawh* of the Ghadir,
Caliphate was made for him manifest and clear,
Only if the throngs opted to obey;
Yet I have never seen such a day,
Nor have I seen such right
Trampled upon, discarded outright;
But the men had sold it, and I never saw
Such a precious thing to sale would go...

[10] This occurs on page 281 of his *Al-Khasa'is al-'Alawiyya*, in a chapter dealing with 'Ali's status in the eyes of Allah, the Exalted, the omni-Scient, and also on

company of the Messenger of Allah (s) when we camped at Ghadir Khumm. The call for congregational prayers was made. The site of two trees was chosen, and it was swept clean. He performed the noon-time prayers then took 'Ali by the hand and asked the crowd: 'Do you not know that I have more authority over the believers than the believers themselves have?' They answered: 'Yes, we do.' He asked: 'Do you know that I have more authority over every believer than the believer himself has?' They answered in the affirmative; then he took 'Ali's hand and said: 'Whoever has accepted me as his master, this 'Ali is his master; O Lord! Befriend whoever befriends him and be the enemy of whoever chooses to be his enemy.' 'Umar met him immediately following that and said to him: 'Congratulations to you, son of Abu Talib! You have become, at dawn and at sunset, the master of every believing man and woman.'"

Al-Nisa'i has quoted 'Ayisha daughter of Sa'd saying that she heard her father saying: "I have heard the Messenger of Allah, peace be upon him and his progeny, on the Day of Juhfa, when he took 'Ali's hand and delivered a sermon, praised and adored Allah, then said: 'O people! I am your *wali*.' They said: 'You have said the truth.' Then he raised 'Ali's hand and said: 'This is my *wali* unto you to discharge the responsibilities of my religion on my own behalf, and I support whoever supports him and am the enemy of whosoever chooses to be his enemy.'"

Sa'd is also quoted saying: "We were in the company of the Messenger of Allah (s). When he arrived at Ghadir Khumm, those who went ahead of him returned to join him, while he waited for those who lagged behind, till all people assembled. Then he said: 'O people! Who is your *wali*?' They answered: 'Allah and His Messenger.' Then he took 'Ali's hand, made him rise and said: 'Whoever has taken Allah and His Messenger as his *wali*, this ('Ali) is his *wali*; O Lord! Befriend whoever befriends him and be the enemy of whoever chooses to be his enemy.'"

---

page 25 of another chapter enjoining acceptance of his *wilayat* and warning against bearing animosity towards him.

The books of traditions recording this incident are numerous and cannot be all cited here. They all contain explicit texts indicating that Ali is the Prophet's vicegerent and successor, just as al-Fadl ibn al-Abbas Abu Lahab has said:[11]

> The one to be recognized as the Vicegerent, generation after generation,
> After Muhammad, is 'Ali; for he was his companion in every occasion.

Sincerely,
Sh

---

[11] These are among poetic lines composed as the answer of al-Walid ibn 'Uqbah ibn Abu Ma'it, quoted by Muhammad Mahmud al-Rafi'i in his Introduction to *Sharh al-Hashimiyyat*, page 8.

Letter 55
Muharram 19, 1330

Why Use it as a Testimonial if not Transmitted Consecutively?

Shi'as apply the principle of consecutive reporting when discussing imamate, due to the fact that they consider consecutive reporting as one of the principles of faith; so why do you quote the Ghadir hadith in support of your argument although such hadith is not consecutively reported according to Sunnis, even if its authenticity is attested to by their *sahih*s?

Sincerely,
S

Letter 56
Muharram 22, 1330

Suffices to prove its application as an argument what we have mentioned in Letter No. 24 above.

I. Natural Laws Necessitate the Consecutive Reporting of Hadith al-Ghadir

The consecutive reporting of the Ghadir hadith is necessitated by the natural laws which Allah has created. Its similitude is like that of any great historical step undertaken by the most important man of a nation who announces, in the presence of thousands of his nationals, the undertaking of a major step, so that they may convey its news to various lands and nations, especially if such an undertaking enjoys the concern of his own family and their supporters in all generations to come, so that such an announcement might receive the widest possible publicity. Can such an announcement, as significant as it is, be transmitted by, say, just one single person? Certainly not. Its news would spread as widely as the early morning sun rays, encompassing the plains as well as the oceans; "And you shall never find any alteration to Allah's order (Qur'an, 33:62)."

II. The Almighty's Benevolence

Hadith al-Ghadir has won the divine concern of Allah, the Dear One, the Sublime, Who inspired to His Messenger, peace be upon him and his progeny, including it in His Qur'an which is recited by Muslims even during the late hours of the night or the early hours of the day, in public and in private, in their supplications and ceremonial prayers, from the top of their pulpits and the heights of their minarets, stating:

> "O Messenger! Convey that which has been revealed unto you from your Lord, and if you do not do so, then you have not conveyed His Message at all, and Allah will protect you from (evil) men." (Qur'an, 5:67)[1]

---

[1] We do not dispute its revelation in reference to 'Ali's *wilayat* on Ghadir Khumm Day, and our narratives from the sources of the purified progeny are consecutive. Suffices you for reference to its narration by others besides the latter what Imam al-Wahid has quoted in his exegesis of Surahal-Ma'ida on page 150 of his book *Asbabul Nuzul* from two respected sources: 'Atiyyah and Abu Sa'id al-Khudri. The author says: "This verse [that is, the one reading: "O Messenger! Convey that which has been revealed unto you from your Lord"] was revealed on Ghadir Khumm Day in reference to 'Ali ibn Abu Talib (as)." The same is narrated by al-Hafiz Abu Na'im who interprets it in his book *Nuzul al-Qur'an* relying on two sources one of which is Abu Sa'id and the other is Abu Rafi'. It is also narrated by Imam Ibrahim ibn Muhammad al-Hamawaini al-Shafi'i in his book *Al-Fawa'id* from various sources ending with Abu Hurayrah. It is quoted by Imam Abu Ishaq al-Tha'labi while explaining the meaning of this verse in his *Al-Tafsir al-Kabir* from two respected sources. What testifies to its reference to 'Ali (as) is the fact that prayers had been already established, *zakat* was enforced, fasting was legislated, the pilgrimage to the House was being conducted, what is permissible was clarified and so was what is forbidden, the Shari'ah was already regulated and its injunctions enforced; so, what else required Allah to place so much emphasis other than on the issue of caliphate, one which prompted Him to pressure His Prophet in a way which was almost similar to threatening? And regarding what, if not caliphate, could the Prophet (s) feel presentiment of dissension if he did not convey it, something which

When he, peace be upon him and his progeny, conveyed the divine Message (implied in this verse), appointing 'Ali as the Imam and entrusting him with the caliphate, Allah Almighty revealed the following verse:

"Today have I perfected your religion (Islam) for you, completed my blessing unto you, and accepted Islam as your religion." (Qur'an, 5:3)[2]

So, congratulations upon congratulations to 'Ali; this is Allah's favour; He grants it to whomsoever He pleases. Anyone who looks into these verses will be profoundly impressed by such divine favours.

III. Concern of the Messenger of Allah (s)

If divine concern is as such, no wonder, then, that the Messenger of Allah, peace be upon him and his progeny, expressed such a profound concern when death approached him, may my life be sacrificed for his sake. It was then that, according to the order which he received from Allah Almighty, he set to announce 'Ali's *wilayat* during his supreme pilgrimage, in the presence of so many witnesses, without being satisfied with similar previous announcements such as his warning in Mecca, or on other occasions with some of which you have by now become familiar. He, therefore, invited the believers to participate in his very last pilgrimage, known as the Farewell Pilgrimage. People from far and wide responded to his invitation, and no less than one hundred

---

required God's own immunity against any harm that might result from discharging it?

[2] *sahih*s documenting the occasion that necessitated the revelation of this verse are consecutive from the sources of the purified progeny (as). We do not doubt what the purified progeny of Muhammad (s) narrates even when al-Bukhari claims that the verse was revealed on the day of 'Arafat, for the members of the Prophet's house know what is revealed in their house.

thousand pilgrims left Medina with him.³ On the standing day at 'Arafat, he informed the attendants that: "'Ali is of me, and I am of 'Ali, and nobody discharges the responsibility [of my religion] on my behalf except I and 'Ali."⁴ And when he came back from the pilgrimage and arrived at the valley of Khumm, trusted Gabriel descended upon him with "*ayat al-tabligh*", verse of conveying the Message, from the Lord of the Worlds. Immediately thereupon, he alighted there till those who lagged behind him, as well as those who went ahead of him, joined him. When they all assembled, he conducted the obligatory prayers then delivered a sermon about Allah, the Dear and the Omniscient, emphasizing the significance of 'Ali's *wilayat*. You have already heard a glittering report of its news, and what you have not heard is even more exact and more explicit; yet what you have heard should suffice you. Its news was carried on behalf of the Messenger of Allah, peace be upon him and his progeny, by all those masses who were present with him there and then and who are estimated to have been over one hundred thousand pilgrims from various lands.

The order of Allah, the Dear and Sublime, which does not suffer any alteration in His creation, necessitates the consecutive reporting of this hadith in spite of all obstacles in conveying it. Yet the Imams of Ahl al-Bayt (as) follow their own wise methods of disseminating it and publicizing for it.

IV. Concern of the Commander of the Faithful

---

[3] Sayyid Ahmad Zayni Dahlan, in a chapter on the Farewell Pilgrimage in his book *Al-Sirah al-Nabawiyya* [Biography of the Prophet], writes: "Ninety thousand - some say a hundred and twenty-four thousand, while others say more - accompanied him, peace be upon him and his progeny, from Medina, and this is just a rough figure of the number of people who accompanied him," to the end of his statement from which you come to know that those who went back with him were more than a hundred thousand, and they all witnessed the Ghadir hadith.

[4] We have quoted this hadith in our Letter No. 48; so, if you refer to it, you will find it *verbatim* numbered 15 in the said reference; the same Letter refers to and comments on it in a way worthy of the attention of researchers.

Referring to the latter, I suggest that you may consider the measure taken by the Commander of the Faithful (as), then Caliph, in gathering people in the spacious meeting place, the Rahba plain. He then said: "I ask in the Name of Allah each Muslim who heard what the Messenger of Allah (s) said on the Ghadir Day to stand and testify to what he heard. Nobody should stand except those who saw the Prophet with their own eyes and heard him with their own ears." Thirty *sahabis*, twelve of whom had participated in the Battle of Badr, stood and testified that the Prophet (s) took 'Ali by the hand and asked people: "Do you know that I have more authority over the believers than the believers themselves have?" They answered in the affirmative. He, peace be upon him and his progeny, then said: "To whomsoever I have been *mawla*, this ('Ali) is his *mawla*; O Lord! Befriend whoever befriends him, and be the enemy of whosoever chooses to be his enemy." You know that accusing thirty *sahabis* of being liars is rejected by reason; therefore, the achievement of consecutive reporting through their testimony is an irrefutable and undeniable proof.

The same hadith was transmitted from those thirty *sahabis* by all those crowds who were then present at the Rahba, and who disseminated it after their dispersal throughout the land, thus providing it with extremely wide publicity. Obviously, the Rahba incident took place during the caliphate of the Commander of the Faithful (as) who received the oath of allegiance in the year 35 A.H. The Ghadir event took place during the Farewell Pilgrimage, 10 A.H. The time period separating the first date from the second is twenty-five years during which many events took place such as a devastating plague, wars, the opening of new countries, and the invasions contemporary to the three righteous caliphs. This time period, one fourth of a century, merely due to its duration, wars and invasions, in addition to a sweeping and devastating plague, had ended the lives of many of those who had witnessed the Ghadir event, especially the elderly among the *sahabah* as well as their youths who were eager to meet their Lord through conducting *jihad* in His way, the Exalted, the Omniscient, and in the way of His Messenger, peace be upon him and his progeny, so much so that their dead outnumbered their survivors. Some of them were scattered throughout the land, and many of those were not present at the Rahba except those who kept company with the Commander of the Faithful (as) in Iraq, and these were only males. In spite of all this, thirty *sahabah*, twelve of whom were participants in the Battle of Badr, had heard hadith al-Ghadir from the Messenger of Allah, peace be upon him and his progeny.

There may have been others who hated to testify, such as Anas ibn Malik[5] and others who received their due punishment in lieu of the prayers of the Commander of the Faithful to Allah to punish those who hid the truth while knowing it. Had he been able to gather all *sahabis* who were alive then, males and females, and address them in the same way which he employed at Rahba, several times that many would have testified; so, what if he had asked people in Hijaz before the passage of such a long time after the incident of the Ghadir? Contemplate upon this fact and you will find it a very strong proof testifying to the consecutive reporting of hadith al-Ghadir.

The books of tradition should suffice you in their documentation of hadith al-Ghadir. Take, for example, what Imam Ahmad has quoted on page 370, Vol 4, of his *Musnad* from Abul Tufayl who has said: "'Ali gathered people at the Rahba, then he said to them: 'I adjure in the name of Allah every Muslim who heard what the Messenger of Allah, peace be upon him and his progeny, had said on the Ghadir Day to state his testimony.' Thirty persons stood up." Abu Na'im has said: "Many stood up and

---

[5] He, peace be upon him, said to him then: "Why don't you stand with other companions of the Messenger of Allah (s) and testify to what you heard of him then?" He answered: "O Commander of the Faithful! I have grown old, and I have forgotten it." 'Ali (as) said: "If you are telling a lie, then may Allah strike you with a white [disease, i.e. leprosy] which your turban cannot conceal." He hardly left before his face was filled with the marks of leprosy; so, he used to say: "I have become the object of a curse invoked by the Righteous Servant." This incident is quite famous, and a testimony for its authenticity exists when Imam Ahmad ibn Hanbal quotes it at the end of page 119, Vol. 1, of his *Musnad*, adding: "They all, except three men, rose to testify; and those three fell under the effect of his curse."

testified how the Prophet (s) took 'Ali by the hand and asked people: 'Do you know that I have more authority over the believers than the believers themselves have?' They answered: 'We do, O Messenger of Allah!' Then he said: 'To whomsoever I have been a *mawla*, this 'Ali is his *mawla*; O Lord! Befriend whoever befriends him and be the enemy of whoever sets himself as his enemy.'" Abul-Tufail continues to say: "I left the place dismayed (disgusted with many people's ignorance of this hadith), and I met Zayd ibn Arqam and said to him: 'I have heard 'Ali say such and such.' Zayd said: 'Then do not deny that you have heard the Messenger of Allah, peace be upon him and his progeny, say so about him.'"

Zayd's testimony stated above, and 'Ali's statement in this regard, may be added to the testimony of the thirty *sahabis*, thus bringing the number of narrators of this hadith to thirty-two *sahabis*. Imam Ahmad has recorded 'Ali's hadith on page 119, Vol. 1, of his *Musnad* as transmitted by Abdul-Rahman ibn Abu Layla. The latter says: "I saw 'Ali at the Rahba abjuring people to testify, emphasizing that only those who had seen and heard the Prophet (s) should stand and testify. Twelve participants in the Battle of Badr, whom I remember so well as if I am looking at them right now, did so." Abdul-Rahman quotes the latter testifying that they had all heard the Messenger of Allah, peace be upon him and his progeny, asking people on the Ghadir Day: "Do not I have more authority over the believers' lives than they themselves do, and my wives are their mothers?" The audience responded: "Yes, indeed, O Messenger of Allah!" Then he said, as Abdul-Rahman quotes him, "Then whosoever takes me as his *mawla* must take 'Ali as his *mawla*; O Mighty Lord! Befriend whoever befriends him and be the enemy of whoever bears animosity towards him!"

Another narration is recorded by imam Ahmad on the same page. It quotes the Prophet (s) saying: "O Lord! Befriend whoever takes him as his *wali* and be the enemy of whoever antagonizes him; support whoever supports him, and abandon whoever abandons him." The narrative goes on to state that with the exception of three men, the witnesses stood to testify. 'Ali invoked Allah to curse those who hid the truth, and his invocation was heeded. If you add 'Ali and Zayd ibn Arqam to the aforementioned twelve participants in the Battle of Badr, then fourteen is obviously the number of witnesses. By tracing the traditions regarding the Rahba incident, 'Ali's wisdom becomes manifest in disseminating hadith al-Ghadir and publicizing for it.

V. al-Husain's Concern

The Master of Martyrs, Abu Abdullah al-Husain, peace be upon him, has left us a legacy of a very memorable stand which he took during the reign of Mu'awiyah. It was then that truth became manifest. It was similar to the stand taken by 'Ali at the Rahba. During the pilgrimage season, al-Husain (as), surrounded by throngs of pilgrims, praised his grandfather, father, mother and brother, and delivered an unprecedented, wise and eloquent speech that captivated his audience and won their hearts and minds. His sermon was inclusive, one wherein he reawakened the masses, traced and researched history, and paid the Ghadir incident its fair and just dues. His great stand, therefore, produced great results, and it became equivalent to hadith al-Ghadir in its fame and wide publicity.

VI. Concern of the Nine Imams (as)

His nine descendants, all sinless Imams, applied their own methods to publicizing and propagating the same hadith. Their methods reflect their wisdom which is comprehended by all those who possess sound senses. They used the eighteenth of Dhul-Hijjah as a special annual feast to congratulate and congratulate one another, merrily and humbly seeking nearness to Allah, the Exalted, the Mighty, through fasting, prayers and supplications. They go beyond limits in their deeds of goodness and acts of righteousness, thanking Allah for the blessings which He bestowed upon them on that Day by virtue of the text that nominated the Commander of the Faithful (as) as Caliph, and His divine promise for him to be the Imam. They used to visit their kin, give more generously to their families, visit their brethren, look after their neighbours, and enjoin their followers to do likewise.

VII. Shi'as' Concern

For this reason, the eighteenth of Dhul-Hijjah of every year is celebrated as a feast by the Shi'as of all times and climes.[6] It is then that they rush to their mosques to offer obligatory and supererogatory prayers, recite the Glorious Qur'an, and read the most celebrated supplications as a token of thanking Allah Almighty for perfecting His religion and completing His blessings upon them by nominating the Commander of the Faithful (as) as the Imam [in the theological as well as the secular sense]. It is then that they exchange visits and happily wish each other the best, seeking nearness to Allah through righteousness and goodness, and through pleasing their kin and neighbours. On that day, every year, they visit the mausoleum of the Commander of the Faithful (as), where no less than a hundred thousand pilgrims come from far and wide. There, they worship Allah on that day in the same way their purified Imams used to worship Him: through fasting, prayers, and remembrance of Allah. They seek nearness to Him through acts of righteousness and the payment of *sadaqat*. They do not disperse before addressing the sacred shrine with a highly commended address authored by some of their Imams. It includes testifying to the glorious stand taken by the Commander of the Faithful (as), honouring his feats and struggle to lay the foundations of the principles of the faith, his service of the Master of Prophets and Messengers (s), and his virtues and merits, among which was the honour which he had received from the Prophet on the Ghadir Day. This is the custom of the Shi'as every year. Their orators have always been referring to hadith al-Ghadir, quoting its tradition or even without reference to them, and their poets are accustomed to

---

[6] Ibn al-Athir, while narrating the significant events that took place in the year 352 in his *Kamil*, says the following on page 181, Vol. 8, of his history book: "On the eighteenth of Dhul-Hijjah of that year, Mu'izz al-Dawla ordered decorations to be installed in Baghdad, fires to be lit at the police quarters, and all merriments be displayed; so, market-places were opened at night just as is customary during Eid nights; he did all that to celebrate Eid al-Ghadir, Ghadir Khumm. Drums were beaten; and trumpets were sounded, and it was quite a memorable day."

compose poems in its commemoration in old as well as modern times;[7] therefore, there is no way to cast doubts about its being consecutively reported from the sources of Ahl al-Bayt (as) and their Shi'as. Their motives to memorize it by heart, their efforts to maintain its pristine text, safeguard its authenticity, publicize and disseminate it.., all have indeed resulted in the achievement of their most aspired objectives. Refer to all the four major Shi'a *Musnad*s, as well as other Shi'a references, containing well-documented and supported traditions, and you will find each one of them reverberating with the same meaning, and each tradition supporting the other. Whoever acquaints himself with these traditions will find out that this hadith is *mutawatir* through their precious sources.

VIII. Its Consecutive Reporting Through the Masses

There is no doubt about its being consecutively reported through Sunni sources, according to natural laws, as you have come to know; "Allah's creation suffers no alteration; this is the Right Guidance, but most people do not know." (Qur'an, 30:30) The author of *Al-Fatawa al-Hamidiyya*, in spite of his

---

[7] Al-Kumait ibn Zayd has said:

On the day of the *dawh*, the Ghadir *dawh* day,
Caliphate was made manifest for him: were they to obey...
Abu Tammam, in a poetic masterpiece which he includes in his *diwan*, says:

On the Day of Ghadir, truth looked clear and bright;
Redolently, with no curtains nor bars to hide;
The Messenger of Allah stood there to invite
Them to come close to what is just and right,
Gesturing with his hands, introducing your *wali*
And *mawla*; yet see what happened to you and me!
He brings the news to people so eloquently,
While they come with grudge and depart grudgingly,
Yet he made the truth eloquently shine,
While they usurped even your right and mine.
You made its destiny the sharp blades of your sword:
And the grave for whoever wanted the truth to uphold...

stubbornness, admits the consecutive reporting of this hadith in his abridged dissertation titled *Al-Salawat al-Fakhira fil Ahadith al-Mutawatira*." Al-Sayyuti and other scholars of exegesis all admit the same. Refer to Muhammad ibn Jarir al-Tabari, author of the famous works titled "Tafsir" and "Tarikh," Ahmad ibn Muhammad ibn Sa'id ibn Aqdah, Muhammad ibn Ahmad ibn 'Uthman al-Dhahabi, have all written critiques of the sources of this hadith. Each one of them has written an entire book on this subject. Ibn Jarir includes in his own book as many as one hundred and five sources for this hadith alone.[8] Al-Dhahabi, in spite of his fanaticism, has testified to the truth of many of its sources. In chapter sixteen of *Ghayat al-Maram*, as many as eighty ahadith transmitted by Sunnis testify to the authenticity of the Ghadir hadith. Yet he did not quote al-Tirmizi, al-Nisai, al-Tabrani, al-Bazzar, Abu Ya'li, or quite a few other reporters who transmit this hadith. Al-Sayyuti quotes this hadith while discussing 'Ali in his book *Tarikh al-Khulafa*' transmitted by al-Tirmizi, adding, "This hadith is also recorded by Ahmad as transmitted by 'Ali (as), and also by Ayyub al-Ansari, Zayd ibn Arqam, 'Umar [ibn al-Khattab], and Thu Murr. Abu Ya'li quotes it from Abu Hurayrah, al-Tabrani from Ibn 'Umar and from Ibn Abbas as transmitted by Malik ibn al-Huwayrith, Habshi ibn Janadah, and Jarir, and also by Ammarah and Buraydah."

A proof of the fame of this hadith is evident from the fact that imam Ahmad records it in his *Musnad* from Riyah ibn al-Harish as transmitted by two sources. It states that a group of men once came to 'Ali (as) and said: "Assalamu Alaikum, our *mawla*." The Imam asked who they were, and they answered him by saying that they

---

[8] The author of *Ghayat al-Maram* says near the conclusion of Chapter 16, page 89, of his book: "Ibn Jarir has quoted the Ghadir hadith from ninety-five sources in a book which he dedicated to this subject, calling it *Al-Wilayat*, and Ibn 'Uqdah has quoted it from one hundred and five sources written down in a book which he also dedicated solely for this subject-matter. Imam Ahmad ibn Muhammad ibn al-Siddiq al-Magharibi has stated that both al-Dhahabi and Ibn 'Uqdah have dedicated a special book solely for this hadith;" so, refer to the sermon in his valuable book titled *Fath al-Malik al-'Ali Bisihhati Babil 'Ilm 'Ali*.

were his subjects. The Imam asked them: "How can I be your *mawla*, while you are [stranger] bedouin Arabs?" They said: "We have heard the Messenger of Allah, peace be upon him and his progeny, on the Ghadir Day saying: 'Whoever I have been his *mawla*, 'Ali is his *mawla*.'" Riyah says that when they left, he followed them and asked them who they were, and that they said to him: "We are a group of the Ansar (Medenite Supporters) in the company of Abu Ayyub al-Ansari." Another proof of its fame is what has been recorded by Abu Ishaq al-Tha'labi while explaining Surah al-Ma'arij in his book *Al-Tafsir al-Kabir*, relying on two very highly respected sources, and stating the following:

The Messenger of Allah, peace be upon him and his progeny, ordered people on the Ghadir Day to assemble, then he took 'Ali's hand and said: "Whoever accepts me as his *mawla*, 'Ali is his *mawla*." The news of this announcement spread throughout the land, and al-Nu'man al-Fahri came to know about this hadith. Riding his she-camel, he came to meet the Messenger of Allah, peace be upon him and his progeny. Having alighted, he said the following to the Prophet: "O Muhammad! You ordered us to bear witness that there is no deity except Allah and that you are the Messenger of Allah, and we obeyed; then you ordered us to offer prayers five times a day, and we agreed; then you ordered us to pay *zakat*, and we agreed; then you ordered us to fast during the month of Ramadan and we agreed; then you ordered us to perform the pilgrimage and we agreed; then, as if all of this is not sufficient, you favoured your cousin to all of us and said 'Whoever accepts me as his *mawla*, 'Ali is his *mawla*;' is this one of your own orders, or is it Allah's?" He, peace be upon him and his progeny, answered: "I swear by the One and only God that this is the command of Allah, the Exalted and Omniscient;" whereupon al-Harith left heading towards his animal murmuring softly to himself: "O Lord! If what Muhammad (s) says is true, then let it rain stones, or let a severe torment descend upon us." He hardly reached his animal before Allah caused a stone to cleave his head, penetrate his body and come out of his anus, leaving him dead on the spot. It is in reference to that incident that Allah Almighty revealed the following verse:

> "A man who brought a question (to the Prophet) asked for a sure penalty - which cannot be warded off by those who reject the truth - from Allah, Lord of the Ways of Ascent."[9] (Qur'an, 70:1-3)

This is how the tradition, quoted *verbatim*,[10] concludes. Its authenticity is accepted by many Sunni scholars as a common fact, Wassalam.

Sincerely,
Sh

---

[9] This is quoted from al-Tha'labi by a group of Sunni dignitaries such as scholar al-Shiblinji of Egypt in a biography of 'Ali in his book *Nurul Absar*; so, you may refer to its eleventh page if you wish.

[10] Refer to what al-Halabi has quoted of the narratives related to the Farewell Pilgrimage in his book of biography known as *Al-Sira al-Halabiyya* and you will find this hadith at the end of page 214 of its third volume.

Letter 57
Muharram 25, 1330

I. Interpreting Hadith al-Ghadir

Believing in the truthfulness of the sahabah requires interpreting hadith al-Ghadir, whether it is consecutively reported or not. For this reason, Sunnis have claimed that "mawla" bears various meanings all of which have been applied in the Holy Qur'an. It may mean "the deserving," as the Almighty says when He addresses the infidels: "Your resort is the Fire; it is your mawla," meaning "You deserve the punishment of the Fire." Another meaning is "the supporter," as Allah, praised be His Name, says: "It is so because Allah is the mawla of those who believe, and the infidels have no mawla." It also means "the heir," as in the statement of the Almighty: "For each We have assigned *mawali* [mawlas] from the inheritance of the parents and the relatives," meaning heirs. It also means "relatives," as is clearly understood from the following verse of the Dear and Mighty One: "I fear the mawali after me," meaning relatives. It also means "friend," as the verse suggests: "On that Day, no mawla will be able to do any good to his mawla." "Wali" also connotes the person who is most qualified to fare with someone else's affairs, as we may say: "Mr. so and so is the wali of the minor." It also means "the supporter" and "the loved one." Some have said: "The gist of the hadith could be 'whoever I have supported, befriended, or loved;' for 'Ali was as such, and this meaning agrees with the prestige enjoyed by the good ancestors, and with the imamate of the three righteous caliphs, may Allah be pleased with them.

II. The Link

It is also possible that some people regarded this hadith to refer to 'Ali simply because one of 'Ali's companions in Yemen noticed his uncompromising policy in executing the commandments of Allah; therefore, he spoke ill of him; for this reason, the Prophet, peace be upon him and his progeny, did not appreciate their attitude and stood up on the Ghadir Day, praised the Imam and lauded his contributions, attracting the attention to his prestige and defending his name against those who intended to chew it. The pretext used by such a group of advocates is that in his sermon, the Prophet (s) praised 'Ali in particular, saying: "Whoever I have been his *wali*, 'Ali is his *wali*," and his Ahl Al-Bayt in general, saying: "I am leaving with you the Two Weighty Things: the Book of Allah and my progeny, my Ahl Al-Bayt;" so, he simply recommended that they should cherish 'Ali in particular and his kin in general. They claim that such a statement neither commits Ali to be his successor, nor does it connote imamate for him, Wassalam.

Sincerely,
S

Letter 58
Muharram 27, 1330

I. Hadith al-Ghadir Cannot be Interpreted

Somehow I have the feeling that your heart is not satisfied with what you yourself have stated, and your soul is not thereby pleased! You revere the Messenger of Allah (s) and cherish his pristine wisdom, infallibility, conclusive Prophethood, believing that he is the master of the wise, and the seal of the prophets: "He does not speak of his own inclination; it is but a revealed inspiration; he has been taught by one mighty in power (Qur'an, 53:3-5)."

Suppose a philosopher from another faith asks you about the Ghadir Day saying:

"Why did he (s) stop all those thousands of companions from proceeding, confining them in midday heat in such a sunbaked plain? Why did he make sure to call back whoever advanced, and wait for whoever lagged behind? Why did he camp with them in such a desolate place where neither water nor vegetation was available? Then why did he preach to them about Allah Almighty in that place and enjoined those who were present there to convey, upon dispersing, what they had heard to those who had not, and why did he start with a self eulogizing sermon, saying: 'It looks like my Lord's Messenger [angel of death, Isra'il] is about to come to call me [to return to my Lord] and I will respond to the call; I am responsible, and so are you,' and what message was the Prophet (s) enjoined to convey and which the nation was enjoined to heed? Why did he ask them: 'Do not you believe that there is no god but Allah and that Muhammad (s) is His Servant and Messenger, that His Paradise is just and His Fire is just, that death is just and the life after death is just, that the Hour is undoubtedly approaching, that Allah will bring to life all those who are lying in their graves?' and they responded in the affirmative? Why did he immediately take 'Ali's hand, lift it till the white hair in his armpit became visible, saying: 'O people! Allah is my *mawla*, and I am the *mawla* of the believers;' then why did he explain his statement 'I am the *mawla* of the believers' by asking them: 'Do not I have more authority over your lives than you yourselves have?' Then why did he say, having made such an explanation, 'Whoever has accepted me as his *mawla*, this ('Ali) is his *mawla*; O Lord! Befriend whosoever befriends him and be the enemy of whosoever antagonizes him; support whosoever supports him and betray whosoever betrays him,' and why did he specifically choose him and pray for him in such a manner which is worthy only of just Imams and truthful successors? And why did he require them to testify by asking them: 'Do I not have more authority over you than you yourselves have?' and they answered in the affirmative; then he said: 'To whomsoever I have been a *mawla*, 'Ali is his *mawla*,' or 'To whomsoever I have been a *wali*, 'Ali is his *wali*, and why did he link the Qur'an to his progeny, thus making them the examples for the wise to follow till the day of Judgment? Why so much concern from such a wise Prophet? What was the mission that necessitated all these introductions, and what was the aspired objective from such a memorable stand? What was the message which Allah Almighty ordered him to convey when He said: 'O Messenger! Convey what has just been revealed unto you from your Lord, and if you do not do so, then you have not conveyed His Message (at all), and Allah will protect you from (evil) men (Qur'an, 5:67),' and what mission required so much emphasis from Allah Who demanded, in a tone so close to threatening, to be conveyed? What was the affair regarding which the Prophet feared dissension if not conveyed by him, one the announcement of which required a profound protection from Allah against the harm of the hypocrites...?"

I ask you, in the name of your grandfather, if you are asked all these questions, will you answer them by saying that Allah, the Omniscient, the All-powerful, simply wanted to explain to the Muslims how 'Ali had been supporting them, and how friendly he was to them? I do not think that you would give such an answer, and I do not think that you would interpret Allah's words, or the words of the master of the wise, the seal of messengers and prophets, as such. You are above thinking that he (s) would exhaust his means and resources in explaining something too clear, according to reason and common sense, to require such an explanation. There is no doubt that you look at the actions and statements of the Prophet (s) in a better light, one which is not derided by the discreet, nor criticized by philosophers or sages. There is no doubt that you appreciate the value of his statements and actions and render them to wisdom and infallibility.

Allah the Almighty has said: "He is a blessed Messenger endowed with strength from the One with the Throne, obeyed, able, and trustworthy; certainly your fellow is not possessed (Qur'an, 81:19-22)." You are above accusing him of clarifying what is already clear, or expounding upon what is already common knowledge, or bringing unusual introductions for such clarifications, or introductions having no bearing over nor correlation thereto. Allah and His Messenger are above that. You, may Allah support the truth through your person, know that what suits such measures, undertaken in the midday heat of that place, ones that are conducive to his actions and statements on the Ghadir Day, is nothing less than the conveying of the divine Message, and the appointment of his vicegerent. Logical proofs and rational explanations unequivocally prove that what he intended to do on that day was nothing other than the appointment of 'Ali as his vicegerent and successor. This hadith, supported by proofs, is an explicit text regarding 'Ali's caliphate, one which does not even require an interpretation, and there is no way to understand it otherwise. This is quite clear for anyone who is "... with a sound mind, attentive, and a witness (Qur'an, 50:37)."

II. Pretext for its Interpretation is Speculative and Misleading

As regarding the pretext they claim, it is nothing but a speculation and an adulteration. It is the sophistry of confusion and embellishment. The Prophet (s) dispatched 'Ali to Yemen twice, the first took place in 8 A.H. It was then that scandalmongers spread rumours about him, and some people complained about him to the Prophet (s) upon their return to Medina. It was then that he resented their complaints,[1] and they saw the sparkle of anger on his face; yet they did not refrain from trying again. The second time took place in 10 A.H. It was then that the Prophet (s) tied a knot on 'Ali's standard, fixed his headwear with his own hands, and said: "Proceed, and do not be distracted;" whereupon 'Ali (as) proceeded to his destination as the divinely guided leader of the rest till he discharged the responsibility entrusted to him by the Messenger of Allah, peace be upon him and his progeny. Then he participated in the Prophet's Farewell Pilgrimage. It was then that the Prophet welcomed him very warmly and even shared with him his own offering. It was then that no scandalmonger dared to open his mouth, nor did any unfair person charge him with anything; so, how can this hadith be necessitated by the objections of those in the opposition party? Or how could it be only an answer to their charges, as some people claim?

Yet mere antagonism to 'Ali is not sufficient for the Prophet to pile praises on him in the way which he has done from a pulpit

---

[1] We have clarified the same in our Letter No. 36; so, refer to it and do not overlook our comment in this regard.

of camel saddles on the Ghadir Day except, Allah forbid, that he risks his own deeds and statements, responsibilities and mission, just to please 'Ali. His divine wisdom is way above that, for Allah, praised be His Name, says: "It is the saying of a glorious Messenger; it is not the speech of a poet; little do you believe; nor is it the speech of a monk; little do you remember; it is but revelation from the Lord of the Worlds." (69:40-43)

Had he desired to just show 'Ali's contributions, and to rebut those who bore grudge against him, he (s) would simply have said: "This is my cousin, my son-in-law, the father of my descendants, the master of my household; therefore, do not harm him," or something like this to show mere admission of status and dignity. But the way this hadith is worded gives no impression other than what we have suggested. It points out rational and deductive proofs. Let the reason be whatever it may be, the statements quite obviously bear explicit meanings which demand no inquiry into their causes.

As regarding his reference to his household in hadith al-Ghadir, it is only to support the same meaning which we have suggested, since he correlated them to the Glorious Book of Allah, setting them as examples for all the wise, saying: "I am leaving with you these which, as long as you adhere to, shall never let you stray: the Book of Allah, and my progeny, my household." He did not do that only so that the nation might realize that it had none to refer to, nor rely upon, after the Prophet, other than both of them. Suffices you for a testimony regarding the Imams from the Prophet's purified progeny (as) is that they are correlated to Allah's Book which no wrong can approach from front nor from back. Just as it is not possible to refer to any book which differs in its judgment from the Book of Allah, the Praised One, the Sublime, it is not possible likewise to refer to an Imam who opposes in his judgment the Imams from the purified progeny (as).

Consider his statement, peace be upon him and his progeny, "They shall never separate till they join me at the Pool;" it is a proof that the earth shall never be without an Imam from his loins who is equivalent to the Book. Anyone who scrutinizes this hadith will find it restricting the caliphate to the Imams from the purified progeny of the Prophet (s). This is supported by the hadith reported by Zayd ibn Thabit and quoted by Ahmad in his *Musnad* at the beginning of page 122, Vol. 5. It states that the Messenger of Allah, peace be upon him and his progeny, has said: "I am leaving you with two successors: the Book of Allah, like a rope extending from heavens to earth, and my household, for they both shall never part from each other till they join me at the Pool." Such a statement is indeed indicative of assigning the caliphate to the Imams from the purified progeny, peace be upon them. You know that the text which emphasizes following the Prophet's progeny implies following 'Ali's leadership, since 'Ali, after the Prophet (s), is the undisputed master, and the obeyed Imam of his household. On one hand, hadith al-Ghadir and others like it imply that 'Ali is the Imam of the Prophet's household whose status, according to Allah and His Messenger, is equal to that of the Holy Qur'an. On the other hand, it gives credit to his own great personality because of which he became the *wali* of all those whose *wali* is none other than the Messenger of Allah (s), Wassalam.

Sincerely,
Sh

Letter 59
Muharram 28, 1330

I. Truth Manifests

I have never seen, in the past or in the present, anyone more gentle in his tone, more strong in his argument, than your own self. Now truth has manifested itself due to the proofs which you have brought forth, thus uncovering the mask of doubt, revealing the pleasant countenance of conviction. No longer do we claim that the meaning of "*wali*" and "*mawla*" in hadith al-Ghadir is "foremost," or that it implies the "supporter," or the like, nor anything akin to what that man who asked for a sure torment had suggested; your view regarding the "mawla" stands on firm grounds, and is taken for granted.

II. Evasion

I wish you agree to our interpretation of the said hadith which is endorsed by a group of learned *'ulama*, including imam Ibn Hajar in his *Al-Sawa'iq al-Muhriqa*, and al-Halabi in his *Sirat*. They argue that even if we agree that he ('Ali) is the worthiest of imamate, the [Prophet's] intention here is futuristic; otherwise, he would have become the Imam in spite of the presence of the Prophet (s) [which is an impossible situation, since the Prophet, as long as he was alive, was the sole Imam tr.], who did not mind the forthcoming of an Imam after him. It is as though the Prophet (s) had said: "'Ali shall be the Imam as soon as he receives the oath of allegiance;" so, such a situation will not collide with the precedence of the three Imams; it thus safeguards the honour of the good ancestors, may Allah Almighty be pleased with them all.

Sincerely,
S

Letter 60
Muharram 30, 1330

Evasion Refuted

You have, may Allah support the truth through your person, asked us to be convinced that the gist of hadith al-Ghadir is that 'Ali is the most worthy of imamate when and if the Muslims choose him as such and swear the oath of allegiance to him, hence his priority to which the hadith hints is futuristic, rather than immediate. In other words, such a priority will take place when and if it is forcibly taken, rather than being actual, so that it does not clash with the caliphate of the three Imams who preceded him [in ruling the Muslims]. We ask you in the light of the truth, the dignity of justice, the honour of fairness, and the logic of fair play, if you yourself are convinced of it so that we may follow suit and follow in your footsteps. Do you agree to give such an explanation yourself, or can it be attributed to you, so that we may follow in your footsteps and do as you do? I do not think that you are convinced or pleased with a view such as this. I am convinced that you yourself wonder about anyone who would accept to derive such a meaning for this hadith when the text does not at all suggest it, nor can anyone conceive it as such; nay, it even challenges the wisdom and discretion of the Prophet (s)..., *astaghfir-Allah*. It neither agrees with his great deeds nor very serious statements made on the Ghadir Day, nor with the irrefutable proofs which we brought forth above, nor with what al-Harith ibn al-Nu'man al-Fahri understood, and what is emphasized by Allah and His Messenger, as well as all the companions.

Yet even the pending priority does not actually agree with the general meaning of this hadith, for it obviously does not necessitate that 'Ali (as) should *not* have been the *mawla* of the three caliphs, nor the *mawla* of anyone who died while being contemporary to any of them. This is exactly the opposite of the conclusion driven home by the Prophet (s) who asked: "Do I not have more authority over the believers than the believers themselves have?" and people answered him in the affirmative; then he (s) said: "To whomsoever

I have been the *mawla* (i.e. master of each and every Muslim individual, without any exception), 'Ali is his *mawla*." So, as you see, nobody is made the exception [other than, of course, the person of the Prophet Himself.] implied in this statement; 'Ali is indeed the *mawla* without any argument. Both Abu Bakr and 'Umar, having heard the words of the Prophet (s) on the Ghadir Day, said to 'Ali:[1] "You have, O son of Abu Talib, become the *mawla* of every believing man and woman," thus admitting that he had become the master of every believing man and woman, generalizing the application to all believing men and women since the sun set on the Day of the Ghadir.

Once 'Umar was asked: "Your conduct with 'Ali is quite different from that of any other companion of the Prophet (s)." 'Umar responded by saying: "Why, he is my *mawla*," as stated by Dar Qutni on page 36 of *Al-Sawa'iq al-Muhriqa*. He thus admitted that 'Ali was his master, and he (Ali) had not been chosen to be a caliph yet, nor had he yet received the oath of allegiance from anyone. Consider how his ('Umar's) statement proved that 'Ali was his *mawla* and the *mawla* of every believing man and woman right then, not by virtue of futurity, since the Messenger of Allah, peace be upon him and his progeny, on behalf of the Almighty Allah, conveyed the same on the Ghadir Day. 'Umar once asked 'Ali to arbitrate in a case brought forth before him involving two bedouins disputants. One of them asked: "Is this man ('Ali) to judge between us?" 'Umar immediately leaped in rage, took the man by the neck and said to him: "Woe unto you! Do you know who this man is? He is your *mawla*, my *mawla*, and the *mawla* of all believers; whoever rejects him as the *mawla* is certainly not a Muslim," as stated near the conclusion of Chapter 11 of Ibn Hajar's *Al-Sawa'iq al-Muhriqa*. Those who have recorded this incident are quite a few.

---

[1] This is quoted by Dar Qutni, as indicated near the conclusion of Section 5, Chapter One, of *Al-Sawa'iq al-Muhriqa* by Ibn Hajar; so, refer to page 26. It is also narrated by many traditionists, each from his own source, and in their own books of traditions. Ahmad has quoted something similar from 'Umar of the ahadith narrated by al-Bara' ibn 'Azib on page 281, Vol. 4, of his *Musnad*, which we have already quoted in Letter No. 54 above.

You, may Allah support the truth through your person, are aware of the fact that had the philosophy of Ibn Hajar and his supporters regarding the Ghadir hadith been accepted, the Messenger of Allah, peace be upon him and his progeny, would have been proven to be tampering with his own mission and responsibility - we seek refuge with Allah against thinking in such a manner - hallucinating in his speeches and deeds - Allah is above letting His Messenger do that - without having, according to such a philosophy, any purpose in that awesome situation other than making an announcement that after 'Ali had been elected as caliph, he would be most fit for it, and that, the theory goes on, nobody should monopolize it, for 'Ali and all other companions, and Muslims in general, are in that respect equal. What characteristic did the Prophet, peace be upon him and his progeny, intend then and there to attribute to 'Ali, and 'Ali alone, from among all others who are well known for their history in serving Islam, if such philosophy, O Muslims, is proven accurate?

As regarding their claim that had 'Ali's priority regarding the Imamate *not* been futuristic, he would have become then *the* Imam in spite of the presence of the Messenger of Allah, peace be upon him and his progeny, we say that such a claim is indeed quite odd; it is the watering down of the truth, an unmatched misrepresentation which ignores the covenants of all prophets, caliphs, kings and princes to their successors. It overlooks the meaning of the hadith: "You to me are like Aaron to Moses except there will be no prophet after me." It is an attempt to forget his statement, peace be upon him and his progeny, in the hadith relevant to his kin when he warned them saying, "Therefore, listen to him [to 'Ali] and obey him," and to other numerous texts in this meaning. Even if we suppose that due to the presence of the Messenger of Allah, peace be upon him and his progeny, 'Ali's priority of the imamate could not be effective immediately, then obviously it had to be effective after his demise, following the unanimously accepted rule of interpreting a statement the absolute truth of which is unattainable by its closest meanings. As regarding the honour of the good ancestors, it is safeguarded without forcing such an interpretation as we will explain if necessary, Wassalam.

Sincerely,
Sh

Letter 61
Safar 1, 1330

Requesting Texts Narrated by Shi'a Sources

As long as the honour and dignity of the good ancestors are protected, then there is nothing wrong with considering all the ahadith regarding the Imam (as), the ones to which you have referred, including hadith al-Ghadir or any other one, without the need for an interpretation. You may also know other ahadith relevant to this subject with which the Sunnis are not familiar; so, may I request you to narrate them so that we may acquaint ourselves therewith? Wassalam.

Sincerely,
S

Letter 62
Safar 2, 1330

Forty Ahadith

Yes, we will narrate to you consecutively reported ahadith with which the Sunnis are not familiar. These are narrated by members of the purified progeny of Muhammad (s), of which we relate forty:[1]

---

[1] This much suffices due to the fact that we have narrated quite a few ahadith from sources such as the Commander of the Faithful 'Ali ibn Abu Talib (as), 'Abdullah ibn 'Abbas, 'Abdullah ibn Mas'ud, 'Abdullah ibn 'Umar, Abu Sa'id al-Khudri, Abul-Darda', Abu Hurayrah, Anas ibn Malik, Ma'ath ibn Jabal, quoting various sources, all stating that the Messenger of Allah, peace be upon him and his progeny, has said: "Whoever teaches my nation forty ahadith related to its faith, Allah will resurrect him on the Day of Judgment in the company of the *faqihs* and the learned." In another wording of the same hadith, "Allah will resurrect him as a learned *faqih*." According to Abul-Darda', the statement reads: "I will include him in my intercession on the Day of Judgment, and he shall be a witness." According to Ibn Mas'ud, "It will be said to him: 'Enter Paradise

1) Al-Saduq Muhammad ibn 'Ali ibn al-Husayn ibn Babawayh al-Qummi has included in his book *Ikmal ad-Din wa Itmam al-Ni'mah*, as transmitted by 'Abdul Rahman ibn Samrah, one particular hadith in which the Messenger of Allah, peace be upon him and his progeny, addresses 'Abdul Rahman thus: "O Abu Samrah! If views differ and opinions vary, then refer to 'Ali ibn Abu Talib, for he is my nation's Imam, and my successor over them after me."

2) In the same reference, i.e. the *Ikmal*, Al-Saduq quotes Ibn 'Abbas narrating one hadith in which the Messenger of Allah, peace be upon him and his progeny, says: "Allah, the Praised One and the Sublime, cast a scrutinizing look at the inhabitants of the earth and chose me from among them to be the Prophet, then he cast another look and chose 'Ali as the Imam and commanded me to take him as my brother, and appoint him as the *wali* and vizier."

3) Al-Saduq, also in the *Ikmal*, traces one hadith to Imam al-Sadiq (as) who quotes his father and ancestors citing the Messenger of Allah, peace be upon him and his progeny, saying: "Gabriel has told me that the Lord of Power, exalted is His Greatness, has said: 'Whoever comes to know that I am the Lord without any partner, and that Muhammad is my Servant and Messenger, that Ali ibn Abu Talib is Muhammad's successor, and that the Imams from his descendants are My Arguments, then I would let him enter Paradise through My Mercy.'"

4) Al-Saduq, also in his *Ikmal*, traces another hadith to Imam al-Sadiq (as) who quotes his father and grandfather citing the

---

from whichever gate you please.'" According to Ibn 'Umar's narration, "... he will be included with the men of knowledge, and be resurrected in the company of martyrs." Suffices us in learning these forty ahadith and others included in all our Letters his statement, peace be upon him and his progeny, "Allah will look after whoever listens to my statement, comprehends it and conveys it just as he heard it." And also his hadith: "Let those of you who witness [my Sunnah] convey it to those who are absent."

Messenger of Allah, peace be upon him and his progeny, saying: "The Imams after me are twelve: The first is 'Ali and the last is al-Qa'im [al-Mahdi]; they are my successors and the executors of my will."

5) Al-Saduq, also in his *Ikmal*, traces yet another hadith to al-Asbagh ibn Nabatah who says that the Commander of the Faithful 'Ali ibn Abu Talib (as) once approached, his hand in the hand of his son al-Hasan, and said: "The Messenger of Allah once came to us and his hand was in mine like this, saying: 'The best of creation after me, and their master, is this brother of mine who is the Imam of every Muslim, the prince of every believer after me.'"

6) Al-Saduq, also in his *Ikmal*, tracing one hadith to Imam al-Rida (as) who quotes his forefathers citing the Messenger of Allah, peace be upon him and his progeny, saying: "Whoever likes to uphold my religion and embark upon the Ark of Salvation after me, let him follow the example of 'Ali ibn Abu Talib, for he is the executor of my will, and my vicegerent over my nation during my lifetime and after my demise."

7) Al-Saduq, also in his *Ikmal*, attributes another hadith by the Messenger of Allah, peace be upon him and his progeny, to Imam al-Rida (as) who quotes his ancestors stating that the Prophet (s) once said: "I and 'Ali are the fathers of this nation; whoever knows us very well also knows Allah, and whoever denies us also denies Allah, the Unique, the Mighty. And from 'Ali's descendants are my grandsons al-Hasan and al-Husayn, who are the masters of the youths of Paradise, and from al-Husayn's descendants shall be nine: whoever obeys them obeys me, and whoever disobeys them also disobeys me; the ninth among them is their Qa'im and Mahdi."

8) Al-Saduq, also in his *Ikmal*, traces another hadith through *isnad* to Imam al-Hasan al-'Askari (as) who quotes his ancestors up to the Messenger of Allah, peace be upon him and his progeny,

addressing Ibn Mas'ud thus: "O Ibn Mas'ud! 'Ali ibn Abu Talib is your Imam after me; he is my successor over you."

9) Quoting one hadith related by Salman, Al-Saduq, also in his *Ikmal*, says that once Salman visited the Messenger of Allah, peace be upon him and his progeny, and found al-Husayn ibn 'Ali (as) sitting on his lap, and the prophet was kissing him and saying: "You are a master, son of a master, an Imam and son of an Imam, brother of an Imam, father of Imams, and you are Allah's Argument, the son of His Argument (*Hujjah*), and father of nine Arguments from your loins, the ninth of them is their Qa'im."

10) Al-Saduq, also in his *Ikmal*, quotes another hadith traced also to Salman who quotes a lengthy hadith by the Messenger of Allah in which he (s) says: "O Fatima! Have you not come to know that we are Ahl Al-Bayt? Allah has made the Hereafter dearer to us than this life, and Allah the Exalted, Praised is His Name, cast a look at the inhabitants of the earth and chose me from among His creation; then he cast a second look and chose your husband and inspired me to marry you to him and take him as *wali* and vizier, and to make him my successor over my nation. So, your father is the best of prophets, your husband is the best of *wasis*, and you are the first to join me."

11) Al-Saduq, also in his *Ikmal*, quotes a lengthy hadith and mentions in it that a meeting of over two hundred men from the *Muhajirun* (Meccan Immigrants) and the Ansar (Medenite Supporters) were seeking knowledge and studying jurisprudence, and that each one of them started bragging about himself, while 'Ali (as) remained silent. They asked him: "O father of al-Hasan, what stops you from saying something?" In response to their question, he (as) only reminded them of a statement made by the Messenger of Allah (s) in which he said: "'Ali is my brother, vizier, heir, executor of my will, successor over my nation, and the *wali* of every believer after me; so, admit all of this about him."

12) Al-Saduq, also in his *Ikmal*, quotes a lengthy hadith narrated by 'Abdullah ibn Ja'far, al-Hasan, al-Husayn, 'Abdulllah ibn 'Abbas, 'Umar ibn Abu Salamah, Usamah ibn Ziyad, Salman, Abu Dharr al-Ghifari, and al-Miqdad who all say that they heard the Messenger of Allah (s) saying: "I have more authority over the believers than the believers themselves have; my brother 'Ali has after me more authority over the believers than the believers themselves have."

13) Al-Saduq, also in his *Ikmal ad-Din wa Itmam al-Ni'mah*, quotes al-Asbagh ibn Nabatah who cites Ibn 'Abbas saying that he heard the Messenger of Allah, peace be upon him and his progeny, saying, "I, 'Ali, al-Hasan, al-Husayn, and nine from the progeny of Husayn are Purified."

14) Al-Saduq has also quoted in his *Ikmal* Ibn Abayah ibn Rab'i citing Ibn 'Abbas saying that the Messenger of Allah, peace be upon him and his progeny, has said: "I am the master of the Prophets, while 'Ali is the master of the *wasis*."

15) Al-Saduq has also quoted in his *Ikmal* one hadith transmitted by Imam al-Sadiq (as) through *isnad* stating that the Messenger of Allah (s) has said: "Allah, the Exalted, the Almighty, favoured me over all other prophets, and favoured 'Ali over all other *wasis*, and favoured from 'Ali's descendants alHasan and al-Husayn, and chose from al-Husayn's progeny the *wasis* who safeguard the faith against the distortion of extermists, the adulteration of liars, and the misinterpretations of those who have strayed."

16) Al-Saduq, also in his *Ikmal*, has quoted 'Ali (as) citing the Messenger of Allah, peace be upon him and his progeny, saying: "The Imams after me are twelve: the first of them is 'Ali,

and the last is al-Qa'im through whom Allah, the Exalted and the Mighty, shall open the east of the earth as well as the west."[2]

17) Al-Saduq has also quoted in his *Amali* a lengthy hadith narrated by 'Ali (as) in which the Messenger of Allah, peace be upon him and his progeny, says, "'Ali is of me, and I am of 'Ali who is created of my own mould; he solves people's disputes regarding my Sunnah; he is the Commander of the Faithful, the leader of the foremost among all men, and the best of *wasis*."

18) Al-Saduq, also in his *Amali*, has quoted another lengthy hadith reported by 'Ali (as) in which the Messenger of Allah, peace be upon him and his progeny, says: "'Ali is the Commander of the Faithful according to the Wilayat of Allah, the Exalted and the Mighty, which He tied in a knot upon His Throne and required the angels to witness; 'Ali is Allah's Vicegerent and Proof [*Hujjatullah*]; he is the Imam of the Muslims."

19) Al-Saduq, also in his *Amali*, has quoted Ibn 'Abbas relating that the Messenger of Allah, peace be upon him and his progeny, has said: "O 'Ali! You are the Imam of the Muslims, the Commander of the Faithful, the leader of the foremost renowned of all men, Allah's Proof after me, and the master of all *wasis*."

20) Al-Saduq, also in his *Amali*, has cited Ibn 'Abbas quoting the Messenger of Allah (s) saying: "O 'Ali! You are my successor over my nation, and you are to me like Seth to Adam."

21) Al-Saduq, also in his *Amali*, has quoted Abu Dharr al-Ghifari saying, ""We were once in the company of the Messenger of Allah (s) at his mosque when he said: 'A man will enter through this door who is the Commander of the Faithful and the Imam of

---

[2] This hadith and the ones before it exist in a chapter containing what has been narrated about the Prophet (s) regarding the Qa'im, and that he is the twelfth in the line of Imams; it is Chapter Twenty-Four of *Ikmal ad-Din wa Itmam al-Ni'mah*, pages 149-167.

the Muslims,' whereupon 'Ali ibn Abu Talib came in, and the Messenger of Allah (s) welcomed him, turned his glorious face to us and said: 'This is your Imam after me.'"

22) In his *Amali*, Al-Saduq has cited Jabir ibn 'Abdullah al-Ansari quoting the Messenger of Allah (s) saying: "'Ali ibn Abu Talib is the foremost among them in accepting Islam, and he is the most learned... He is the Imam and successor after me."

23) In his *Amali*, Al-Saduq has also quoted one hadith correct through *isnad* related by Ibn 'Abbas who quotes the Messenger of Allah (s) saying: "O people! Whose words are better than Allah's? Your Lord, Mighty is His Grace, has commanded me to assign 'Ali over you as the most outstanding Imam, as my own successor and executor of my will, and that you should regard him as my brother and vizier."

24) In his *Amali*, Al-Saduq also quotes one hadith correct through *isnad* narrated by Abu 'Ayyash who says: "The Messenger of Allah (s) once ascended the pulpit and delivered a sermon in which he said: 'My cousin 'Ali is also my brother, vizier, successor, and the one who pays my dues on my own behalf.'"[3]

25) In his *Amali*, Al-Saduq has also quoted one hadith correct through *isnad* reported by the Commander of the Faithful who says: "Once, the Messenger of Allah (s) delivered a sermon in which he said: 'O people! The month of Allah has approached,' and he continued his sermon recounting the attributes of the month of Ramadan. I asked: 'O Messenger of Allah! What is the best of deeds in this month?' He replied: 'It is staying away from whatever Allah has forbidden you,' then he burst weeping, so I inquired: 'What grieves you, O Messenger of Allah?' and he answered: 'O

---

[3] This hadith, together with the four preceding it, is quoted from al-Saduq's *Ghayat al-Maram*. These are quite lengthy, and we have quoted from them whatever testifies to our argument. As regarding the ahadith which succeed it, they are to be found in Chapter 13 of *Ghayat al-Maram*.

'Ali! I am grieving at what horrible forbidden things that will happen to you in the same month,' adding, 'You are my *wasi*, the father of my descendants, and my successor over my nation during my lifetime and after my death; your bidding is as good as mine, and so is your forbidding.'"

26) In his *Amali*, Al-Saduq has quoted another hadith narrated by 'Ali, peace be upon him, thus: "The Messenger of Allah (s) has said: 'O 'Ali! You are my brother and I am yours; I have been chosen to be the Prophet while you have been chosen to be the Imam; I take charge of the revelation [of the Holy Qur'an] while you take charge of its implementation; you are the father of this nation. O 'Ali! You are my *wasi* and vicegerent, my vizier and heir, and the father of my offspring.'"

27) In his *Amali*, Al-Saduq has also quoted one hadith the *isnad* of which is authentic as transmitted by Ibn 'Abbas who says: "While the Ansar were assembling at Quba' Mosque, the Messenger of Allah (s) said: 'O 'Ali! You are my brother and I am yours; you are the executor of my will and my own successor, and the Imam of my nation after me: Allah will assist whoever assists you, and He will be the enemy of whoever antagonizes you.'"

28) In his *Amali*, Al-Saduq has also quoted a lengthy hadith narrated by Umm Salamah in which the Messenger of Allah (s) addresses her thus: "O Umm Salamah! Listen and bear witness: This 'Ali ibn Abu Talib is the executor of my will; he is my successor, the one who tries my enemies, and the one who safeguards my Pool [of al-Kawthar]."

29) In his *Amali*, Al-Saduq has also quoted Salman al-Farsi saying, "I have heard the Messenger of Allah (s) saying: 'O Muhajirun and Ansar! Shall I lead you to that which, as long as you adhere to, shall never let you stray after me?' They said: 'O yes, Messenger of Allah!' He (s) said: 'This 'Ali is my brother and the executor of my will, my vizier, heir and successor; he is your

Imam; therefore, love him as much as I love him, and respect him as much as I respect him, for Gabriel has enjoined me to say so to you.'"

30) In his *Amali*, Al-Saduq has also quoted through *isnad* one hadith related by Zayd ibn Arqam in which the Messenger of Allah (s) is quoted saying: "Shall I lead you to that which, as long as you adhere to, will protect you against annihilation and straying? Your Imam and *wali* is 'Ali ibn Abu Talib (as); therefore, do support him, listen to his counsel, and believe in him, for Gabriel has ordered me to say so to you."

31) In his *Amali*, Al-Saduq has quoted Ibn 'Abbas relating one hadith in which the Messenger of Allah (s) says: "Allah, the Praised, the Sublime, has inspired to me: 'I have selected from your nation a brother and heir for you, a successor and executor of your will.' I inquired: 'O Lord! Who is he?' He replied: 'It is he who loves me and I love him...,' till He said in His divine statement: 'It is 'Ali ibn Abu Talib.'"

32) In his *Amali*, Al-Saduq has quoted Ibn 'Abbas citing another hadith related by his ancestors in which the Messenger of Allah (s) says: "During my *isra'* (night journey), my Lord, Exalted is His Might, promised me that 'Ali is the Imam of the pious, the leader of the foremost among renowned men, the religion's chief."

34) In his *Amali*, Al-Saduq has quoted one hadith through *isnad* to Imam al-Rida (as) who quotes his ancestors citing the Messenger of Allah (s) saying: "'Ali is of me, and I am of 'Ali; may Allah wage war against those who fight 'Ali; 'Ali, indeed, is the Imam of creation after me."

35) Abu Ja'far Muhammad ibn al-Hasan al-Tusi, the sect's *shaykh*, in his *Amali* quotes one hadith narrated by 'Ammar ibn Yasir in which the Messenger of Allah (s) is quoted telling 'Ali, "Allah has decorated you in a way that is most dear to Him: through

asceticism to the extent that you do not feel deprived of any of this life's pleasures, and none of them feels deprived of you, and He has endowed you with the love for the destitute, making their fellowship welcomed by you, and they welcome you as their Imam; therefore, congratulations to whoever loves you and believes in you, and woe unto whoever hates you and tells lies about you."

36) In his *Amali*, Shaykh Al-Saduq has also quoted one hadith through *isnad* to 'Ali (as) who has said while preaching from Kufa's pulpit: "O people! The Messenger of Allah (s) granted me ten attributes that are dearer to me than anything upon which the sun shines: He (s) has said to me: 'O 'Ali! You are my brother in this life and the life hereafter, and you are the closest to me among all creation on the Day of Resurrection; your residence in Paradise faces mine; you are my heir, the executor of my will after me, faring with both my foes and family; you protect my family on my own behalf during my absence; you are my nation's Imam; you execute justice among my followers; you are my friend, and my friend is the friend of Allah; your enemy is my enemy, and my enemy is surely the enemy of Allah.'"

37) In Al-Saduq's book titled *Al-Nusus 'ala al-A'Imma*, which contains texts relevant to the Imams, al-Hasan ibn 'Ali (as) is quoted saying: "I have heard the Messenger of Allah (s) say the following to my father: 'And you are the inheritor of my knowledge, the substance of my own judgment, and the Imam after me.'"

38) Also in his work containing texts about the Imams, Al-Saduq quotes 'Umran ibn Hasin saying: "I have heard the Messenger of Allah (s) say to 'Ali, 'You are the Imam and successor after me.'"

39) Also in his same work, Al-Saduq quotes 'Ali (as) citing the Messenger of Allah (s) saying to him: "O 'Ali! You are the

wasi over those who have died among my household, and the caliph of those who are alive among my nation."

40) Also in the same reference cited above, Al-Saduq quotes al-Husayn ibn 'Ali (as) saying: "When Allah revealed the verse: 'And those who are kin of each other are more worthy of each other in the Book of Allah,' I asked the Messenger of Allah to interpret it, and he said: 'You are the kin; when I die, your father 'Ali is the most worthy of me and my station; when your father dies, your brother al-Hasan is most worthy of it; and if al-Hasan dies, then you are most worthy of his station.'"

This is the conclusion of what we wanted to quote in such a hurry. Its ratio to the remainder of the texts is like that of one bouquet to the remainder of all flowers, or the drop of water to the ocean; yet a portion should suffice; praise be to the Lord of the worlds, Wassalam.

Sincerely,
Sh

Letter 63
Safar 3, 1330

I. Shi'a Texts Rejected as Testimonials
As long as these texts are not quoted by non-Shi'as, Sunnis are not bound to accept them as testimonials.

II. Why Have Others Refrained from Quoting Them?
Had they been verified, why has nobody else quoted them?

III. Asking for More Texts
Let us refer only to the hadith narrated by Sunnis in this regard, Wassalam.

Sincerely,
S

Letter 64
Safar 4, 1330

I. Above Texts were Quoted upon Request
We have cited those texts in order to acquaint you with them and in response to your own request.

II. Sahihs are Proofs against the Majority
Our own testimonial against your argument is what we have already quoted from your own *sahih*s.

III. Not Quoted Because of Their Existence in Our Own Sahihs
The reason why those texts were not included is due to the prejudice, with which we are familiar, of those who concealed their

grudge, and hid their animosity, from the party of Pharaoh during the early epoch of Islam, worshippers of authority and domination who spent everything they possessed of might and means to hide the contributions of Ahl Al-Bayt and put out their light in every land. They forced people to deny their feats and attributes through means and methods of both tempting and terrorizing, through their wealth once, and through their positions and political stature another. They bestowed their favours upon those who denied these merits, dismissing, banishing or even murdering those who believed in them.

You know that the texts related to the imamate, and the promises of caliphate, are held with apprehension by those who fear that such texts may jeopardize their thrones or undermine the very foundations of their governments. The safety of these texts against the tampering of such people, of that of their followers and flatterers, and their ability to reach us through many sources and methods, is, indeed, a miracle testifying to their own truth. This is so due to the fact that those who denied the status of Ahl Al-Bayt, usurped the positions rightly and divinely assigned to them, used to incur the worst punishment upon anyone who showed love for Ahl Al-Bayt. They would shave his beard, convey him on the back of a donkey and tour the marketplaces, humiliating him, beating him and depriving him of even the most simple and basic human right, till he would lose all hope for justice from those rulers and despond of having friends in the community.[1] So, if anyone spoke well of 'Ali (as), he would be disowned, and retribution would fall upon him; therefore, his possessions would be confiscated, and he would be executed. How many tongues praising 'Ali were cut off? How many eyes which looked at him with respect were gouged? How many hands which pointed out to him were amputated? How many feet which walked towards him affectionately were sawed?

---

[1] Refer to page 15, Vol. 3, of *Sharh Nahjul Balaghah* by Ibn Abi al-Hadid, and you will find out what atrocities befell Ahl al-Bayt (as) and their Shi'ahs in those days. Imam al-Baqir (as) has made a statement in this regard to which we refer the researchers.

How many homes of his followers were burnt? And how many of their families were banished...?

Among the narrators of hadith and "protectors of the legacy" were people who worshipped those monarchs and tyrants as well as their rulers other than worshipping Allah, the Exalted, the Sublime, and they sought nearness to them with all their resources of scholarship, thus distorting, testifying for the authenticity of this or against the authenticity of that, just like many whom we see these days of flatterers among shaykhs, hired scholars, bad judges who race to please the rulers by endorsing their policies, be they just or unjust, calling their edicts correct, be they truly correct or corrupt; so, the ruler does not even have to ask them for a verdict in support of his regime or to indict his opponents, for they do so according to his own wish and according to the requirements of his policy, even if this means opposing the Book and the Sunnah, thus violating the nation's consensus, out of their own eagerness to safeguard their positions, or due to their coveting of a position they aspire to acquire. What a distance separates these from those! The latter did not value their governments, while the others needed their monarchs so badly, since they would use them to fight Allah and His Messenger. For this reason, they enjoyed with the monarchs and rulers a special lofty status, and their word was heeded; therefore, they commanded authority and prestige, and they were fanatical against the accurate ahadith if the latter pointed out to an attribute of 'Ali (as) or of other members of the household of Prophethood; so, they would reject it strongly, dropping it violently, attributing to its narrators Rafidism - and Rafidism is the worst vice according in their judgment. This is their policy towards the traditions lauding 'Ali, especially if they are held in high esteem by the Shi'as.

As regarding the flatterers, these have had friends in the especially high class in every land; they would speak highly of them, and they have for followers' secular scholars who would publicize their views, from among those who make a show of asceticism and piety, among the leaders and tribal chiefs. When the latter hear what they say regarding rejecting those authentic ahadith, they would hold their statements as gospel revealed and would publicize them among the commoners and the ignorant, thus making them well known in every land and using them as principles upheld in every time. There is another group of people who were custodians of hadith in those days, and who were forced by fear to overlook the ahadith praising 'Ali and Ahl Al-Bayt (as). If those poor folks were asked about what those flatterers were saying regarding rejecting the accurate *sunan* containing 'Ali's contributions and those of Ahl Al-Bayt (as), they would fear, if they told the general public of what they knew, that a blind, deaf and dumb dissension might occur. They were, therefore, forced out of fear to seek shelter by side-tracking the subject for fear of being rebuked by the flatterers and those who publicize for them, and for fear of those who repeat their words like parrots from among the populace and ignorant commoners.

Kings and rulers ordered people to denounce the Commander of the Faithful. They pressured them to do so once by tempting them with money, and once by threatening them with their armies and dreadful promises of retribution, thus forcing them to belittle him and his lineage, so much so that they painted a disgusting picture of him in their books and narrated ahadith whereby ears feel offended, making the cursing of his name from the pulpits a tradition followed by the Muslims during both Eids and on Fridays. The Light of Allah cannot be put out, and the contributions of His *walis* cannot be hidden; otherwise, those traditions would not have reached us through the sources of both groups, accurately and explicitly implying his caliphate. No texts are more consecutively reported than the texts in his praise, and I, by Allah, wonder about the favours which He has bestowed upon 'Ali ibn Abu Talib, His servant and the brother of His Messenger, how his light pierced through the clouds, the pitch of darkness, and survived the tumultuous waves, letting its ray shine on the world like midday sun!

4) You may refer, in addition to all the irrefutable proofs you have heard, to the text of inheritance, for it by itself is an irrefutable proof, Wassalam.

Sincerely,
Sh

Letter 65
Safar 5, 1330

Requesting the Ahadith Relevant to the Inheritance

Please narrate to us the hadith of inheritance as transmitted by Sunnis, Wassalam.

Sincerely,
S

Letter 66
Safar 5, 1330

Ali is the Prophet's Heir

There is no doubt that the Messenger of Allah, peace be upon him and his progeny, has left 'Ali with a legacy of knowledge and wisdom as much as the Almighty permitted His prophets and *wasis* to inherit, so much so that the Messenger of Allah (s) has said: "I am the city of knowledge and Ali is its gate; therefore, whoever wishes to attain knowledge, let him approach through the gate."[1]

He, peace be upon him and his progeny, has said: "I am the storehouse of wisdom, and 'Ali is its door... 'Ali is the gateway of my knowledge, the one who explains after me the Message with which I have been sent; loving him is indicative of genuine faith, and hating him is hypocrisy." According to Zayd ibn Abu 'Awfah, he, peace be upon him and his progeny, has addressed 'Ali thus: "You are my brother and heir;"[2] whereupon 'Ali inquired: "And what will you bequeath unto me?" He, peace be upon him and his progeny, answered: "Whatever Prophets before me used to bequeath." In another hadith, he, peace be upon him and his

---

[1] We have quoted this hadith and the couple before it in Letter No. 48 above. Refer in that Letter to ahadith number 9, 10 and 11, and do not overlook our comments.

[2] We have quoted the said hadith in Letter No. 32.

progeny, according to Buraydah, has said: "The heir of my knowledge is 'Ali."[3] Refer also to the hadith on the day of warning. During the lifetime of the Messenger of Allah, peace be upon him and his progeny, 'Ali (as) used to say: "By Allah, I am his brother, successor and cousin, and the heir of his knowledge; so, who is more worthy of all this other than myself?"[4]

Once 'Ali was asked: "How did you come to inherit your cousin rather than your uncle?" He answered: "The Messenger of Allah, peace be upon him and his progeny, gathered the descendants of 'Abdul Muttalib, who were quite a few, and each one of them had such an appetite that would consider tree trunks edible and would drink water though not potable, and he prepared for them a *mudd*[5] of food (a dry measure approximately Tangier 46.61, about one and three quarters of a pound); yet they all ate till they were satisfied, while the food looked as if it was not touched. Then he, peace be upon him and his progeny, said: 'O descendants of 'Abdul Muttalib! I have been sent to you in particular, and to all people in general; so, who among you pledges to be my brother, friend and heir?' Nobody stood; so, I stood, though the youngest among the attendants, but he (s) told me to sit. He repeated his statement twice, and each time, I was the only one who stood up, and every time he would tell me to sit. On the third time, he shook hands with me; thus did I come to inherit my cousin instead of my uncle.'"[6]

---

[3] Refer to it in Letter No. 68 above.

[4] This statement *verbatim* is confirmed as being 'Ali's. It is quoted by al-Hakim on page 126, Vol. 3, of his *Al-Mustadrak* through a narration endorsed by al-Bukhari and al-Muslim. Al-Dhahabi, in his *Talkhis al-Mustadrak*, has admitted the same.

[5] It is an ancient measurement of volume from the Islamic world. One 'Sa' is equal to 4 mudds. The Sa of the Prophet" (ṣa' an-nabi) is exactly 4.2125 liters. Converting this measure to the weight of wheat it is a value of 3.24 kg.

[6] This hadith stands on firm grounds, and it is a lengthy one. It has been quoted by al-Diya' al-Maqdisi in his *Al-Mukhtara*, and by Ibn Jarir in his *Tahthib al-Athar*. It is hadith number 6155 on page 408, Vol. 6, of *Kanz al-'Ummal*. It is also quoted by al-Nisa'i on page 18 of his *Al-Khasa'is al-'Alawiyya*, and it is transmitted by Ibn Abul-Hadid from al-Tabari's *Tarikh* near the end of the commentary on the "*Qasi'a*" sermon, page 255, Vol. 3, of *Sharh Nahjul*

According to al-Hakim's *Al-Mustadrak*,[7] and to al-Dhahabi's *Talkhis*, who both testify to its authenticity, Qatham ibn al'Abbas was asked once: "How did 'Ali come to inherit the Messenger of Allah (s) rather than your own selves?" He answered: "It is so due to his being the foremost among us in following him, and in keeping company with him more than anyone of us."

It was well known that 'Ali, rather than his uncle al'Abbas or any descendant of Hashim, was the heir of the Messenger of Allah, peace be upon him and his progeny. They accepted that as a fact, though they were informed of the reason why such inheritance was confined to 'Ali alone, who was the Prophet's cousin, rather than to al'Abbas, his uncle, or to any other uncle or relative of the Prophet, peace be upon him and his progeny. For this reason, they used to ask 'Ali (as) once and once Qatham, and the latter used to answer them as stated above in a way that is satisfactory to the understanding of those inquirers. Otherwise, the answer would be that Allah, the Exalted and Omniscient, looked upon the people of the earth and chose from among them Muhammad (s) and elevated him to be the Prophet, then He cast another look and selected 'Ali and inspired to His Messenger, peace be upon him and his progeny, to take him as his heir and successor.

On page 125, Vol. 3, of *Al-Mustadrak*, al-Hakim, having quoted Qatham stating the above, says: "The judge of judges [supreme judge, or grand mufti], Abul-Hasan Muhammad ibn Salih al-Hashimi, has told me that he once heard Abu 'Umar the judge saying: 'I heard Isma'il ibn Ishaq the judge, having been informed of what Qatham had said, saying that a man inherits another through either a blood relationship or sincere loyalty, and men of knowledge do not dispute the fact that [under normal circumstances] a cousin does not become the heir while the uncle [his father] is still alive.' According to such consensus, 'Ali inherited the Prophet's knowledge rather than they." As a matter of

---

Balaghah. Refer also to page 159, Vol. 1, of Imam Ahmad ibn Hanbal's *Musnad* where you will find the same hadith conveying this meaning.

[7] It occurs on page 125 of its third volume. It is also quoted by Ibn Abu Shaybah, and it is hadith number 6084 on page 400, Vol. 6, of *Kanz al-'Ummal*.

fact, chroniclers are sequential in narrating such a fact, especially through the sources of the purified progeny, and suffices us for proof is the Will (of Prophet (s)) and its clear texts, Wassalam.

Sincerely,
Sh

Letter 67
Safar 6, 1330

Where is the Prophet's Will?
Sunnis are not familiar with any will left for 'Ali, nor are they acquainted with any of its contents; so, please oblige and tell us its story, Wassalam.

Sincerely,
S

Letter 68
Safar 9, 1330

The Will's Texts
The texts regarding the will are consecutively reported through the Imams of the purified progeny (as); so, refer to what has been stated in this regard by others as mentioned in Letter No. 20 that quotes the statements of the Messenger of Allah, peace be upon him and his progeny, who took 'Ali (as) by the neck and said: "This is my brother and successor; he shall succeed me in faring with you; therefore, listen to him and obey him."

Muhammad ibn Hamid al-Razi quotes Salamah al-Abrash, Ibn Ishaq, Abu Rabi'ah al-Ayadi, Ibn Buraydah, ending with the latter's father Buraydah citing the Messenger of Allah, peace be upon him and his progeny, saying: "For every Prophet there is a successor and an heir; my successor and heir is 'Ali ibn Abu Talib."[1] In his *Kabir*, and through *isnad* to Salman al-Farsi, al-Tabrani quotes the latter citing the Messenger of Allah, peace be

---

[1] Al-Dhahabi has quoted this hadith while discussing the biography of Sharik in his book *Mizan al-I'tidal*, falsifying it and alleging that Sharik could not have tolerated narrating such a hadith. He said: "Muhammd ibn Hamid al-Razi is not trustworthy." Our answer to his allegation is that Imam Ahmad ibn Hanbal, Imam Abul Qasim al-Baghwi, Imam Ibn Jarir al-Tabari, the Imam of critics and verifiers Ibn Ma'in, and others of their caliber, have all trusted Muhammad ibn

upon him and his progeny, saying: "My successor, my confidant, the best man I leave behind me to fulfil my promise and implement my religion, is 'Ali ibn Abu Talib (as)."[2] This is a clear text proving that he is the successor, and an obvious testimony that he is the best of people after the Prophet (s). It contains an obligatory instruction that he should succeed him, and that people should obey him, as is clear to the wise.

Abu Na'im al-Hafiz, in his *Hilyat al-Awliya'*,[3] quotes Anas saying that the Messenger of Allah, peace be upon him and his progeny, said to him: "O Anas! The first to enter this door is the Imam of the pious, the leader of Muslims, the chief of religion, the seal of successors of prophets, and the leader of the most pious among renowned men." Anas says that 'Ali came in, and the Messenger of Allah, peace be upon him and his progeny, stood up with excitement, hugged 'Ali and said to him: "You will discharge my responsibility, convey my instructions, and explain all that in which they will dispute after me."

Al-Tabrani, in his *Al-Kabir*, quotes Abu Ayyub al-Ansari citing the Messenger of Allah, peace be upon him and his progeny, saying that the Prophet (s) addressed Fatima once thus: "O Fatima! Have you not come to know that Allah, the Dear One, cast a look at the inhabitants of the earth and chose your father from among them and sent him as His Messenger, then He cast a second look

---

Hamid and narrated his hadith, for he is their mentor. A reliable authority such as al-Dhahabi admits the same in his biography of Muhammd ibn Hamid in his *Al-Mizan*. The man cannot be charged with Rafidism or Shi'ism, but the critic is a predecessor of al-Dhahabi; so, there is no reason for initiating such an accusation regarding this hadith.

[2] This hadith *verbatim* is numbered 2570 at the end of page 155, Vol. 6, of *Kanz al-'Ummal*, and the author quotes it again in his *Muntakhab al-Kanz*; so, refer to *Al-Muntakhab*, footnote on page 32, Vol. 5, of Ahmad's *Musnad*.

[3] It exists on page 450, Vol. 2, of *Sharh Nahjul Balaghah*, and we have quoted it in Letter No. 48.

and selected your husband and inspired me to marry him to you and appoint him as my successor?"[4]

Notice how Allah selected 'Ali (as) from among all other inhabitants of the earth, immediately after selecting from among them the Seal of His Prophets (s), and see how the selection of the successor is conducted in the same sequence to the selection of the Prophet. Also see how Allah inspired His Prophet to solemnize his marriage and appoint him as his successor. See if successors of prophets were any other than the latter's own *wasis*. Is it fitting to push aside [when it comes to selecting a caliph] one who is the best among Allah's servants, the *wasi* of the master of His Prophets, and prefer someone else over him? Is it fitting if someone else, other than he, should rule the Muslims and make him simply one of his own commoners and subjects? Is it possible, by virtue of reason, that one elected by people should be obeyed by that who was selected by Allah, just as He selected His Prophet? How is it possible that both Allah Himself and His Messenger choose him while we elect someone else? "No believing man nor woman, after Allah and His Messenger have decreed an edict, should practice free will regarding their affairs; and whoever disobeys Allah and His Messenger surely strays manifestly (33:36)."

Narratives abound that state that as soon as those who were hypocritical, envious, and interest seeking came to know that the Messenger of Allah, peace be upon him and his progeny, was going to marry his daughter Fatima al-Zahra', mistress of the women of paradise and equal only to Mary (as), to 'Ali, they envied 'Ali and were extremely concerned, especially after many of them had unsuccessfully sought her hand.[5] They said that that was indicative

---

[4] This hadith, *verbatim*, as well as its source are also in hadith number 2541 on page 143, Vol. 6, of *Kanz al-'Ummal*, and it is quoted in *Muntakhab al-Kanz* as well; so, refer to the latter and read the footnote on page 31, Vol. 5, of Ahmad's *Musnad*.

[5] Ibn Abu Hatim has quoted Anas saying: "Abu Bakr and 'Umar sought Fatima's hand from the Prophet, but he remained silent and did not tell them anything; so, they went to 'Ali to inform him."

of 'Ali's status; so, nobody had any hope of being his peer, and they even plotted and schemed. They sent their women to the Mistress of the Women of the World trying to turn her against 'Ali. Among what they said to her was that 'Ali was poor and did not have much of this world's possessions, but she, peace be upon her, was quite aware of their scheming and ill intentions as well as those of their men. In spite of all this, she did not offend them in any way, till the Will of Allah Almighty and Omniscient and of His Messenger was carried out. It was then that she desired to show those women the status enjoyed by the Commander of the Faithful (as) whereby Allah will shame his enemies, and she said: "O Messenger of Allah! Why did you marry me to a poor man who has no money?" He, peace be upon him and his progeny, answered her in the way stated above.

> When Allah wishes to publicize
> A virtue hidden from the eyes,
> He facilitates to it one very well-known
> To covet and envy everyone.

Al-Khatib quotes one author whose *isnad* is unanimously agreed upon, and who is very highly respected, namely Ibn 'Abbas, saying: "When the Prophet (s) solemnized the marriage of Fatima and 'Ali, Fatima said: 'O Messenger of Allah! You have married me to a poor man who does not have anything.' The Prophet (s)

It is also transmitted from Ibn Abu Hatim by many reliable authorities such as Ibn Hajar at the beginning of Chapter 11 of his *Al-Sawa'iq al-Muhriqa*. Many other authorities have quoted something similar to it from Ahmad through *isnad* to Anas. Abu Dawud al-Sajistani, as stated by Ibn Hajar in Chapter 11 of his *Al-Sawa'iq al-Muhriqa*, while discussing the twelfth verse, says that Abu Bakr sought Fatima's hand, and the Prophet (s) turned him down; then 'Umar did the same, and he turned away from him, too; so, they both informed 'Ali of it. 'Ali himself is quoted saying: "Abu Bakr and 'Umar sought Fatima's hand from the Messenger of Allah, but he (s) rejected them. 'Umar then said: 'You, 'Ali, are worthy of her.'" This hadith is quoted by Ibn Jarir. Al-Dulabi has quoted it, admitting its authenticity while discussing the Prophet's purified progeny, and it is hadith number 6007 on page 392, Vol. 6, of *Kanz al-'Ummal*.

said to her: 'Are you not pleased that Allah has chosen from among the inhabitants of the earth two men one of whom is your father and the other is your husband?'"[6] Recounting the attributes of 'Ali, al-Hakim, on page 129, Vol. 3, of his *Al-Mustadrak*, quotes Sarij ibn Yunus citing Abu Hafs al-Abar, alA'mash, Abu Salih, and ending with Abu Hurayrah who quotes Fatima (as) saying: "O Messenger of Allah! Why have you married me to a poor man with no money?" He (s) answered: "O Fatima! Are you not pleased that Allah, the Exalted and Sublime, cast a look at the inhabitants of the earth and chose two men one of whom is your father and the other is your husband?" Ibn 'Abbas is also quoted saying that the Messenger of Allah (s) has said the following to Fatima: "Are you not pleased that I have married you to the one who is the foremost among Muslims in accepting Islam and the one endowed with more knowledge? You are the Mistress of the women of my nation, just as Mary was the mistress of the women of her nation; are you not pleased, O Fatima, that Allah cast a look at the people of the earth and chose two men from among them: one of them is your father and the other is your husband?"[7]

The Messenger of Allah (s), whenever the Mistress of the women of the world suffered any hardship, would remind her of Allah's favour and that of His Messenger unto her, since he married her to the best of his nation, thus solacing her and removing from her chest whatever pain time had brought her. Suffices you for a testimonial on this subject what Imam Ahmad has stated on page 26, Vol. 5, of his *Musnad* where he quotes one particular hadith narrated by Ma'qil ibn Yasar in which the Prophet (s) is reported to have visited Fatima (as) when she fell sick and said to her: "How

---

[6] This hadith, *verbatim*, with reference to its narrator, is hadith number 5992 on page 391, Vol. 6, of *Kanz al-'Ummal*, where the author admits the reliability of its narrator.

[7] This hadith, *verbatim*, with reference to its narrator, is hadith number 2543 on page 153, Vol. 6, of *Kanz al-'Ummal*, where the author quotes it from Ibn 'Abbas and Abu Hurayrah. Al-Tabrani, in his *Al-Muttafaq*, has transmitted it from al-Khatib who quotes Ibn 'Abbas; so, refer to *Al-Muntakhab* and read the first line of footnote on page 39, Vol. 5, of Ahmad's *Musnad*.

do you feel?" She answered: "By Allah, my grief has intensified, my want has worsened, and my sickness has lasted for too long." He (s) said to her: "Yet are you not satisfied that I have married you to the one who is the foremost among my nation in accepting Islam, the one endowed with more knowledge, and the greatest in clemency?" Narratives relating this issue are numerous, and there is no room to state all of them in this letter, Wassalam.

Sincerely,
Sh

Letter 69
Safar 10, 1330

Argument of the Will's Deniers

Those who follow the Sunnah and consensus deny this will simply because of what al-Bukhari has narrated in his *Sahih* where he quotes al-Aswad saying, "It was said once to 'Ayesha, may Allah be pleased with her, that the Prophet (s) had made a will regarding 'Ali,[1] and she responded: 'Who said so? I have seen the Prophet, while I was reclining him to my chest, when he ordered a washbowl to be brought to him; I hardly noticed how fast he collapsed and died; so, how could he have made a will to 'Ali?"[2] In the same reference, the author quotes other sources citing 'Ayesha saying, "The Messenger of Allah breathed his last while being between my stomach and under my chin," and she is often noted as saying, "He died reclining on my chest," and she may have

---

[1] This hadith is quoted by al-Bukhari in his treatise on "*Al-Wasaya* (wills)," page 83, Vol. 2, of his *Sahih*, and in his chapter on the sickness and demise of the Prophet (s), page 64, Vol. 3, of the same book. It is quoted by Muslim on page 64, Vol. 3, of his *Sahih*, and it is also quoted by Muslim in his treatise of the Prophet's will on page 14, Vol. 2, of his *Sahih*.

[2] You probably already know that both shaykhs have intentionally narrated this hadith while discussing the Prophet's will to 'Ali, for those who stated at that time that the Prophet had left a will to 'Ali had not yet split from the ranks of the nation. They were either among the *sahabah* or the *tabi'in* who had the courage to reveal what would make the mother of believers unhappy and would oppose the politics of the time; for this reason, she, may Allah be pleased with her, was shaken a great deal when she heard their hadith. Such a reaction is seen in her own statement in response to it, a statement which is one of the feeblest of answers. Imam al-Sindi, in his comment on this hadith in al-Nisai's *Sunan*, as indicated on page 241, Vol. 6 (the Egyptian Press at al-Azhar), said: "It is quite obvious that such hadith [by the mother of the believers 'Ayesha] does not rule out the existence of the will prior to her statement, nor does it prove that he (s) had died suddenly without being able to leave a will or could have thought of doing so, since he came to know that his end was approaching even before falling sick, then he remained sick for days....," up to the conclusion of his statement. If you scrutinize this statement, you will find it quite strong.

said: "He died while his head was on my thigh."³ So, had there been any will, she would have come to know about it. In Muslim's *Sahih*, in a treatise on the subject of wills on page 14, Vol. 2, the author quotes 'Ayesha saying, "The Messenger of Allah (s) left neither a dinar nor a dirham, nor a male nor a female camel, nor did he leave any will." In both *sahih*s, in a treatise on wills, Talhah ibn Masrif is quoted saying, "I asked 'Abdullah ibn Abu 'Awfah: 'Did the Prophet leave any will at all?' He answered: 'No.' I asked him: 'How did he enjoin people to write their wills while he himself did not do so?' He answered: 'His will is the Book of Allah.'" Since these ahadith are more authentic than the ones which you have cited, and are included in both *sahih*s, while the ones you have cited are not, they can be brought forth as irrefutable arguments, Wassalam.

Yours,
S

Letter 70
Safar 11, 1330

I. The Will Cannot be Repudiated

The Prophet's will regarding 'Ali cannot be repudiated, for there is no doubt that he entrusted him, having bequeathed to him his knowledge and wisdom, as indicated in Letter 66 above, to wash his corpse, enshroud it and bury it,⁴ and to pay his dues, fulfil

---

³ Her statements "He died on my chest," and "He died between my belly and chin," are recorded in a chapter dealing with his sickness and demise (s) in Bukhari's *Sahih*. As regarding her statement "He died while his head was on my thigh," this exists in another chapter in which the author discusses his sickness and demise without an intervening chapter.

⁴ On page 66, Part Two, Vol. 2, of his *Tabaqat*, Ibn Sa'd quotes 'Ali saying: "The Prophet (s) had instructed that nobody other than myself should give him the ceremonial bath [for the dead]." Both Abul Shaykh and Ibn al-Najjar, as stated on page 54, Vol. 4, of *Kanz al-'Ummal*, quote 'Ali (as) saying: "The Messenger of Allah (s) had instructed me saying: 'When I die, bathe me and use seven water skins.'" Ibn Sa'd, while discussing giving the Prophet (s) his last

ceremonial bath, on page 63, Part Two, Vol. 2, of his *Tabaqat*, quotes 'Abdul-Wahid ibn Abu 'Awanah saying that when the Messenger of Allah (s) fell sick prior to his demise, he said: "O 'Ali! You should bathe me when I die." 'Ali said: "I conducted the ceremonial bath for him, and each part of his body was very responsive to my touch." Both al-Hakim, on page 59, Vol. 3, of his *Al-Mustadrak*, and al-Dhahabi in his *Talkhis*, quote 'Ali saying: "I gave the Messenger of Allah his bath, and I waited to see how death would affect his body, but I sensed no change: his body smelt in death as fragrantly as it did when he was still alive." This hadith is quoted by Sa'id ibn Mansur in his books of traditions, by al-Marwazi in his *Jana'iz*, by Abu Dawud in his *Marasil*, by Ibn Mani', Ibn Abu Shaybah in his books on traditions, and it is hadith number 1094, page 54, Vol. 4, of *Kanz al-'Ummal*. Al-Bayhaqi, in his books of traditions, quotes 'Abdullah ibn al-Harith saying: "'Ali gave the Prophet (s) the ceremonial bath while the Prophet's corpse was wrapped in a shirt," and it is hadith number 1104, page 55, Vol. 4, of *Kanz al-'Ummal*, and Ibn 'Abbas is quoted saying: "'Ali has four chracteristics nobody else has had: he is the first to pray in the company of the Messenger of Allah; he accompanied him in all his campaigns; he remained with him when others ran away for their own lives, and he is the one who administered the ceremonial bath to him and placed him in his grave." This is quoted by Ibn 'Abd al-Birr is his biography of 'Ali in the *Isti'ab*, and by al-Hakim on page 111, Vol. 3, of *Al-Mustadrak*. He also quotes Abu Sa'id al-Khudri saying that the Messenger of Allah, peace be upon him and his progeny, has said to 'Ali: "O 'Ali! You are the one who should bathe me, cancel my debts, and entomb me in my grave." This is quoted by al-Daylami, too, and it is hadith number 2583, page 155, Vol. 4, of *Kanz al-'Ummal*. 'Umar is quoted saying that the Messenger of Allah (s) said to 'Ali (as) once: "You are to bathe me and bury me," according to the hadith on page 393, Vol. 6, of *Kanz al-'Ummal*. In the footnote to page 45, Vol. 5, of Ahmad's *Musnad*, 'Ali is quoted saying: "I have heard the Messenger of Allah (s) saying: 'I have been granted five of my own wishes regarding 'Ali the like of which no other Prophet before me had been granted regarding anyone. The first is that he is the one who would cancel my debt and bury my body...,'" up to the end of the hadith quoted at the beginning of page 403, Vol. 6, of *Kanz al-'Ummal*. And when he was placed on the bed and people desired to perform the ritual burial prayer rites, 'Ali said: "Nobody should be the Imam in leading such prayer, for the Messenger of Allah is your Imam alive and dead." People used to enter in groups and stand in prayers in a row without an Imam. They would make the *takbir* as 'Ali stood near the corpse of the Messenger of Allah (s) saying: "Peace be unto you, O Messenger, and Allah's Mercy and Blessings; we bear witness, O Mighty Lord, that he has conveyed what You have revealed unto him, provided advice to his nation, and struggled in the way of Allah till He, the Exalted, the omni-Scient, elevated His faith, and his mission was accomplished. O Lord! Include us among those who follow what You have revealed to him, make us strong in our conviction, and his promise on his behalf, defray his outstanding debts,[5] and explain to people after him whatever matters in which they differed regarding the commandments and injunctions of Allah, the Exalted

---

rejoin our souls in his company," and people would respond with "Amin, Amin." This continued till all men, then women, then children, said their prayers. This hadith *verbatim* is quoted by Ibn Sa'd in his discussion of how the Prophet was given his ceremonial burial bath in his own *Tabaqat*. The first who entered to pay respects were the descendants of Hashim, then the Immigrants (*Muhajirun*), then the Supporters (*Ansar*), then other people. The first men who performed the ritual funeral prayers on his departed soul were 'Ali and al-'Abbas who stood beside each other and made five *takbirs*.

[5] Narratives in this regard are consecutively reported from the purified progeny (as). Suffices you what is quoted in *Al-Kabir* by al-Tabrani from Ibn 'Umar, and by Abu Ya'li in his *Musnad* from 'Ali (as). The first quotes one particular hadith in which the Messenger of Allah (s) says: "O 'Ali! You are my brother and vizier, and you shall pay my dues on my behalf, fulfill my commitment, and set my conscience to ease." You can find this hadith on page 155, Vol. 6, of *Kanz al-'Ummal* narrated by Ibn 'Umar. On page 404, Vol. 6, of the same reference, 'Ali (as) is quoted stating likewise. Many have quoted al-Buwaisiri saying that the narrators of this hadith are all trustworthy. Ibn Mardawayh and al-Daylami, as stated on page 155, Vol. 6, of *Kanz al-'Ummal*, quote Salman al-Farsi saying that the Messenger of Allah (s) has said: "'Ali ibn Abu Talib fulfills my commitments on my own behalf, and he cancels my debt." Al-Bazzaz, as stated on page 153, Vol. 6, of *Kanz al-'Ummal*, indicates the same. It is also quoted by Imam Ahmad ibn Hanbal on page 164, Vol. 4, of his *Musnad* from Habashi ibn Janadah who says: "I have heard the Messenger of Allah (s) saying: 'Nobody pays my dues except I or 'Ali.'" Ibn Mardawayh, as stated on page 401, Vol. 6, of *Kanz al-'Ummal*, quotes 'Ali (as) saying that when the verse "And warn thy near in kin" was revealed, the Messenger of Allah (s) said: "'Ali pays my debt, and fulfills my promise on my own behalf." Sa'd says that on the Juhfa day, the Messenger of Allah (s), having taken 'Ali by the hand, and delivered a sermon, praised and glorified Allah then said: "O people! I am your *wali*." They said: "You have spoken the truth, O Messenger of Allah." Then he raised 'Ali's hand and said: "This is the one chosen to be my *wali*; he shall pay my debt on my behalf." Qatadah is quoted saying, "'Ali has carried out after the prophet (s) a few errands (on behalf of the Prophet) one of which is said to have been the payment of [debts totalling] five hundred thousand dirhams." 'Abdul-Razzaq was asked: "Did the Prophet (s) leave a will in this regard?" He answered: "Yes; I do not doubt at all that the Prophet (s) has, indeed, left a will to 'Ali; otherwise, nobody would have let him pay the Prophet's debt all by himself." This hadith is quoted by the author of *Kanz al-'Ummal* on page 60, Vol. 4, who numbers it 1170.

and the Sublime.⁶ He also entrusted the nation to take 'Ali (as) as his (s) successor,⁷ brother,⁸ the father of his descendants,⁹ his

---

⁶ Authentic texts have unanimously stated that he (s) has entrusted 'Ali (as) to clarify to his nation whatever ambiguous matters in which they disputed after him. Suffices you for proofs ahadith number 11 and 12 quoted in Letter No. 48, in addition to others which we have already quoted, as well as others which we have not quoted due to their being too well-known.
⁷ This is explained in Letters 36, 40, 54, and 56 above.
⁸ The brotherhood between the Prophet and the wasi is *mutawatir*, and suffices you for proof for its authenticity what we have quoted in Letters No. 32 and 34.
⁹ His being the father of his descendants is understood. He (s) has said to 'Ali (as): "You are my brother, and the father of my descendants; you shall fight for my Sunnah." This hadith is quoted by Abu Ya'li in his *Musnad*, as stated on page 404, Vol. 6, of *Kanz al-'Ummal*, and its narrators are all trustworthy as admitted by al-Busairi. It is also quoted in Ahmad's *Manaqib*, as stated at the conclusion of Section Two, Part 9, page 74, of Ibn Hajar's *Al-Sawa'iq al-Muhriqa*. He (s) has also said: "Allah has placed the progeny of every prophet in his own loin, and He has placed mine in 'Ali's loins." This hadith is quoted by al-Tabrani in his *Al-Kabir* as narrated by Jabir, and by al-Khatib in his *Tarikh* from Ibn 'Abbas. It is hadith number 2510, page 152, Vol. 6, of *Kanz al-'Ummal*. And he (s) has said: "All descendants of women belong to the latter's men except Fatima's, for I am their *wali* and father." This is quoted by al-Tabrani from al-Zahra' (as) and is included among the ahadith quoted by Ibn Hajar in Section 2, Part 11, of his *Al-Sawa'iq al-Muhriqa*, page 112. It is also quoted by al-Tabrani from Ibn 'Umar as referred to on the same page. Al-Hakim quotes something like it on page 164, Vol. 3, of his *Al-Mustadrak*, adding: "The narrators of this hadith are trustworthy, though they [Bukhari and Muslim] did not record it." He (s) has said in one hadith quoted by al-Hakim in his *Al-Mustadrak*, and al-Dhahabi in his *Talkhis al-Mustadrak*, both admitting its authenticity due to the endorsement of both shaykhs, "As regarding you, O 'Ali, you, indeed, are my brother and the father of my descendants; you are of me and for me," up to the end of the list of such authentic texts.

vizier,[10] confidant,[11] the executor of his will,[12] his vicegerent,[13] the gateway of his knowledge, according to hadith number 9 cited in Letter 48 above, the gateway of his wisdom, according to hadith number 10 cited in Letter 48, the Gate of Salvation of his nation, according to hadith number 14 cited in Letter 48 above, its security and the ark of its salvation, as testified by the traditions we quoted in Letter 8 above. Obeying Ali is as important as obeying the Prophet himself: disobedience to him is a sin equal to that of

---

[10] Refer to the texts regarding 'Ali's government such as his (s) statement: "You to me are in the same status like that of Aaron to Moses," as we explained in Letter No. 26, and in others. And also his saying (s) in the hadith of warning his household, "Who, then, among you would support me in my mission?" 'Ali answered: "I, O Messenger of Allah, would like to be your supporter in this matter," as quoted in our Letter No. 20. May Allah reward Imam Abu-Sayri for his poetic masterpiece in which he says:

And the vizier of his cousin in endeavours sublime,
And by their own households are viziers prime;
Uncovering the lid did not his conviction increase,
Like the sun, nothing can cause his rays to decrease.

[11] The nation's consensus has decreed that there is one verse in the Book of Allah implemented by nobody other than 'Ali till the Day of Judgment. It is the verse of elevation [*najwa*] in Surah al-Mujadila. This is agreed upon by both his supporters and opponents who quote in this regard many texts held to be authentic according to both shaykhs, known by the pious among the nation as well as the libertine. Suffices you what is quoted by al-Hakim on page 482, Vol. 2, of his *Al-Mustadrak*, and by al-Dhahabi in his *Talkhis al-Mustadrak*. Refer also to the exegesis of this verse as recorded by books of exegesis authored by al-Tha'labi, al-Tabari, al-Sayyuti, al-Zamakhshari, al-Razi, and others. In the forthcoming Letter No. 74, you will come to know of two ahadith narrated by Umm Salamah and 'Abdullah ibn 'Umar regarding the confidential dialogue between the Prophet (s) and 'Ali (as) immediately prior to the Prophet's demise, and you will be acquainted with their confidential discussion on the day of Ta'if, and the statement of the Messenger of Allah (s) then: "It is not I who has confided in him; it is Allah Who has done so," and also to their confidential talks during 'Ayesha's time; so, contemplate upon that.

[12] Suffices you for a text proving that he is his *wali* his statement (s), quoted by Ibn 'Abbas and referred to in Letter No. 22: "You are the *wali* on my behalf in this life and the life hereafter." This hadith stands on firm grounds according to the demands of the religion of Islam; therefore, there is no need to go into details.

[13] Suffices you of the texts of the will what you have heard in Letter No. 68.

disobeying the Prophet according to hadith number 16 cited in Letter 48 and according to others. Following him is equal to following the Prophet; abandoning him is abandoning the Prophet, according to hadith number 17 cited in Letter 48 above and according to others, that he [Prophet] is on peaceful terms with whoever is peaceful with him, and he is an enemy of whoever bears animosity towards him,[14] the friend of whoever befriends him and the enemy of whoever antagonizes him;[15] whoever loves him is loved by Allah and His Messenger, and whoever hates him does in turn hate Allah and His Messenger, according to ahadith 19, 20 and 21 cited in Letter 48 above and according to others. Whoever befriends him befriends them both, and whoever antagonizes him in fact antagonizes them both, according to hadith 23 cited in the same Letter; whoever harms him harms them too;[16] whoever denounces him does in fact denounce both Allah and His

---

[14] This is quoted by Imam Ahmad from Abu Hurayrah's hadith on page 442, Vol. 2, of his *Musnad*. He says that the Messenger of Allah (s) looked at 'Ali, Fatima, al-Hasan, and al-Husayn, peace be upon them, then said: "I declare war on whoever fights you, and peace unto whoever is peaceful towards you." In another authentic hadith, he (s) has also said when he covered them with a blanket, "I declare war on whoever fights them, and peace unto whoever is peaceful towards them." This hadith is transmitted by Ibn Hajar while explaining the first verse which he states to have been revealed in their honour in Section One, Part 11, of his *Al-Sawa'iq al-Muhriqa*, giving detailed explanation for his (s) statement: "Fighting 'Ali is fighting me, too, and making peace with 'Ali is making peace with me."

[15] Refer to hadith 20 in Letter No. 48. His consecutive statement: "O Lord! Befriend whoever befriends him, and be the enemy of whoever sets himself as his enemy" should, by the Grace of Allah, suffice. You have heard in Letter No. 36 his (s) statement as quoted by Buraydah: "Whoever hates 'Ali hates me, too, and whoever abandons 'Ali abandons me, too." Another *mutawatir* hadith is his (s) statement: "Nobody loves him ['Ali] except a believer, and nobody hates him except a hypocrite." It is by Allah the covenant of the Ummi Prophet (s).

[16] Consider his statement (s), which is quoted by 'Umar ibn Shash, "Anyone who hurts 'Ali hurts me, too," which is quoted by Ahmad on page 483, Vol. 3, of his *Musnad*, and by al-Hakim on page 123, Vol. 3, of his *Al-Mustadrak*, and by al-Dhahabi in *Talkhis al-Mustadrak* where he admits its authenticity. Al-Bukhari has quoted it in his *Tarikh*, Ibn Sa'd in his *Tabaqat*, Ibn Abu-Shaybah in his *Musnad*, and al-Tabrani in his *Kabir*. It exists on page 400, Vol. 6, of *Kanz al-'Ummal*.

Messenger (s), according to hadith 18 cited in Letter 48 above, and according to others. He is the Imam of the righteous and the annihilator of the debauchees; whoever supports is in fact divinely supported, and whoever betrays him is betrayed by the Almighty, according to the first hadith cited in the same Letter and according to others; he is the master of Muslims and the Imam of the righteous, the leader of the pious among the most renowned men, according to ahadith 2, 3, 4, and 5 in Letter 48; he is the banner of guidance, the Imam of Allah's servants, the lighthouse of whoever obeys Allah's commandments, the Word which Allah has enjoined upon the pious, according to hadith 6 in the same Letter and according to others; he is the supreme Siddiq, the nation's Faruq, and the believers' chief, according to hadith 7 in the same Letter and according to others. His status is like that of the Great Furqan (Qur'an) and the Wise Remembrance.[17] He is to the Prophet in the same position which Aaron held in comparison to Moses, as clarified in Letters No. 26, 28, 30, 32, and 34, and to the Prophet's status with his Lord, according to hadith 13 of Letter 48, and according to others, and like the position of the Prophet's head to his body, according to the hadith quoted in Letter 50 and to others, to which we refer you, suggesting that you may observe our comment. He is like unto his own self according to the verse of Mubahala and to the hadith quoted by Ibn 'Awf which is reproduced in Letter 50. Allah the Exalted and the Sublime cast a look at the inhabitants of the earth and chose him from among them as is clear from the traditions which we have quoted in our Letter 68. Suffices you his covenant on the standing day at 'Arafat during the Farewell Pilgrimage, and that nobody discharges the Prophet's responsibility other than the Prophet himself or 'Ali,[18] up to the

---

[17] Consider in this regard what you have heard in Letter No. 8 quoting Sihah al-Thaqalain, for they show the truth to those who have eyes to see, and you have already come to know in Letter No. 50 that "'Ali is with the Qur'an and the Qur'an is with 'Ali; they shall never separate from each other."

[18] Reason alone rules it impossible that the Prophet (s) would order something and strongly requires his nation to adhere to it while he himself is in dire need to act upon it. He needed a will in order to appoint his representative, and take into consideration the orphans who most badly need a care-taker. Allah is above

end of so many such attributes which nobody else can claim other than a *wasi*, and those who enjoy a special status with the Prophet; so, how can any wise person deny the Prophet's will, or overlook it, other than an interest seeker? What is a will other than entrusting a person with some such matters?

II. Why Denied

As regarding the followers of the four sects, whoever denies it from among them does so thinking that accepting it will jeopardize the legitimacy of the caliphate of the three Imams.

III. Deniers' Arguments not Binding

We cannot accept their argument just because it is based upon what al-Bukhari and others have said. They quote Talhah ibn Masrif saying: "I asked 'Abdullah ibn Abu 'Awfah: 'Did the Prophet leave any will at all?' He answered: 'No.' I asked: 'How did he enjoin people to write their wills while he himself did not do so?' He answered: 'His will is the Book of Allah.'" This hadith is not confirmed through our sources; it is but a fabrication necessitated by certain politicians. Regardless of that, the *sahih*s of the purified progeny are *mutawatir* regarding the issue of the will; so, let all texts which disagree with them be discarded.

IV. Reason and Intellect Require it

Yet the issue of the will does not even require any argument due to the dictates of reason and common sense.

---

neglecting his precious legacy, which includes Allah's legislations and commandments, and Allah is above leaving his orphans and widows, who are residents of the earth far and wide, struggling in the dark, going and coming as they desired, without a *qayyim* through whom Allah's argument becomes complete against them. Yet even common sense by itself rules that he should have left a will for 'Ali (as), since we have found the prophet (s) entrusting him to bathe and embalm his corpse, to clothe and bury it, then to pay his outstanding debts and clear his conscience, and clarify to people what they differ regarding their faith after him... etc., as referred to at the beginning of this Letter.

If something elongates, it stands by itself - in form and hue;
For surely the sun dissipates all that seems to be untrue.

As regarding al-Bukhari's narrative from Ibn Abu 'Awfah who claims that the Prophet, peace be upon him and his progeny, has left the Book of Allah as his will, it is a statement the tail of which is cut off, for he, peace be upon him and his progeny, had recommended to his nation to uphold both Weighty Things spontaneously, warning it of the danger of straying if it did not do so, informing it that they both would never part from each other till they reached him at the Pool. Our *sahih*s in this regard are consecutively reported from the sources of the purified progeny; so, you may refer to other *sahih*s as quoted in our Letters No. 8 and 54, Wassalam.

Yours,
Sh

Letter 71
Safar 10, 1330

Why Reject the Hadith of the Mother of Believers and the best Among the Prophet's Consorts?

Why did you - may Allah forgive you - turn away from the mother of believers and the best of the Prophet's consorts and discarded her hadith, leaving it to oblivion, while her statement is the final and just judgment? In spite of this, you may give us your own viewpoint to consider, Wassalam.

Sincerely,
S

Letter 72
Safar 12, 1330

I. She Was Not the Best of the Prophet's Consorts

The mother of the believers 'Ayesha enjoys a special status, and she has her own contribution standing to her credit, but she is not the best of the Prophet's wives. How can she be the best since one authentic hadith quotes her saying, "The Messenger of Allah, peace be upon him and his progeny, once mentioned Khadija, and I objected by saying: 'She was an old woman, and such and such, and Allah has granted you someone better than her [meaning herself].' He said: 'Not at all; Allah has not granted me better than her; she believed in me when people denounced me, and she believed in me when people called me a liar; she shared her wealth with me when people deprived me, and Allah blessed me with children by her while depriving me of the children of all others'"? 'Ayesha is also reported as having said, "The Messenger of Allah, peace be upon him and his progeny, never left home before mentioning Khadija and praising her. One day, he mentioned her, and I felt jealous. I said: 'Was she but an old woman, while Allah has blessed you with someone better than her?' He became so offended that his front hair shook in anger, then he said: 'No, by

Allah! Allah did not bless me with anyone better than her! She believed in me when people disbelieved; she held me truthful when people called me a liar; she gave me an equal share of her wealth when people deprived me, and Allah blessed me with children by her while depriving me the children of other women.'"[1]

II. The Best is Khadija

The best of the Prophet's (s) consorts, therefore, is Khadija al-Kubra, the truthful of this nation, the foremost in believing in Allah and His Book, and in solacing His Prophet. Allah has inspired His Messenger (s) to convey the good news to her that she had in Paradise a house built of stalks of gold and silver,[2] and that she had been a favourite of Allah. The Almighty said of her: "The best of the women of Paradise are Khadija daughter of Khuaylid, Fatima daughter of Muhammad, Asiya daughter of Muzahim, and Mary daughter of 'Umran (Amram)." He, peace be upon him and his progeny, has said: "Among all the women of the world, commended are Khadija daughter of Khuaylid, Fatima daughter of Muhammad, Asiya daughter of Muzahim, and Mary daughter of 'Umran." There are other ahadith which are among the most authentic and reliable emphasizing the same.[3] It cannot also be said that 'Ayesha was the best among the mothers of believers save Khadija. Reliable traditions and recorded events refuse to favour her over the others, as is obvious to the wise. She probably thought of herself as being superior to all others, and the Prophet, peace be upon him and his progeny, did not agree with her self assessment. The same happened with Safiyya daughter of Huyay when the Messenger of Allah, peace be upon him and his progeny, entered

---

[1] This hadith and the one that follows it are among detailed ahadith narrated by Sunnis. Refer to them in the discussion of Khadija al-Kubra (as) in the *Isti'ab*, and you will find them as we have quoted them here *verbatim*. They are quoted by al-Bukhari and Muslim in their *sahih*s in almost similar wording.

[2] As narrated by al-Bukhari in his chapter on women's jealousy and sentimentality, near the conclusion of his treatise on marriage, page 175, Vol. 3, of his *Sahih*.

[3] We have quoted it in the second paragraph of our celebrated statement, and anyone who wishes to research is referred thereto.

her room once and found her weeping. He asked her: "What grieves you?" She answered: "I have come to know that both 'Ayesha and Hafsa speak ill of me and say that they are better than me." He, peace be upon him and his progeny, said: "Couldn't you have told them: 'How can you be better than me, since my father is Aaron, my uncle is Moses, and my husband is Muhammad?'"[4] Whoever traces the mother of the believers 'Ayesha in her deeds and statements will find her as we indicate here.

III. A General Hint to the Reason Why her Hadith was Discarded

The reason why we have discarded her hadith regarding the will is due to the fact that it does not constitute an argument, and please do not ask me to elaborate on this point, Wassalam.

Sincerely,
Sh

---

[4] This is quoted by al-Tirmizi from Kinanah, slave of the mother of believers Safiyya, and it is transmitted by Ibn 'Abd al-Birr in his biography of Safiyya in the *Isti'ab*, Ibn Hajar in her biography in *Al-Isabah*, by Shaykh Rashid Rida at the end of page 589, Vol. 12, of his *Manar*, in addition to many other traditionists.

Letter 73
Safar 13, 1330

Requesting an Explanation to our Rejection of 'Ayesha's Hadith

You are not one who deceives, cheats, or pretends, nor are you one who falsely charges someone. You are above being charged or accused as being as such. I, praise be to Allah, neither criticize nor disprove, nor do I look for someone's faults nor shortcomings; truth is my pursuit. I cannot help asking you why you turn away from her ['Ayesha's] hadith, and your documented answer to this question is unavoidable.

> Convey your message, and have no worry,
> Let thy eyes be cooled, and be merry.

The argument I press in this regard is embedded in the meaning of this verse of the Holy Qur'an: "Those who have concealed what We have revealed of clear signs and guidance after We had made them clear to mankind in the Book: these have been cursed by Allah and by those who curse (2:159)"..., Wassalam.

Sincerely,
S

Letter 74
Safar 14, 1330

I. Explaining Why We Reject her Hadith

You have, may Allah assist you, insisted that I should elaborate, and you have left me no option except doing just that. Due to the wealth of your knowledge, you know where we come from. Here lies the fountainhead of the will; here lies the battle-ground of explicit texts; here lies the annihilation of the *khums*, inheritance, and creed; here lies the cause of sedition; here lies the reason of discord; here lies the root of dissension...[1] While fighting the Commander of the Faithful, she toured the lands, leading a huge army in order to usurp his government and put an end to his rule.

> What happened has happened; I am no narrator of that;
> So have good thoughts, and do not ask who, when or what.

To argue in support of denying the will to 'Ali using her own statement, the most bitter of his enemies that she was, is an attempt not expected at all from any fair-minded person. And that was not the only incident that demonstrated her animosity towards 'Ali (as). Denying the will to 'Ali is much less significant than the Lesser Camel (Jamal) Battle[2] and the Greater Camel Battle in which evil intentions surfaced and the curtain removed. Likewise, her attitude was manifest even before going out to fight him, the man who was her own *wali*, and her Prophet's wasi, till the news

---

[1] This agrees with Sunni books of traditions; so, refer to al-Bukhari's *Sahih*, his chapter on the households of the Prophet's wives, his treatise on holy wars and traditions, page 125, Vol. 2, and you will find the details.

[2] The dissension of the Lesser Camel Battle took place in Basra five days before the end of Rabi'ul-Thani, 36 A.H., before the arrival of the Commander of the Faithful (as) there, when the city was attacked by the mother of believers ['Ayesha] accompanied by Talhah and al-Zubayr. 'Ali's governor of Basra then was 'Uthman ibn Hanif al-Ansari. Forty supporters of 'Ali (as) were killed at its mosque, and seventy others elsewhere. 'Uthman ibn Hanif, who was one of the most respectful *sahabah*, was taken captive, and his captors wanted to kill him but feared revenge from his brother Suhayl and the rest of the Ansar; so, they shaved his beard, moustache, eyebrows, and head; they beat him, imprisoned him, then they expelled him from Basra. They were fought by Hakim ibn Jablah, with a group of his tribe 'Abd Qays, of whom he was chief. Hakim was a man of wisdom, discretion, and prestige, and he was followed by a group of Banu Rabi'a who refused to cease fighting till each and every one of them was martyrded, including Hakim, in addition to his most honourable son, his brave brother, and Basra fell in the hands of the invading army. When 'Ali (as) came, he had to face 'Ayesha's army, and so did the Greater Camel Battle take place. The details of both battles are preserved in books of history written by Ibn Jarir, Ibn al-Athir, and in many others.

of his death reached her, whereupon she prostrated to thank God (for his martyrdom) and composed these lines:[3]

> She laid down her rod, happy and pleased,
> Her heart joyful, her mind eased;
> As a traveller arrives home, of burdens relieved;
> Never say 'Ayesha, by Ali's death, was grieved.

If you desire, I may quote for you of her hadith what proves to you that she was in remote error. She has said: "When the Messenger of Allah, peace be upon him and his progeny, became seriously sick, he went out dragging his feet, reclining on two persons; one of them was 'Abbas ibn 'Abdul Muttalib and another man."[4] The narrator of this hadith comments adding: "I informed 'Abdullah ibn 'Abbas about what 'Ayesha had said, and he responded to me saying, 'Do you know the name of the man whom 'Ayesha did not name?' I said: 'no.' Ibn 'Abbas said: 'He was 'Ali ibn Abu Talib.'" The narrator continues to say that 'Ayesha does not wish 'Ali any good.[5]

If she did not wish any good to a man with whom the Messenger of Allah, peace be upon him and his progeny, walked, how could she then be expected to feel good about mentioning the will which contains a great deal of good for 'Ali? On page 113, Vol. 6, of his Musnad, Imam Ahmad quotes 'Ata' ibn Yasar saying:

---

[3] As quoted by trustworthy chroniclers such as Abul-Faraj al-Isfahani at the conclusion of his discussion of 'Ali in his book *Maqatil al-Talibiyyin*.

[4] As quoted by al-Bukhari about her in his section on the Prophet's (s) sickness and demise, page 62, Vol. 3, of his *Sahih*.

[5] This statement in particular, i.e. Ibn 'Abbas saying that 'Ayesha does not wish him any good, is left out by al-Bukhari who stops his quotation at its preceding statements, following his customary habit in such situations, but many authors of books of tradition have quoted it through their authentic reporters. Consider what Ibn Sa'd records on page 29, Section Two, Vol. 2, of his *Tabaqat*, where he cites a chain of narrators including Ahmad ibn al-Hajjaj, 'Abdullah ibn Mubarak, Younus, Mu'ammar, al-Zuhri, 'Ubaydullah ibn Atbah ibn Mas'ud, whose sources end with Ibn 'Abbas. Reporters of this hadith are considered trustworthy according to the consensus of scholars.

"A man came and spoke ill of both 'Ali and 'Ammar to 'Ayesha who responded by saying, 'As regarding 'Ali, I have nothing to say to defend him; but concerning 'Ammar, I have heard the Messenger of Allah, peace be upon him and his progeny, say that whenever 'Ammar had to opt between two options, he always chose the most reasonable of them.'"

Have you noticed that?! The mother of the believers warns about plotting against 'Ammar due to the saying of the Messenger of Allah, peace be upon him and his progeny, "Whenever 'Ammar had to opt between two options, he always chose the most reasonable of them," while refraining from warning against plotting to harm 'Ali who is the brother and successor of the Prophet, his Aaron and confidant, the most just among his nation, the foremost to believe in his message, the one whose merits are the most...! As if she is not aware of his status in the eyes of Allah, the Exalted and Mighty, or his position in the heart of the Messenger of Allah, peace be upon him and his progeny, or his status in Islam, his great efforts for its promotion, and his handsome contributions. As if she never heard anything in the Book of Allah nor the Sunnah of His Messenger (s) in his praise, so that she would place him at par with 'Ammar!

By Allah, my mind is perplexed when I consider her statement: "I have seen the Prophet (s), while on my chest, ordering a wash-bowl to be brought to him; I hardly noticed how fast he collapsed and died; so, how could he have made a will to 'Ali?" I do not know which aspect of her statement I should criticize, being scrutinized as a whole from various angles. I wonder how anyone can presume that since his death took place the way she described, he could not have left a will. Did she think that a will is valid only at the time of death?! No, but it is the excuse of one who is fighting the irrefutable truth, whoever he or she may be, while Allah has said in His Glorious Book, addressing His revered Messenger (s), "It is prescribed unto you when death approaches someone to leave something good, a will (Qur'an, 2:180 and 5:106)." Did the mother of the believers ever see him, peace be upon him and his progeny, going against the instructions of the Book of Allah or ignoring its injunctions? God forbid. She saw him following its guidance, adhering to its verses, rushing to obey its bidding and forbidding, reaching the ultimate end of adherence to all its injunctions. There is no doubt in my mind that she must have heard him saying: "No believer who knows that he is leaving something behind him should sleep even two nights without having his will written,"[6] or something in this meaning, for his instructions regarding the writing of wills have undoubtedly come from him. It does not fit him or any other Prophet, blessings of Allah be upon all of them, to bid something without doing it himself, or forbid something while doing the opposite thereof; Allah is above selecting such individuals for conveying His message.

As regarding what Muslim and others have quoted 'Ayesha saying: "The Messenger of Allah (s) left neither a dinar nor a dirham, neither a male nor a female camel, nor did he leave any will," it is just like its previous "hadith." Yet it is not correct to assume that what she meant was that he (s) did not leave any will at all, but rather that he did not have possessions which required a will, for, indeed, he did not leave much of this world's wares, the most ascetic person that he was. He joined his Lord, the Exalted and the Sublime, leaving a few outstanding debts,[7] and a few items, in addition to things entrusted to him by other people which required a will [regarding who they belonged to. He also left of his own possessions something that would help defray his debts, and the fulfilment of his promises, with a remnant that required being

---

[6] As quoted by al-Bukhari at the beginning of his treatise on wills in his *Sahih*, page 83, Vol. 2. It is also quoted by Muslim in his section on the record of the [Prophet's] will, page 10, Vol. 2, of his *Sahih*.

[7] Mu'ammar quotes Qatadah saying that 'Ali (as) had taken care, on behalf of the Prophet (s), of certain matters after his demise, most of which was a debt estimated at five hundred thousand dirhams; so, refer to this hadith on page 60, Vol. 4, of *Kanz al-'Ummal*, and it is hadith number 1170 among the ones which he narrates.

handed over to his heir. The proof for that is what Fatima al-Zahra', peace be upon her, rightfully demanded of her father's inheritance.[8]

II. Reason Confirms the Will

The Messenger of Allah, peace be upon him and his progeny, left things which demanded a will, things which no other human being ever left. Suffices you that he left the upright religion of Allah, while still at the beginning of its growth and early inception, and that by itself demanded an heir more than did gold or silver, a house or a real estate, lands or cattle. The entire nation became his orphans and widows, seeking refuge with his successor to take his place to fare with them and manage their religious and secular affairs. It is impossible that the Messenger of Allah, peace be upon him and his progeny, should have entrusted Allah's religion, while still in its cradle, to inclinations and presumptions, or left the protection of its legislation to personal motives and interests, without a successor to look after religious as well as secular affairs, someone upon whom he could rely to represent him before the public. He is above leaving his orphans, who inhabited spacious lands, like frightened cattle in a rainy winter night, without anyone to look after them. He is above abandoning the will especially after having received instructions in its regard from his Lord and thus strongly commanded his nation to do so. Reason does not listen to the claim that no will was made, even if such a claim comes from a highly respected person.

At the dawn of the Islamic era, the Messenger of Allah, peace be upon him and his progeny, made a will to 'Ali (as) even before his mission was publicized in Mecca, immediately following the revelation of the verse saying: "And warn your near kin (26:214)," as we explained in Letter 20. He continued repeating his will time and over again, emphasizing it through many covenants to which we had referred. When he finally wished, while in his last hours, may I sacrifice my parents for his own sake, to write his will to

---

[8] As quoted by al-Bukhari at the and of his chapter on Khaybar's campaign in his *Sahih*, page 37, Vol. 2.

'Ali (as) to emphasize his previous verbal covenants, and to back his previous verbal statements in this regard, he, peace be upon him and his progeny, said: "Bring me some writing material so that I may write for you something to protect you against straying," but they disputed, while no dispute is permitted in the presence of a Prophet, and said: "The Messenger of Allah (s) is delirious."[9] It was then that he (s) realized, after they had made such a statement, that no trace would remain of his intended order, if implemented, other than dissension; therefore, he told them to clear his room, feeling satisfied with the verbal covenants which he had made to 'Ali (as).

In spite of all this, however, he made three recommendations at the time of his death: that they should select 'Ali as his successor; that they should turn the polytheists out of the Arabian Peninsula; and that they should reward the envoys in the same way he (s) used to reward them. But the dictates of politics at that time did not permit the traditionists to narrate his first will, claiming that they had forgotten it. Al-Bukhari, at the conclusion of the hadith containing the charge that the Messenger of Allah (s) was delirious, said *verbatim*: "And his (s) will at the time of his death contained three instructions: to turn the polytheists out of the Arabian peninsula, to reward the envoys in the same way which he used to reward them..., and the third one was forgotten."[10] This is how Muslim puts it in his *Sahih*, and so do all other authors of sunan and musnads.

III. Her Claim that the Prophet Died on Her Chest is Refuted

The claim of the mothers of believers that the Messenger of Allah, peace be upon him and his progeny, joined his Lord while

---

[9] This is quoted *verbatim* by Muhammad ibn Isma'il al-Bukhari in his section on generosity towards envoys in his book *Al-Jihad wal-Siyar*, page 118, Vol. 2, of his *Sahih*.
[10] Refer to it in the chapter dealing with rewarding the emissaries on page 118, Vol. 2, of *Al-Jihad wal-Siyar*.

being on her chest is opposed by the authenticated tradition stating that he (s) joined the Supreme Companion while being on the chest of his brother and friend (*wali*) 'Ali ibn Abu Talib (as), according to all consecutively reported *sahih*s from the Imams of the purified progeny which are supported by Sunni *sahih*s, as is well known to researchers, Wassalam.

Sincerely,
Sh

Letter 75
Safar 17, 1330

I. Mother of the Believers is not Ruled by Emotions

The axis upon which your argument, regarding the mother of the believers in her frank hadith denying a will to 'Ali, revolves is two folded:

One is your allegation that her biased indisposition against the Imam bids her to deny the will. Our rebuttal is that those who are familiar with her lifestyle deny the allegation that she yields to emotion while narrating hadith about the Messenger of Allah, peace be upon him and his progeny, or that she seeks a special interest; so, she cannot be accused while quoting the Prophet's hadith, albeit if the subject matter of such hadith is someone she likes or someone she does not. God forbid that interests dominate her mind to the extent that she lies while quoting hadith from the Messenger of Allah, peace be upon him and his progeny, preferring to promote her own interest rather than telling the truth.

II. The Pleasant and the Ugly are Denied by Reason

The other is that reason alone refuses your claim that this hadith is authentic, for it is neither logical nor permissible to conclude that the Messenger of Allah, peace be upon him and his progeny, would leave the religion of Allah, the Exalted and the Sublime, in its cradle, while Allah's servants are following a new creed, without having made a will instructing them regarding their affairs. The answer to your claim is that this matter is based on rational goodness and ugliness, and the Sunnis disclaim it, for reason according to their judgment does not at all determine whether something is pleasant or ugly; rather, they believe that jurisdiction is the one that determines it. They believe that whatever the jurisdiction labels as good, they accept it as good, and whatever the jurisdiction describes as bad, they consider it as such, and reason cannot be relied upon at all in such matters.

III. Why Oppose the Claim of the Mother of Believers?

As regarding what you have mentioned at the conclusion of your Letter 74, concerning your rejection of the claim of the mother of believers that the Prophet died on her chest, we are not familiar with any hadith narrated by Sunnis which disproves it; so, if you are aware of any such hadith, please oblige and state it, Wassalam.

Sincerely,
S

Letter 76
Safar 19, 1330

I. Her Yielding to Sentiment

You have stated, while dealing with the first issue, that it is well-known from the lady's lifestyle that she does not yield to emotion, and that she does not seek any special interest. Please free your own self from the shackles of convention and sentimentality and carefully and studiously research her method of dealing with those whom she liked, as well as with those whom she did not like, for there you will see sentimentality most manifestly. Do not forget her dealing with 'Uthman ibn 'Affan by word and deed,[1] her secret and public schemes against 'Ali, Fatima, al-Hasan and al-Husayn (as), and her behaviour towards other mothers of the believers; nay, even with the Messenger of Allah, peace be upon him and his progeny, himself; for in these there is a great deal of manifestations of her sentiments and interest-seeking.

Suffices you for a proof what we, proving how sentimentality tempts some people into misbehaving, have cited regarding the

---

[1] Refer to page 77, Vol. 2, of *Sharh Nahjul Balaghah* by the Mu'tazilite scholar, and pages 457 and its succeeding pages of the same volume, and you will find her conduct towards 'Uthman, 'Ali and Fatima depicting sentimentality in its most manifest forms.

masters of conspiracy and purgery, out of animosity towards Lady Mary [the Copt, consort of the Prophet] and her son Ibrahim, peace be upon him, till Allah, the Almighty and the Exalted One, cleared them of such unjust accusations at the hands of the Commander of the Faithful (as), in a manner that is tangible and clear:[2] "And Allah turned the spiteful disbelievers back empty-handed (Qur'an, 33:25). " If you desire, I may recount more proofs and state the fact that, following her own sentiments, she once said to the Messenger of Allah, peace be upon him and his progeny, "It seems as if you reek of the odour of maghafir [odorous tiny flowers],"[3] so that he might not taste some honey at the house of the mother of believers Zainab bint Jahsh, may Allah be pleased with her. If a trivial reason like this permits her to address the Messenger of Allah, peace be upon him and his progeny, in such a manner, how can she be relied upon when she denies that he (s) left a will for 'Ali (as)? Do not also forget her yielding to sentiment when Asma' bint al-Nu'man was wedded to the Messenger of Allah, peace be upon him and his progeny. She said to her: "When the Prophet (s) weds a woman, he likes to hear her say: 'I seek refuge with Allah against you,'"[4] aiming thereby to turn the Prophet, peace be upon him and his progeny, against his wedding altogether and make him hate the poor woman, as if she allowed herself to attribute statements to the Messenger of Allah, peace be upon him and his progeny, as long as such statements served her own purpose, even when her purpose

---

[2] Whoever wishes to be familiar with the details of this calamity must research the biography of Lady Mary [or Mariyya, the Copt, wife of the Prophet (s)], peace be upon her, on page 39, Vol. 4, of al-Hakim's *Al-Mustadrak*, or to his *Talkhis* by al-Dhahabi.

[3] From what al-Bukhari has quoted in his explanation of Surah al-Tahrim in his *Sahih*, page 136, Vol. 3; so, refer to it and be amazed. There are several ahadith quoted from 'Umar stating that the two women who conspired against the Messenger of Allah (s) were 'Ayesha and Hafsa. There is a lengthy hadith dealing with this issue.

[4] As quoted by al-Hakim in his biography of Asma' in his *Sahih Al-Mustadrak*, page 37, Vol. 4, and is quoted by Ibn Sa'd who discusses her biography on page 104, Vol. 8, of his *Tabaqat*, and the incident is very well known. It is narrated in the biography of Asma' by both authors of *Isti'ab* and *Al-Isabah*, and it is quoted by Ibn Jarir and others.

was petty or prohibitive. Once he, peace be upon him and his progeny, asked her to see how a particular woman was doing, and she informed him of the opposite of what she had observed, seeking her own self interest.[5] Once she complained about him, peace be upon him and his progeny, to her father, succumbing again to her sentiments, saying, "Do not now be biased,"[6] whereupon her father slapped her so hard that her clothes became soaked with her blood. Once, having felt angry with him (s), she said: "... and you claim to be Allah's Messenger...,"[7] in addition to many such incidents the narrative of which would require a much larger space, and what we have quoted here must suffice.

II. Rationale Regarding the Pleasant and the Unpleasant

You have said, while commenting on the second point, that Sunnis do not subscribe to what is called rationally pleasant or unpleasant, etc. I think of you as being above making such a statement which is reminiscent of sophists who deny even concrete facts. Among our deeds are those of whose goodness we are quite sure, and they are praiseworthy and rewardable due to their own merits, such as charity and fairness, since we know what they are, while there are others with whose ugliness we also are familiar, and they demand repudiation and punishment because of their own evil, such as injustice and aggression, since they are what they are. The wise know that there is a need that necessitates such judgments, and the wise are as certain regarding these matters as they are certain that the single is half the pair. Simple common

---

[5] The details of this incident are preserved in the books of traditions and history; so, refer to page 294, Vol. 6, of *Kanz al-'Ummal*, or page 115, Vol. 8, of Ibn Sa'd's *Tabaqat*, where he also states the biography of Sharaf daughter of Khalifah.

[6] This issue is quoted by the authors of books of tradition and history; so, refer to hadith number 1020 of the ones narrated in *Kanz al-'Ummal*, page 116, Vol. 7, and it is quoted by al-Ghazali in the third section of his treatise on marriage on page 35, Vol. 2, of *Ihya'ul-'Ulum*. It is also quoted in section 94 of his book *Mukashafatul Qulub*, at the conclusion of page 238.

[7] As quoted by al-Ghazali in both sections of the books cited above.

sense always determines the distinction between your treatment of someone who is good to you and of someone who is not. Reason determines the goodness of the first person's treatment to you and its being praiseworthy by you, as well as the ugliness of the second and its being worthy of renunciation and punishment. Whoever doubts this is a rebel against his own reason.

Had the goodness or the evil of what we have mentioned here been matters of the legislative code, then they would not have been adopted and implemented by those who denied all divine codes such as atheists and secular rulers. In spite of their denial of religion, the latter still condone equity and goodness, determining thereupon their praise and rewards, without doubting at all the ugliness of injustice or aggression, nor the necessity to denounce such deeds and to punish their doers. Their criterion in their judgment is nothing other than reason; so, talk no more about those who belittle reason and conscience, nor of those who deny what all wise men know, ruling in the contrary of what the human nature dictates, the nature which Allah, the Praised One, has created and embedded within His servants. He has enabled them thereby to realize facts that are discernible by their faculty of reason, just as He made them able to recognize matters through their senses and feelings. Their nature, then, demands that they should be able to rationally judge equity and the like as good, and injustice and its peers as ugly, just as being able to distinguish through the sense of taste between the sweetness of honey and the bitterness of colocynth [*Citrullus colocynthis*], and through their sense of smell can they distinguish between the fragrance of musk [*Chenopodium botrys*] and the stink of cadaver, and through their sense of touch can they distinguish between what is soft and what is rough, and through their faculty of seeing can they tell the difference between a pleasant and an ugly view, and through their faculty of hearing can they tell the difference between the music of the pipe and the braying of a donkey. Such is the nature which Allah has created: "He created people in such a way; indeed, there is no way anyone can change His creation; this is the straight religion, though most people do not know (30:30)."

The Ash'aris desired to exaggerate the power of faith in the legislative system and the attitude towards a total submission to its judgment; therefore, they denied the judgment of the wise, saying that there is no judgment other than what is legislated. Thus did they become oblivious of the absolute rational theory stating that "Whatever a wise person decides should be the decision of the legislator," and heedless of the fact that they by doing so in fact left no excuse for their own selves, thus discarding any criterion whereby they might ascertain a legislative code or discard it altogether. This is so due to the fact that to arrive at such a conclusion through legislative proofs is like running in a circle, and no pretext can be applied therewith. Had there been no authority for reason, implementing tradition or consecutively reported hadith would have been rejected. Nay! Had there been no intellect, nobody would have worshipped Allah nor come to know Him. Expounding in this subject has been recorded in a library containing works of our renowned scholars.

III. Rejecting the Claim of the Mother of Believers

As regarding the claim of the mother of the believers that the Prophet, peace be upon him and his progeny, died on her chest, it is a claim which we reject based upon *sahih*s sequentially reported by members of the purified progeny (as). Refer to what others have stated as quoted by Ibn Sa'd. He quotes 'Ali (as) saying: "The Messenger of Allah, peace be upon him and his progeny, during his ailment [preceding his demise], said: 'Fetch me my brother,' so I came to him and he asked me to come closer, and so did I; thereupon, he reclined on me. He continued reclining on me thus and talking to me, so much so that some of his saliva fell on me, then the Messenger of Allah, peace be upon him and his progeny, breathed his last;" as stated on page 51, Part Two, Vol. 2, of the author's *Tabaqat*, in a section about those who said that the Messenger of Allah died in 'Ali's lap. It is hadith number 1107 on page 55, Vol. 4, of *Kanz al-'Ummal*. Abu Na'im in his *Hilyat al-Awliya'*, Abu Ahmad al-Fardi in his *Naskh*, and many other authors of books of traditions have all quoted 'Ali (as) saying: "The Messenger of Allah, peace be upon him and his progeny, taught me," meaning during that sickness, "a thousand doors each one of which leads to a thousand others." It is hadith number 6009 quoted at the end of page 392, Vol. 6, of *Kanz al-'Ummal*. Whenever 'Umar ibn al-Khattab was asked about anything regarding these matters, he would say nothing other than: "Ask 'Ali, since he is the one who can handle it."

Jabir ibn 'Abdullah al-Ansari is quoted saying that Ka'b al-Ahbar once asked 'Umar: "What were the last words of the Messenger of Allah, peace be upon him and his progeny?" 'Umar answered: "Ask 'Ali." Ka'b did so, and 'Ali (as) said: "I let the Messenger of Allah, peace be upon him and his progeny, recline his head on my flanks till he finally uttered: 'Prayers! [i.e. uphold prayers] Prayers!" Ka'b said: "This, indeed, is the call of all prophets, and for this purpose are they sent." Then Ka'b asked 'Umar who gave the ceremonial funeral bath to the Prophet's corpse, and his answer was again: "Ask 'Ali." When Ka'b asked 'Ali (as), 'Ali answered that it was he who did so, as stated by Ibn Sa'd on page 51, Part Two, Vol. 2, of *Tabaqat*, and it is hadith 1106 in *Kanz al-'Ummal* quoted on page 55, Vol. 4. Ibn 'Abbas was asked once: "Have you seen when the Messenger of Allah, peace be upon him and his progeny, died, if his head was on anyone's lap?" He answered: "He died reclining on 'Ali's chest." It was said to him that 'Urwah narrates a tradition from 'Ayesha saying that he (s) died reclining on her chest, and Ibn 'Abbas denied it, asking the person who put the question forth: "Do you believe it?! By Allah, the Messenger of Allah, peace be upon him and his progeny, died reclining his head on 'Ali's chest, and Ali is the one who gave him his bath," as quoted by Ibn Sa'd on the same page mentioned above, and it is hadith number 1108 of the ones enumerated in *Kanz al-'Ummal*, page 55, Vol. 4. Ibn Sa'd cites Imam Abu Muhammad 'Ali ibn al-Husayn Zainul'Abidin (as) saying: "The Messenger of Allah, peace be upon him and his progeny, breathed his last while his head was in 'Ali's lap," as quoted by Ibn Sa'd on page 51.

Traditions documenting this subject are consecutively reported from all Imams of the purified progeny (as). Many of those who opted to deviate from their path admit that, too, so much so that Ibn Sa'd has quoted al-Sha'bi saying: "The Messenger of Allah, peace be upon him and his progeny, passed away while his head was in 'Ali's lap; and it was 'Ali who gave him his [funeral] bath," as mentioned on the page referred to above in *Al-Tabaqat*. The Commander of the Faithful, peace be upon him, used to declare the same publicly; therefore, you may refer to his statement in one of his sermons where he says: "Custodians of the hadith among the companions of the Messenger of Allah, peace be upon him and his progeny, know very well that I never hesitated to implement the commandments of Allah, nor lagged in discharging the orders of His Messenger, not even for one hour. I, by the Grace of Allah, on many occasions risked my own life defending his, when even heroes retreated and feet slowed down, and he (s) breathed his last while his head rested on my chest, and even his saliva fell on my hand, whereupon I rubbed it on my face. I took care of washing his corpse, the angels assisting me, and the house and its courtyards became full of the noise of angels descending and ascending..., and I never ceased hearing their prayers unto him, till we buried him; so, who is more worthy of him alive or dead than I?" as stated at the conclusion of page 196, Vol. 2, of *Nahjul Balaghah*, and on page 590, Vol. 2, of Ibn al-Hadid's *Sharh Nahjul Balaghah*.

So is his speech when he, peace be upon him, was burying the Mistress of all Women, peace be upon her. He said:

"Peace be upon you, O Messenger of Allah, from me and from your daughter who has come now to be your neighbour, rushing to reunite with you... My patience, O Messenger of

Allah, about the death of your chosen one has run out, and my consolation has waned and withered. Deep, indeed, is my grief for being separated from you, and great is the calamity, while the extent of your grief is a source for consolation, for I laid you to sleep in the tomb of your grave, after your soul had parted from your body that was resting on my chest; therefore, we are God's, and unto Him is our return,"

Up to the end of his statement which is stated at the end of page 207, Vol. 2, of *Nahjul Balaghah*, and on page 590, Vol. 2, of *Sharh Nahjul Balaghah* by Ibn Abi al-Hadid. Umm Salamah has also narrated an authentic hadith saying: "By the One by Whom alone do I swear, 'Ali was the closest to the Messenger of Allah (s) upon his death. We [she and Ali] visited him one afternoon, and he happily and repeatedly said: 'Ali has come! 'Ali has come!' Fatima (as) inquired whether 'Ali had been sent on an errand. Later on, 'Ali came again, and I thought that probably he needed to have some privacy with the Prophet (s); so, we came out and sat at the door. I was closer to the door. The Messenger of Allah (s) bent his head over 'Ali and started talking to him confidentially, addressing him affectionately, till he passed away; so, 'Ali was the last person to be with him before his death."[8]

Abdullah ibn 'Umar narrates the following:

"During his sickness, the Messenger of Allah, peace be upon him and his progeny, asked that his brother be fetched; so, Abu Bakr came in, but he turned away from him and reiterated his request. This time 'Uthman was brought in, but he turned away from him, too. Then 'Ali was called in his

---

[8] This hadith is quoted by al-Hakim at the beginning of page 139, Vol. 3, of his authentic *Al-Mustadrak*, succeeded by his comment: "This hadith is authentic, but they [Bukhari and Muslim] did not publish it." Al-Dhahabi, too, has admitted its authenticity when he quoted it in his *Talkhis al-Mustadrak*. It is also quoted by Ibn Abu Shaybah in his *Sunan*, and it is hadith number 6096, page 400, Vol. 6, in *Kanz al-'Ummal*.

presence. The Prophet (s) covered him with his own robe and reclined on him. When he came out of his room, people asked him what the Prophet (s) had said, and he answered: 'He taught me a thousand subjects each one of which leads to a thousand others.'[9]

You know that this hadith portrays a behaviour typical of prophets, while the other one portrays a man ruled by his lust. If a shepherd dies on his wife's chest, between her chin and navel, or on her thigh..., having laxed in looking after his herd, he would surely be labelled as wreckless and irresponsible. May Allah forgive the mother of the believers. I wish that she, while denying 'Ali such a will, had attributed the denial to her father, whom she thinks is more worthy of such a will, but her father was already in the army raised by the Messenger of Allah, peace be upon him and his progeny, under his own honourable patronage; he was in Usama's army which was then camping at Jurf. Anyhow, the claim that he (s) died in her lap is attributed to nobody other than 'Ayesha, whereas the claim of his demise, may I sacrifice my parents for his sake, is narrated through 'Ali (as), Ibn 'Abbas, Umm Salamah, 'Abdullah ibn 'Umar, al-Sha'bi, 'Ali ibn al-Husayn (as), and all Imams of the progeny of Muhammad (as), thus

---

[9] This is quoted by Abu Ya'li through a chain of narrators including Kamil ibn Talha, Ibn Lahi'ah, Hay ibn 'Abdul-Maghafiri, Abu 'Abdul-Rahman al-Habli, ending with 'Abdullah ibn 'Umar. It is quoted by Abu Na'im in his *Hilyat al-Awliya'*, by Abu Ahmad al-Fardi in his own version as stated on page 392, Vol. 6, of *Kanz al-'Ummal*. Al-Tabrani, in his book *Al-Tafsir al-Kabir*, has stated that when the Ta'if campaign was underway, the Prophet (s) took his time in confiding with 'Ali, so much so that when Abu Bakr passed by them, he said: "O Messenger of Allah! Your confidential talk with 'Ali has lasted for quite some time." He (s) said: "It is not I who has confided in him; it is Allah..." This is hadith number 6075, page 399, Vol. 6, of *Kanz al-'Ummal*. He often used to sit with 'Ali (as) and confide in him. Once 'Ayesha entered and found them engaged in a confidential conversation. Said she: "O 'Ali! I spend one day out of nine [in the company of my husband]; so, why don't you, son of Abu Talib, leave me alone on that day?" The Prophet's face immediately showed the redness of anger. Refer to this incident at the beginning of page 78, Vol. 2, of *Sharh Nahjul Balaghah* by al-Hamidi.

making it more reliable and more fit of the personality of the Messenger of God (s).

IV. Preference of Umm Salamah's Hadith over Hers

Had 'Ayesha's hadith been disproved by Umm Salamah alone, the latter's hadith would have been preferred over hers for many reasons besides the ones mentioned above, Wassalam.

Sincerely,
Sh

Letter 77
Safar 20, 1330

Why Prefer Umm Salamah's Hadith to 'Ayesha's?

As if your preference of Umm Salamah's hadith to that of 'Ayesha, may Allah be pleased with them both, according to what you have stated, is not sufficient, you went a step further to claim that the reasons for such a preference are more than what you have already indicated. What are these reasons? State them, may Allah have mercy on you, no matter how many, and do not leave any, for our aim is to research and learn, Wassalam.

Sincerely,
S

Letter 78
Safar 22, 1330

More Reasons for Preferring Umm Salamah's Hadith

Not only did Lady Umm Salamah believe wholeheartedly in the great Book of Allah, which distinguishes between right and wrong and enjoins repentance to Allah Almighty, as the Holy Qur'an testifies,[1] she is not rebuked in the Qur'an for insubordination to the Prophet nor because of her supporting the enemies of his wasi,[2] nor did Allah, Gabriel, the true believers, and the angels, all side by His Prophet against her, nor did Allah threaten to divorce her and compensate His Prophet with a better

---

[1] This is a reference to the following verse in Surah al-Tahrim: "If you both repent to Allah, then your hearts have submitted to Allah."

[2] Her insubordination to the vicegerent is manifested by her denial of the existence of the Prophet's will to him, and by bearing grudge towards him as long as he lived. As regarding her insubordination to the Prophet (s), and Allah's readiness to side with His Prophet (s) against her, this is proven by the verse saying: "If they become insubordinate to him, then (suffices him that) Allah is his Mawla, and so are Gabriel and the righteous among the believers, and even the angels support him (Qur'an, 66:4)."

wife than her,³ nor did He bring the example of the wives of Nuh and Lut as being in her own category,⁴ nor did she try to instigate the Prophet to make unlawful unto himself that which Allah has made lawful unto him,⁵ nor did the Prophet (s) preach once and point to her residence saying: "Right there is the dissension, disunity, and discord...; from there will the devil's horn come out,"⁶ nor did her manners permit her to stretch her legs before the Prophet while performing the rite of prayers, thus showing disrespect to him and to the rite of prayers, without removing them from the place of his prostration till he beckoned her to do so, then when he beckoned her, she lifted her leg till he stood up, then she put it down again...!⁷

This is how she was. As if she did not scandalize and arouse people against 'Uthman, calling him "Na'thal," saying, *verbatim*, *"Uqtulu Na'thal faqad kafar!"* ("Kill Na'thal, for he has turned *kafir* [disbeliever]."⁸ As if she did not go out of her house, after

---

[3] This hadith and the one that precedes it is a reference to the verse "It could be that if he divorces you, his Lord will bless him with wives better than you, submitting to Allah, truly believing in Him."

[4] This is a reference to the statement of the Almighty: "Allah has struck for those who disbelieved the example of the wife of Nuh and the wife of Lut," to the end of the chapter.

[5] This is a reference to the verse: "O Messenger! Why do you make unlawful what Allah has made lawful unto you, seeking to please your wives (Qur'an, 66:1)?"

[6] This is quoted by al-Bukhari in his section dealing with stories about what went on at the homes of the Prophet's wives in his dissertation on the issues of holy wars and the Prophet's biography in his *Sahih*. It also is on page 125, Vol. 2, following his chapter on the injunction of the *khums* and its payment. Its wording in Muslim's *Sahih* is as follows: "The Messenger of Allah came out of 'Ayesha's house and said: 'Satan's horn shall come out of this place;'" so refer to page 503 of its second volume [original Arabic text].

[7] Refer to Bukhari's *Sahih*, his section dealing with what deeds are lawful while performing the prayers, page 143, Vol. 1.

[8] Her scandalizing 'Uthman and denouncing many of his actions, her calling him names, and her statement: "Kill Na'thal, for he has turned infidel," are hardly overlooked by any book containing such events and affairs. Suffices you what exists in the books of history by Ibn Jarir, Ibn al-Athir, and by others. Some

having been commanded by Allah Almighty to settle therein,[9] ride her camel 'Askar and lead an army,[10] descending a hill or ascending a mountain. Yet she did not yield to advice but insisted on leading the army which she had raised to fight the Imam.[11] Her statement that the Messenger of Allah (s) died on her chest, therefore, is as good as her statement claiming that the Messenger of Allah (s) saw a few Sudanese men playing at their mosque with their shields and spears, and he supposedly asked her if she liked to have a look at them, to which invitation she responded in the affirmative. 'Ayesha goes on to say: "He let me stand behind him,

---

individuals denounced her behaviour and composed poetry in this regard such as:

You started something and schemed,
Like winds blown and rain streamed;
You ordered them to slay the Imam,
Claiming he reneged from Islam...

Up to the conclusion of these verses which are quoted on page 80, Vol. 3, of Ibn al-Athir's *Al-Kamil*, after reference was made as to how the Battle of the Camel started.

[9] That is, when the Almighty says: "And remain at your homes, and do not decorate your selves as you used to do during the days of jahiliyya (Qur'an, 33:33)."

[10] The camel 'Ayesha was riding during the Basra incident was called 'Askar. It was brought to her by Ya'li ibn Umayyah, and it was huge, masculine. When she saw it, she liked it, but when she came to know that its name was 'Askar, she changed her mind and said: "Return it, for I have no need for it." She stated that the Messenger of Allah (s) had informed her of such name and forbidden her from riding it; so, they changed its saddle and brought it back to her saying: "We have found another one for you, larger and stronger." Thus, she was pleased with it. This incident is mentioned by a number of writers of history and of biographies; so, refer to page 80, Vol. 2, of *Sharh Nahjul Balaghah* by the Mu'tazilite scholar.

[11] The hadith in this regard is quite famous, and it is one of the signs of true prophethood and miracles of Islam. It has been summarized by Imam Ahmad ibn Hanbal while quoting 'Ayesha's hadith in his *Musnad*, pages 52 and 97, Vol. 6. Hakim did likewise, quoting it on page 120, Vol. 3, of his authentic *Mustadrak*, and al-Dhahabi admitted the same when he quoted it in his *Talkhis al-Mustadrak*.

my cheek on his, and said: 'O Sons of Arfada, keep on!'" supposedly encouraging them to play so that the lady mighty be entertained, till he asked her if she saw enough. Upon saying "Yes," he told her to leave.[12] And it is similar to her other story in which she claims: "The Messenger of Allah (s) came in once when I had two concubines singing for me excitingly. He lay down on the bed. Abu Bakr entered and rebuked me saying: 'Do I hear Satan's pipe being played in the presence of the Messenger of Allah?!' The Messenger of Allah (s) approached him and told him to leave them alone."[13]

Yet similar to it is another story. She says: "The Prophet raced with me once and I outran him. We kept doing so for years during which I gained weight, and when he outran me, he said: 'This [game] cancels that!'" as quoted by Imam Ahmad in 'Ayesha's hadith on page 39, Vol. 6, of his Musnad. Or like her statement: "I used to play with girls, and some of my friends would come to play with me, and the Messenger of Allah used to let them in so that I would play with them," which is quoted by Imam Ahmad who discusses 'Ayesha on page 75, Vol. 6, of his *Musnad*. Or like yet another story of hers quoted by Ibn Abu Shaybah, and it is hadith number 1017 of the ahadith narrated by Ibn Abu Shaybah in Vol 7 of *Kanz al-'Ummal*: "I have acquired seven merits no woman, other than Mary daughter of 'Umran, was endowed with: The angel of revelation descended in my own form; the Messenger of Allah married me as a virgin whom no man ever touched before; the revelation descended upon him while we were having intercourse; he loved me more than any other woman; several verses of the Qur'an were revealed on my behalf that almost caused the nation to perish; I saw Gabriel while none of the other wives of the

---

[12] This hadith about her is undisputed. It is quoted by both shaykhs in their *sahih*s; so, you may refer to Bukhari's *Sahih*, the beginning of his section on both *'Eid*s, page 116, Vol. 1, and refer to Muslim's *Sahih*, his section on permissible sports during the days of the eid, page 327, Vol. 1. Also refer to Ahmad's *Musnad*, page 57, Vol. 6.

[13] This is quoted by al-Bukhari, Muslim, and Imam Ahmad from 'Ayesha's hadith which we referenced in the footnote above.

Prophet saw him besides me; and he breathed his last in my house while nobody was there except I and the angel of death."[14] Other "ahadith" which she has narrated go in more details about her "merits," all falling in the same pattern.

As regarding Umm Salamah, suffices her for a merit her loyalty to her *wali* and her Prophet's *wasi*. She was well-known for her terse opinion and great intellect, her strong faith, her suggestion on the Day of Hudaybiya which testified to her intellectual prowess, her wise judgment, and her lofty status; may Allah have mercy and blessings upon her, Wassalam.

Sincerely,
Sh

---

[14] It is unanimously agreed upon that he (s) died in the presence of 'Ali (as), and that 'Ali (as) was nursing him and aiding him; so, how can it be accurate to claim that he died while nobody was there except 'Ayesha and the angel of death? Where were 'Ali (as) and 'Abbas then? And where were Fatima (as) and Safiyya? Or where were the Prophet's consorts and all the descendants of Hashim? How did they leave him to 'Ayesha alone? It is also quite obvious that Mary, peace be upon her, did not really possess any of the seven virtues the mother of believers attributes to her; so, what is the wisdom of her using her as the only exception?

Letter 79
Safar 23, 1330

Consensus Endorses al-Siddiq's Caliphate

If what you have said about the covenant and the will, as well as the clear texts, is proven accurate, then what can you say about the nation's consensus to nominate [Abu Bakr] al-Siddiq? Its consensus is an unequivocal proof that testifies to his statement (s): "My nation's consensus shall never occur regarding anything wrong," and his statement, peace be upon him and his progeny, "My nation's word shall never be misleading;" so, what do you have to say about that?

Sincerely,
S

Letter 80
Safar 24, 1330

No Consensus

We say that the meaning of his (s) statements: "My nation's consensus shall never occur regarding anything wrong," and "My nation's word shall never be misleading," is that he (s) negates the error, or the misguidance, of the issue regarding which the nation arbitrates; thus, the nation will be reaching a unanimous endorsement in that issue's regard. This is the meaning of such traditions, and nothing else. As regarding the matter which is considered by a group of individuals of the nation who decided to carry it out, successfully forcing it even on those who had a say, their carrying it out does not prove its validity. The pledge of allegiance taken at the *saqifa* was not an issue regarding consultation; rather, it was something which was undertaken by the second caliph and by Abu 'Ubaydah and a group of their friends, then they took by surprise those who actually had the authority to do and undo, assisted by contemporary circumstances. Thus did they finally achieve what they had aspired. Abu Bakr himself declared that the oath of allegiance which he had received was conducted neither in accordance with consultation nor wisdom. He did so when he delivered a sermon at the dawn of his caliphate in which he apologized to the public saying: "The allegiance which I have received is a rash slip from the evil of which Allah has protected us, and there was a presentiment regarding dissension."[1] ʿUmar testified to the same fact in front of many eye-witnesses when he delivered a sermon from the pulpit of the Prophet's Mosque one Friday shortly before the conclusion of his reign, a sermon the news of which became widely publicized. Al-Bukhari has included it in his *Sahih*,[2] and I would like to quote it for you here *verbatim*:

> "It has come to my knowledge that someone[3] has said that if ʿUmar dies, he will swear the oath of allegiance to so-and-so; therefore, let nobody hesitate from saying that the oath of allegiance to Abu Bakr was a slip that was driven home, for it was exactly so, yet Allah protected us from the evil of its consequences... Whoever swears the oath of allegiance to

---

[1] This is quoted by Abu Bakr Ahmad ibn ʿAbdul-ʾAziz al-Jawhari in his book *Al-Saqifa* and by Ibn Abi al-Hadid on page 132, Vol. 1, of his *Sharh Nahjul Balaghah*.

[2] Refer to the *sahih*, his chapter on the stoning of the woman who becomes pregnant out of adultery if she gets married, page 119, Vol. 4. It is also quoted by several authors of books of tradition and history such as Ibn Jarir and al-Tabari who discuss the events of the year 11 in the *tarikh* [history] book of each, and it is transmitted by Ibn Abi al-Hadid on page 122, Vol. 1, of his *Sharh Nahjul Balaghah*.

[3] The one who is making a statement is Ibn al-Zubayr, and his statement is: "By Allah! As soon as ʿUmar dies, I will swear the oath of allegiance to ʿAli, for allegiance to Abu Bakr was a slip by the nation that safely passed by." ʿUmar, therefore, was extremely angry, and he delivered the said sermon. This is stated by many of those who have commented on al-Bukhari. Refer to the explanation of this hadith in al-Qastalani's *Sharh*, page 352, Vol. 11, and you will find the author quoting al-Balathiri with regards to surnames, admitting the authenticity of this hadith according to its endorsement by both shaykhs.

someone prior to consulting others, doing so only out of fear of being killed if he did not, then he should not do it at all [and accept death instead]...[4] One of the rumours circulated about us when Allah took His Messenger (ṣ) away from us is that the Ansar differed from us in their views; they all assembled at the *saqifa* [shed] of Bani Sa'idah; besides them, 'Ali (as) and al-Zubayr, and their followers, differed, too..."

He continued to point out what had happened at the shed, the disputes and differences of opinion, the voices that rose out of concern for the safety of the religion, etc. It was under those circumstances that 'Umar swore allegiance to Abu Bakr.

It is a fact well-known by those who research the events that prevented the members of the Prophet's household (as), the custodians of the Message, from attending the allegiance [inauguration] ceremony. They were detained at 'Ali's house together with Salman, Abu Dharr al-Ghifari, al-Miqdad ibn al-Aswad al-Kindi, 'Ammar ibn Yasir, al-Zubayr ibn al-Awwam, Khuzaymah ibn Thabit, Abu ibn Ka'b, Farwah ibn 'Amr ibn

---

[4] In his commentary on this hadith, Ibn al-Athir has stated that the statement's gist is that they feared being murdered. The meaning of the whole hadith, therefore, is something like: "The allegiance must come as a result of consultation and consensus; so, if two men split from the group and one of them swears the fealty of allegiance to the other, then they both have departed from the group and consensus. If one receives the oath of allegiance, then he should not be one of them; rather, they both have to be isolated from the group that agrees to distinguish its own Imam from the rest. Otherwise, if one of them receives the oath of allegiance, after having committed a heinous act which caused the group to do without them, then there is no guarantee that both persons will commit murder." It is one of the dictates of the justice described by 'Umar who passed such a judgment on himself and his friend just as he passed it on others. Prior to his said sermon, he had stated the following: "Swearing the oath of allegiance to Abu Bakr was a slip against whose evil Allah has protected us; so, you should kill whoever repeats it." This statement became extremely famous, and many narrators of historical events transmitted it, including scholar Ibn Abi al-Hadid on page 123, Vol. 1, of his *Sharh Nahjul Balaghah*.

Wadqah al-Ansari, al-Bara' ibn 'Azib, Khalid ibn Sa'd ibn al-'As al-Amawi, and many others. So, how can it be said that there was a consensus in spite of the fact that all these men, including Muhammad's progeny (as), who are to the nation like the head to the body, the eyes to the face, the descendants of the Messenger of Allah (s) and the custodians of his knowledge, the ones who are peers only to and the companions of the Book of Allah, the arks of the nation's redemption, and the gates of its salvation, the nation's protection against straying, and the standard-bearers of its guidance, as we have proven above...,[5] did not attend? But their dealing requires no proof if conscientiously discerned.

Both al-Bukhari and al-Muslim,[6] in their *sahih*s, in addition to many other renowned traditionists and historians, have all proven the fact that 'Ali (as) did not participate in the allegiance process, and that he did not reconcile and make peace except after the mistress of the ladies of the world (as) had joined her father (s) [in Paradise], six months thereafter, compelled by the general Islamic interest during those very critical circumstances. The testimony to these facts comes from 'Ayesha herself who says: "Al-Zahra' (as) boycotted Abu Bakr and did not speak to him after the demise of the Messenger of Allah (s) till she died, and when 'Ali (as) made peace with them, he accused them of depriving him of his place in the caliphate." This hadith, as you can see, does not mention anything about his swearing the oath of allegiance to them. How thought-provoking his statement is when he addresses Abu Bakr thus:

If you had argued with them, kinship claiming,

---

[5] Refer to Letter No. 6 and its following pages up to the end of Letter No. 12, and you will come to know the prestige meted to Ahl al-Bayt, peace be upon them.

[6] Refer to al-Bukhari's *Sahih*, and read the last lines of his chapter on Khaybar's campaign on page 39, Vol. 3. Also refer to Muslim's *Sahih*, to his chapter on the Prophet's statement: "We do not leave behind us anything, for whatever we leave is for charity," in his treatise on holy wars and biographies on page 72, Vol. 2, and you will find the matter as we have detailed it.

Then others are closer to the Prophet and more deserving;
And if through consultation you took control,
How so when those with counsel were not there at all?![7]

Al-'Abbas ibn 'Abdul Muttalib had used the same argument with Abu Bakr, as Ibn Qutaybah discusses him on page 16 of his book *Al-Imama wal Siyasa*, telling him once: "If you demanded what you demanded through kinship to the Messenger of Allah (s), then you had confiscated our own. If you had demanded it due to your position among Muslims, then ours is a more prestigious than yours. If this affair is accomplished when the believers are pleased with it, then it cannot be so as long as we are displeased therewith."

So; tell me where is the consensus you are talking about, having heard what the uncle of the Messenger of Allah (s), the one who was his father's peer, stated, in addition to the statement of his cousin, brother and executor of his will, as well as the statements of all his household and kin?

Sincerely,
Sh

---

[7] Both of these poetic verses are included in *Nahjul Balaghah*. Ibn Abi al-Hadid has said so while explaining them in his *Sharh Nahjul Balaghah*, page 319, Vol. 4, adding, "His statement is addressed to Abu Bakr, for Abu Bakr argued with the Ansar at the *saqifa*, saying: 'We are the progeny of the Messenger of Allah (s) and his nutshell;' so, when he argued about the allegiance, claiming that it was done by those who had a say, 'Ali (as) said: 'As regarding your argument with the Ansar saying that you belong to the progeny of the Messenger of Allah (s) and are among his kin, others are closer in kinship to him than you; as regarding your argument of being elected and that the masses are pleased with you, there many *sahaba* who were not present there; so, how can it be called consensus?'" Shaykh Muhammad 'Abdoh has made two comments on these verses summarizing what Ibn Abi al-Hadid has said while explaining them.

Letter 81
Safar 28, 1330

Consensus Concluded When Dispute Dissipated

Sunnis do not deny the fact that the allegiance was not taken after consultation or serious consideration. Rather, they admit that it took place suddenly and unexpectedly. They do not deny going against the wish of the Ansar and their preference of Sa'd, nor in opposing the descendants of Hashim and their followers from the Muhajirun and Ansar who joined the Imam (as) in his boycott. But they say that the caliphate was finally vested upon Abu Bakr who was accepted by everyone as the Imam; dispute dissipated, hostilities halted, and everyone became determined to support al-Siddiq and provide him with counsel in secrecy and in public; therefore, they fought in his wars, they supported him when he concluded a peace treaty, and they carried out his orders. Nobody at all differed in that regard, thus a total consensus was finally reached, and the consignment of caliphate was accomplished; praise be to Allah for having united their word after their dissension, and for unifying their hearts after their discord, Wassalam.

Sincerely,
S

Letter 82
Safar 30, 1330

Consensus Was Not Concluded; Dissension Did Not Dissipate

Their consolidation in supporting al-Siddiq, and their providing him with counsel in secrecy and in public, is one thing; the validity of the consignment of the caliphate through consensus is quite another. They are not correlated judged by reason or tradition, for 'Ali and all the infallible Imams from his descendants (as) have a well-known policy in supporting the Islamic authority; it is the same whereby we worship Allah. I mention it here in answer to what you have stated. It may be summed up thus: They believe that the Muslim nation can never rise to glory except through a state that unites its populace, mends any crack in its structure, protects its borders, and safeguards its undertakings. Such a state cannot be established except by subjects who support it with their lives and possessions. If it is possible for such a state to be led by a legitimate statesman who represents in the true sense of the word the government of the Messenger of Allah, then he is the one to be assigned for such a responsibility rather than anyone else. But if this becomes impossible, and the government is usurped by someone else, then the nation has to support him in every issue upon which the dignity and fortitude of Islam hinges, and so do the protection of the borders of the Islamic state, and the safeguarding of its national security.

It is not permissible to divide the Muslims or create discord among them by opposing him; rather, the nation has to treat him, albeit if he is a slave with amputated limbs, the treatment meted to rightful caliphs, entrusting him with the land's *khiraj* tax and his share thereof, the *zakat* of cattle and other items, etc. It has the right to take the same from him through the sale and purchase, as well as all means of property transfers, such as by way of awards, gifts, and the like.

There is no doubt about the clearing of conscience of one who pays him liabilities, as though he is paying them to the Imam of truth, and the rightful caliph. This is the path of 'Ali and the purified Imams from his descendants (as). The Messenger of Allah (s) has said: "There will be after me favouritism, and unpleasant matters," as stated in one hadith narrated by 'Abdullah ibn Mas'ud which is quoted by Muslim on page 118, Vol. 2, of his *Sahih*, and by many authors of *sahih*s and *sunan*. People asked him (s): "O Messenger of Allah! What do you enjoin one of us who witnesses them to do?" He (s) answered: "Perform your obligations, and pray

Allah for the attainment of what rightfully belongs to you." Abu Dharr al-Ghifari, may Allah be pleased with him, is also quoted by Muslim in Vol. 2 of his *Sahih* as saying, "My friend the Messenger of Allah (s) advised me to listen and to obey even [a ruler who is] a slave whose limbs are amputated." Salamah al-Ju'fi is quoted by Muslim and others asking the Messenger of Allah (s): "O Messenger of Allah! Suppose we are ruled by those who require us to discharge our duties towards them while they themselves decline to grant us our rights, what do you advise us to do then?" He (s) answered him saying, "Listen and obey, for they will bear the burden of their sins, and you will bear yours." In one particular hadith quoted by Muslim on page 120, Vol. 2, of his *Sahih*, which is narrated by all authors of books of traditions, Huzayfah al-Yemani, may Allah be pleased with him, quotes the Prophet (s) saying: "There will be rulers after me who will neither guide according to my guidance, nor follow my Sunnah; and there will be among them men whose hearts are like those of the devils' clad in human form." Huzayfah asked him (s): "What shall I do then, O Messenger of Allah, if I happen to witness that?" He (s) answered: "You shall listen to the ruler and obey him; if he whips your back and confiscates your property, you will still have [no choice but] to listen and obey." Similar to this hadith is one narrated by Umm Salamah thus: "There will be [unjust] rulers over you, and you will either acknowledge [their being unjust] or deny it. Those who acknowledge shall be considered innocent, while those who deny it will be saved from chastisement."[1] They asked him (s): "Are we not supposed to fight them?" He answered: "No, as long as they uphold their prayers."

*Sahih*s are consecutively reported in narrating the above quoted traditions, especially through the purified progeny (as). For

---

[1] This hadith is quoted by Muslim on page 122, Vol. 2, of his *Sahih*. The meaning of his phrase (s) "Whoever knows it is innocent" is that whoever knew the abomination and identifies it as such will have a path leading to dissociation from its sin and punishment by changing it with his own hand or tongue, but if he cannot, then let him abhor it by his heart.

this reason, the latter remained persevering as they saw eye-sores, and they kept tongue-tied, acting upon these sacred commandments and upon others whereby they were bound. They were enjoined to persevere while suffering as they felt forced to overlook eye-sores, safeguarding the unity of the nation, and keeping it intact. They abided by the gist of these texts while dealing with those who were entrusted with faring with the affairs of the Muslims. While being aware of the fact that they themselves were more worthy of being in their shoes, they tasted the bitterness of colocynth, hoping they might be able one day to lead them to the Right Path. The ascension of those individuals to power was more painful to them than the blows of sharp swords, yet they tolerated it only to fulfil the covenant, discharge the commitment, and carry out their duties as far as the Shari'a is concerned, favouring - while opposing such rulers - to prefer what is most important over what is more important. For this reason, the Commander of the Faithful (as) tried his best to provide counsel to all three caliphs, exerting himself in providing them with advice.

Whoever acquaints himself with his policy during their epoch will come to know that he, having lost all hope to get his indisputable right to succeed the Messenger of Allah (s), willingly took to reclusion, preferring to make asylum with those in authority. He did not fight them while seeing his promised throne in their grip, nor did he oppose them openly. He did so only in order to maintain the solidification of the nation and safeguard the creed, always keeping the religion's interest in mind, preferring the life hereafter to this one. He suffered from agonies which nobody else suffered. He was agonized by two calamities: the caliphate in its texts and commandments was earnestly pleading to him in a heart-rending voice on one hand, and, on the other hand, oppressive discord was warning him against a possible mutiny in the peninsula. There was a possible danger of bedouin Arabs renouncing their religion, thus annihilating the Islamic creed. The faith was being threatened by the hypocrites of Medina in whose nature hypocrisy was immersed, and who were aided by the hypocritical bedouins around them, according to the text of the Book (Qur'an). Nay, the latter party was even worse in disbelief and hypocrisy than the first, so much so that it was better they did not know the limits of what Allah had revealed to His Messenger (s).

The loss of the Prophet (s) emboldened the latter, and Muslims became in the aftermath like frightened cattle in a winter night, surrounded by wolves and ferocious brutes. While their fellows were quite active in their attempts to wipe out the religion of Islam and crush the Muslims, the Romans, the Kisras and others were waiting in anticipation, to the end of the list of such thronging elements that bore grudge against Muhammad, the progeny of Muhammad, and the companions of Muhammad (s). These parties bore animosity towards and felt jealous of the message of Islam; they desired to demolish its foundations, and undermining its might. In such endeavour, they would be very quick, seeing that they had their golden opportunity in the departure of the Prophet to his Supreme Companion. The chance had ripened then for them to make use of the chaos before Islam had recovered its strength and organization. It was then that the Commander of the Faithful (as) realized both dangers, and it was only natural that he would sacrifice his own right in order to sustain the religion of Islam, thus preferring the general interest to that of his own.

This is how such confusion ended, and the dispute between him and Abu Bakr was suspended, for he dreaded nothing save the disunity of Muslims and was concerned only that the Muslims should have the upper hand. So, he, all members of his household, their supporters from the Immigrants and Ansar, remained patiently tongue-tied even as they saw eye-sores. His speech after the Messenger of Allah (s) had departed is very frank in reflecting this attitude, and relevant reports are consecutive through the Imams of the purified progeny.

But the head of the Ansar, Sa'd ibn 'Abadah, never made asylum with the first two caliphs, and he was never seen in public accompanying either of them during an Eid celebration or on a Friday, and he never subscribed to their views, nor did he ever yield to their orders, till he was assassinated in Huran during the reign of the second caliph, and his assassins claimed that he was killed by the jinns. He made a memorable statement during the *saqifa* incident, but we see no need to quote it here.[2]

As regarding his friends such as Haban ibn al-Munthir[3] and other Ansaris, these succumbed unwillingly, yielding to pressure; so, do you consider the actions dictated by the fear of the sword or the burning by the fire[4] as a belief in the consignment of the

---

[2] Sa'd ibn 'Abadah, Thabit's father, was one of those present at the taking of the allegiance at 'Aqaba. He is also a participant in Badr and other battles. He was chief of al-Khazraj and their envoy, a generous man and a chief among the Ansar. His statement, to which we have referred, fills books of biographies and histories. Suffices you what Ibn Qutaybah has said in his treatise on *Imamate and politics*, Ibn Jarir al-Tabari in his *Tarikh*, Ibn al-Athir in his *Al-Kamil*, Abu Bakr Ahmad ibn 'Abdul-'Aiz al-Jawhari in his book *Al-Saqifa*, and others.

[3] Habab was one of the chiefs of the Ansar and a hero of Badr and Uhud, a man of feats and a glorious record. He is the one who said: "I am [as strong and firm as] a wooden post rubbed by camels, and a sweet fruit very much coveted. I am the son of a lion in his own den; by Allah, if you so desire, we would go back to wage a war that would grind even youngsters." He said other much stronger statements, and we thought it would be wiser to refrain from quoting them here.

[4] Their threat to 'Ali to burn his house is proven by absolute *tawatur*. Consider what Imam Ibn Qutaybah has said at the beginning of his chapter on Imamate and politics, Imam al-Tabari in two places where he discusses the events of the year 11 A.H. in his famous *Tarikh*, Ibn 'Abd Rabbih al-Maliki in his hadith of the *saqifa* as quoted in Vol. 1, page 134, of *Sharh Nahjul Balaghah*] by al-Hamidi al-Hadidi, al-Mas'udi in *Muruj al-Thahab* quoting 'Urwah ibn al-Zubayr when the latter apologized on behalf of his brother 'Abdullah who almost started setting the houses of the descendants of Hashim on fire because they boycotted his allegiance, al-Shahristani who quotes al-Nizam while discussing the Nizami group in his book *Al-Milal wal-Nihal*. Abu Mikhnaf has dedicated for the narratives related to the *saqifa* an entire book in which he details what we have summarized here, not to mention the fame and *tawatur* of this hadith, in addition to these poetic verses by al-Hafiz Ibrahim which are famous as the "'Umari poem":

allegiance? Or is it a testimony to such "consensus" implied in the statement of the Prophet (s) saying "My nation shall never commit an error in its consensus of opinion"? Please state your verdict; may Allah reward you, Wassalam.

 Sincerely,
 Sh

A statement 'Umar said to 'Ali; so think for a while;
Its listener venerates, respect the speaker and bear:
"Shall I burn your house and make of its ashes a pile
Should you choose to be stubborn and not swear
The oath of allegiance, even if and while
The Chosen One's daughter is inside there?"
None other than Abu Hafs was the speaker
Addressing Adnan's knight and protector...

Thus did they treat the Imam (as) without whose agreement, consensus according to our view can never be binding; so, we ask all those who are fair minded how can their "consensus" be binding upon us, since the case is as such?

Letter 83
Rabi'ul-Awwal 2, 1330

Can You Compromise the Text's Accuracy with the Companions' Truthfulness?

Those who are endowed with a discreet insight and keen comprehension regard the companions as being above doing anything contrary to the wish of the Prophet (s) in whatever he bids or forbids, neither do they permit anything other than such a policy. Therefore, they could not have heard the text regarding the Imam once, twice or thrice, then deviated therefrom. And how can you describe such companions to be truthful had they heard the text about him then refrained from following it? I do not think that you are able to compromise both [contradictory] situations, Wassalam.

Sincerely,
S

Letter 84
Rabi'ul-Awwal 5, 1330

I. Compromising the Text's Accuracy with Their Truthfulness

Our legacy of traditions, which has been left to us by those companions, indicates that the latter adhered to all texts as long as they were relevant to the faith, concerned about the matters related to the Hereafter, such as his (s) hadith regarding the obligatory fast during the month of Ramadan rather than any other month, facing only the *qibla* while performing the obligatory prayers, the number of obligatory prayers during the day or the night, the number of rak'at [prostrations] in each, as well as how to perform them, his hadith that the ceremonial *tawaf* around the House [Ka'ba] is seven times, and such ahadith aiming at the achievement of divine rewards in the life to come.

As regarding his texts that deal with political matters such as succession, government, administration, legislation, invasions, etc., they did not see that they had to follow or adhere to them in all circumstances; rather, they allowed themselves to practice a measure of research, discretion, and *ijtihad*. If they saw in opposing such texts a promotion of their cause, or an advantage to their power, they would oppose them. They may even seek to please the Prophet by doing just so. They were convinced that the Arabs would neither accept 'Ali's rule nor follow a text in such a matter, since he pressured them a great deal while enforcing the Will of Allah in their regard, spilling their blood with his sword in while promoting the Word of Allah, dismantling all their masks while defending the truth, till Allah's Will became dominant in spite of every infidel. So, they would not obey him willingly, nor would they follow such texts except by force, having attributed to him the spilling of all blood in the way of Islam during the lifetime of the Prophet (s), according to their custom of retaliation in such circumstances, for they saw him as the only candidate upon whom they would seek revenge, especially since seeking revenge is usually done to the best among the foe's tribesmen, and the choicest of its clans. They knew that he was the best among the Hashimites, after the Messenger of Allah (s), without any doubt or dispute. For this reason, the Arabs waited for a chance to annihilate him; they sought means to deal with him, and they bore a great deal of grudge against him and his descendants, till they leaped over them in a way that became well-known everywhere, and its shame filled the earth and the skies.

There is another reason: Quraysh in particular and the Arabs in general used to criticize 'Ali's might in dealing with the enemies of Allah, the forcefulness of his method of dealing with those who trespass the limits of Allah or permit what He prohibited. They feared his enjoining right and forbidding wrong; they dreaded his justice in dealing with the subjects and his equity in every public issue. Nobody hoped for his concession nor dreamed of his compromise. The mighty and powerful are weak till he executes justice on them, and the weak and downtrodden are strong and dignified when he grants them what is rightfully theirs. So, how can the Arabs willingly submit to a man like that while "They are the foremost in disbelief and hypocrisy, so much so that they ought not know the limits of what Allah has revealed unto His Messenger (Qur'an, 9:97)," and "Among the people of Medina are those who are stubborn in hypocrisy; you [O Our Prophet Muhammad] do not know them; We know them (Qur'an, 9:101), and among them are those who do not hesitate to commit anything insane.

There is still another reason. Quraysh in particular and Arabs in general used to envy him for the favours Allah bestowed upon him. He has been uplifted by Allah, His Messenger and the wise, to a sublime status due to his knowledge and feats; peers fall short of their attainment; those qualified hesitated to attempt to compete with him. He has, through his feats and attributes, won a status from Allah and His Messenger coveted by the hopeful, and a prestige unattainable by the most ambitious. For these reasons, jealousy filled the hearts of the hypocrites. The spiteful, ungrateful, and unequitable hypocrites, in addition to opportunists, all agreed not to discharge their responsibility towards him; therefore, they left these texts behind their backs, entrusting them to oblivion.

It was what it was, I shall never discuss the views;
So, entertain good thoughts; do not ask about the news.

Also, Quraysh and all other Arabs had by then coveted political dominance for their own respective tribes, and their ambition extended thereto. For this reason, they decided to discard the covenant and were determined to ignore the will. So, they all collaborated to forget the text, pledging not to mention it at all. They all agreed to divert the caliphate, since its inception, from its rightful candidate, who was assigned to it by their Prophet, and make it through election and choice, so that each one of their quarters might have a justification for hoping to attain it, though after a while. Had they followed the text and advanced 'Ali to succeed the Messenger of Allah, peace be upon him and his progeny, such caliphate would never have left his purified progeny, since he had equated his progeny on the Ghadir Day, as well as on other occasions, to the perfect Book of Allah, describing them as models for the wise till the Day of Judgment.

The Arabs would not have been able to tolerate the confinement of caliphate to one particular dynasty, especially when all their tribes coveted it, and it was sought by all those who wanted it for their own camps.

> It has, indeed, withered, weakened, and waned:
> A skeleton unwanted even by one whose funds drained.

Also, whoever knows the history of Quraysh and the Arabs at the dawn of Islam would come to know that they did not yield to the Hashimite Prophethood except after being annihilated, being powerless; so, how could they have agreed that Hashim's descendants should monopolize both prophethood and caliphate? 'Umar ibn al-Khattab once said to Ibn 'Abbas in a dialogue between them: "Quraysh hated that both prophethood and caliphate should be confined to your household for fear you might oppress other people."[1]

II. Rationalizing the Imam's Reluctance to Demand his Right

The good ancestors then could not force those folks to implement the spirit of the text for fear they might rebel if they did, and in apprehension of the dire consequences of disputing regarding such an issue. Hypocrisy surfaced immediately after the demise of the Messenger of Allah, peace be upon him and his progeny, and the might of the hypocrites increased by such a loss.

---

[1] This is quoted by Ibn Abul-Hadid on page 107, Vol. 3, of *Sharh Nahjul Balaghah*, while discussing an issue worthy of the attention of researchers which is also discussed by Ibn al-Athir near the conclusion of 'Umar's biography on page 24, Vol. 3, of his *Al-Kamil* before discussing the story of the "consultation."

The dark souls of the infidels grew darker, the foundations of the faith weakened, and the hearts of the Muslims waned, so much so that they became like frightened cattle in a winter night, surrounded by wolves and ferocious beasts. One group among the Arabs reneged, while another contemplated doing so, as we explained in Letter No. 82 above. Under such circumstances, 'Ali (as) feared dire consequences resulting from rushing matters if he took upon himself to take charge, knowing how people's hearts were, as we have described, with the hypocrites being what they were, biting their fingers in rage, and the renegades as we have clarified, while the polytheist nations were just as we have previously indicated. The Ansars had differed and deviated from the Muhajirun, saying, "Let us choose our ruler and you choose yours, etc." His concern about the faith prompted him to refrain from demanding the caliphate for himself and overlooking certain matters, knowing that demanding the caliphate under such circumstances would endanger the nation and jeopardize the safety of the faith; so, he opted to refrain just in preference of the interest of Islam and that of the common welfare, of the good of the future to that of the present.

He, therefore, remained at home, refusing to give his allegiance till he was forced to leave, just to silently enforce his own right, silently defying those who forsook him. Had he rushed to give his allegiance, he would have had neither argument nor pretext, but he, by doing so, safeguarded both religion and his own right to rule the believers, thus proving the originality of his mind, his overwhelming clemency, his patience and preference of the public interest to that of his own. Any soul that gives so much while facing so much affliction is sure to be rewarded by Allah with divine rewards. His objective was indeed to seek the pleasure of Allah in that epoch as well as in the epochs to come.

As regarding the three caliphs and their supporters, these have interpreted the text regarding his succession in the manner which we have indicated above. This should not surprise us at all once we come to know how they interpret and personally comprehend other texts of the Prophet, peace be upon him and his progeny, regarding issues such as succession, government, administration, legislation, etc. They probably did not consider them to be religious issues; so, it was easy for them to practically oppose them. When they finally took charge, they stuck to a policy of overlooking such texts, promising to punish those who would mention or even allude to them. When they succeeded in enforcing order, the dissemination of the religion of Islam, the invasion of nations, and the acquisition of wealth and power, they did not become corrupt in their own personal desires, and that elevated them and caused them to win people's respect, confidence, and love. People followed suit in forgetting about that text, and when Banu Umayyah succeeded them, the latter's main objective became the extinction and annihilation of the Prophet's household. In spite of all this, a few correct texts have reached us and have been protected in authentic books of traditions; these suffice for proof; praise be to Allah, Wassalam.

Sincerely,
Sh

Letter 85
Rabi'ul-Awwal 7, 1330

Requesting Narration of Incidents Wherein They did not Follow the Texts of Hadith

I have received your latest letter and found it miraculous in proving possible what we thought to be impossible, amazing in its portrayal of imagery in the most explicit depiction; so, praised be the One Who has simplified for you even the most complex demonstration, bestowing upon you the reins of elucidation, till you achieved what cannot be achieved by all means and won what cannot be won by the hopeful. We thought that the causes are not related to what the authentic texts have implied, and that there is no way to explicitly prove that they deviated therefrom. Yet I wish you had recounted the incidents wherein they did not follow the explicit texts, so that appropriateness becomes obvious, and the path of guidance manifests itself. I request you, therefore, to elaborate on this matter, in the light of their well-known traditions, digesting whatever is written in the books of chronicles regarding their way of thinking. Wassalamo Alaikum.

Sincerely,
S

Letter 86
Rabi'ul-Awwal 8, 1330

I. Thursday's Calamity

The incidents in which they did not follow the texts of hadith are innumerable. Take, for example, the calamity on Thursday, which is the most famous of such incidents and the most abominable among them. It is narrated by all authors of *sahih*s and *sunan*, and it was documented by all traditionists and historians. Suffices you what al-Bukhari, in his section dealing with the statement of the ailing Messenger (s): "Get away from me," on page 5, Vol. 4, of his *Sahih*, where the author relies on the authority of 'Ubaydullah ibn Abdullah ibn 'Utbah ibn Mas'ud who quotes Ibn 'Abbas saying that when death approached the Messenger of Allah, peace be upon him and his progeny, his house was full of men including 'Umar ibn al-Khattab. The Messenger of Allah, peace be upon him and his progeny, said: "Let me write you something that will forever protect you against straying after me 'Umar said: "The Prophet is under the influence of pain, and you have with you the Qur'an; so, the Book of Allah suffices us." Those who were present there argued among themselves, and their argument developed into a dispute. Some of them said: "Come close to the Prophet so that he may write something for you that will safeguard you against straying after him," while others repeated what 'Umar had said. When the argument and dispute intensified in the presence of the Prophet, the Messenger of Allah, peace be upon him and his progeny, said to them: "Get away from me." Ibn 'Abbas used to say: "The calamity, the real calamity, is what caused the Messenger of Allah (s) to desist from writing what he wished to write, due to their argument and dispute."

There is no dispute regarding the authenticity of this hadith nor the occasion whereupon it was invoked. Al-Bukhari quotes it in his treatise on knowledge on page 22, Vol. 1, of his work, and it exists in many other places with which the researchers are familiar. He quotes it in several places of his *Sahih*. Muslim, too, quotes it at the conclusion of the Prophet's will in his *Sahih* on page 14, Vol. 2. Ahmad narrates Ibn 'Abbas's hadith in his own Musnad. Refer to page 325 of its first volume. It is narrated by all authors of traditions and books of history, each writer editing it yet retaining its gist, reiterating the fact that the Prophet (s) was described as "hallucinating," or "delirious." But they also mentioned that 'Umar had said: "The Prophet (s) has been overcome by pain" just to sanitize the statement and undermine the sentiments of those who found it abominable. Supporting this fact is what Abu Bakr Ahmad ibn 'Abdul-'Aziz al-Jawhari has said in his book titled *Al-Saqifah*, relying on the authority of Ibn 'Abbas and quoting him saying,

"When death approached the Messenger of Allah, there were men present at his house among whom 'Umar ibn al-Khattab was one. The Messenger of Allah said: 'Bring me ink and a tablet so that I may write you something that will safeguard you against straying after me.' Those present at his house differed among themselves and disputed, some saying 'Come close and watch the Prophet write you something,' while others repeated what 'Umar had said. When the argument and dispute increased, the Messenger of Allah, peace be upon him and his progeny, became angry and said: 'Get away from me," as stated on page 20, Vol. 2, of *Sharh Nahjul Balaghah* by the Mu'azilite scholar [Ibn Abi al Hadid].

As you notice from this narrative, it is explicit in indicating that some individuals reported 'Umar's opposition in meaning, not *verbatim*. This also proves that the traditionists who did not wish to state the name of the person who opposed had nonetheless quoted his statement *verbatim*. In a chapter on rewarding the envoys, in his book *Al-Jihad wal Siyar*, page 118, Vol. 2, al-Bukhari states:

"Qabsah narrated a tradition to us from Ibn 'Ayinah, Salman al-Ahwal, and Sa'id ibn Jubayr, all consecutively quoting Ibn 'Abbas saying: 'On a Thursday - what a day that Thursday was...,' and he burst sobbing till his tears drenched the stones, then he went on to say, "...the pain of the Messenger of Allah intensified on a Thursday; so, he ordered us to bring him some writing material so that he might write us something whereby we would be protected against straying after him, but people disputed, knowing that nobody should dispute in the presence of any Prophet, and they said: 'The Messenger of Allah is delirious.' He, peace be upon him and his progeny, then said: 'Leave me, for the pain which I am suffering is more tolerable than what you are attributing to me,' and he left in his will prior to his demise three items: to get the polytheists out of the Arab land, to reward the envoys the same way he (s) used to reward them,' and I forgot the third one."[1]

The same hadith is narrated also by Muslim at the conclusion of a chapter dealing with the will in his *Sahih*, and by Ahmad in Ibn 'Abbas's ahadith on page 222, Vol. 1, of his work, and by all other traditionists. In his chapter on the will, in his *Sahih*, Muslim quotes Sa'id ibn Jubayr in one place, and Ibn 'Abbas in another, saying, "That Thursday, O what a day that Thursday was...," and his tears kept pouring down till they looked like pearls arrayed in a formation, then he continued to say: "The Messenger of Allah, peace be upon him and his progeny, said: 'Bring me a tablet and an ink-pot,' or a plate and some ink, 'so that I may write you something whereby you shall never be misguided;' so, some people said: 'The Messenger of Allah is delirious.'"[2]

Anyone who researches this abominable incident in the *sahih*s will soon come to find out that the first person who said that the Messenger of Allah was delirious was indeed 'Umar, and some of those who were present there and then followed suit. In the first hadith, you have heard Ibn 'Abbas saying:[3] "Those present at his house differed among themselves and disputed, some saying 'Come close and watch the Prophet writing you something,' while others repeated what 'Umar had said," i.e. "The Messenger of Allah is delirious." In another tradition narrated by al-Tabrani, in his *Awsat*, and on page 138, Vol. 3, of *Kanz al-'Ummal*, 'Umar is quoted saying: "When the Prophet became sick, he said: 'Bring me a tablet and an ink-pot, so that I may write you something after which you shall never stray;' so, the women behind the curtain said:

---

[1] The third is none other than the matter which the Prophet (s) desired to write down in order to protect them from misguidance, but politics forced the traditionists to "forget" it, as the Hanafi *mufti* of Sur, Hajj Dawud al-Dadah, suggested.
[2] This hadith is quoted *verbatim* by Ahmad on page 355, Vol. 1, of his *Musnad*, in addition to many other reliable authors of books of traditions.
[3] This is what al-Bukhari has quoted from 'Ubaydullah ibn 'Abdullah ibn 'Utbah ibn Mas'ud from Ibn 'Abbas, and it is also quoted by Muslim and others.

'Have you not heard what the Messenger of Allah, peace be upon him and his progeny, is saying?'" 'Umar goes on to say: "I said to them: 'You are like the women who admired Joseph; when the Messenger of Allah falls sick, you squeeze your eyes, and when he is healthy, you ride his neck!" He also continues to say: "The Messenger of Allah then said: 'Leave them, for they are better than you.'"

You can see that they never implemented the spirit of this hadith. Had they done so, they would have been protected against misguidance. We wish they had stopped at just being insubordinate and not answering him by saying: "The Book of Allah suffices us," as if he did not know the status of Allah's Book among them, or that they were more knowledgeable than him about its characteristics and merits. We wish they had been satisfied with all of that rather than surprising him with their rude statement: "The Messenger of Allah is delirious," just when he was suffering the agony of death. What a farewell statement to the Messenger of Allah (s)! They did not follow the Prophet's command due to their being satisfied with the Book of Allah as they claimed, as if they never read the verse: "Whatever the Messenger hands over to you, take it, and whatever he forbids you therefrom, obey him (Qur'an, 59:7)." They said: "The Messenger of Allah is delirious," as if they never read the verse: "It is the speech of an eminent Messenger, empowered by the One with the Throne, peaceful to those who obey Him; verily, your fellow is not possessed (Qur'an, 81:19-22)," and His statement, the Exalted, the Omniscient, "It is the speech of an eminent Messenger, not of a poet; little do you believe; nor is it the speech of a priest; little do you remember; it is but the Revelation from the Lord of the Worlds (Qur'an, 69:40-43)," and His statement, the Almighty, the Sublime, "Your fellow has neither strayed, nor has he yielded to temptation; he utters nothing out of his own inclination; it is but what is revealed unto him of the Revelation; he is taught by One mighty in powers (Qur'an, 53:2-5)," in addition to many such verses laden with divine wisdom, all testifying to his being divinely protected from delirium.

Yet even reason by itself testifies to the same, but they were aware of the fact that he, the Messenger of Allah, peace be upon him and his progeny, wished to strengthen the covenant of caliphate, and emphasize its being the monopoly of 'Ali in particular, and the Imams among his purified progeny in general; so, they stood as a stumbling block in his way to do so, as admitted by none other than the second caliph himself in a private conversation which he held with Ibn 'Abbas...! It exists in line 27, page 114, Vol. 3, of *Sharh Nahjul Balaghah* by Ibn Abul Hadid.

If you consider his statement, peace be upon him and his progeny, "Bring me a tablet and an ink-pot, so that I may write you something whereby you shall never stray after me," and his statement in the hadith of the Two Weighty Things: "I am leaving with you that which, as long as you uphold, will never let you stray: the Book of Allah and my progeny, my Ahl al-Bayt," you will come to know then that the purpose of both traditions is the same, and that he, peace be upon him and his progeny, wished, even while being sick, to write for them the details of the injunctions implied in the hadith of the Two Weighty Things [*al thaqalain*].

II. The Reason Why the Prophet Repealed His Order Then

He repealed his order to them due to their statement with which they surprised him, forcing him to change his mind, since after uttering it there would be no effect for his writing them anything other than dissension and dispute, leading them to argue be he really delirious - God forbid - or not, just as they did even in his own presence and while he could still see things, so much so that he could not tell them more than to get away, as you have heard. Had he insisted on writing it, they would have resorted to their claim that he had written it in delirium, and many of their followers would have gone to extremes in their attempts to prove that he did so while being delirious - God forbid - and fill their books with such allegations, only to reject his writing and use it as a pretext for not implementing it.

For these reasons, his marvellous wisdom decreed that he, peace be upon him and his progeny, should forget about such writing for fear those opposing his wish and their followers might open a door to casting doubts about Prophethood itself; we seek refuge with Allah, and we pray for His protection. He, peace be upon him and his progeny, saw how 'Ali (as) and his followers submitted to the spirit of such writing, whether he had written it down or not, while others would not act upon it anyway even if he had written it. Wisdom, therefore, necessitated abandoning it since it would have no effect at all over the opposition that arose other than dissension, as is obvious, Wassalam.

Sincerely,
Sh

Letter 87
Rabi' al-Awwal 9, 1330

Justifying and Discussing the Calamity

When he, peace be upon him, ordered them to bring him a blank sheet of paper and an ink-pot, he did not really intend to write anything in particular; he intended only to test them, that's all. Therefore, Allah guided al-Faruq, from among all other companions, to forbid them from bringing them to him. Such an opposition, therefore, must be considered to be in agreement with his Sublime Lord, and be counted among his divinely-endowed spiritual powers, may Allah be pleased with him. This is the argument of many renowned personalities. But his statement, peace be upon him, "... you shall never stray," rejects such an argument if the principle of fairness is to be implemented, for it is a supplementary command which means "If you bring me the blank sheet and the ink-pot, and if I write you something, then you shall never stray after it." It is obvious that interpreting such an order as being indicative of a test is a sort of flagrant lying from which Prophets are immune, especially where bringing the blank sheet and the ink-pot is more fit for the one who receives the order than his seeking such an excuse; therefore, another alibi is needed.

All that can be said is that the issue is not an invitation to a party, so that whoever refuses may simply be blamed, but it is an issue of consultation. They used to consult him ['Umar], peace be upon him, in a few matters. And 'Umar knew that he deep down in his heart was successful in choosing what is best for the interest of Muslims, and that itself was inspired by Allah Almighty. He simply desired not to let the Prophet burden himself with the pain resulting from writing something in the state of sickness and agony, and he, peace be upon him, thought that it would be better not to bring the blank sheet and the ink-pot. He may also have feared that the Prophet might write things that would be quite impossible for people to carry out, thus making them liable for punishment, since such things would be texts for which the principle of ijtihad is not possible. Or he may have feared that the hypocrites might cast doubts about the authenticity of such writing due to its being done under the influence of sickness, thus becoming a cause of dissension; therefore, he said: "The Book of Allah suffices us," supporting the verse of the Almighty: "We have not left aught (without explaining it) in the Book (Qur'an, 6:38)" and also "Today have I completed your religion for you (Qur'an, 5:4)," out of his own concern, peace be upon him, for this nation against straying after Allah had completed His religion for it and complemented His blessing unto it.

Such was their answer. His saying "... you shall never stray" indicates determination and a positive attitude. The endeavour to bring about security against straying, whenever possible and without any doubt, is a must. His disappointment with them and his telling them to leave him since they did not carry out his order is another proof that the matter was simply a response to a consultation.

So, if you say that had it been a must, the Prophet, peace be upon him, would not have repealed it simply because they disobeyed him, just like he did not stop preaching due to the opposition of the unbelievers..., if you say all this, then we would say that the case is so had the order been carried out, for it indicates that the writing of that matter was not obligatory on the Prophet, peace be upon him. This of course does not imply that they should not have brought him the sheet and the ink-pot when he ordered them to, explaining to them that its benefits would include security for them against straying and a source of continuous guidance. The main point is that those receiving his order should have obeyed it, especially when the benefit was for the one receiving the order, and it is the reason for the statement, not for its enforcement.

Yet it is also possible that it was obligatory on him, too, and such an obligation was removed due to their insubordination and their saying that he was speaking in delirium, for the fate of such writing was then reduced to dissension, as you yourself have wisely stated.

It is also possible that some people may say that 'Umar, may Allah be pleased with him, did not take the meaning of the Prophet's statement to imply that such writing would result in protecting each and every member of the nation from straying, so much so that none of them at all would be misguided. Rather, he understood "... you shall never stray" to mean "... you shall never agree all of you to walk the path of misguidance, nor will misguidance, after such writing, would inflict anyone among you." Rather, he, may Allah be pleased with him, was convinced that they would never all concede to tread the path of misguidance. This is why he found no reason why the Prophet should write anything else, thinking that the intention of the Prophet was simply an additional precaution in the matter, since he was so well-known to be overflowing with kindness and compassion.

This is all that has been said in the manner of finding an excuse for that initiation. Whoever scrutinizes it will be positive in thinking that it is far from being rational, for the simple fact that his statement, peace be upon him, "... you shall never stray" indicates that the matter required proper attention, as we have said, and his disappointment with them is a proof that they became derelict regarding one of their obligations. It is, therefore, more fitting to say that such an incident took place when they, indeed, behaved contrarily to their custom, just like their previous slip, and it is one mistake that is not at all typical of them, and we do not really know how accurate the whole story is. Allah is the Guide to the Straight Path, Wassalamo Alaikum.

Sincerely,
S

Letter 88
Rabi'ul-Awwal 11, 1330

Pretexts Refuted

Any fair minded person ought to yield to the truth and utter what is right. There are other views regarding the rejection of these arguments which I desired to put forth to you, so that the final judgment will be left entirely to you.

Their first pretext states that he, peace be upon him and his progeny, having ordered them to bring the ink-pot, did not really intend to write something but rather desired to test them, that's all. We say, in addition to what you yourself have stated, that this incident took place shortly before his demise, as the tradition itself suggests; there was simply no time for testing, but there was time for a last minute warning and justifying, time for a will containing a very significant matter, a piece of complete advice for the nation. Anyone who is dying is certainly far from testing or jesting; he would be concerned about his affairs and those of his own kin, especially if he is a Prophet.

If he, as long as he lived, did not have enough time to test them, how could he have found time to do so when he was about to die? His statement, peace be upon him and his progeny, telling them to get away from him when they fussed and argued in his presence, is surely indicative of his disappointment with them. Had those who opposed him been right, he would have appreciated their opposition and expressed his pleasure therewith. Anyone who studies this tradition, especially their saying that the Messenger of Allah was delirious, will be positively sure that they were aware of his intention to do something they hated; so, they surprised him with such a statement, and they persisted fussing, arguing, and disputing, as is quite obvious. Ibn 'Abbas's tears, and his labelling the incident a catastrophe disproves this argument.

Those who seek excuses by arguing that 'Umar was divinely inspired in assessing the public interest of Muslims, that he was inspired by Allah, are talking nonsense, and their argument is dismissed in such a discussion since it suggests that he, not the Messenger of Allah, peace be upon him and his progeny, was on the right track in this incident, and that his so-called "inspiration" was more accurate than the revelation which he (s), the truthful and trustworthy that he was, uttered.

They say that it was intended to relieve the Prophet, peace be upon him and his progeny, from the burden of writing while feeling sick. You, may Allah support the truth through your person, know that writing such matters would only bring the Prophet peace of mind, tranquillity, and the pleasure of his eyes. He would feel happy for ensuring a security for his nation, peace be upon him and his progeny, against misguidance. The commands to be obeyed, the divine will, and the physical presence were all his. He, being more precious than my parents, wished to have access to a sheet of paper and an ink-pot; he issued an order and nobody was supposed to oppose his wish; "Neither a believing man nor a believing woman has any right, when Allah and His Messenger decree a matter, to follow their own views, and whoever disobeys Allah and His Messenger is surely in manifest misguidance (Qur'an, 33:36)."

Yet their insubordination in such an extremely significant matter, and their fussing, arguing, and disputing in his presence, were to him more painful than writing what he wished to write in order to protect his nation against misguidance. How can anyone who feels pity for him because of the pain of writing something opposes him and surprise him by saying that he was speaking in delirium?

They say that 'Umar thought that not to bring the sheet and the ink-pot was wiser. This is a most odd statement. How can it be wiser while the Prophet himself had ordered that they should be brought forth? Did 'Umar think that the Messenger of Allah would order something which would be better left out?

Yet even more strange is their argument that 'Umar feared that the Prophet might write things which would be impossible to implement and whose abandoning would require chastisement. How can it thus be feared in spite of the Prophet's statement "...

you shall never stray"? Do people who thus argue think that 'Umar assesses the consequences more correctly than the Prophet himself, and that he is more cautious about and compassionate to his nation than the Prophet (s)? Certainly not.

They also say that it is possible that 'Umar feared the hypocrites might cast doubts about the authenticity of such writing, since it would be written during the Prophet's sickness, and that it would be a cause for dissension. You, may Allah support the truth through your person, know that such an insinuation is impossible since the Prophet, peace be upon him and his progeny, has stated: "... you shall never stray," thus clearly stating that such writing would bring them security against straying; so, how can it be a reason for dissension just because the hypocrites might cast doubts about its authenticity? Had he ['Umar] feared such hypocrites and their casting doubts about the authenticity of what the Prophet wished to write, why did he then plant the seed of such doubts himself when he opposed and objected and even said that the Prophet was delirious?

As regarding their interpretation of verses cited in support of 'Umar's statement: "The Book of Allah suffices us," such as the verse: "We have left nothing unexplained in the Book (Qur'an, 6:38)," and "Today have I completed for you your religion (Qur'an, 5:4)," it is erroneous, for neither verse suggests a security against misguidance, nor do both verses guarantee guidance for people; so, how can relying on these verses justify abandoning the implementation of the texts whose writing the Prophet wished to record? Had the presence of the dear Qur'an been to bring security against misguidance, then neither misguidance nor dissension, the removal of which is as hopeless as can be, would have ever taken place.[1]

---

[1] You, may Allah support the truth through your person, know that the Prophet (s) did not say: "I would like to write down the tenets," so that it may be said to him: "Suffices us the Book of Allah, the Exalted One." Even if we suppose that he wished to write down those tenets, it could very possibly be that his own

In their final argument, they say that 'Umar did not understand the tradition to imply that such writing would be a cause for protecting each and every member of his nation from misguidance; and that rather he understood that it would, after its writing, safeguard them against erring in their consensus. They claim that 'Umar, may Allah be pleased with him, knew that the error in their consensus would never occur, albeit if such writing had taken place or not, and that for this reason he opposed its writing thus.

Besides what you have said, we may add that 'Umar did not lack such a degree of understanding, and he was not blind to the implication of the tradition which became obvious to all people. Urban residents as well as bedouins understood the intention of the Prophet (s) that it would be a complete prescription for the protection of every individual against misguidance... only had it been written. This is the meaning which anyone can comprehend of this tradition. 'Umar knew for sure that the Messenger of Allah, peace be upon him and his progeny, was not worried about his nation making an error in its consensus views, since he, may Allah be pleased with him, had heard him, peace be upon him and his progeny, saying: "The consensus of my nation shall never be in misguidance nor in error," and his statement: "One group from my nation shall always stand opposing what is just," and he was aware of the verse saying: "Allah has promised those who believe among

---

writing thereof would be a cause for security against misguidance; therefore, there is no reason to avoid his text and be satisfied with the Qur'an alone. If the text he wished to write was only to safeguard them against misguidance, it would not be appropriate to leave it, shun it, and rely on the fact that Allah's Book includes everything. You know very well how the Muslim nation has no option besides referring to the sacred Sunnah in spite of the fact that it holds the Book of Allah, the Exalted, as indispensable, and although it is inclusive and is divinely protected, for deriving injunctions from it is not within the reach of every ordinary person. Had the Book of Allah been completely sparing us from referring to its own explanations as put forth by the Prophet (s), then Allah Aighty would not have commanded him to explain it to people when He said: "We have revealed unto you the Book so that you may explain to people what has been revealed for them."

you and do good deeds that He will let them inherit the earth just as He let those before them be the successors, and He will firmly set the roots of the faith which He has approved, and He will exchange their fear with security; they shall worship Me, without associating anything with Me (Qur'an, 24:55)," In addition to many such texts in both the Book and the Sunnah. They all are clear in implying that NOT the entire nation shall err in its consensus views; so, it is not feasible, in spite of all this, that 'Umar or anyone else would conceive that when the Prophet, peace be upon him and his progeny, asked for a blank sheet of paper and an ink-pot, was worried about his nation erring in its consensus views. What 'Umar is liable to have understood of this hadith is what anyone else would, not what is contrary to the authentic Sunnah, nor to the perfect verses of the Qur'an. But the disappointment of the Prophet, peace be upon him and his progeny, was obvious when he told them to get away from him, and it proved that what they had shunned was indeed a sacred obligation. Had 'Umar's objection been due to his misunderstanding of this hadith, as they claim, then the Prophet would have helped him remove his misunderstanding, and he would have clarified his objective to him. Nay, even if the Prophet was convinced that he would be able to convince them to carry out his order, he would not have ordered them out. Again, Ibn 'Abbas's tears and genuine agony provide the greatest rebuttal to such claims.

Justice refuses to find an excuse for those who had permitted such a calamity to take place. Had it been, as you described, a simple slip like another one before it, and a rare occurrence, the matter would have been a lot more tolerable, but it was the catastrophe of the century that split the nation's spine; so, we are Allah's, and to Him is our return.

Sincerely,
Sh

Letter 89
Rabi'ul-Awwal 14, 1330

I. Admitting the Falsehood of Such Pretexts
You have closed the avenues in the way of permitting the falsehood of such pretexts.

II. Requesting Narration of Other Incidents
Go ahead, then, and state all other incidents in which they used their own judgment regarding the Prophet's Hadith, Wassalam.

Sincerely,
S

Letter 90
Rabi'l-Awwal 17, 1330

Usamah's Regiment
If you have truly submitted to the truth, without fearing any blame, then you are the ultimate goal and the true objective. You are above getting confused about what is right and what is not, and you are above hiding the truth. You are even more than that, more honourable, and more virtuous.

You have, may Allah raise your status of honour, asked me to narrate for you all other incidents in which they preferred to follow their own views rather than submitting to divine orders; therefore, consider the incident of the regiment of Usamah ibn Zayd ibn Harithah dispatched to invade the Romans. It was the last regiment contemporary to the Prophet (s) who paid it a great concern, ordering his companions to prepare for it, earnestly urging them to do so. He raised the army in his own pure person in order to give those enlisted in it a great deal of moral encouragement and address their conscience. He did not spare any dignitary from among the Muhajirun nor the Ansar, such as Abu Bakr, 'Umar,[1] Abu 'Ubaydah, Sa'd, and their peers, from enlisting.[2]

It took place on Safar 26, 11 A.H. The next day, he called upon Usamah and said: "Go to the place where your father had been murdered and let your cavalry roam it, for I have vested upon you the leadership of these troops; therefore, invade Ubna[3] in the morning, burn their homes and come back faster than the tidings of your deeds. If Allah grants you the upper hand over them, do not stay there too long. Take road guides with you; dispatch others to collect information for you, and let the scouts escort you."

---

[1] Authors of books of tradition and history have unanimously accepted the fact that Abu Bakr and 'Umar, may Allah be pleased with them, were enlisted in the same army, stating such a fact in their books unreservedly, and this is one of the instances in which they have never disputed. Refer, therefore, to any book which contains information about this particular expedition such as Ibn Sa'd's *Tabaqat*, the books of history by al-Tabari and Ibn al-Athir, *Al-Sira al-Halabiyya*, *Al-Sira al-Dahlaniyya*, and others, so that you may find out for yourself. When al-Halabi discusses this campaign in Vol. 3 of his *Sira* [biography book], he mentions an interesting anecdote which we would like to quote here as he words it:

> When the caliph al-Mahdi entered Basra, he happened to see Iyas ibn Mu'awiyah, who is proverbial in sharpness of intellect, and who was then a young boy surrounded by as many as four hundred men of knowledge and prestige, al-Mahdi asked him: "What beards! Couldn't they find an older sage to follow rather than this teenager?" Then al-Mahdi turned to him and asked him how old he was. He answered: "I am, may Allah prolong the presence of the commander of the faithful among us, the same age Usamah ibn Zayd ibn Harithah was when the Messenger of Allah (s) entrusted him to lead the army in which both Abu Bakr and 'Umar served." Al-Mahdi said: "Come close, may Allah bless you." He was then seventeen years old.

[2] 'Umar used to say to Usamah: "The Messenger of Allah (s) has died leaving you in command over me." He is quoted by a group of renowned scholars such as al-Halabi while discussing Usamah's army in his *Al-Sira al-Halabiyya*, in addition to many other traditionists and historians.

[3] It is a territory in Balqa' between 'Ashkelon (a seaport in southwest Palestine) and Ramallah (in Jordan's West Bank), near Mu'ta where Zayd ibn Harithah and Ja'far ibn Abu Talib, of the two wings in Paradise, peace be upon him, were martyred.

On Safar 38, his death fever intensified, and he started suffering from headaches. On Safar 29, he found them reluctant to leave; therefore, he went out to urge them to expedite the campaign. He (s) tied the flag for Usamah with his own eminent hands in order to stir their conscience and manipulate their determination. Then he said: "Go in the Name of Allah, in the Path of Allah, and fight those who disbelieve in Allah." Usamah took the tied flag and handed it to Buraydah, then he camped at Jurf. Even there, they slackened and did not leave, in spite of all the clear statements of the Prophet (s) urging them to expedite the campaign, such as: "... invade Ubna in the morning," and "... come back faster than the tidings of your deeds," in addition to many such orders which they never followed in reference to that regiment. Moreover, even some of them started questioning the wisdom of selecting Usamah for its leadership, just as they had questioned that of his father's, making several remarks to that effect, in spite of their witnessing the Prophet (s) vesting upon him such a responsibility, and their hearing the Prophet (s) saying to him: "I have vested upon you the leadership of these troops," and their seeing him tying the flag for him, which is the symbol of authority, with his own eminent hands, and all of that he (s) did in spite of his fever.

All of the above did not stop them from casting doubts about the wisdom of selecting him as the regiment's commander, so much so that their grumbling angered the Prophet (s) who went out one day, his head bandaged,[4] wrapped in a blanket, suffering the pain of fever, on a Saturday, the 10th of Rabi'ul-Awwal, only two days before his demise, and ascended the pulpit. Having seated

---

[4] Every traditionist and author of biography and history books who has mentioned this regiment has also mentioned their resentment of the Prophet's appointment of Usamah as the commander over them, and that he (s) became extremely angry when he came to know about such resentment, hence he delivered the *khutba* which we have quoted earlier; so, refer to the chapter on Usamah's regiment in Ibn Sa'd's *Tabaqat*, both Sira books of al-Halabi and al-Dahlani, and other books dealing with this topic.

himself on the pulpit, he (s) praised Allah and glorified Him, then, according to the consensus of historians and scholars, he said:

> "O people! It has come to my knowledge that some of you have felt uneasy about my appointment of Usamah [as the commander]. If you cast doubts about his appointment, you had done so before when I appointed his father who, by Allah, was worthy of such authority, and so is his son after him."

He urged them to start marching, and they in fact did start bidding him farewell and leaving to join the troops stationed at al-Jurf, while he was still urging them to rush. Then his sickness worsened, yet he kept saying: "Usamah's army! Complete the mission of Usamah's army! Dispatch Usamah's troops!" He kept repeating these orders even while they were still reluctant to respond. On the 12th of Rabi'ul-Awwal, Usamah left his temporary quarters at al-Jurf and visited the Prophet (s) who ordered him to start his mission immediately, saying: "Tomorrow, by the blessing of Allah, the Exalted One, leave early in the morning," so he bade him farewell and left for the camp. Accompanied by 'Umar and Abu 'Ubaydah, he went back again to see the Prophet. The three men reached the Prophet who was breathing his last. He died, may my life and those of the world be sacrificed for his sake, on the same day, and the army returned to Medina and considered cancelling the campaign altogether.

They discussed this matter with Abu Bakr, pressuring him a great deal to endorse their idea of cancellation, in spite of witnessing all the emphasis the Prophet (s) had placed on rushing the mission, having heard his statement stressing that they should expedite sending the troops in a way too fast to allow the enemy to know about it, spending so much effort raising the army personally, appointing Usamah to take charge of it, and tying its flag with his own hands, saying: "Tomorrow, by the blessing of Allah, the Exalted One, leave early in the morning," till he died, as you have come to know. Had it not been for the newly appointed successor of the Prophet (s), they would have all decided to cancel the campaign and untie the flag's knot, but the caliph [Abu Bakr] refused to do so, and when they saw him determined to carry on the mission, 'Umar approached him and requested him on behalf of the Ansar to depose Usamah from the post of the army's leader and appoint someone else.

It was not long since they had angered the Prophet and annoyed him by their displeasure with his appointment of Usamah as the commander of the regiment, nor since his going out of his house for the same reason, painfully feverish, bandaged, wrapped in a blanket, unable to walk steadily, his legs hardly carrying him due to the pain from which he was suffering; having ascended the pulpit, breathing heavily, fighting his pain, he said: "O people! It has come to my knowledge that some of you have felt uneasy about my appointment of Usamah [as the commander]. If you cast doubts about his appointment, you had done so before when I appointed his father who, by Allah, was worthy of such an authority, and so is his son after him." Thus did he, peace be upon him and his progeny, emphasize, by swearing by Allah, that they should submit to what he had decreed. They did not. The new caliph [Abu Bakr] refused to yield to their pressure to remove Usamah from his post. He leaped and took 'Umar by the beard saying: "May your mother lose you, and may she be deprived of you as a son! He has been appointed by the Messenger of Allah (s) and you still ask me to depose him?!"[5] They reluctantly dispatched Usamah's regiment. The total number of his troops was no more than three thousand, including one thousand cavaliers.[6] It was dodged by many of those

---

[5] This is quoted by al-Halabi and al-Dahlani in their respective Sira books, and by Ibn Jarir al-Tabari while discussing the events of the year 11 in his *Tarikh*, in addition to other authors of books of history.

[6] He raided Ubna, burnt their homes, cut their palm-trees, his cavalry trampled upon their residential quarters, killing a few and capturing a few others. Among those whom he killed was his father's assassin. Nobody among the Muslims was killed; so, praise be to Allah, Lord of the Worlds. Usamah was then riding his father's horse. Their banner then said: "O you who is divinely supported, take

who had been drafted by the Messenger of Allah (s) himself. According to Shahristani's fourth Introduction to his book *Al-Milal wal Nihal*, the Prophet (s) is quoted saying: "Draft in Usamah's army; may Allah curse its draft dodgers."

You may also know that initially they were reluctant to go with the regiment; then they finally dodged, just to firmly lay the foundations of their political structure and set its bases, preferring it to the carrying out of the orders of the Prophet. They saw that such a political structure was more worthy of their concern and attention, since their reluctance to draft would not cancel the dispatching of the troops, nor would the draft dodgers either. As regarding the caliphate, they would certainly miss it had they participated in the campaign before the Prophet's demise. He (s) had desired that they should leave the capital in order to clear the way for the establishment of the caliphate for the Commander of the Faithful Ali ibn Abu Talib (as) peacefully and quietly. So, when they would come back, such caliphate would have already been established and settled down for Ali, and there would have been no chance for them to dispute or question it.

The Prophet (s) had selected Usamah, who was seventeen years old,[7] to be their commander simply in order to subdue the stiff necks of some of them, and out of his own desire to contain the ambition of others, and also as a safeguard for protecting the peace in the future against the dispute of those who were obviously ambitious and hopeful, had he chosen one of them instead. But they were intelligent enough to be aware of what he (s) was planning; so, they questioned the appointment of Usamah, reluctantly refused to accompany him, and did not leave Jurf till the soul of the Prophet (s) returned to its Lord. It was then that they decided

---

their lives," which was the Prophet's banner during the Battle of Badr. He distributed two shares of the booty to cavalry soldiers and one to the infantry, taking for himself the same.

[7] This is most likely. Some say he was eighteen years old, others say nineteen, and still others say twenty, but nobody said he was older than that.

to cancel the campaign and untie the flag's knot on one hand, and to depose Usamah on the other. Moreover, many of them became draft dodgers, as you have come to know. These are five reasons why they did not act upon the Prophet's hadith, preferring their own political interests, and following their own judgment rather than implementing the spirit of his hadith, Wassalam.

Sincerely,
Sh

Letter 91
Rabi' al-Awwal 19, 1330

I. Justifying Their Behaviour Towards Usamah's Regiment

Yes, the Messenger of Allah (s) had urged them to rush to participate in Usamah's campaign, ordering them to expedite, as you have mentioned, emphasizing his order till he told Usamah to invade Ubna in the morning, not allowing him to wait till the evening, telling him to go and emphasizing his order once more by telling him to rush. But he, peace be upon him, according to all narrations, fell sick and started breathing very heavily, so much so that they started worrying about him and feeling too upset to leave him in such condition. They remained at Jurf waiting to know the condition of his health out of their own fear for his life and due to their attachment to him. They, therefore, are excused for having waited, and they should not be blamed.

As regarding their questioning the Prophet's appointment of Usamah after his death, in spite of what they remembered of his statements and his emphasis by word and by action, with which they were familiar, it was nothing more than their objection to his being too young, to his being a youth among middle-aged and old men. The latter naturally find it very difficult to receive orders from the young, and they by nature feel resentful towards submitting to their judgment. Their hatred of his appointment was not an innovation but simply due to the human nature; so, consider that.

As regarding their demand after the demise of the Messenger to depose Usamah, this is justified by some scholars among those who expected the Siddiq [Abu Bakr] to agree with them. These persons thought that such deposition would, in their view, serve the public interest. Yet, for the sake of fairness, I personally cannot rationalize their request to depose him after seeing how angry the Prophet (s) was when they requested the same, and his going out, feverish, bandaged and wrapped in a blanket, to denounce such a notion in his sermon from the pulpit. They knew that such an incident was, indeed, a historical milestone; so, their real motive is not known except by Allah.

As regarding their determination to cancel the campaign, and their pressuring al-Siddiq to do so, in spite of seeing how much emphasis the Prophet had placed on its dispatch, his concern about expediting its departure, as well as his repeated statements to this effect, is but their own caution about the capital of Islam else it should be assaulted by the polytheists around it once vacated from a protecting force, while the army was far away from it, especially since hypocrisy surfaced as soon as the Prophet (s) died, and the hopes of the Jews and Christians were revived, and a group among the Arabs renegaded, while other groups refused to pay *zakat*. The companions of the Prophet, therefore, spoke to our master al-Siddiq and requested him to forbid Usamah from leaving, but he refused and said: "It is better for me that birds snatch my flesh away rather than start my rule by overruling the command of the Messenger of Allah (s)."

This is what our fellows have said regarding al-Siddiq. As regarding others, they are not to be blamed for trying to stop the campaign since their objective was nothing other than a genuine concern about the safety of the religion of Islam.

As regarding the question why Abu Bakr, 'Umar, and others who were drafted in the regiment, lagged behind when Usamah proceeded, it was only to lay the firm foundations of the Islamic government, support the law of Muhammad (s), and protect the caliphate, which was the only protector of both faith and the faithful.

II. No Hadith Curses its Draft Dodgers
As regarding what you have quoted of Shahristani's book *Al-Milal wal Nihal*, we have found it to be narrated without the name of its narrator. Both al-Halabi and Sayyid al-Dahlani, in their

respective books of traditions, have said that in fact there was no such hadith at all in that meaning. If you, may Allah protect you, are able to narrate hadith from Sunnis supporting it, then lead me to it, Wassalam.

Sincerely,
S

Letter 92
Rabi' al-Awwal 22, 1330

I. Their Pretexts do not Contradict our Statement

You have, may Allah Almighty protect you, admitted that they lagged behind Usamah's regiment and were at Jurf reluctant to proceed in spite of being ordered by the Prophet (s) to rush and expedite. You also admit that they did, indeed, raise questions about the [Prophet's] wisdom in appointing Usamah in spite of what they had seen and heard of deeds and words regarding his appointment.

You have further admitted that they did, indeed, request Abu Bakr to depose him even after seeing how angry the Prophet (s) was when he noticed their questioning his appointment, his going out to them, feverish, bandaged, wrapped in a blanket, to deliver a sermon from the pulpit in which he repudiated their grumbling, a sermon you yourself have described as one of the significant historical events, one wherein he described Usamah as being worthy of such a post.

You have accepted the fact that they requested the caliph to cancel the regiment dispatched by the Messenger of Allah (s), and untie the knot he, with his own eminent hands, had tied, in spite of seeing his concern about dispatching it and his complete care about expediting it, in addition to several statements he made regarding the necessity of doing so.

You have, moreover, admitted that some of those who had been drafted in that army by the Prophet (s) himself who ordered them to enlist under Usamah's leadership had lagged behind. You have admitted all these facts which are written down in the books of history and are matters of consensus among the traditionists and historians, saying that they were not to be blamed for all what they had done. The summary of their pretext, as you have put it, is that they had preferred in those matters the interest of Islam according to their own views, not according to the Prophet's statements in their regard. We did not intend in this matter to state anything more than that. In other words, the topic of our discussion is whether they used to follow all the Prophet's statements or not. You have chosen the first, while we have chosen the second, and now your admission that they did not follow such statements proves our own viewpoint. Their being excused or not is obviously besides the point.

Since it has been proved according to your views that they preferred, in the incident of Usamah's regiment, the interest of Islam, following their own views rather than those of the Prophet as embedded in his statements, then why don't you likewise say that they preferred in the issue of caliphate to follow their own views regarding what is good for Islam to those of the Prophet (s) as stated in his Ghadir hadith and the like? You have found excuses for those who cast doubts about Usamah's appointment, saying that they did so only because of his young age and their being middle-aged and old, and that old folks are naturally made to resent taking orders from the young; so, why don't you apply the same argument to those who did not follow the Ghadir texts appointing Ali (as), who was a young man, to take charge of middle-aged and elderly companions, who considered him young at the time when the Messenger of Allah, peace be upon him and his progeny, died just as they considered Usamah young when the Prophet (s) appointed him as their commander in that regiment? What a big difference between caliphate and the leadership of a regiment! If their nature refused to accept the leadership of a youth in commanding one regiment, they were more liable to refuse the lifetime leadership of a youth in all religious and secular matters.

But your argument that middle-aged and elderly folks naturally resent receiving orders from the young is rejected if you apply it to all matters, since those whose faith is strong among elderly believers certainly do not resent being commanded by Allah and His Messenger to take orders from a youth, or in any other matter. "Nay! By thy Lord, they shall never truly believe till they totally accept your judgment in all their disputes, then they do not feel any hardship in accepting your judgment, submitting thereto wholeheartedly (Qur'an, 4:65)." "Whatever the Messenger grants you, take it, and abstain from whatever he forbids you (Qur'an, 59:7)."

II. Al-Shahristani's Hadith is Documented

As regarding al-Shahristani who discusses those who dodged the draft in Usamah's army, narrating their story as a generally accepted fact, it has been narrated in one hadith documented by Abu Bakr Ahmad ibn 'Abdul-Aziz al-Jawhari in his book *Al-Saqifa*, from which I quote here this much for you *verbatim*:

> "Ahmad ibn Ishaq ibn Salih has narrated a tradition to us from Ahmad ibn Siyar from Sa'd ibn Kathir al-Ansari whose men quote 'Abdullah ibn 'Abdul-Rahman saying that when the Messenger of Allah (s) fell sick shortly before his death, he appointed Usamah ibn Zayd ibn Harithah to take charge in leading an army most of which were men from the Muhajirun and the Ansar. Among them were: Abu Bakr, 'Umar, Abu 'Ubaydah ibn al-Jarrah, 'Abdul-Rahmn ibn 'Awf, Talhah, and al-Zubayr, and ordered him to invade Mu'ta, where his father Zayd had been murdered, and to invade the valley of Palestine .Usamah slackened, and so did the rest of the army, and the Messenger of Allah, peace be upon him and his progeny, though sick, kept emphasizing that the army must rush there, till Usamah said to him: 'O

Messenger of Allah! Would you permit me to stay for a few days till Allah Almighty heals you?' He answered: 'Go and proceed, supported by the blessings of Allah.' He said: 'O Messenger of Allah! If I proceed while you are sick like that, I will be going with a heart swollen with pain.' He (s) said: 'Proceed towards victory in good health.' Usamah persisted: 'But I hate to keep asking the travellers about your condition.' He said: 'Proceed to carry out my orders,' then he, peace be upon him and his progeny, fainted. Usamah left and prepared to proceed. When the Messenger of Allah (s) regained his consciousness, he immediately inquired about Usamah, and he was told that he and his men were preparing to proceed, whereupon he kept repeating: 'Carry out Usamah's mission; the curse of Allah be upon whoever dodges its draft.' Usamah finally left the city, the flag above his head, surrounded by the companions, till he reached Jurf. In his company were Abu Bakr, 'Umar, and most of the Muhajirun and the Ansar such as Asid ibn Hadr, Bashir ibn Sa'd, and many other dignitaries. Then he received a messenger sent by Umm Ayman who informed him to go ahead and enter the city because the Prophet (s) was dying. He immediately left for Medina with the standard still in his hand. Having reached the Prophet's residence, he planted it at the door just when the Prophet (s) had died."

This has been written down by a group of historians such as the Mu'tazilite scholar Ibn Abul-Hadid at the conclusion of page 20 and the succeeding page in Vol. 2 of his *Sharh Nahjul Balaghah*, Wassalam.

Sincerely,
Sh

Letter 93
Rabi' al-Awwal 23, 1330

Requesting Narration of Other Incidents

We seem to have elaborated on Usamah's regiment, just as we elaborated on the Thursday calamity, till truth became distinct from falsehood, and the rays of the dawn became visible to those who can see; so, now let us hear about other incidents, Wassalam.

Sincerely,
S

Letter 94
Rabi' al-Awwal 25, 1330

His Order (s) to Kill the Renegade

Suffices you in response to your request what is recorded by a group of the nation's scholars and the imams of narrators, such as imam Ahmad ibn Hanbal who writes on page 15, Vol. 3, of his *Musnad*, quoting Abu Sa'd al-Khudri saying that Abu Bakr once came to the Messenger of Allah, peace be upon him and his progeny and said: "O Messenger of Allah! I was passing through a valley when I saw a man, solemn and properly attired, saying his prayers." The Prophet, peace be upon him and his progeny, said to him: "Go and kill him." So Abu Bakr went there, and when he saw the man like that, he hated to kill him; therefore, he returned to the Messenger of Allah, peace be upon him and his progeny, without carrying out his order. The Prophet, peace be upon him and his progeny, said to 'Umar: "Go and kill him," and 'Umar went there and saw him in the same way Abu Bakr had described, and he, too, came back without killing the man and said: "O Messenger of Allah! I have seen him saying his prayers very solemnly; so, I hated to kill him." The Prophet (s) then said to 'Ali: "'Ali, you go and kill him," whereupon 'Ali went to the place and returned only to say: "O Messenger of Allah! I could not find the man." The

Prophet, peace be upon him and his progeny, then said: "This man and his friends read the Qur'an only pronouncing its words [just to impress people]; they depart from the faith as swiftly as the arrow departs from the bow, and they do not go back till the arrow goes back to the bow anew. Kill them, for they are the worst among the living."

In his *Musnad*, Abu Ya'li, as stated in the biography of Dhul-Thadya by Ibn Hajar in his *Isaba*, quotes Anas ibn Malik saying: "We used to admire the piety and *ijtihad* of a man who was contemporary to the Messenger of Allah (s), and we mentioned him by name to the Messenger of Allah, peace be upon him and his progeny, but he did not know him. We described him to the Prophet (s), but he still did not recognize him. While we were talking about him, he came into sight and we said that it was he. He (s) said: 'Are you talking to me about a man on whose face Satan has placed his mark?' The man approached till he stood before them without greeting them. The Messenger of Allah, peace be upon him and his progeny, asked him: 'I ask you in the Name of Allah if you have told yourself when you approached that there is nobody among us better than or superior to you?' The man answered: 'Indeed, I have,' and he came in to say his prayers.

The Messenger of Allah, peace be upon him and his progeny, asked who would be willing to kill the man, and Abu Bakr said he would. When Abu Bakr entered, he found the man engaged in saying his prayers; so, he wondered how he could kill a man who was saying his prayers. When the Messenger of Allah (s) asked him what he did, he answered: 'I hated to kill him while he was saying his prayers, and you yourself had ordered us not to kill those who pray.' The Prophet (s) asked for a volunteer, and this time 'Umar responded. 'Umar entered and found the man prostrating and said to himself that Abu Bakr was better than him; therefore, he went out. When the Prophet (s) asked him if he did what he had promised to do, he told him that he had found the man placing his forehead on the ground prostrating to God. The Prophet (s) once more asked: 'Who can kill this man?' 'Ali answered in the affirmative, and when he entered looking for him, he found out that he had already left; so, he went back to the Messenger of Allah (s) and told him that the man had already left. It was then that the Prophet (s) said: 'Had this man been killed, no couple among my nation would have disputed with one another.'"

This incident has been recorded by al-Hafiz Muhammad ibn Musa al-Shirazi in his book wherein he combines the *tafasir* of Y'aqub ibn Hayyan, 'Ali ibn Harb, al-Sadi, Mujahid, Qatadah, Waki', and Ibn Jurayh. Its authenticity is considered common knowledge by trustworthy traditionists such as Imam Shihabud-Din Ahmad, who is better known as Ibn 'Abd Rabbih al-Andalusi, who quotes it at the conclusion of his chapter on those who follow their own inclinations in the first volume of his book *Al-'Iqd al-Farid*. At the conclusion of this incident as he narrates it, he says that the Prophet (s) has said: "This is the first horn [of the devil] coming out in my nation. Had you killed him, no two men would have disputed with each other. The children of Isra'il split into seventy-two groups, and this nation shall split into seventy-three groups all of which, except one, will go to Hell."[1]

Another almost similar narration of this incident is recorded by authors of books of traditions[2] who cite 'Ali (as) saying: "Some people from Quraysh came once to the Prophet (s) and said: 'O Muhammad! We are your neighbours and allies, and some of our slaves had come to you without a genuine desire to learn your religion or jurisprudence; they simply escaped from our possession; so, return them to us.' He asked Abu Bakr his opinion, and Abu Bakr said: 'They are right in saying that they are your

---

[1] The words "*firqa*" and "Shi'ah" are, if you count the times each one of them is repeated, synonymous, for the total number of each one of them is 385, making the majority of that group hopeful.
[2] Such as Imam Ahmad near the conclusion of page 155, Vol. 1, of his *Musnad*, Sa'id ibn Mansur in his *Sunan*, and Ibn Jarir in *Tahthib al-Athar*, all testifiying to its authenticity. It is quoted from all of them by al-Muttaqi al-Hindi on page 396, Vol. 6, of his book *Kanz al-'Ummal*.

neighbours;' whereupon the Prophet's face changed colour [i.e. became red with anger], and he asked 'Umar what he thought. 'Umar repeated Abu Bakr's words, and again his face changed colour and said: 'O people of Quraysh! By Allah! Allah will send you a man the faith of whose heart is tested by Allah, and he will fight you in order to safeguard the faith.' Abu Bakr inquired if he meant him, and his answer was negative. Then 'Umar inquired if it was he about whom the Prophet (s) was talking, and his answer was: 'No, it is the man who is mending the sandal;' the Prophet (s) had given me his sandal to mend," Wassalam.

    Sincerely,
    Sh

Letter 95
Rabi' al-Awwal 26, 1330

Justifying not Killing the Renegade

They, may Allah be pleased with them, may have understood the Prophet's order to be a recommendation rather than an obligation, and this is why they did not kill the man. Or maybe they thought that killing him was to be handled by a more qualified companion, since such were present then, and they did not refrain from killing him out of fear that he might flee, having refrained from telling him about anyone's intention to kill him, Wassalam.

Sincerely,
S

Letter 96
Rabi' al-Awwal 29, 1330

Justification Rejected

The order was one that required its execution as such; so, nobody would understand it any other way; therefore, calling it a recommendation is not proved by any argument at all. On the contrary, proofs emphasize its real meaning, i.e. as an order; so, look carefully into those traditions and you will find out that what we say here is the truth. Suffices you his statement (s): "This man and his men read the Qur'an only pronouncing its words [just to impress people]; they depart from the faith as swiftly as the arrow departs from the bow, and they do not go back till the arrow goes back to the bow anew. Kill them, for they are the worst among the living," and also his statement, peace be upon him and his progeny, "Had he been killed, no two men of my nation will have ever disputed with one another." Such statements were not said except when there was a serious command greatly emphasizing that the man be killed.

If you refer to Ahmad's *Musnad,* you will find the order to kill the man was directed to Abu Bakr in particular, then to 'Umar in particular; so, how can the obligation be ruled out?

Yet traditions are indeed explicit in indicating that those companions refrained from killing the man only because they hated to do so for no reason other than the fact that he was engaged in prayer and supplication. They did not feel well even though the Prophet (s) himself felt well about getting rid of him. They did not abide by the order which they had received from the Prophet (s) to kill the man. This incident, therefore, is just another proof testifying to the fact that they used to prefer to follow their own opinions rather than the instructions of the Prophet (s), Wassalam.

Sincerely,
Sh

Letter 97
Rabi' al-Awwal 30, 1330

Requesting Narration of all Such Incidents

Narrate all the rest of such incidents, without leaving any one of them out, so that we do not have to request you again, even if this means that your letters will be lengthy, Wassalam.

Sincerely,
S

Letter 98
Rabi' al-Thani 11, 1330

I. Glittering Proofs

Consider the Hudaybiya Treaty, Hunayn's booties, the taking of ransom from the captives of the Battle of Badr, his (s) order to slaughter a few camels when they had a severe shortage of food rations during the Battle of Tabuk, some of their own affairs on Uhud and its valley, the incident when Abu Hurayrah started conveying glad tidings to all those who believed in the Unity of Allah, the incident of performing ritual prayers for a hypocrite, the incident of their questioning the *sadaqat* and their inquiries about debauchery, their interpretation of the verses dealing with the *khums* and *zakat*, the two verses dealing with the *mut'a* [temporary] marriage. The verse dealing with the divorce thrice, their interpretation of the traditions regarding the extra prayers during the month of Ramadan, the latter's methods and numbers, the method of calling the *athan*, the number of *takbirs* during funeral prayers..., to the end of the list that is too lengthy to be dealt with in detail here. Add to this their opposition regarding the matter pertaining to Hatib ibn Balta'ah, their opposition to what the Prophet (s) did at Ibrahim's *maqam*, the addition of the houses of some Muslims to the building of the mosque, the enforcement of the blood money of Abu Khirash al-Hathli to be paid by the people of Yemen, the banishment of Nasr ibn al-Hajjaj al-Salami, the penalty enforced on Ja'dah ibn Salam,[1] the method to regulate the *jizya*, the covenant to conduct the *shura* in the well-known manner, roaming at night and spying during day-time, the compensation in performing the rituals..., to the end of the list of innumerable issues in which they aspired to achieve power and control, as well as special interests. We have dedicated in our book *Sabil al-Mu'minin*[2] a lengthy chapter to deal with them.

II. Reference to Other Incidents

Yet there are other texts dealing particularly with 'Ali and the purified progeny (as) besides the ones related to the caliphate which they did not honour either; rather, they acted to the contrary of the latter, as researchers know very well. So, no wonder to see how they used their own judgment to interpret the texts related to his caliphate; after all, isn't it just another text which they subjected to their own views and preferred their own thinking rather than acting upon it? Wassalam.

Sincerely,
Sh

---

[1] Refer to 'Umar's biography in Ibn Sa'd's *Tabaqat* and you will see how Ja'dah was executed for no complaint brought against him nor a witness other than a sheet on which there were verses written by an anonymous poet accusing Ja'dah of committing adultery.

[2] If you did not have a chance to read *Sabil al-Muminin*, try not to miss reading *Al-Fusul al-Muhimma*, for it contains precious benefits which no other book contains. We have dedicated a complete chapter to those who interpret it; it is Chapter 8, pages 44 to 130 of the second edition, where these matters are explained in detail.

Letter 99
Rabi' al-Thani 5, 1330 A.H.

I. Their Preference of the Common Interest in Those Instances

Anyone endowed with wisdom does not suspect their good intentions, and their preference of the common interest to all other considerations in their conduct regarding those instances. They always thought of what would be the best for this nation and the wisest for its faith, the best for its unity; so, they are not to be blamed for whatever they did, albeit if they followed certain texts or used their own judgment regarding them.

II. Requesting the Rest

We had requested you to narrate all the instances, but you have narrated only a few, stating that there are texts regarding the Imam and his progeny (as) besides the ones pertaining to his caliphate which our ancestors did not honour. We wish you had stated them in detail and spared us requesting you again to do so, Wassalam.

Sincerely,
S

Letter 100
Rabi' al-Thani 8, 1330

I. The Debater Digresses from the Subject-Matter

You have admitted their conduct regarding those well-known instances, and you have believed what we had said first; so, all praise is due to Allah. As regarding their good intentions and their preference of the common interest, their seeking of what is best for the nation, its faith and unity, this is a departure from our main topic, as you yourself know.

II. Responding to His Request

In your latest letter, you have requested the details of the authentic ahadith regarding 'Ali (as) in matters other than the imamate which they did not follow; nay, they did not even pay them any attention. You are the imam of traditions of our time; you are well acquainted with them; you have spent a great deal of effort in tackling the details of what we have summed up, and who else is more knowledgeable than you of the details of what able to compete with you regarding the Sunnah? Certainly not; yet, the matter is just what the axiom says: "How often do people ask about things with which they are familiar?"

You know very well that there are quite a few companions who hated 'Ali and were his enemies. They deserted him, hurt him, cursed and wronged him, opposed him, fought him, struck his face and the faces of his Ahl al-Bayt as well as those of their followers with their swords, as is well-known by necessity from the history of the ancestors. The Messenger of Allah, peace be upon him and his progeny, has said:

- "Whoever obeys me obeys Allah, and whoever disobeys me disobeys Allah;
whoever obeys 'Ali obeys me, and whoever disobeys 'Ali disobeys me too."
- "Whoever deserts me deserts Allah, and whoever deserts you, O 'Ali, deserts me, too."
- "O 'Ali! You are a leader in this life and a leader in the life hereafter; I love whoever loves you, and the one I love is loved by Allah; your enemy is my enemy, and my enemy is the enemy of Allah; woe unto whoever hates you after me."
- "Whoever denounces 'Ali denounces me, too, and whoever denounces me denounces Allah."
- "Whoever hurts 'Ali hurts me, too, and whoever hurts me hurts Allah."

- "Whoever loves 'Ali loves me, and whoever hates 'Ali hates me."
- "Nobody loves you, O 'Ali, except a true believer, and nobody hates you except a hypocrite."
- "O Allah! Befriend whoever befriends him, and be the enemy of whoever sets himself as his enemy; support whoever supports him, and forsake whoever forsakes him."

One day, he looked at 'Ali, Fatima, al-Hasan and al-Husayn (as) and said: "I fight whoever fights you, and I am peaceful unto whoever is peaceful to you." Having covered them with a blanket, he (s) said: "I fight whoever fights you, and grant asylum to whoever seeks peace with you; I am an enemy of your enemy." There are many such traditions which quite a few companions did not implement; nay, the latter's actions contradicted their injunctions in preference of their own desires since they sought their own self-interest. Those whose insight is keen know that all the very well-known traditions in honour of 'Ali - which are several hundreds, such as the ones enjoining acceptance of his taking charge, forbidding everyone from becoming his enemy - are all proofs testifying to his great status and prestige, and to his lofty position in the eyes of Allah and His Messenger. We have narrated quite a few of them in these Letters, and what we have not narrated is many times more.

You are, by the Grace of God, among those who are very well familiar with traditions and their meanings. Have you found any tradition which enjoins opposition and enmity towards him, or any particular one indicative of harming him, hating him, or bearing animosity towards him, or anything like hurting him and wronging him, denouncing him from the Muslims' pulpits, or making that a tradition followed by the preachers who preach during Fridays and eids? Certainly not. But those who did all of these things never paid any attention to such traditions in spite of their abundance and sequential narration. They did not hinder them from behaving in any way that would best serve their political interests. They knew that he was the brother and friend of the Prophet (s), his heir and confidant, the chief of his progeny, his Aaron over his nation, his son-in-law in his own right, the father of his descendants, the foremost to accept Islam, the most sincere in faith, the most knowledgeable, the most diligent in doing good deeds, the most clement, the strongest in conviction, the hardest worker in the cause of God, the most courageous, the most virtuous, the one possessing the most feats, the most cautious about the interest of Islam, the nearest to the Messenger of Allah, the closest to him (s) in guidance, manners, and loftiness, the most exemplary in his deed, speech, or silence... But personal interests were to them above any other argument or consideration; so, why then the amazement at their preference to follow their own personal views regarding the imamate to following the spirit of the Ghadir hadith, for example? Yet isn't the Ghadir hadith but just one of several hundred others which they saw only through their own glasses, preferring their own views and considering their own interests?

The Messenger of Allah, peace be upon him and his progeny, has also said: "The similitude of my Ahl al-Bayt among you is like that of Noah's ark; whoever boards it is saved, and whoever lags behind it is drowned," and "The similitude of my Ahl al-Bayt among you is like the Gate of Salvation to the children of Isra'il: forgiven are the sins of whoever enters through it." He, peace be upon him and his progeny, has also said: "The stars are the security of the inhabitants of the earth against drowning, and my Ahl al-Bayt are the nation's security against dissension; so, if any Arab tribe opposes them, they will all dispute with each other and become the party of Iblis (Eblis)," in addition to many such traditions all of which were ignored completely by them..., Wassalam.

Sincerely,
Sh

Letter 101
Rabi' al-Thani 10, 1330

Why didn't the Imam Cite the Ahadith of Caliphate and Wisayat on the Saqifa Day?

Truth has manifested itself; praise to Allah, Lord of the Worlds. There remains only one last issue the nature of which seems to be disguised, wrapped in obscurity. Please mention it to uncover its veil and make its secret known. It is the fact that the Imam, during the incident of the saqifa, did not cite any of the texts regarding the caliphate and wisayat, to which you give so much attention, to al-Siddiq and the allegiance to him; so, are you more familiar with such texts than he is? Wassalam.

Sincerely,
S

Letter 102
Rabi' al-Thani 11, 1330

I. Why the Imam Abstained on the Saqifa Day from Citing Such Texts

Everybody knows that neither the Imam nor any of his supporters among the descendants of Hashim and others witnessed such an allegiance, nor did they enter that saqifa then. They were distracted from it and whatever went on inside it. They were totally preoccupied by their tremendous calamity: the demise of the Messenger of Allah, and their conducting of the appropriate funeral preparations for him, peace be upon him and his progeny, paying no attention to anything else. As soon as they finished burying him in his sacred resting place, those at the saqifa had already commenced their act, conducted the allegiance, and tightly tied their knot, being extremely careful in forbidding any speech or deed that would weaken their allegiance, affect their deal, or annoy their commoners; so, where were the Imam during the events of the saqifa, the giving or the taking of allegiance to al-Siddiq so that he might argue with them? How can he or anyone else be expected to argue after the allegiance had already been taken, and those who had a say had taken such measures? Can any one person in our present time face the authorities, uproot their power, and abolish their government? Would they leave such a person alone if he attempted to do so? Impossible. So, compare the past with the present, for neither people nor times have changed much.

Yet 'Ali (as) did not expect his arguments with them then to cause anything other than dissension. He preferred to lose what was his over its attainment under such circumstances. He feared that such dissension might harm Islam and its *kalima*, as we have previously explained, saying that he was inflicted in those days more than anyone else by two major catastrophes: On one hand, caliphate, in its texts and wills, cried unto him and invoked him in a complaint that would make the heart bleed, and the oppressive dissension on the other warned him of an uprising in the peninsula, a possible rebellion of the Arabs that would sweep Islam away, threatening it with the hypocrites among the residents of Medina who were accustomed to hypocrisy, supported by the bedouins who, according to the text of the Book of Allah (9:101), are hypocrites, nay, even worse in disbelief and hypocrisy, so much so, that it would be better for them not to know the limits of what Allah has revealed unto His Messenger (9:97). These have become stronger by the loss of the Prophet (s), peace be upon him and his progeny, and Muslims became like frightened cattle in a winter night, surrounded by assaulting jackals and wild beasts. Musaylamah the Liar, conspirator Talhah ibn Khuwaylid, and sorceress Sajah daughter of al-Harath, in addition to their rogues and hoodlums, were all trying their best to wipe Islam out and crush the Muslims. Add to this the fact that the Romans, the followers of Kisra and Caesar, besides many others, were plotting against the Muslims. Still add to these other elements full of grudge against Muhammad, his progeny and companions, and full of hatred towards the message of Islam. All these parties desired to uproot Islam's foundations. These were active in doing so, rushing their steps, seeing that the wind was finally blowing in their direction, and the opportunity because of the departure of the Prophet (s) to the Sublime Companion had come; so, they wished to make use of that opportunity before Islam regained its strength and resumed order. 'Ali (as) was aware of both dangers, and it was only natural that he would offer his own right on the altar of sacrifice for the sake of the Muslims.[1]

But he also wanted to maintain his right for the caliphate and argue with those who departed from it in a way that would neither harm the Muslims, nor cause dissension among them, nor encourage their enemy to take advantage thereof. He, therefore, remained at home till he felt obligated, not forced, to leave it. Had he rushed to them, he would not have had any argument, nor would his followers have had any proof, but he secured, by taking such a stand, both the protection of the faith, and the maintaining of his own right to rule the Muslims. When he saw that preserving Islam and responding to the plots of its enemies depended during those days on calm and peace, he paved in person the way for calmness,

---

[1] He, peace be upon him, has declared so in a letter which he sent to the people of Egypt with Malik al-Ashtar when he vested on him its government. He said in it: "Allah, praise be to Him, has sent Muhammad (s) as a warner to the worlds and as master of all Messengers. When he, peace be upon him, left (this world), Muslims after him disputed among themselves. By Allah, I never dreaded nor expected the Arabs to remove such responsibility from his Household, nor would they distance me therefrom after him, but what alarmed me most was their leaning towards that person to swear allegiance to him; so, I controlled myself till I saw that people had deviated from Islam and started inviting everyone to wipe out Muhammad's faith. I, therefore, feared that if I did not support Islam and Muslims while witnessing the structure of Islam cracked or partially demolished, the catastrophe on me would be greater than missing your government which is nothing but the enjoyment of a few days after which it would vanish like a mirage, or disappear like summer clouds;" so he rose in those events till wrongdoing was removed, and the religion became deeply rooted and settled. Refer to his statement in *Nahjul-Balaghah*.

preferring to make peace with those who had a say just to protect the nation and out of his concern about the faith, being concerned about religion and in preference of the good to come to the present one, implementing his juristic as well as moral obligation to prefer, while still opposing, what was most important to what was more important, since the circumstances then permitted neither the use of the sword, nor the response through one argument against another.

II. Reference to his and his Followers' Arguments Despite Obstacles

In spite of all this, he and his descendants (as), in addition to the learned among his followers, used to follow wisdom when mentioning the will, publicizing for its clear texts, as is obvious to those who research, Wassalam.

Sincerely,
Sh

Letter 103
Rabi' al-Thani 12, 1330

Looking for His and His Followers' Arguments

When did the Imam do so? And when did his kin and supporters do that? Please acquaint us with a portion of it, Wassalam.

Sincerely,
S

Letter 104
Rabi' al-Thani 15, 1330

I. A Few Incidents When the Imam Argued

The Imam used to be quiet in publicizing the texts pertaining to him, without using them for personal gains against his opponents out of his own concern about the safety of Islam and to safeguard the strength of Muslim. He often used to defend his silence and reluctance to demand it, in such circumstance, by saying: "A man is not blamed if he takes his time in obtaining what is his; the blame is on that who takes what does not belong to him."[1] He used to apply certain methods crowned with manifest wisdom in disseminating the texts in his honour.

Have you noticed what he did in the incident of the Rahba, when he gathered people during his caliphate to celebrate the Ghadir Day? He said to them: "I ask each Muslim of you who heard the Messenger of Allah, peace be upon him and his progeny, say on the Ghadir Day what he said to stand and testify to what he had heard, and nobody should stand except those who have seen him;" thirty companions, including twelve participants in the battle of

---

[1] This statement is a short one dealing with his noble ojective, and it is included in *Nahjul Balaghah*. Refer to what the Mu'tazilite scholar has said while explaining it on page 324, Vol. 4, of his *Sharh Nahjul Balaghah*.

Badr, testified to what they had heard of the Ghadir hadith as we have indicated above in Letter No. 56. This is the maximum that he could do under such critical circumstances due to 'Uthman's murder, and the mutiny in Basra and Syria. It is, indeed, the peak of wisdom in such publicity in those days, and what a praiseworthy effort that revived the Ghadir tradition from its tomb and brought it to life after it was almost buried for good! The crowds at the Rahba were reminiscent of those who witnessed the Prophet (s) (s) on Ghadir Khumm day taking 'Ali (as) in his own eminent hand and addressing a hundred thousand or more of his nation to convey to them the message that he would be his successor. Thus, the Ghadir tradition is one of the most reliable among consecutive traditions; so, observe the Prophet's wisdom when he exhorted him in front of such thronging crowds, and be mindful of the wisdom of the *wasi* on that Friday when he asked them to testify, thus highlighting the truth in a quiet manner dictated by circumstances, and by a peaceful method the Imam preferred. Thus was his method in disseminating the covenant and publicizing for the tradition. He was the type of person who would attract the attention of the unaware through means which did not require making a lot of noise or creating bad feelings among people.

Consider what the authors of books of traditions have quoted of his own hadith, peace be upon him, during the incident of the feast arranged by the Messenger of Allah, peace be upon him and his progeny, at the house of his uncle, the most dignified man among the people of Mecca, when he warned his near in kin. It is a lengthy and sacred tradition people have always considered as one of the proofs of Prophethood and the miracles of Islam due to its inclusion of the Prophetic miracle of feeding a large number of people with very little food. We have already quoted it in Letter No. 20. It concludes by stating that the Messenger of Allah, peace be upon him and his progeny, took 'Ali (as) by the neck and said: "This is my brother, *the* executor of my will, and my own successor; so, listen to him and obey him." He used quite often to tell how the Messenger of Allah, peace be upon him and his progeny, said to him: "You are the *wali* of every believer after me," and he also quite often used to narrate this statement of the Prophet (ṣ): "Your status to me is like that of Aaron to Moses, except there will be no Prophet after me," and, reminiscing of Ghadir Khumm, "Do not I have more authority over the believers than the believers themselves have?" They said: "Yes, indeed." He then said: "To whomsoever I have been a *wali*, this ('Ali (as)) is his *wali*," in the words of Ibn Abu 'Asim, as we explained at the conclusion of Letter No. 23, in addition to many such irrefutable texts. They have been publicized by the most trustworthy and reliable traditionists. This is all that he was able to do during those circumstances. ["Purposeful wisdom; so, how can the *nuthur* be of any use?"]

On the Day of Shura, he discharged his responsibility and warned others, sparing none of his own attributes or feats without using it as an argument. During the days of his caliphate, he often complained about the gross injustice done to him, painfully announcing his complaint from the pulpit, saying: "By God, that person vested it upon himself, knowing that my place from it was like the axle from the quern: From me does the stream of knowledge flow, and birds do not soar higher; so, I lowered against it my curtain and kept aloof therefrom. I had to opt between either fighting with an amputated arm, or be patient about a blind calamity in which the grown-ups become elderly and the youngsters grow gray hair, one wherein a *mu'min* sweats till he meets his Lord. I decided that to be patient was wiser; so I became patient while seeing eye sores, tongue-tied, witnessing my inheritance being plundered," to the end of his *shaqshaqi* sermon, which is *khutba* 3 in *Nahjul Balaghah*, page 25, Vol. 1. He often said: "O Lord! I seek Thy assistance against Quraysh and those who support them, for they have cut my flesh, demeaned my status, and disputed with me about what is mine, then they said: 'It is only right that we take it, and that you should abandon it.'" Refer to either *khutba* 167 or page 103, Vol. 2, of *Nahjul Balaghah*. In the same *khutba*, someone said to him: "You seem to be so much concerned about this matter." The Imam (as) answered: "No; by

God you are more concerned about it than I am. I have demanded one of my own rights, while you have stood between it and my attaining thereof." He, peace be upon him, has also said: "By Allah, since the time when Allah took the life of his Messenger, peace be upon him and his progeny, till today, I have always been pushed away from my right, while others are preferred over me," as in *khutba* 5, page 36, Vol. 1, of *Nahjul Balaghah*.

He, peace be upon him, said once: "We have a right; if we do not attain it, we will have to mount old camels even if the journey is lengthy."[2] He, peace be upon him, said in a letter he wrote to his brother 'Aqil: "May the One who affects justice retaliate on my behalf against Quraysh who have separated me from my own kin and deprived me the support of my own maternal brother," as stated in letter 36, page 67, Vol. 3, in *Nahjul Balaghah*. He, peace be upon him, quite often used to say: "I looked around and found no supporter other than my Ahl al-Bayt whom I preferred to protect against death, overlook against my wish, and I remained patient, containing my anger though it is more bitter than colocynth [*Citrullus colocynthis*]," as in *khutba* 25, page 62, Vol. 1, of *Nahjul Balaghah*.

Some of his friends asked him once: "How did you keep your folk away from that post knowing that you have more right to it than anyone else?" He, as stated on page 79, Vol. 2, of *Nahjul Balaghah*, statement 157, answered: "O fellow of Banu Asad! You are disturbed by such a mysterious matter to the extent that you ask your question awkwardly. Yet we are obligated to you due to our kinship, and you have the right to ask such a question. You have asked, so be informed that as regarding some people oppressing us in this regard, while they know that we are superior in lineage to them, and stronger in blood ties to the Messenger of Allah (s), this

---

[2] This statement is number 21 of his statements in the chapter dealing with "choice gems of his wisdom," page 155, *Nahjul Balaghah*. Sayyid al-Radi has commented on it in a very valuable commentary, and so has Shaykh Muhammad 'Abdoh. Both deserve the attention of any scholar.

came due to the selfishness of certain people who were supported by others. The government is only to Allah, and the return is unto Him on the Day of Judgment; so, do not ask me about the usurpation called for even inside his [Prophet's] own chambers..." He, peace be upon him, has also said: "Where are those who claim that they are more deeply rooted in knowledge than we are? They tell lies about us and flagrantly oppress us though Allah has raised our status and lowered theirs, granted us and deprived them, and permitted us to enter while ordering them out, and through us has He taken them out of the darkness of blindness into the light of guidance. The seeds of imamate have been planted in the wombs of the descendants of Hashim of Quraysh; it suits nobody else, and caliphate is appropriate for nobody other than them...," to the conclusion of statement 140, on page 36 and the succeeding pages, Vol. 2, of *Nahjul Balaghah*.

Consider his statement in one of his sermons: "When the Messenger of Allah, peace be upon him and his progeny, passed away, some people turned back [in their covenant to him], aiming to take various paths [rather than just one Right Path], relying on treachery, favouring those who were not his kin, abandoning the path they were ordered to take in order to please him, thus moving the foundation stones of Islam from their places, using other sinful substances in the building of its structure. They have entered into Islam through the doors of those who follow their own inclinations, going to extremes in their bewilderment, distracted like drunkards, following the *sunnah* of the descendants of Pharaoh, worshippers of this life, those who have deliberately abandoned their religion." Refer to this statement, which is cited at the beginning of page 25; it concludes sermon 2, Vol. 1, of *Nahjul Balaghah*, which he delivered after receiving the oath of allegiance, for it is one of the greatest. In it, he says: "Nobody can be compared with the progeny of Muhammad, peace be upon him, from all the members of this nation, and nobody can be the peer of those who have received His blessing. They are the corner-stones of the faith, the pillars of conviction; through them does the extremist return to moderation, and through them does the one who has left knowledge behind him retracts; they possess the characteristics of those who deserve to rule, and in them lie the covenant and the legacy. Now right has returned to its people and transferred back to its appropriate place." Add to this his statement cited in the context of sermon 84, page 145, Vol. 1, of *Nahjul Balaghah* in which he wonders about those who oppose him: "How amazed I am to see the error of these groups, disputing in their arguments about their religion, neither following in the footsteps of the Prophet (s), nor the example of his *wasi*...!"

II. The Argument of al-Zahra' (as)

Al-Zahra', peace be upon her, delivered very wise arguments in this regard. Two of her own statements were in wide circulation among Ahl al-Bayt (as), so much so that they used to require their children to memorize them just as they required them to memorize the entire text of the Holy Qur'an. They deal with those who "moved the foundation stones of the faith from their bases" and built them somewhere else. She said:

> "How dare they? Where have they moved it [caliphate] to, building it somewhere else other than at the haven of the Message, the foundations of Prophethood, the place where the faithful spirit [Gabriel] descends, the one who is the authority about secular as well as religious matters? This, indeed, is the manifest loss. Why do they hate al-Hasan's father so much? By Allah, they hate the strength of his sword, his might and astounding deeds, and his extraordinary effort in supporting the religion of Allah. By Allah, had they all yielded to his leadership,[3] he would have taken them to the easy path, without harming anyone. He would

---

[3] The reins passed on to him by the Messenger of Allah are those of governing the nation in the matters pertaining to its religion as well as the daily life. The meaning is that had they all been in consensus in submitting to such a government, yielding to such a leader, they would have been protected from harm.

have brought them to an overflowing fountain of goodness, advised them in secrecy and in public, neither filling his belly with their own sustenance, nor satisfying his thirst nor hunger out of their own toil. The gates of mercy of the heavens and the earth would have been widely opened for them. Allah will punish them for the sins they were committing; so, come and listen to the story, and so long as you live, be amazed, and when you are amazed, the incident bemuses you... Where have they gone, and which nitche have they clung to? What an evil guardian they have taken, and what an evil bunch! How evil is the end of the oppressors who traded the tails for the hoofs, and the rumps for the chests! So, dusted are the noses of those who think that they have done well; they are the ones who fill the world with corruption without knowing it. Woe unto them! 'Isn't that who guides to the truth worthier of being followed than the one who does not guide? What is the matter with you? How do you judge?'"[4]

Up to the conclusion of her sermon which is a specimen of the speech of the purified progeny in this regard, and you may judge the rest by this one, Wassalam.

Sincerely,
Sh

---

[4] This is quoted by Abu Bakr Ahmad ibn 'Abdul-'Aziz al-Jawhari in his book *Al-Saqifa and Fadak*, from a chain of narrators including Muhammad ibn Zakariyya, Muhammad ibn 'Abdul-Rahman al-Muhallabi, 'Abdullah ibn Hammad ibn Sulayman who quotes his father, 'Abdullah ibn al-Hasan who quotes his mother Fatima bint Husayn, ending with al-Zahra', peace be upon her. It is also narrated by Imam Abul-Fadl Ahmad ibn Abu Tahir, who died in 280, on page 23 of his book *Balaghat al-Nisa'* through Harun ibn Muslim ibn Sa'dan, from al-Hasan ibn Alwan from Atiyyah al-'Awfi who narrated this *khutba* from a chain of narrators including 'Abdullah ibn al-Hasan from his mother Fatima bint al-Husayn, from her grandmother al-Zahra', peace be upon her. Our own fellows narrate this *khutba* from Suwayd ibn Ghaflah ibn Awsajah al-Ju'fi from al-Zahra', peace be upon her. Al-Tibrisi has quoted it in his book *Al-Ihtijaj*, and al-Majlisi in his book *Biaar al-Anwar*, and it is narrated by many other trustworthy narrators.

Letter 105
Rabi' al-Thani 16, 1330

Requesting Narration of Other Such Incidents

We aspire to complete the benefit if you quote others besides the Imam and al-Zahra', and you will thus do us a favour, Wassalam.

Sincerely,
S

Letter 106
Rabi' al-Thani 18, 1330

I. Ibn 'Abbas's Argument

May I invite your attention to the dialogue between Ibn 'Abbas and 'Umar in which the latter, in a lengthy conversation between both men, asked: "O Ibn 'Abbas! Do you know what stopped your folks [from demanding the caliphate] after Muhammad (s)?" Ibn 'Abbas narrates saying: "I hated to answer 'Umar's question, so I said to him: 'If I do not know, the commander of the faithful [i.e. 'Umar] knows.'" 'Umar said: "[Some people simply] hated that both prophethood and caliphate be confined to your House; so, they were happy about their scheme. Quraysh sought it for themselves, and were able to obtain it." I said: "O commander of the faithful! Do you permit me to say something and promise to control your anger?" He answered in the affirmative; therefore, Ibn 'Abbas said: "As regarding your statement, O commander of the faithful, that Quraysh sought it for themselves and were successful in obtaining it, I say that had Quraysh sought what Allah had chosen for them, their choice would have been unobjectionable and unblamed. As regarding your statement that they hated to see both prophethood and caliphate in our House, I say that Allah, the Exalted and the Sublime, has described some people to be malicious, saying, '...

that is so because they hated what Allah has revealed, so He rendered their deeds vain.'" 'Umar then said: "Impossible, O Ibn 'Abbas, for I heard things about you which I hate to believe else your status in my eyes should be reduced." I asked: 'What are they, O commander of the faithful? If they are true, they should not lower my status in your esteem, and if they are not, I am capable of defending myself against false charges.' 'Umar then said: 'It has come to my knowledge that you say that they have deprived you of it [caliphate] out of envy, oppression and injustice.' I said: 'As regarding your statement, O commander of the faithful, that it was oppression, then that has become quite obvious to those who are ignorant as well as to those who are clement. As regarding your statement about envy, then Adam was envied, and we are his descendants who also are envious.' 'Umar then said: 'Impossible, impossible; your hearts, O descendants of Hashim, have become filled with envy that can never dissipate.' I therefore said: 'Wait, O commander of the faithful, do not attribute this to the hearts of those whom Allah has purified with a perfect purification.'"[1]

He argued with him in another incident, asking: "How did you leave your cousin?" Ibn 'Abbas said he thought 'Umar meant 'Abdullah ibn Ja'far; so, he answered: "I left him in the company of his friends." He said: "I did not mean him; I meant the greatest among you, Ahl al-Bayt." Ibn 'Abbas said: "I left him exiled, irrigating while reciting the Qur'an." 'Umar said: "O 'Abdullah! I implore you not to be shy but tell me if he is still concerned about the issue of caliphate." He answered in the affirmative. Then 'Umar asked: "Does he claim that the Messenger of Allah (s) has selected him for it?" Ibn 'Abbas answered: "Yes, indeed; moreover, I even asked my father if there was any statement made by the Messenger of Allah regarding selecting him for the caliphate, and my father informed me that that was the truth."

---

[1] We have quoted it *verbatim* from *Al-Tarikh al-Kamil* by Ibn al-Athir who includes it at the conclusion of 'Umar's biography among the events of the year 23 A.H., page 24, Vol. 3, and it is also quoted by the Mu'tazilite scholar in 'Umar's biography, too, page 107, Vol. 3, of *Sharh Nahjul Balaghah*

'Umar then said: "The Messenger of Allah held him in very high esteem through his speeches and actions in a way that left no argument nor excuse for anyone,[2] and he kept testing the nation regarding him for some time;[3] nay, even when he was sick [prior to his demise], he wished to nominate him for it, but it was I who stopped him."[4]

In a third dialogue between both men, 'Umar said: "O Ibn 'Abbas! I can see how wronged your friend ['Ali (as)] is." Ibn 'Abbas said: "O commander of the faithful, then affect justice on his behalf." Ibn 'Abbas said: "But 'Umar pulled his hand from mine and went away whispering to himself for a good while. Then he stopped; so, I rejoined him, and he said to me: 'O Ibn 'Abbas! I do not think that his people denied him [the caliphate] for any reason other than his being too young for it.' I said to him: 'By Allah, neither Allah nor His Messenger regarded him as too young when they both ordered him to take Surat Bara'a (Qur'an, Chapter 9) from him [from Abu Bakr].' Having heard this, he turned away from me and started walking fast; so, I left him alone."[5]

How often has 'Abdullah ibn 'Abbas, who is the scribe of the Muslim nation, the spokesman of the Hashimites, and cousin of the Messenger of Allah (s), encountered such stances? In Letter No. 26, you have come to see how he argues with the oppressive party by citing a tradition that counts ten exclusive merits of 'Ali (as). It is a lengthy and eminent tradition in which he quotes the Prophet

---

[2] He means that the speech of the Messenger of Allah (s) praising 'Ali indicates that 'Ali enjoys quite a lofty status, obviously an admission by 'Umar.
[3] He means that the Prophet (s), due to praising 'Ali in such wise words, is testing the nation to see if it would accept him as his successor.
[4] This is quoted by Imam Abul-Fadl Ahmad ibn Abu Tahir in his book *Tarikh Baghdad*, indicating his reliable source to be Ibn 'Abbas. It is also quoted by the Mu'tazilite scholar who discusses 'Umar in his *Sharh Nahjul Balaghah*, page 97, Vol. 3.
[5] This dialogue is quoted by authors of books of biographies in their discussions of 'Umar, and we have quoted it here from *Sharh Nahjul Balaghah* by the Mu'tazilite scholar; so, refer to page 105 of its third volume.

(s) asking his cousins: "Who among you would be my supporter in [matters related to] this life and the life hereafter?" They declined, but 'Ali (as) said: "I support you in this life as well as the life to come." The Prophet (s) then said to 'Ali (as): "You are my *wali* in this life and the life to come." In another tradition, Ibn 'Abbas narrates that during the Tabuk raid, the Messenger of Allah (s) went out, accompanied by many people, and 'Ali (as) asked him: "Shall I accompany you?" The Messenger of Allah denied his request; so, 'Ali (as) wept; whereupon the Prophet (s) said to him: "Are you not pleased that your status to me is like that of Aaron to Moses, except there is no Prophet (s) after me? I ought not leave except after you represent me in my absence." The Messenger of Allah has also told him: "You are the *wali* of every believer after me," and "Whoever accepts me as his *wali*, 'Ali (as) [henceforth] is his *mawla*."

II. Arguments of al-Hasan and al-Husayn

The dignitaries among the descendants of Hashim often argued likewise. Once al-Hasan ibn 'Ali (as) came to Abu Bakr who had seated himself on the pulpit of the Messenger of Allah (s) and told him to get down from a place his father was more worthy of. Al-Husayn (as) is reported to have said similarly to 'Umar who was also seated on the same pulpit.[6]

III. Arguments of Prominent Shi'ah Sahabah

Books written by imamites who dealt with this topic cite many incidents wherein the Hashimites and their followers among the *sahabah* and *tabi'in* argued likewise, and they ought to be reviewed by those who are interested in their contents. Suffices here to cite the book of arguments by imam al-Tibrisi in which he

---

[6] Ibn Hajar has quoted both cases in his fifth *maqsad* of the verse enjoining kindness to the Prophet's kin, and it is verse 14, of the ones dealt with in Chapter 11 of his book *Al-Sawa'iq al-Muhriqa*; so, refer to page 160 of this reference. Al-Dar Qutni has quoted the case of al-Hasan with Abu Bakr, and Ibn Sa'd has quoted the case of al-Husayn with 'Umar in his biography of the latter in his *Tabaqat*.

quotes statements made by the Umayyad Khalid ibn Sa'id ibn al-'As,[7] Salman al-Farsi, Abu Dharr al-Ghifari, 'Ammar ibn Yasir, al-Miqdad, Buraydah al-Aslami, Abul-Haytham ibn al-Tihan, Sahl and 'Uthman sons of Hanif, Khuzaymah ibn Thabit of the two Shahadas, Ubayy ibn Ka'b, Abu Ayyub al-Ansari, and many others among those who researched the history of Ahl al Bayt and of their followers. Yet they never missed any opportunity to prove their point by citing explicit or implicit references, strongly or smoothly worded, speeches and writings, poetry and prose, according to whatever their circumstances, though critical, permitted.

IV. Reference to their Applying the Will as an Argument

They repeatedly referred to the will, using it as an argument, as is well-known by researchers, Wassalam.

Sincerely,
S

---

[7] Khalid ibn Sa'id ibn al-'As was among those who rejected Abu Bakr's caliphate; he refused for three months to swear allegiance to him, as stated by a group of reliable Sunnis such as Ibn Sa'd in his biography of Khalid in his *Tabaqat*, page 70, Vol. 4, adding that when Abu Bakr dispatched troops to Syria, he prepared the standard for him and came in person to his house, but 'Umar said to Abu Bakr: "Do you give charge to Khalid after having heard what he has said?" He continued trying till he sent Abu 'Arwah al-Dawsi with the message that "The successor of the Messenger of Allah (s) asks you to return our standard." He did so saying: "Your government has never pleased us, nor has your deposition harmed us." Having heard such a statement, Abu Bakr came to him to apologize, and he earnestly requested him not to mention 'Umar in public. All writers who mention the incident of this campaign to Syria mention this incident as well, for it is one of such detailed incidents.

Letter 107
Rabi' al-Thani 19, 1330

When did they Mention the Will?

When did they mention the will to the Imam, and when did they use it in their argument? I do not think that they mentioned it other than in the presence of the mother of the believers who denied it, as we explained before, Wassalam.

Sincerely,
S

Letter 108
Rabi' al-Thani 22, 1330

The Recommendation as Evidence

Yes, indeed, they did. The Commander of the Faithful (as) mentioned it while preaching from the pulpit, and we have in Letter No. 104 quoted its text. Anyone who quotes the tradition of the Household on the day of warning has done so, quoting 'Ali (as). We have also quoted it in Letter No. 20. It contains the explicit text recommending him for the caliphate. Imam Abu Muhammad al-Hasan (as), grandson of the Prophet (s), and master of all the young of Paradise, delivered a sermon when his father the Commander of the Faithful (as) was assassinated in which he said: "I am the descendant of the Prophet (s), and the son of his vicegerent," as quoted by al-Hakim on page 172, Vol. 3, of his authentic *Mustadrak*. Imam Ja'far al-Sadiq (as), as on page 254, Vol. 3, of *Sharh Nahjul Balaghah*, at the end of the commentary on the *qasi'a* sermon, has said: "Even before the [Islamic] Message became public, 'Ali (as), while in the company of the Messenger of Allah (s), used to see the light and hear the voice [of angels]." He also quotes him (s) saying: "Had I not been the seal of Prophets, you ['Ali (as)] would have been made a partner in my Prophethood; yet since you cannot be a prophet, you certainly are the *wasi* and the heir of a Prophet ," according to Buraydah. Such usage is common among all the Imams of Ahl al-Bayt, and it is a necessity among them and their followers from the time of the *sahabah* till now.

Salman al-Farsi is reported saying that he heard the Messenger of Allah (s) saying: "The one who is my *wasi*, confidant, the best I leave behind me to execute my will and cancel my debts, is 'Ali ibn Abu Talib (as)." Abu Ayyub al-Ansari has reported a tradition in which he says that he heard the Messenger of Allah (s) saying to Fatima (as): "Have you not come to know that Allah, the Exalted and Omniscient, cast a look at the inhabitants of the earth and chose your father for His Messenger, then He cast a second look and chose your husband, then He inspired me to marry you to him and take him as my vicegerent?" Buraydah has narrated a tradition in which he says that he heard the Messenger of Allah (s) saying: "For every Prophet there is a vicegerent and heir, and my vicegerent and heir is 'Ali ibn Abu Talib (as)," and both ahadith of Abu Ayyub and Salman have already been quoted above in Letter No. 68. Whenever Jabir ibn Yazid al-Ju'fi narrated a tradition from Imam al-Baqir (as), he used to say, as stated in Jabir's biography in al-Dhahabi's *Al-Mizan*, "The *wasi* of *wasi*s has narrated a tradition to me..., etc." Umm al-Khayr daughter of al-Harish al-Bariqi delivered an eloquent speech in Siffin urging the Kufians to fight Mu'awiyah in which she said: "Hurry, may Allah be merciful unto you, to support the just Imam, the faithful *wasi*, the greatest truthful," as quoted by Imam Abul-Fadl Ahmad ibn Abu Tahir al-Baghdadi on page 41 of his work *Balaghat al-Nisa'* stating his source to be al-Sha'bi.

This is what some ancestors have quoted while lauding the recommendation in their sermons and speeches, and whoever researches their biographies will find them applying the title "*wasi*" to the Commander of the Faithful (as) as freely as they would call anything by its name, so much so that the author of *Taj al-'Arus* says on page 392, Vol. 10, while explaining the term "*wasi*":

"[Pronounced] like *ghani*, *wasi* is the title of 'Ali (as), may Allah be pleased with him."

As regarding dealing with this theme in their poetry, this cannot all be cited here due to its abundance, but we quote of it what serves the purpose to make a point. 'Abdullah ibn 'Abbas ibn 'Abdul-Muttalib has described him as:

> The Messenger's *wasi*, chosen from his Household;
> His valiant knight when a challenge is posed.

Al-Mughirah ibn al-Harith ibn 'Abdul Muttalib has said these verses in which he encourages the people of Iraq to fight Mu'awiyah in Siffin:

> The *wasi* of the Messenger of Allah is your chief,
> His son-in-law, promoted Allah's Mushaf Sharif.

'Abdullah ibn Abu Sufyan ibn al-Harth ibn 'Abdul Muttalib has said:

> Among us is 'Ali (as), hero of Khaybar, now in ruin,
> The hero of Badr, too, when troops retreated;
> He is *wasi* of the Chosen Prophet (s) and his cousin,
> So, who can attain his lofty status, only to him meted?

Abul-Haytham ibn al-Tihan, one of the heroes of Badr, composed verses to recite during the Battle of the Camel in which he said:

> The *wasi* is our Imam and *wali* in word and deed,
> No secret left; what was hidden is now revealed.

Khuzaymah ibn Thabit, of the two *Shahadas*, a hero of Badr, recited verses which he, too, composed during the Battle of the Camel in which he said:

> O *wasi* of the Prophet! The battle has shaken the foes,
> And caravans have been dispatched to deal blows.

He, may Allah be pleased with him, has also said:

> O 'Ayesha! Leave 'Ali and the names you call him, too,
> For what you call him is certainly not true;
> He is but the *wasi* from the Prophet's clan,
> The one to testify to that is but you, says everyone.

'Abdullah ibn Badil ibn Warqa' al-Khuza'i, a hero among the *sahabah*, who was martyred in Siffin together with his brother 'Abdul-Rahman, said the following on the incident of the Battle of the Camel:

> O my people! What a great calamity Satan brought,
> Battle the enemy, for the *wasi* of the Prophet is fought.

Among the verses said by the Commander of the Faithful himself in Siffin were these:

> If Ahmad were told that his *wasi* is indeed
> Equalled to a wretch, he would surely be displeased.

Jarir ibn 'Abdullah al-Bijli, a *sahabi*, sent verses to Shurhabil ibn al-Samt in which he mentioned 'Ali (as) saying:

> Among all other members of the Prophet's clan,
> He is *wasi* of the Messenger of ar-Rahman,
> His Messenger's protecting knight,
> A man proverbial in courage and might.

'Umar ibn Harithah al-Ansari, in a poem lauding Muhammad, son of the Commander of the Faithful, better known as Ibn al-Hanafiyya, said:

Like the *wasi*, and after the Messenger named,
The colour of his standard is crimson red.

When people swore the oath of allegiance to 'Ali (as) after 'Uthman, 'Abdul-Rahman ibn Ja'il said these verses:

I swear you have allied yourselves to one
Whose concern about the faith is well-known,
Supported by the Almighty: virtuous, with no sin,
'Ali, *wasi* of the Chosen one and his cousin,
The first to offer ritual prayers,
One endowed with piety and honours.

A man of the Azd tribe said the following during the Battle of the Camel:

This is 'Ali;
The Prophet's *wasi*
On the Day of Salvation;
The Prophet told the nation:
"This is a brother of mine!
"And successor when my sun ceases to shine."
The wise heeded and kept it in mind,
The wretch forgot and left it behind.

During the Battle of the Camel, a young man from the tribe of Zabbah, who was trained in 'Ayesha's camp, came out and said:

We are children of Zabbah, enemies of 'Ali,
The one who is known for long as the *wasi*,
A brave knight during the time of our Nabi,
I am not blind about the virtues of 'Ali,
I only mourn the murder of the son of 'Uthman, the *taqi*.

Sa'id ibn Qays al-Hamadani, who fought in 'Ali's camp, said the following on the Battle of the Camel:

What a battle that has kindled a fire!
Breaking the spears of every knight,
Tell the *wasi*: Qahtan approaches in desire,
Call upon them to aid Hamadan with their might,
They are their kin,
They are their children.

Ziyad ibn Labid al-Ansari, one of 'Ali's companions, composed these verses during the Battle of the Camel:

How do you see the Ansar in a fierce battle faring?
We are people never afraid to die;
In supporting the *wasi*, we attack with daring,
The Ansar are serious, their spirits high.
'Ali son of 'Abdul-Muttalib do we support
Against those who, about him, lied in their import.
Tell the liars, whose conscience is cheap,
A miserable harvest shall they forever reap.

Hajar ibn 'Adi al-Kindi said on the same occasion:

Lord! Protect 'Ali whose deeds You bless,
The pious believer, the caller for Your Oneness.
This is the view not of a depraved nor a deceiver,
He is but a divinely inspired and guided leader,
Protect him, Lord, and protect Your Prophet's Call
Through his *wali* and the *wasi* of each and all.

'Umar ibn Ahjiyah composed a poem lauding the address of al-Hasan, delivered after that of Ibn al-Zubayr, during the Battle of the Camel saying:

Hasan of goodness, like your father in virtue and grace,
Among us you have taken a lofty, exemplary place.
You have delivered a speech whereby Allah exposed

The lies of the enemies of your father who posed

Prattling, like Ibn al-Zubayr, the man of shame.
Ask even skeptics, and they will tell you his name.
Allah has insisted to lower in infamy his head,
And raise that of the clement son of *al-wasi* instead.
Thou hast undoubtedly chosen Thy own Nabi,
And Thou also appointed his honourable *wasi*.

Zajr ibn Qays al-Ju'fi composed these verses also during the Battle of the Camel:

The Lord salutes Ahmad, Messenger of the King
Who grants him many a blessing
After the Messenger of the King our Caliph will succeed,
A man worthy of authority-a knight true in word and deed:
Ali I meant, the Prophet's *wasi*, bringing to the Path
All the depraved and strayers who incurred the divine Wrath.

Al-Ash'ath ibn Qays al-Kindi has said:

The messenger of the Imam has come to us, so be it
That every Muslim in Ali's army speedily enlist,
He is messenger of the *wasi*, the *wasi* of the Messenger,
Foremost in feats, virtues, piety of every believer.

... and Also:

A message from the Imam we have received
From Ali the virtuous, Ali of Hashim,
Son-in-law of the Prophet (s), his vizier indeed,
The best in the nation and in every realm.

Al-Nu'man ibn al-'Ajlan al-Zarqi al-Ansari said the following during the Battle of Siffin:

Since the *wasi* is our leader, how can there be division?
Nay! No bewilderment, no confusion, do not slacken;
So, leave the depraved Mu'awiyah and follow the religion
Of the *wasi*, and praise the Lord of man and jinn.

'Abdul-Rahman ibn Thu'ayb al-Aslami has said the following in a poem threatening Mu'awiyah with the Iraqi troops:

They are led by none other than the *wasi*
To rid you of misguidance and uncertainty.[1]

'Abdullah ibn Abu Saufyan ibn al-Harith ibn 'Abdul-Muttalib has said:

The one in charge after Muhammad is 'Ali who
On all occasions did defend, support and stand.
He is the *wasi* of the Messenger, nothing is new;
His peer, the first to pray with him and lend him hand.

Khuzaymah ibn Thabit, of the two *shahadas*, has said:

He is *wasi* of the Messenger out of all his clan

---

[1] This verse, and all the poetic verses and martials which precede it, are quoted in the books of biographies and chronicles, especially the ones dealing with the battles of the Camel and Siffin. They have been quoted in their entirety by the researching scholar Ibn Abi al-Hadid on page 47 and its following pages up to page 50, Vol. 1, of his *Sharh Nahjul Balaghah*, Egyptian edition, where he explains the *khutba* of the Commander of the Faithful (as) referring to Muhammad's progeny (as) and to what they have said about him, including the following: "They have the distinction of being divinely granted the right to rule, and in them the Prophet's will is preserved, and they are the ones who inherit his legacy." Having quoted these verses and martials, he says *verbatim*: "The verses containing this word 'wasiyya' [will] are nUmarous, but we have mentioned here some of them where there is reference to the two parties (meaning Abu Mikhnaf's book dealing with the Battle of Camel, and Nasr ibn Muzahim's book dealing with the Battle of Siffin); besides these, the references are uncountable and innUmarable. We would have filled many pages of them had we not feared boredom and monotony."

His defending knight since the very beginning,
The first to pray, preceded by no man
Save the Lady chosen by the One Who Grants blessing.

Zafar ibn Huzayfah al-Asadi has said:

Surround Ali, O men, and support him,
For he is the *wasi* and the first Muslim.[2]

Abul-Aswad al-Du'ali has said:

I love Muhammad passionately, and to me
Very dear are: 'Abbas, Hamzah, and the *wasi*.

Al-Nu'man ibn 'Ajlan, an Ansar poet and dignitary, said these verses in a poem addressed to Ibn al-'As narrated by al-Zubayr ibn Bakkar in his *Muwaffaqiyyat*. It is transmitted by the Mu'tazilite scholar on page 13, Vol. 3, of his *Sharh Nahjul Balaghah*, but Ibn 'Abd al-Birr quotes this poem stating the biography of al-Nu'man in his *Isti'ab*, omitting the name of the witness from it ("... and thus do they behave (Qur'an, 27:34)":

You underestimated Ali who is the most fit,
Albeit if you knew, or did not know it;
For he, assisted by Allah, guides unto Him and indeed
Forbids debauchery, oppression and every wrongful deed;
The *wasi* of the Chosen Prophet (s) and his cousin
Killer of knights who are misguided, unbelieving.

---

[2] Zafar's verse, and both couplets composed by Khuzaymah before it, in addition to the couplets composed by Abu Sufyan which preceded them, are all narrated by Imam al-Iskafi in his book *Naqd al-'Uthmaniyya*, and they are transmitted by Ibn Abi al-Hadid at the end of his commentary on the *qasi'a* sermon on page 258 and the pages following it, Vol. 3, of *Sharh Nahjul Balaghah*, Egyptian edition.

Al-Fadl ibn al-'Abbas has said these verses which are quoted by Ibn al-Athir at the end of the latter's discussion of 'Uthman, on page 43, Vol. 3, of his work *Al-Tarikh al-Kamil*, commenting that 'Uthman is "the best of people besides the three men of the [Prophet's] house."

> The best of people and of every believer
> After the one chosen to be Messenger
> Is the *wasi* according to people who remember.
> And he is first to perform the rite of prayer
> And the like of the Messenger;
> The first at Badr to deal a deadly blow
> To those who broke the divine Law.

Hassan ibn Thabit has said these verses in which he praises Ali on behalf of all the Ansar. They are quoted by al-Zubayr ibn Bakkar in his *Muwaffaqiyyat*, and recorded by Ibn Abi al-Hadid on page 15, Vol. 2, of his work *Sharh Nahjul Balaghah*:

> You are the most faithful to the Prophet among us
> Worthy of his recommendation; for who else surpass
> You in it, who else? Aren't you his brother
> In true guidance, and his *wasi*,
> The best scholar of the Qur'an and all other
> Ahadith of the blessed Nabi?

Some poets said these verses addressing al-Hasan ibn 'Ali (as), peace be upon both of them, as quoted by Shaykh Muhammad 'Ali Hashshu al-Hanafi al-Saydawi in the footnote to page 65 of his book *A'thar Thawat al-Siwar*, when he discussed both Ghanima daughter of 'Amir, and Mu'awiyah, saying that she recited this verse before Mu'awiyah in a statement she made responding to his own:

> The most dignified of men, son of the *wasi*,
> Grandson of the Prophet, son of Ali.

Umm Sinan daughter of Khayth'amah ibn Kharsha'ah al-Mathhaji has said the following verses addressing and lauding Ali (as); they are mentioned by Imam Abul-Fadl Ahmad ibn Abu Tahir al-Baghdadi when he discusses Umm Sinan on page 67 of *Balaghat al-Nisa'*. They are also quoted from Umm Sinan by Shaykh Muhammad 'Ali Hashshu al-Hanafi al-Saydawi at the end of page 78 of his *?thar Thawat al-Siwar*.

> You were among us, after Muhammad, his trusted successor
> He selected you, and of his trust you proved a protector.

This much of the poetry contemporary to the Commander of the Faithful (as) is what we have been able to quote in such a short letter. If we review the poetry composed after him, then we will be authoring a voluminous book beyond the writing of which we would still apologize for our work being incomplete. Yet to quote all such poetry may become boring, and it may cause us to digress from the main subject-matter. So, let us be satisfied with quoting only the most famous poets, and let us judge the rest according to what is quoted here.

In his celebrated poem, al-Kumait ibn Ziyad has thus lauded the descendants of Hashim:

> He is the *wasi* protecting the throne of the nation
> Against collapse and disintegration,[3]

---

[3] When scholar Shaykh Muhammad Mahmud al-Rafi'i came to the conclusion of his commentary on this verse in his own commentary on the verses composed by the poet al-Kumait in praise of the descendants of Hashim, he said: "Meaning 'Ali, may Allah glorify his countenance, who is named *wasi* because the Messenger of Allah *awsa* [left a will] regarding him." The same is narrated about Ibn Buraydah who quotes his father citing the Prophet (s) saying: "For every Prophet there is a *wasi*, and 'Ali is my *wasi* and the heir of my legacy." Al-Tirmizi states that the Prophet (s) is quoted saying: "To whomsoever I have been a master, this 'Ali is his master." Al-Bukhari quotes Ibn Sa'd saying that the Messenger of Allah (s) headed to Tabuk, leaving 'Ali (as) behind. 'Ali (as) asked him: "Do you thus leave me with children and women?" He said: "Are you not pleased that your status to me is like that of Aaron to Moses, except there will be no prophet after me?" Ibn Qays al-Raqiyyat has said:

> The embodiment of virtue, glory and goodness,
> Solving the problems with order and firmness.
> The *wasi*, the *wali*,[4] the knight
> Courageous, brave: his star was bright,
> The *wasi* of the *wasi*, determined and wise
> In battle-fields, you hear his enemy's agony cries.

Kuthayyir ibn 'Abdul-Rahman ibn al-Aswad ibn 'Amir al-Khuza'i, better known as Kuthayyir 'Azza, has said:

> The *wasi* of the Chosen Prophet and his cousin; he
> Emancipates those in bondage, and judges with equity.

Abu Tammam al-Ta'i has said the following in one of his poems the rhyme of which rhymes with "r's":[5]

> You plotted against his *wasi* and deceived before;
> You cooked it, unprecedented, unmatched in lore,
> Against the Prophet's brother, son-in-law, who bore
> Feats of valour, while your plots opened the door
> To mischief: peerless in brother, son-in-law...; say no more;
> To the Prophet he was like Aaron to Moses of yore...

Among us are: Ahmad the Prophet, the truthful, the pious, the man of wisdom;

And 'Ali and Ja'far with two wings: They are the *wasi*, and the man of martyrdom.

This is something which poets used to always say about 'Ali (as) with a great elaboration. Then he testifies to the poetry we have first quoted by Kuthayyir 'Azzah.

[4] Muhammad Mahmud al-Rafi'i, the commentator, says *verbatim*: "Meaning vicegerent after the Messenger of Allah."

[5] The poem starts with: "Gazelles that made the dusty dunes glitter like stars," which is included in his *diwan* (collection of poems).

Du'bal ibn Ali al-Khuza'i has said the following in his eulogy of the Master of Martyrs [Imam Husayn (s)]:

> The head of the son of Muhammad's daughter and his *wasi*,
> O men, is being raised atop a spear for all to see...!

Abul-Tayyib al-Mutanabbi, when rebuked for stopping his praise of Ahl al-Bayt, as recorded in his diwan (collection of poems) said:

> I have no pretext for leaving the praise of the *wasi*
> His light dominates, his shade expands unto you and me:
> For when something elongates, it stands on its own,
> Attributes of the sun's light are never gone.

He also said the following verses in his praise of Abul-Qasim Tahir ibn al-Husayn ibn Tahir al-'Alawi, as also recorded in his *diwan*:

> He is son of the Messenger of Allah and of his *wasi*,
> Alike unto them when I diligently compare and see.

Verses such as these are innumerable, uncountable, Wassalam.

Sincerely,
Sh

Letter 109
Rabi' al-Thani 23, 1330

Why do Some Fanatics Question the Derivation of the Shi'a School of Muslim Law from the Imams of Ahl al-Bayt (as)?

We, in our Letter No. 19, had indicated that some fanatics question the derivation of your school of thought, in its roots and branches of religion, from the Imams of Ahl al-Bayt, and we wished to ask you about this matter. Now is the time to ask such a question; so, could you please answer it in a way that would refute their claim? Wassalam.

Sincerely,
S

Letter 110
Rabi' al-Thani 29, 1330

I. Shi'ah Faith is Sequentially Derived from the Imams of Ahl al-Bayt

All those endowed with wisdom and discretion know by necessity that the derivation of the roots and branches of the Shi'ah imamite faith is from their forefathers and ancestors ending with the purified progeny. Their views, therefore, are conducive to those of the Imams of the purified progeny in the roots and branches of the faith, as well as all deductions arrived at from studying the Book and the Sunnah, or in any matter related to them or to all branches of theological science. They do not rely in their understanding of the latter except upon such progeny, and they refer to none other than them. They worship Allah, the Exalted, and seek nearness to Him, Praised be He, through the faith of the Imams of Ahl al-Bayt, without seeing any deviation therefrom, nor desiring any substitute. This has been the policy of their good ancestors since the time of the Commander of the Faithful, al-Hasan, al-Husayn, and the nine Imams from the progeny of al-Husayn (as) till our time. Those who have learned the roots and branches of the faith from Ahl al-Bayt are quite a few reliable Shi'ahs, and the number of those who learned from the latter is much larger. The number of those known for piety, verification and correction is more than sequential. They have narrated all this to those who succeeded them through *tawatur*, and after them it was thus narrated to others, and so on. This has been the case with each and every generation, till it reached us as clear as mid-day sun, without any cloud obstructing it.[1]

We now, in understanding the roots and branches, are followers of the Imams from the progeny of the Messenger (s). We have quoted our forefathers who all quote them. This has been the case in all generations till the time of the Naqis, 'Askaris, Rizas, Jawads, Kazims, Sadiqs, 'Abidins, Baqirs, both grandsons of the Prophet (s), peace be upon all of them, and finally the Commander of the Faithful (as), not counting Shi'ah ancestors who kept company with the Imams of Ahl al-Bayt (as), learning the religious injunctions from them, quoting them while discussing Islamic knowledge.

There is no room here to count all of them and read their roll call. Suffices you what the pens of their renowned scholars have written of interesting works a list of which does not fit in this narration. They derived all that from the light of the Imams of guidance, the progeny of Muhammad, peace be upon him and them, quoting it from their own oceans of knowledge, hearing it directly from them. They are the scribes of their knowledge and wisdom. Their works were authored during the life-time of those purified ones, and such works became references for all Shi'ahs who succeeded them. Through them, the superiority of the sect of Ahl al-Bayt manifested itself over all other Islamic sects.

---

[1] *Al-Huda*, the Iraqi magazine, quoted this Letter and published it in series in its first and second volumes in a column signed by the humble author.

We do not know any follower of the four Sunni Imams, for example, who authored a book during the life-time of their Imams. Rather, people authored works in abundance dealing with their faith after those Imams had left this world, when it was decided that *taqlid* should be confined to their sects alone. During their life-time, they were just like any other contemporary jurist or traditionist, not enjoying any distinction over others of their class; therefore, nobody among their contemporaries was interested in exerting an effort to record their speeches like that exerted by Shi'ahs in recording the statements of the Infallible Imams (as). Ever since the inception of the Shi'ah sect, nobody was permitted to refer in the religious matters to anyone other than their Imams. For this reason, such an effort was unavoidable, and they became the sole source of religious scholarship. A great deal of effort and resources were spent in recording their verbal statements, and many exhausted their resources in doing so in a manner that is unmatched so that they might preserve the knowledge which, according to such sect, is the only one accepted by Allah. The books authored during the life-time of Imam al-Sadiq (as) alone numbered four hundred dealing with four hundred different topics containing the religious verdicts [*fatawa*] issued by al-Sadiq (as) during his life-time. The disciples of al-Sadiq (as) have written many, many times this number, as you will hear in detail shortly, Insha-Allah.

As regarding the four Sunni imams, nobody looks at them in the eyes Shi'ahs look at the Imams of Ahl al-Bayt. Nay; they did not even have followers during their own life-time! They did not live to enjoy the status given to them after they had died, as stated by Ibn Khaldun al-'Arabi in a chapter he dedicated to the science of *fiqh* in his famous Introduction, and it is a fact admitted by many of their renowned scholars. In spite of all this, we do not doubt that their followers followed anyone other than them, for theirs are, indeed, the views of the followers of those Imams, the ones held reliable in dealing with their affairs by every generation. They recorded them in their books because their followers knew their sects best, just as Shi'ahs best know the sect of their Imams, those who worship Allah accordingly, believing that it is the only way to seek nearness to Him.

II. Advancement of Shi'ahs in Recording Knowledge During the Sahabah's Epoch

Researchers unhesitatingly accept the fact that Shi'ahs were the pioneers in recording the branches of knowledge, more so than anyone else. As a matter of fact, nobody in the first century of Islam besides 'Ali (as) and those endowed with the gift of knowledge among his Shi'ahs did so. The reason for this could be attributed to the differences of opinion among the companions in permitting or forbidding the writing of knowledge. According to al-'Asqalani in his Introduction to *Fath al-Malik al-'Ali Bisihhati Babil 'Ilm 'Ali*, and according to others, 'Umar ibn al-Khattab and a few others disliked the idea for fear hadith might be mixed with the Book, versus the permission granted by 'Ali (as), and after him al-Hasan al-Mujtaba (as), grandson of the Prophet (s), and a group of other companions, to such writing. During that time, Ibn Jurayh authored in Mecca the first book dealing with the legacies in which he quotes Mujahid and 'Ata'. Al-Ghazali says that it is the first book authored in Islam. The truth of the matter is that it is the first book authored by a non-Shi'ah in Islam. After it, Mu'ammar ibn Rashid, of San'a, Yemen, wrote his, then Malik authored his *Mawti'*. The Introduction of *Fath al-Malik al-'Ali Bisihhati Babil 'Ilm 'Ali* states that al-Rabi' ibn Sabih was the first to compile information, and that he lived at the sunset of the time of the tabi'in. **Anyhow, the consensus of opinion is that Sunnis did not author a single book during the first Islamic century.**

As regarding 'Ali and his Shi'ahs, these spent a great deal of effort and time to attain that end during the first century of Islam. The first writing of the Commander of the Faithful was the Book of Allah, the Exalted, the Praiseworthy. Having finished the rituals pertaining to the preparation for the departure of the Prophet (s) from this world, 'Ali (as) decided not to dress except to either say the prayers or compile the Qur'an. He, therefore, compiled it arranged in the order of its revelation. He pointed out its general and specific meanings, absolute and restrictive, perfect and those that seem to be alike, revocation and what revokes it, emphasis and relaxation, injunctions and instructions, pointing out the occasions which necessitated the revelation of its perfect verses, explaining what might be confusing to other people. Ibn Sirin used to always say: "If you are lucky enough to obtain that book, then you will find in it abundant knowledge." This is cited by Ibn Hajar in his *Al-Sawa'iq al-Muhriqa*, and by many other renowned writers. Several companions who could read took pains to compile the Holy Qur'an, but they could not compile it in the order of its revelation, nor could they mark it the way explained above, leaving 'Ali's compilation more than just a compilation - rather an exegesis.

Having finished working on the Book of the Dear One, he authored a book which he dedicated to the Mistress of the Women of Mankind. It came to be known to her purified sons as "Mushaf Fatima," Fatima's book, which contained axioms, pieces of wisdom and counsel, morals, historical events and unique occurrences, written as a solace for her after being bereaved by the loss of her father the Prophet (s). After that, he authored a book dealing with blood monies which he titled *Al-Sahifa*. It is referred to by Ibn Sa'd at the end of his work titled *Al-Jami'* giving the credit of authorship to the Commander of the Faithful. Both al-Bukhari and Muslim mention this work and quote it in several places of their Sahih. Among their narrative is what they have quoted from al-A'mash from Ibrahim al-Taymi who quotes his father saying: "'Ali (as), may Allah be pleased with him, told me once: 'We have no book for you to read, besides Allah's Book, other than this *Sahifa*.' Then he brought it to me. It contained matters related to wounds and camel teeth. Also among its contents is a statement reading: 'Medina is a sanctuary from sir to Thawr; anyone who desecrates it, or shelters a desecrator, will incur the curse of Allah, the angels, and man.'" This is the wording of al-

Bukhari in his section dealing with the sins of those who disown their mawali, in his chapter on ordinances, page 111, Vol. 4, of his *Sahih*, and it is referred to in the chapter on Medina's sanctity, when the pilgrimage is discussed on page 523, Vol. 1, of Muslim's *Sahih*. Imam Ahmad ibn Hanbal repeatedly refers to the narrative regarding this Sahifa in his *musnad*. He quotes 'Ali (as) on page 100, Vol. 1, of his *Musnad*, transmitted by Tariq ibn Shihab who says: "I have witnessed 'Ali, peace be upon him, telling people from the pulpit: 'By Allah! We have nothing to recite for you other than the Book of Allah the Exalted, and this Sahifa,' which he was attaching to his sword, 'I have learned its contents from the Messenger of Allah.'"

Quoting 'Abdul-Malik, al-Saffar narrates: "Abu Ja'far asked to have 'Ali's book brought to him, and his son Ja'far brought something bulky shaped like a thigh. Among its contents was a sentence reading: 'If a man dies, his women will not inherit any of his estates.' Abu Ja'far said: 'This, by Allah, is the hand writing of 'Ali (as) and the dictation of the Messenger of Allah (s)!'"A group of Shi'ahs who were contemporary to the Imam (as) followed in the footsteps of the Commander of the Faithful (as) and authored a number of books. Among those authors were: Salman al-Farsi and Abu Dharr al-Ghifari, as stated by Ibn Shahr Ashub who says: "The first to author in Islam is 'Ali ibn Abu Talib (as), then Salman al-Farsi, then Abu Dharr."

Among the latter is Abu Rafi', freed slave of the Messenger of Allah (s), and treasurer of *baytul-mal* [state treasury] during the rule of the Commander of the Faithful, peace be upon him. He was among the elite of his followers who sought his guidance. He wrote a book dealing with traditions, ordinances and other matters which he compiled mostly from 'Ali's hadith. It enjoyed a prestigious status among our ancestors who used it as a source of quotations and narrations. Among them is 'Ali ibn Abu Rafi' who, according to his biography in Isaba, was born during the life-time of the Prophet (s) who named him 'Ali. He authored a book on the science of *fiqh* according to the teachings of Ahl al-Bayt who, peace be upon them, used to cherish that book and refer their Shi'ahs to it. Musa ibn 'Abdullah ibn al-Hasan has said: "A man inquired about *tashahhud* from my father. My father told me to fetch the book written by Abu Rafi'. He took it and dictated to us from it."

The author of *Rawdat al-Jannat* concludes his discussion by stating that the latter was the first book dealing with *fiqh* written by Shi'ahs, but he, may Allah have mercy on him, has certainly erred. Among them is 'Ubaydullah ibn Abu Rafi', a scribe and a follower of 'Ali (as), who learned from the Prophet (s) and narrated to Ja'far his (s) saying: "Your form and manners are similar to mine." This is quoted by a group of scholars including Ahmad ibn Hanbal in his *Musnad*. Ibn Hajar has mentioned it in Part 1 of his *Isaba* under the heading "'Ubaydullah ibn Aslam." The name of the father of Rabi' is Aslam. This 'Ubaydullah authored a book dealing with the *sahaba* who fought the Battle of Siffin on 'Ali's side, from which Ibn Hajar quotes extensively in his own Isaba;[2] so, you may refer to it. Also among them is Rabi'ah ibn Sam' who wrote a book dealing with *zakat* on cattle herds derived from the hadith of the Prophet (s) which is narrated by 'Ali (as). They include 'Abdullah ibn al-Hurr al-Farsi who narrates a glitter of ahadith all reported by 'Ali (as) from the Messenger of Allah (s). And among them is al-Asbagh ibn Nabatah, a friend and disciple of the Commander of the Faithful (as) who quotes the Imam's instructive epistle to Malik al-Ashtar and his will to his son Muhammad. Both are recorded by our fellows in their authentic books of traditions directly from him. Among them is Salim ibn Qays al-Hilali, a companion of 'Ali (as), who quotes his hadith and that of Salman. He wrote a book dealing with imamate which is mentioned by Imam Muhammad ibn Ibrahim al-Nu'mani in his book *Al-Ghayba*, saying: "Nobody among all Shi'ah scholars and narrators of the hadith of the Imams disputes the fact that the book

---

[2] Refer to the biography of Jubayr ibn al-Habab ibn al-Munthir in Part One of *Al-Isabah*.

written by Salim ibn Qays al-Hilali is a major bibliography of works dealing with *usul* [basics of jurisprudence] narrated by scholars and traditionists from Ahl al-Bayt, and one of the pioneers in its subject-matter. It is one of the major sources to which Shi'ahs refer and upon which they rely." Our fellows have also recorded the names and works of those of the same calibre among their good ancestors who authored books, in addition to the indices and biographies to whose authors everyone is referred.

III. Their Authors Contemporary to the Tabi'in and the Latter's Followers

As regarding the authors among our ancestors who belong to the second generation, i.e. that of the tabi'in, this Letter falls short of elaborating on them, and the best to do in getting to know them, their works and sources in detail, is to refer to the bibliographies and biographies compiled by our scholars.[3]

Upon that class did the light of Ahl al-Bayt (as) brightly shine, whereas it was earlier obstructed by the clouds of the oppression of oppressors. The calamity of the Taff disclosed the enemies of the progeny of Muhammad (s), and made them lose face before the wise. It also drew attention to the atrocities meted to Ahl al-Bayt (as) since losing the Messenger of Allah (s). Their horrible implications forced people to look for the reasons and obligated them to research the causes. Thus did they come to know the seeds and roots of the calamity. Those among them who were blessed with a conscience rose to protect the status of Ahl al-Bayt (as) and support them [both Imams], for the human nature is made to assist the wronged and dislike wrong-doing. Muslims, in the aftermath of that catastrophic incident, entered a new era in which they rushed to support Imam 'Ali ibn al-Husayn Zaynul-'Abidin (as), refer to him in their quest for answers regarding the roots and

---

[3] Such as al-Najashi's Index, Shaykh Abu 'Ali's *Muntahal Maqal fi Ahwalir Rijal*, Mirza Muhammad's *Minhajul Maqal fi Tahqiqi Ahwalir Rijal*, and many other books dealing with this branch of knowledge, and they are quite few.

branches of the faith, and to all Islamic sciences derived from the Book and the Sunnah. After his death, they started referring to his son Imam Abu Ja'far al-Baqir (as). Followers of both Imams, i.e. Zaynul-'abidin and al-Baqir (as), among ancient Imamis, wrote innumerable books, but those scholars whose names and biographies were recorded in biography books were about four thousand heroes, and their works numbered approximately ten thousand[4] or more which are narrated by our friends in every generation quoting them from reliable sources. A group among the elite of those heroes won the honour of serving them, while the rest served Imam al-Sadiq, peace be upon all of them, and luck had it that a large number of them reached their ultimate objective of attaining authentic knowledge.

Among the latter is Abu Sa'id Aban ibn Taghlib ibn Rabah al-Jariri, the famous reciter of the Qur'an, the traditionist, lexicographer, and linguist who was one of the most reliable among scholars. He was contemporary to three Imams from whom he transmitted a great deal of knowledge and a large number of traditions. Suffices you the fact that he narrates from al-Sadiq (as) alone thirty thousand ahadith, as stated by al-Mirza Muhammad in his biography of Aban in his work *Manhaj al-Maqal* wherein he quotes Aban ibn 'Uthman citing al-Sadiq, peace be upon him. He enjoyed their respect and high esteem. Al-Baqir, peace be upon him, said to him, while they were both at the sacred city of Medina, "Take your place at the mosque, and issue your verdicts to people, for I love people to observe a man of my own Shi'ahs like you." Al-Sadiq (as), peace be upon him, said to him once: "Debate with the people of Medina, for I love to see men like you among my narrators and friends." Whenever he came to Medina, people came to him in large numbers and arranged for him to sit where the Prophet (s) used to sit. Al-Sadiq (as) said to Salim ibn Abu Habbah: "Visit Aban ibn Taghlib, for he has learned a large number of ahadith from me, and whatever he narrates to you, you should

---

[4] Indicated so by many masters of the art such as Shaykh al-Baha'i in his *Wajiza*, and many other renowned personalities.

narrate, too." He, peace be upon him, has said to Aban ibn 'Uthman: "Aban ibn Taghlib has narrated thirty thousand ahadith from me; so, quote the same from him." Whenever Aban ibn Taghlib visited al-Sadiq (as), the Imam would hug him, shake his hand, and order a couch to be given to him to lean on, and he would lend him his full attention. When the news of his death was brought to him, he, peace be upon him, said: "By Allah! My heart is aching because of the death of Aban." He died in 141 A.H. Aban has narrated traditions from Anas ibn Malik, al-A'mash, Muhammad ibn al-Munkadir, Sammak ibn Harb, Ibrahim al-Nakh'i, Fudayl ibn 'Umar, and al-Hakam. He is relied upon by Muslim and all authors of the four books of traditions, as we explained while discussing him in Letter No. 16.

Aban is not harmed by al-Bukhari's reluctance to rely on his authority, for his solace is that the man does not rely on the authority of the Imams of Ahl al-Bayt (as) such as al-Sadiq, al-Kazim, al-Rida, al-Jawad, al-Taqi, and al-Hasan al-'Askari al-Zaki, peace be upon all of them, either. Bukhari does not consider these men reliable; nay, he even does not rely on the authority of the elder grandson of the Prophet (s) and the master of the young of paradise! On the other hand, he relies on men like Marwan ibn al-Hakam, 'Umran ibn Hattan, 'Ikramah al-Barbari and their likes; so, we are Allah's, and to Him is our return. Aban has written very interesting books. One of them is [exegesis of what is unusual in the Qur'an], whose contents are mostly Arabic verses of poetry cited to testify to the truth contained in the Perfect Revelation. Later, 'Abdul-Rahman ibn Muhammad al-Azdi al-Kufi combined the contents of Aban's book with those of Muhammad ibn al-Sa'ib al-Kalbi and Ibn Rawaq 'Atiyyah ibn al-Harith and published them in one volume, highlighting the views in which they differed among themselves as well as those they agreed upon. He once quotes Aban independently, and once he quotes what agrees with 'Abdul-Rahman's views. Our friends have quoted both books through various reliable sources. Aban has authored a book dealing with moral excellences, and one dealing with the Battle of Siffin, and he has authored one of the major reference books on which the Imamites rely in their derivation of juristic injunctions. All his books have been reported with reference to his authorship thereof. Their details are in bibliography books.

Among them is Abu Hamzah al-Thumali ibn Dinar, a trustworthy authority and a dignitary among our ancestors. He derived his knowledge from three Imams: al-Sadiq (as), al-Baqir, and Zaynul-'Abidin, peace be upon them. He remained in close contact with them, and won their respect. Al-Sadiq (as), peace be upon him, lauded him saying: "In his age, Abu Hamzah is like Luqman in his own time." He has written a book on the exegesis of the Qur'an, and I noticed imam al-Tibrisi quoting him in his *tafsir* titled *Mujma'ul Bayan fi Tafsir al-Qur'an*.[5] He has also written a book on rare ahadith, another on asceticism, and a dissertation on rights[6] narrated from Imam Zaynul-'abidin 'Ali ibn al-Husayn from whom he narrates his own invocation recited at early dawn which shines brighter than the sun and the moon. He also narrates from Anas and al-Sha'bi. He in turn is quoted by Waki', Abu Na'im, and a group of their class who are our own friends, and from others, as we stated in his biography in Letter No. 16

There are other valiant men who did not live to meet Imam Zaynul-'Abidin, but they won the honour of serving both al-Baqirs, peace be upon them.

---

[5] Refer to al-Tibrisi's *Mujma'Bayan fi Tafsiril Qur'an* in the section dealing with the exegesis of the verse reading: "Say: 'I do not ask you for any reward for it other than being kind to my kin'" in Surat al-Shura, and you will find him quoting Abu Hamzah's own *tafsir*.
[6] Our fellows have reported all of Abu Hamzah's books, giving him credit for the narration, and the details are in their books. Our dignitary-authority Sayyid Sadr ad-Din al-Musawi has abridged *Risalat al-Huquq* and published it in order to be memorized by heart by Muslim youths, and he has done a very good job; may Allah enable the Muslims to enjoy the fruits of his concern and the magnitude of his effort.

Among these are: Abul-Qasim Bard ibn Mu'awiyah al-'Ajli, Abu Basir al-Asghar Layth ibn Murad al-Bakhtari al-Muradi, Abul Hassan Zararah ibn 'Ayan, Abu Ja'far Muhammad ibn Muslim ibn Rabah al-Kufi al-Ta'ifi al-Thaqafi, and many other standards of guidance and lighthouses that shone in the dark. To elaborate on them is not possible here.

As regarding these four men, they have, indeed, achieved a special status and won the coveted prize and a lofty station. When Imam al-Sadiq (as), peace be upon him, mentioned them once, he said: "I find nobody who kept our name alive like Zararah, Abu Basir Layth, Muhammad ibn Muslim, and Burayd; without them, nobody would have learned as much." Then he added: "These are the custodians of the faith who were trusted by my father to safeguard what Allah has decreed as permissible or forbidden. They are the ones who are foremost in seeking our company in this life, and they will be the foremost in joining us in the Hereafter." Once, he, peace be upon him, recited: "Convey the glad tidings to those who pray for attaining Our Paradise (Qur'an, 22:34),"and he followed his recitation by naming these four persons, adding, in a lengthy statement lauding them, "My father is said to have trusted them to safeguard Allah's permissible and forbidden matters, and they were the custodians of his knowledge; today, they are my faithful confidants and the true friends of my father; they are the stars of my Shi'ahs alive or dead; through them does Allah dispel every innovation. They protect this religion from the lies of the innovators, and the interpretations of the extremists," in addition to other eminent statements he made in which he credited them for their contributions, honour, dignity, and true service in a way which we cannot describe. In spite of all this, they were charged by the enemies of Ahl al-Bayt (as) with every possible false charge, as we have explained in our work *Mukhtasar al-Kalam fi Mu'allifi al-Shi'ah min Sadr al-Islam*. This does not undermine their lofty status and great significance in the eyes of Allah, His Messenger, and the believers. Those who envied the Prophet (s)s only increased the loftiness of those Prophets' status, without affecting their canons other than their promotion thereof among those who recognize and follow the truth, making them acceptable to those endowed with wisdom.

During the lifetime of al-Sadiq (as), peace be upon him, knowledge was disseminated like never before, and the Shi'ahs of his forefathers (as) rushed to him from far and wide. He approached them with a pleasant countenance, making them feel at home, sparing no effort to educate them and acquaint them with the secrets of knowledge, the particulars of wisdom, and the nature of matters, as admitted by Abul-Fath al-Shahristani in his book *Al-Milal wal Nihal*. When he mentions al-Sadiq (as), he comments: "He was a man very much informed of the religion, endowed with perfect manners in wisdom, extreme renunciation of this world, and a complete abstinence from temptations."[7] He has also said of him: "He stayed in Medina for some time instructing the Shi'ahs belonging to his faith, lavishing the secrets of knowledge upon those who were loyal to him. Then he went to Iraq and stayed there for a period of time during which he did not publicly criticize nor covet authority... Whoever drowns in the oceans of knowledge never desires to see the shore, and whoever ascends to the peak of reality never fears descending," up to the end of his statement; "And truth makes itself manifest to the fair minded, and to the obstinate."

A large number of the companions of al-Sadiq (as) achieved ultimate wisdom, and they became leaders to righteousness, lanterns in the dark, oceans of knowledge, stars of guidance. Among those whose names and biographies are stated in biography books are four thousand men from Iraq, Hijaz, Iran, and Syria. They are authors of works very well known by Imamite scholars. Among them are the four hundred books of basics of jurisprudence mentioned above which deal with four hundred subjects, all written during the time and derived from the verdicts of al-Sadiq (as). They

---

[7] He does so when he mentions the Baqiriyya and Ja'fariyya among Shi'ah sects in his book *Al-Milal wal-Nihal*.

were rendered indispensable for both theoretical and practical knowledge, so much so that a group of the nation's scholars and emissaries of the Imams summarized their contents in special books to facilitate their comprehension by students and make them more accessible. The best among such compilations are the four books which are the major sources for the Imamites in referring to the roots and branches of their faith. They have been referring to them since the first century of Islam, and these are: *Al-Kafi, Al-Tahthib, Al-Istibsar,* and *Man la Yahdaruhul Faqih*. All are sequentially narrated, and the authenticity of their contents is never doubted. *Al-Kafi* is the oldest among them, the greatest, the best, and the most authentic. It contains sixteen thousand one hundred and ninety-nine ahadith which include all what now exists in the six *sahih* books [al-*Sihah al-sitta* of the Sunnis], as admitted by al-Shahid in his *Al-Thikra*, and by many other renowned scholars. One of the companions of al-Sadiq (as) and al-Kazim (as), authored several books ninety-nine of which became quite famous. They are narrated by our friends who quote him, and their details exist in our book *Mukhtasar al-Kalam fi Muallifi al-Shi'ah min Sadr al-Islam*. They all are very interesting books, dazzling in the clarity of their contents and the glitter of their arguments. They deal with both roots and branches of the faith, and with *tawhid* and rational philosophy; they rebut the atheists, heretics, pantheists, predestinarians, determinists, and those who are extremist in their beliefs regarding Ali (as) and Ahl al-Bayt (as). They also rebut the Kharijites and Nasibis, those who denied that a will [by the Prophet] was made regarding Ali (as), those who obstructed his way to attain the caliphate, and those who preached that someone else should be elected as caliph before Ali (as), in addition to other topics.

In the second century, Hisham was the most knowledgeable person in the science of speech, divine wisdom, and all rational and deductive sciences. He was distinguished in *fiqh* and hadith, surpassing everyone else in tafsir and all other sciences and arts. He is the one who discussed the concept of imamate and cultivated the sect through observation. He quotes al-Sadiq (as) and al-Kazim, and he enjoys a special status in their eyes which cannot be described. He won such praise from them that elevated his status to high heaven. He was first a Jehmi, then he met al-Sadiq (as) and came to see the light of guidance through him, so, he joined his party, then he followed al-Kazim and surpassed all the disciples of both Imams. Those who desire to put out Allah's light, out of envy of Ahl al-Bayt (as), and out of malice, accused him of saying that the Almighty has a physical form, and of other serious charges. We are most knowledgeable of his sect. We have within our reach reports of his life-style and norm of speech. He has written works defending our sect as referred to above; so, nothing of his speech can be known to others and not to us, since he is among our ancestors and descendants, while his critics are far from his sect and taste. What al-Shahristani has quoted in his *Al-Milal wal-Nihal* of Hisham's speech does not imply his belief in a physical form for Allah. Let me quote for you what he has quoted him:

"Hisham ibn al-Hakam has studied *usul* in depth. We must not forget his arguments with the Mu'tazilites, for the man is above what his opponent charges, and beneath what similitude he strikes, for he argued with al-'Allaf saying: 'You claim that the Creator is the One Who knows, and His knowledge is His own essence; so, He then becomes a knowledgeable person who is different from the world [His creation]; why then don't you say that He has a form unlike all other forms?'"

It is no secret that this statement, if true, proves only that he opposes al-'Allaf's views. Not everyone who argues about something is a believer therein, since it is possible that his purpose is to test al-'Allaf's beliefs and sift his knowledge, as al-Shahristani suggests, saying: "The man is above what his opponent accuses him and beneath what similitude he strikes." If we suppose that it is proved that Hisham believes as such, this could be before his going back to the true guidance [through Imam al-Sadiq (as)]. You have come to know that he used to believe like the Jehmis, then he saw the light of guidance through Muhammad's progeny (as), and became an Imam of those who followed their Imams. Nobody among our ancestors has found any proof of what the opponent attributes to him, yet we find some traces of what they have attributed to Zararah ibn 'Ayan, Muhammad ibn Muslim, Mu'min al-Taq, and their peers. This comes in spite of the fact that we spared no effort to research the accusation and found its bases nothing more than injustice and animosity, intrigue and false allegation; "Do not think that Allah is unmindful of what the oppressors do."

As regarding what al-Shahristani has alleged of Hisham's belief in Ali (as) as Allah, this is a joke that causes even a bereaved woman whose child has just died to burst in laughter. Hisham is above such nonsense and superstition. Hisham's statements dealing with *tawhid* call for the glorification of Allah above being reduced to a physical form of any nature, and His sublimity above what the ignorant allege. His statements dealing with imamate and *wisayat* reflect his preference of the Messenger of Allah, peace be upon him and his progeny, over Ali (as). He declares that Ali (as) is just a member of the Prophet's nation and a subject, his vicegerent and successor, and that he is a servant of Allah who has been wronged and overcome and was unable to secure what is rightfully his, being forced to succumb to the power of his opponents, continuously afraid about his safety, having neither supporter nor helper; so, how can al-Shahristani say: "Hisham ibn al-Hakam has studied *usul* in depth. We must not forget his arguments with the Mu'tazilites, for the man is above what his opponent charges, and beneath what similitude he strikes, for he argued with al-'Allaf saying: 'You claim that the Creator is the One Who knows, and His knowledge is His own essence; so, He then becomes a knowledgeable person Who is different from the world [His creation]; why then don't you say that He has a form unlike all other forms?'" He then attributes to Ali (as) the allegation that he is Allah Almighty! Isn't this a clear self-contradiction? Is it proper for Husham, in spite of his abundant knowledge and contributions, that such nonsense is attributed to him? Certainly not. But these people have insisted on piling charges out of their own envy and animosity towards Ahl al-Bayt (as) and those who follow their views; so, we are Allah's, and unto Him is our return.

Authorship flourished during the lifetime of Imams al-Kazim, al-Rida, al-Jawad, al-Hadi, al-Hasan al-Zaki al-'Askari, peace be upon them, in a way that was never preceded, and traditionists quoting them and other Imams spread far and wide throughout the land, trying their best reasoning to attain knowledge, in pursuit of it and of its secrets, enumerating its issues, verifying its facts, saving no effort to record the arts and collect particles of knowledge.

Al-Muhaqqiq, in his *Al-Mu'tabar*, says: "Among the students of al-Jawad, peace be upon him, were virtuous men like al-Husayn ibn Sa'id and his brother al-Hasan, and also Ahmad ibn Muhammad ibn Abu Nasr al-Bazanti, Ahmad ibn Muhammad ibn Khalid al-Barqi, Shathan, Abul-Fadl al-'Ami, Ayyub ibn Nuh, Ahmad ibn Muhammad ibn 'Isa and others whose list is quite lengthy... Their books till today are in current circulation among the companions reflecting their abundant knowledge."

Suffices you the fact that al-Barqi's books outnumber a hundred, and al-Bazanti has authored his renowned work titled *Jami' al Bazanti*, while al-Husayn ibn Sa'id has written thirty books. It is not possible in such a Letter to count what has been written by the students of the six Imams who descended from Imam al-Sadiq (as), peace be upon them, but I refer you to the available biographies and bibliographies; so, read about the biography of Muhammad ibn Sinan, 'Ali ibn Mahziyar, al-Hasan ibn Mahbub, al-Hasan ibn Muhammad ibn Sam'ah, Safwan ibn Yahya, 'Ali ibn Yaqtin, 'Ali ibn Fadal, 'Abdul-Rahman ibn Najran, al-Fadl ibn Shathan (who authored two hundred books), Muhammad ibn Mas'ud al-'Ayyashi (who wrote more than two hundred titles), Muhammad ibn 'Umayr, Ahmad ibn Muhammad ibn 'Isa (who quoted one hundred companions of al-Sadiq (as), peace be upon him), Muhammad ibn 'Ali ibn Mahbub, Talhah ibn Talhah ibn Zayd, 'Ammar ibn Musa al-Sabati, 'Ali ibn al-Nu'man, al-Husayn ibn 'Abdullah, Ahmad ibn 'Abdullah ibn Mahran who is better known as Ibn Khaniba, Sadfah ibn al-Munthir al-Qummi, 'Ubaydullah ibn 'Ali al-Halabi who brought his book to al-Sadiq (as), peace be upon him, to edit and verify, which he appreciated and said: "Do you see these folks having a book like this one?!" Add to them Abu 'Amr the physician, 'Abdullah ibn Sa'id who brought his book to Abul-Hasan al-Rida, peace be upon him, for the same purpose, and Unus ibn 'Abdul-Rahman who brought his book to Imam Abu Muhammad al-Hasan al-Zaki al-'Askari, peace be upon him.

Anyone who researches the biographies of the followers of the progeny of Muhammad, peace be upon him and them, and researches those who kept company with the nine Imams from the descendants of al-Husayn, counting their works contemporary to their respective Imams and reviewed by those they quoted, disseminating the hadith of Muhammad's progeny in every branch and root of religion..., will come across thousands of such men. Then if he gets acquainted with these sciences in every class as handed down from the time of the nine Infallible Imams (as) till our time, he will certainly be convinced then that the sect of these Imams is *mutawatir* (consecutively reported), dispelling any doubt he might have about the fact that our worship of the Almighty Allah in the roots and branches of the faith is derived from the Messenger's Household. Nobody doubts this fact except one who is arrogant and prejudiced or dumb ignorant; so, praise be to Allah Who has guided us to this, for without His guidance, we would not have been thus guided; Wassalam.

Sincerely,
Sh

Letter 111
Jamadi al-Ula 1, 1330

Conviction

I bear witness that you, in the roots and branches of the faith, are followers of the Imams from the Messenger's progeny. You have clarified this matter and rendered it obvious, unveiled whatever was obscure thereof; so, to doubt you is madness, and to mistrust you is misguidance. I have scrutinized your letter and found it very pleasing. I verified it and was able to inhale its divine fragrance which nourished me with its sweet scent. Before knowing you, I used to be confused about your beliefs due to what I hear of allegations from scandal-mongers; now I have found it to be a lantern that dispels the darkness, and I am leaving you victorious, successful; so, how great is the blessing which Allah has bestowed upon me, and how great your benefit unto me! Praise to Allah, Lord of the Worlds, Wassalamo Alaikum.

Sincerely,
S

Letter 112
Jamadi al-Ula 2, 1330

Appreciation

I bear witness that now you are acquainted with the matter, capable of handling it. You have surpassed all others in comprehending it and researching it minutely, scrutinizing it carefully, turning it to all sides, discerning its inner implications, seeking its essence and nature, without being swayed by nationalistic biases, nor motivated by personal interests. So, the attributes of your clemency cannot be harmed, nor can your mind be dominated. You have dealt in depth researching it with a clemency that is more than pleasing, and with a mind more spacious than this world, minutely verifying, without minding the view of kith or kin, till what is hidden has surfaced; truth has manifested itself, and morning rays have appeared to all those who can see; so, all praise is due to Allah for guiding us to His religion, and for being successful to attain what He has enjoined us to attain of His Path: THE RIGHT PATH, and may He send blessings unto Muhammad and the progeny of Muhammad, and many salutations.

Sincerely,
Sh

Glossary

Azan: the call for prayers; *muazzin* is one who performs *azan*.

Athbat: plural of *thabat*, one who is widely recognized as an authority in his own field.

'Atiyya: gift, present, grant, boon

'Awl: one sought during the time of need, a reliable helper.

Bada': starting point, the very beginning of something, the onset

Bara'ah: dissociation or renunciation

Baytul-Mal: Islamic government's state treasury.

Diwan: a collection of poems.

Faqih: jurist, one who is knowledgeable in Islamic jurisprudence.

Fatawa: plural of *fatwa*, a religious edict or decision.

Fiqh: the science of Islamic jurisprudence.

Firqa: group, party, sect

Furu': branches of the faith

Hadith: (singular) tradition, a statement made by Prophet Muhammad (s); its plural is: *ahadith*

Hajj: Islamic pilgrimage to Mecca during the prescribed period.

Ihram: pilgrimage garb, white unwoven cotten shroud worn by pilgrims.

Ijtihad: the degree one reaches in order to be qualified as a *mujtahid*, one who is capable of deriving religious decisions on his own.

Imam: leader of an *ummah*, a group of people (small or big); he may be the one who leads others in congregational prayers, or a supreme religious authority, or one of the Twelve Infallible Imams (as).

Isnad: the method whereby one *hadith* is traced and in the end attributed to a *muhaddith*, traditionist, one who transmitted it the first time.

Jahiliyya: pre-Islamic period of ignorance.

Janaba: uncleanness caused by seminal discharge.

Jihad: a struggle, an effort exerted, or a war waged in defence of Islam.

Jizya: a protection tax paid by non-Muslims living under Muslims' control in exchange for their exemption from the military service.

Kafir: infidel, apostate, atheist, one who does not believe in the existence of the Creator.

Kalam: the science of logic.

Kalima: synonymous to "shahada," it is a Muslim's declaration of faith (that is, to testify that there is no god except Allah, and that Muhammad (s) is the Messenger of Allah), and it is always pronounced in Arabic.

Khiraj: the combination of all religious taxes collected at the end of the Islamic lunar year.

Khums: one-fifth of one's savings (usually paid by Shi'a Muslims) set aside from annual income.

Khutba: lecture, sermon; a speech delivered on a specific occasion.

Kufr: apostasy, infidelity, disbelief

Kunyat: usually applied for a parent, it is the way of calling him or her by the name of his or her oldest son (such as saying "father of so-and-so" or "mother of so-and-so"), or it may be applied out of respect, a tradition usually followed in Arab countries, and it is applied as a prefix to one's name.

Maqam: standing place, a place where one usually stands to preach or address the public.

Mawla: depending on its usage, it may mean either "master" or "slave," or it may mean one who is most fit for a specific position of honour and prestige. Derived from the adjective *awla* (one who is best qualified), it means: the person who is best suited to be the religious and temporal leader of all Muslims.

Mu'min: believer, one who has *iman*, conviction, true belief

Mujtahid: one who acquires the degree of *ijtihad* and thus becomes capable of deriving religious decisions on his own.

Musnad: a compilation of traditions (*ahadith*) which are consecutively and chronologically traced to their transmitters.

Mut'a: temporary marriage

Mutawatir: consecutively reported, traced by a perfect chronological chain of ascertained narrators of *hadith*.

Najasa: uncleanness, impurity

Najwa: a silent supplication

Nuthur: plural of *nathr*, one's pledge to do something very good to show appreciation for the Almighty's favourable response to his supplication and the attainment of his worldly wish.

Qayyim: person in charge of something, one charged with authority.

Qibla: direction towards the Ka'ba, Mecca.

Sadaqa: (singular) charity offered voluntarily; its plural is: *sadaqat*

Sahabah: (singular) companions of the Holy Prophet Muhammad (s); its plural is: *sahabi*

Shari'a: Islam's legislative system.

Shubha: (singular) doubt, suspicion; its plural is: *shubuhat*

Shura: the principle of mutual consultation, Islam's form of democracy.

Siqaya: the act of providing water to the thirsty free of charge.

Sunan: plural of *sunnah*: a highly commended act of worship or way whereby a Muslim seeks nearness to Allah.

Tabi'i: (singular) one who accompanied for a good period of time and learned from a *sahabi*, a companion of the Holy Prophet Muhammad (s); its plural is: *tabi'in*

Tafsir: (singular) exegesis or explanation of Qur'anic verses; its plural is: *tafasir*

Tahara: purification, the act of removing *najasa*, uncleanness or impurity.

Takbir: the act of glorifying Allah by declaring in an audible voice: "Allaho Akbar!" Allah is Great!

Taqiyya: one's way of exerting precaution in order to save his life when it is in jeopardy, Shi'as' way of trying to survive against the presence of sure perils.

Taqlid: the concept of following a *mujtahid* or an authority recognized as the *a'alam*, the most knowledgeable in Islamics.

Tashahhud: the testimony regarding Allah being the Lord and Muhammad (s) being His Servant and Messenger; it is the uttering of "Ashhadu an la ilaha illa-Allah, wa ashhadu anna Muhammad abdohu wa rasooloh."

Tawatur: consecutive reporting, the tracing of one particular *hadith* to its respective chronological chain of narrators.

Tawhid: the concept of the absolute Unity of God, the belief that God is One and indivisible, One – and Only One – God.

Tawwabin: the penitent ones, those who repented their reluctance to go to the rescue of Imam Husain (as) when he was confronted with Yazid's armies and who enlisted under the military command of al-Mukhtar and pursued those who massacred Imam Hussain ibn Ali ibn Abu Talib (as) and killed them.

Thiqat: plural of *thiqah*, a trustworthy authority.

'Ulama: plural of *'alim*, scholar-theologian.

Usul: the basics of jurisprudence.

Waqf: a piece of property dedicated for the promotion of any particular good cause.

Wilayat: supreme authority that combines both temporal and religious authority.

Zakat: Literally, it means "purification;" it is a compulsory 2.5% tax on one of three categories of wealth: 1) metal coins (gold, silver, etc.), 2) grain crops (barley, wheat, grain, rice, etc.), and 3) animals raised for food consumption. *Zakat* is somehow a complicated issue, and for details, readers are advised to consult books dealing with *fiqh*. Among its types are: *zakat al-mal* (taxable wealth accumulated during one full year), and *zakat al-fitr* (a tax to be paid by the head of a household at the commencement of the fast of the month of Ramadan).

And surely Allah knows best...

Index

'Abbad ibn al-Abbas, 66
'Abdul Birr, 167
'Abdul-'Aziz ibn 'Umar ibn Aban, 127
'Abdul-'Aziz ibn Abu Salamah, 122, 154
'Abdul-'Aziz ibn Sayah, 77
'Abdul-Ghafir ibn Isma'il al-Farsi, 203
'Abdul-Hamid ibn Abul 'Ishrin, 135
'Abdul-Husayn Sharafuddin, I
'Abdullah al-Ansari, 125
'Abdullah al-Darmi, 110, 122
'Abdullah al-Hamidi, 138
'Abdullah ibn 'Abbas, 76, 96, 100, 273, 317, 417, 423
'Abdullah ibn 'Abdul-Rahman, 87, 389
'Abdullah ibn 'Amir, 127
'Abdullah ibn 'Ubaydullah, 126
'Abdullah ibn 'Umar, 98, 188, 273
'Abdullah ibn Aban, 118
'Abdullah ibn Abu Awfah, 112
'Abdullah ibn Abu Sufyan, 423
'Abdullah ibn Abu Talha, 128, 176
'Abdullah ibn Ahmad, 77, 103, 123, 150
'Abdullah ibn al-Hurr al-Farsi, 441
'Abdullah ibn al-Mubarak, 94, 103
'Abdullah ibn Badil ibn Warqa' al-Khuza'i, 424
'Abdullah ibn Buraydah, 99
'Abdullah ibn Dawud, 101
'Abdullah ibn Hammad ibn Sulayman, 413
'Abdullah ibn Hantab, 22
'Abdullah ibn Hasan, 111
'Abdullah ibn Hashim, 139
'Abdullah ibn Idris, 92
'Abdullah ibn Ja'far, 102, 277, 416

'Abdullah ibn Mas'ud, 63, 94, 100, 273, 348
'Abdullah ibn Maymun, 104
'Abdullah ibn Mu'it', 136
'Abdullah ibn Mubarak, 317
'Abdullah ibn Namir, 74, 81
'Abdullah ibn Sa'd, 139
'Abdullah ibn Sa'id, 451
'Abdullah ibn Shabramah, 95
'Abdullah ibn Shaddad, 102
'Abdullah ibn Yasar, 88
'Abdullah ibn Yazid, 112, 120
'Abdullah ibn Yazid al-Khadmi, 120
'Abdul-Malik al-Mas'udi, 74
'Abdul-Malik ibn 'Ayan, 108, 109
'Abdul-Malik ibn 'Umayr, 95
'Abdul-Malik ibn Abjar, 100
'Abdul-Malik ibn Abu Ghaniya, 79
'Abdul-Malik ibn Abu Sulayman, 87
'Abdul-Rahman al-Hamadani, 101
'Abdul-Rahman ibn 'Awf, 182, 183
'Abdul-Rahman ibn Abu Hatim, 117
'Abdul-Rahman ibn Abu Layla, 78, 138, 139
'Abdul-Rahman ibn Abu Sa'id al-Khudri, 133
'Abdul-Rahman ibn Bishr, 139
'Abdul-Rahman ibn Ja'il, 425
'Abdul-Rahman ibn Mahdi, 127
'Abdul-Rahman ibn Muhammad, 102, 444
'Abdul-Rahman ibn Muhammad al-Azdi, 444
'Abdul-Rahman ibn Najran, 451
'Abdul-Rahman ibn Salih al-Azdi, 104
'Abdul-Rahman ibn Sulayman, 103
'Abdul-Rahman ibn Thu'ayb al-Aslami, 428

'Abdul-Rahman ibn Yazid, 63, 87, 115
'Abdul-Razzaq, 72, 105, 106, 107, 108, 110, 222, 304
'Abdul-Razzaq ibn Humam, 105
'Abdul-Salam ibn Harb, 94
'Abdul-Wahid ibn Ayman, 122
'Adi ibn Thabit, 88, 111, 122
'Aflah ibn Sa'id, 83
'Ali ibn 'Abis, 81
'Ali ibn al-Husain, 52
'Ali ibn al-Ja'd, 77, 115, 123
'Ali ibn al-Madini, 125, 136, 139
'Ali ibn al-Mubarak, 138
'Ali ibn al-Munthir, 117
'Ali ibn al-Nu'man, 451
'Ali ibn Badimah, 115
'Ali ibn Dawud, 79, 127
'Ali ibn Fadal, 451
'Ali ibn Ghurab, 116
'Ali ibn Hajar, 95, 137
'Ali ibn Hakim, 93, 95
'Ali ibn Harb, 393
'Ali ibn Hashim, 103, 118, 126, 134
'Ali ibn Ja'far al-Sadiq, 53
'Ali ibn Khashram, 91
'Ali ibn Mahziyar, 451
'Ali ibn Muhammad al-Khatib, 188
'Ali ibn Musa al-Rida, 129
'Ali ibn Mushir, 81
'Ali ibn Qadim, 117
'Ali ibn Salih, 77, 78, 87, 116
'Ali ibn Yaqtin, 451
'Ali ibn Yazid, 116
'Ali ibn Zaid, 115
'Alqamah, 62, 63, 114, 115
'Amara daughter of Hamzah, 102
'Amil,, II
'Amis al-Khayth'ami,, 102
'Ammar al-Thihni,, 95
'Ammar ibn Musa al-Sabati,, 451
'Ammar ibn Yasir, 31, 229, 282, 343, 419
'Ammar ibn Zurayq, 119
'Ammarah ibn al-Qa'qa', 95
'Amr ibn 'Abdullah, 119
'Amr ibn 'Awf, 136
'Amr ibn al-'Aas, 139
'Amr ibn al-Salim, 85

'Amr ibn Bahr, 150
'Amr ibn Dinar, 100, 128
'Amr ibn Jahsh, 206
'Amr ibn Malik, 133
'Amr ibn Maymun, 120, 191
'Amr ibn Murrah, 84, 89
'Amr ibn Dharr, 69
'Amr ibn Wa'ilah, 99
'Aqaba, 352
'Arrak ibn Malik, 78
'Asakir, 31, 49, 56, 178, 182, 184, 227, 228, 231
'Ashkelon, 378
'Asim al-Ahwal, 65, 77
'Askar, 337
'Ata' ibn Abu Rabah, 78, 87
'Ata' ibn Yasar, 317
'Ata' ibn Yasin, 76
'Atban ibn Malik, 182
'Atiyyah al-'Awfi, 112, 113
'Umar, 46, 47, 62, 63, 68, 69, 72, 73, 76, 78, 84, 85, 89, 91, 94, 96, 98, 99, 100, 102, 103, 104, 107, 113, 117, 136, 138, 154, 161, 166, 167, 170, 177, 182, 183, 185, 186, 187, 188, 189, 193, 210, 228, 242, 255, 269, 277, 293, 297, 298, 303, 304, 305, 306, 307, 325, 329, 331, 332, 342, 343, 352, 358, 362, 363, 364, 369, 371, 372, 373, 374, 375, 378, 380, 381, 386, 389, 391, 392, 394, 396, 398, 415, 416, 417, 418, 419, 424, 426, 438, 443
'Umran ibn Hasin, 74, 99, 133, 191, 283
'Umran ibn Hattan, 24, 444
'Umran ibn Maysarah, 127
'Urwah, 95, 101, 110, 117, 118, 125, 139, 329, 352
'Utbah, 50, 362, 364
'Utbah ibn Mas'ud, 362, 364
'Utbah ibn Rabi'ah, 50
'Uthman, 68, 70, 72, 77, 83, 85, 89, 90, 95, 97, 100, 101, 103, 104, 111, 115, 117, 120, 121, 137, 138, 182, 185, 255, 316, 324, 331, 336, 408, 419, 425, 430, 443
'Uthman ibn 'Umayr, 111
'Uthman ibn Abu Hamid, 111

459

'Uthman ibn Jabalah, 95
'Uthman ibn Qays, 111
Uyun al-Akhbar, 150
A Treatise on Islam, 150
Aaron, 162, 163, 166, 169, 170, 176, 177, 178, 179, 180, 181, 186, 188, 189, 203, 270, 305, 308, 313, 318, 402, 409, 418, 432
Aban ibn 'Uthman, 443
Aban ibn Taghlib, 39, 62, 79, 90, 140, 443
Abbad al-Ahwazi, 101
Abbad ibn al-Abbas, 65
Abbad ibn Ya'qub, 74, 94, 100
Abbas al-Duri, 104
Abbas ibn 'Abdul-'Azim, 105
Abbas ibn 'AbdulMuttalib, 317
Abd al-Hakam, 70
Abd al-Qays, 96
Abd ibn Hamid, 81, 110, 122
Abdah ibn Sulayman, 103
Abdoh, 12, 13, 14, 410
Abdul-Ghani, 35, 182
Abdullah ibn al-Hasan, 53, 113, 413, 440
Abdullah ibn Lahi'ah, 103
Abdullah ibn Salam, 41
Abdul-Razzaq, 72, 105, 106, 107, 108, 110, 223
Abraham, 40, 48, 195
Abu 'Abdullah Ahmad ibn Hanbal, 231
Abu 'Abdullah al-Qarashi, 222
Abu 'Abdullah al-Sadiq, 43, 56, 127
Abu 'Abdul-Rahman, 82, 122, 126, 332
Abu 'Ali al-Tibrisi, 45
Abu 'Arwah al-Dawsi, 419
Abu 'Awanah, 67, 70, 79, 92, 191, 303
Abu 'Ayyash, 279
Abu 'Ubaydah, 31, 63, 177, 341, 378, 380, 389
Abu 'Ubaydah ibn al-Jarrah, 177, 389
Abu Ahmad al-Fardi, 332
Abu Ayyub al-Ansari, 228
Abu Bakr, 36, 39, 46, 48, 49, 66, 67, 68, 72, 76, 85, 94, 103, 104, 105, 110, 123, 125, 132, 139, 170, 177, 182, 189, 193, 210, 219, 220, 224, 228, 269, 297, 298, 331, 332, 338, 341, 342, 343, 344, 345, 347, 351, 352, 362, 378, 380, 381, 385, 386, 387, 389, 391, 392, 393, 396, 413, 417, 418, 419
Abu Bakr ibn Mardawayh, 49
Abu Balj Yahya ibn Salim al-Fizari, 191
Abu Barzah al-Aslami, 217
Abu Basir al-Asghar, 445
Abu Dawud, 62, 63, 68, 70, 71, 74, 80, 81, 84, 87, 89, 92, 101, 102, 104, 110, 111, 113, 116, 117, 118, 119, 127, 129, 132, 133, 134, 140, 191, 297, 303
Abu Fakhita, 69
Abu Hamzah al-Thumali ibn Dinar, 444
Abu Hurayrah, 43, 98, 107, 246, 255, 273, 299, 307, 397
Abu ibn Ka'b, 343
Abu Ishaq al-Subay'i, 88, 220
Abu Ishaq al-Tha'labi, 150, 188, 246, 256
Abu Ja'far al-Baqir, 442
Abu Ja'far al-Iskafi, 153
Abu Khirash al-Hathli, 397
Abu Lahab, 33, 149, 243
Abu Mikhnaf, 352, 428
Abu Na'im, 30, 31, 42, 43, 44, 49, 53, 69, 77, 110, 114, 121, 122, 123, 132, 149, 151, 185, 216, 217, 227, 228, 230, 251, 296, 329, 332, 445
Abu Rafi', 43, 126, 188, 229, 246, 440
Abu Sa'd, 107, 122, 127, 138, 167, 391
Abu Sa'id, 21, 25, 43, 66, 113, 133, 138, 167, 188, 210, 228, 230, 238, 246, 273, 303, 443
Abu Sa'id al-Khudri, Abul-Darda', 273
Abu Salamah, 124, 175, 277
Abu Shaybah, 21, 68, 70, 81, 83, 93, 110, 122, 125, 127, 137, 138, 139, 154, 185, 192, 293, 303, 331, 338
Abu Sufyan, 107, 137, 206, 429
Abu Tammam al-Ta'i, 432
Abu Dharr al-Ghifari, 343
Abul-'Abbas al-Sarraj, 103

Abul-Aswad al-Du'ali, 98, 429
Abul-Darda'ah, 115
Abul-Fadl al-'Ami, 451
Abul-Faraj al-Asfahani, 317
Abul-Fath al-Shahristani, 446
Abul-Fida, 150
Abul-Hasan al-Kazim, 79
Abul-Hasan al-Rida, 451
Abul-Haytham ibn al-Tihan, 419, 423
Abul-Mu'ayyad, 50
Abul-Qasim, 65, 433, 445
Abul-Tayyib, 433
Ahl al-Bayt, 15, 16, 17, 26, 32, 34, 38, 41, 43, 44, 45, 81, 88, 93, 94, 98, 120, 123, 132, 143, 144, 145, 146, 147, 155, 162, 165, 168, 201, 238, 239, 248, 254, 286, 344, 366, 400, 402, 410, 412, 416, 422, 433, 435, 436, 437, 440, 441, 442, 444, 446, 448, 450
Ahmad al-'Ajli, 112, 115
Ahmad al-Nisa'i, 112
Ahmad al-Wak'i, 127
Ahmad ibn 'Abdah, 139
Ahmad ibn 'Abdul-'Aziz al-Jawhari, 342, 362, 413
Ahmad ibn 'Abdullah ibn Mahran, 451
Ahmad ibn 'Ali Khaythamah, 110
Ahmad ibn 'Umar, 75
Ahmad ibn 'Umar al-Muhammasani, 75, 91
Ahmad ibn 'Uthman al-'Awdi, 81
Ahmad ibn Abu Khayth'amah, 106
Ahmad ibn Abu Sarij, 110
Ahmad ibn Abu Tahir, 413, 417, 422, 431
Ahmad ibn al-Azhar, 106
Ahmad ibn al-Furat, 117
Ahmad ibn al-Hajjaj, 317
Ahmad ibn Hanbal, 30, 62, 89, 107, 108, 111, 112, 115, 116, 118, 132, 136, 137, 139, 168, 178, 186, 192, 210, 218, 226, 240, 250, 293, 295, 304, 337, 391, 439, 441
Ahmad ibn Ibrahim al-Nishapuri, 203
Ahmad ibn Mani', 137
Ahmad ibn Muhammad ibn 'isa, 451

Ahmad ibn Muhammad ibn Abu Nasr, 451
Ahmad ibn Muhammad ibn Khalid al-Barqi, 451
Ahmad ibn Muhammad ibn Sa'id ibn Aqdah, 255
Ahmad ibn Rashid, 86
Ahmad ibn Sinan, 125
Ahmad ibn Siyar, 389
Ahmad ibn Yahya al-Halwani, 222
Ahmad ibn Yunus, 77
al 'Alawiyyah, 151
Al Fusul Al Muhimmah, VI
al'Askari, 276
al-'Abbas, 46, 51, 105, 107, 149, 186, 189, 304
al-'Allaf, 449, 450
Al-'Aqili, 132, 133
al-'Ayyashi, 40, 451
Al-'Iqd al-Farid, 150, 393
al-A'mash, 43, 79, 82, 84, 89, 90, 91, 92, 95, 101, 107, 110, 111, 112, 117, 119, 120, 122, 125, 130, 138, 154, 439, 443
al-Amawi, 42, 344
al-Amidi, 165, 168, 169
al-Ansari, 112, 139, 175, 188, 218, 255, 256, 316, 343, 389, 419, 422, 424, 426, 427
Al-Arba'in, 22, 25, 33, 225
Al-Arba'in al-Nawawiyya, 225
Al-Asalib Al-Badi'ah fi Rujhan Ma'atim Al-Shi'a, X
al-Asbagh ibn Nabatah, 86, 141, 275, 277, 441
al-Ash'ari, 5, 7
Al-Ash'ath ibn Qays al-Kindi, 427
al-Azhar, V
al-Balathiri, 342
al-Baqir, 39, 41, 42, 43, 45, 53, 55, 69, 80, 108, 129, 210, 229, 286, 422, 444
al-Bara' ibn 'Azib, 112, 120, 182, 187, 188, 241, 269, 343
al-Barqi, 44, 451
al-Bayhaqi, 149, 151, 217, 226, 228
al-Dahlani, 379, 381, 386
al-Daylami, 218, 224, 225, 227, 229, 234, 238, 303, 304

461

Al-Fadl ibn al-'Abbas, 430
al-Fadl ibn Shathan, 451
al-Faruq, 369
Al-Fatawa al-Hamidiyya, 255
Al-Fawa'id, X, 246
Al-Fawa'id wal Fara'id, X
Al-Ghayba, 441
al-Ghifari, 98, 180, 188, 203, 229, 277, 349, 419, 440
al-Hafiz, 296
al-Hafiz Abu Na'im, 39, 246
al-Hafiz ibn Hajar, 154
al-Hafiz Ibrahim, 352
al-Hafiz Muhammad ibn Musa al-Shirazi, 393
al-Hafiz Salahud-Din al-'Ala'i, 218
al-Hakim, 21, 22, 25, 31, 33, 52, 53, 107, 125, 162, 177, 183, 185, 192, 193, 195, 199, 210, 215, 218, 219, 221, 222, 223, 225, 227, 228, 233, 239, 292, 303, 305, 306, 307, 325, 331, 421
Al-Halabi, 44
al-Hamawani al-Shafi'i, 43
al-Hamidi, 332, 352
al-Harish al-Bariqi, 422
al-Harith ibn Hasirah, 73, 74, 229
Al-Hasan ibn 'Ali, 79
al-Hasan ibn Alwan, 413
al-Hasan ibn Badr, 177
al-Hasan ibn Mahbub, 451
al-Hasan ibn Muhammad, 451
al-Hasan ibn Muhammad ibn Sam'ah, 451
al-Husayn, 113, 275, 276, 277, 435, 451
al-Husayn ibn 'Ali, 71, 92, 276, 283
Al-Husayn ibn 'Ali al-Ju'fi, 85
al-Husayn ibn 'Ali al-Sukuni, 92
Ali ibn Abu Talib, 30, 31, 43, 49, 51, 52, 65, 93, 145, 147, 167, 182, 184, 186, 188, 191, 192, 219, 224, 227, 231, 238, 246, 273, 274, 275, 276, 279, 281, 288, 295, 304, 317, 322, 382, 422, 440, 459
Ali ibn al-Husayn, 53, 78, 274, 329, 332, 442, 445
Ali ibn Ja'far, 48, 71
'Ali ibn Zayd ibn Jath'an, 107

Al-Ihtijaj, 413
Al-Imama wal Siyasa, 345
Al-Isabah, 96, 97, 113, 192, 229, 313, 325, 441
al-Iskafi, 85, 150, 153, 429
Al-Istibsar, 447
Al-Jami' al-Kabir, 31
Al-Jami' al-Saghir, 218
Al-Jami' Bayna Rijalul Sahihain, 107, 109, 115, 116
Al-Jihad wal Siyar, 363
Al-Juhfa, 22
Al-Kafi, 447
al-Kalbi, 47
Al-Kamil, 105, 109, 149, 217, 337, 352, 358
Al-Kashshaf, 34
al-Kazim, 48, 53, 56, 128, 444, 448, 450
Al-Khasa'is, 194
Al-Khatib, 118, 202
al-Kumait ibn Ziyad, 431
Al-Ma'rifa, 178, 185
al-Majlisi, 413
al-Malla, 32, 64, 86, 121
Al-Maqasid, 166
al-Mahdi, 26
Al-Milal wal Nihal, 76, 84, 120, 134, 140, 382, 386, 446
al-Miqdad, 47, 277
al-Mirza Muhammad, 443
Al-Mu'tabar, 450
Al-Mujma' al-Kabir, 29
Al-Mukhtara, 151
Al-Muntakhab, 179, 183, 184, 185, 187, 296, 299
Al-Musnad, 21
Al-Mustadrak, 21, 22, 25, 31, 44, 52, 53, 107, 161, 165, 166, 167, 181, 182, 183, 185, 186, 187, 192, 193, 195, 210, 215, 221, 222, 223, 225, 227, 228, 231, 233, 239, 292, 293, 299, 303, 305, 306, 307, 325, 331
Al-Muttafaq wal-Muftaraq, 184, 226
al-Muttaqi al-Hindi, 178, 179, 183, 185, 187, 192, 194, 196, 218, 393
al-Muwaffaq, 49
al-Nabhani, 32, 33, 36
al-Najaf al-Ashraf, II

al-Nishapuri, 44, 125, 232
al-Nu'man al-Fahri, 256
Al-Nu'man ibn 'Ajlan, 429
Al-Nusus 'ala al-A'Imma, 282
Al-Nusus Al-Jaliyyah, IX
al-Qawariri, 135
al-Qawshaji, 41, 202
al-Qaysarani, 64, 104, 107, 109, 116
al-Rabi' ibn Sabih, 438
al-Ramadi, 105
al-Razi, 54, 73, 86, 226, 234, 295, 306
al-Rida, 46, 53, 56, 444, 450
al-Sa'luki, 125
al-Sabban, 32
al-Sadi, 41, 77, 393
al-Sadiq, 39, 41, 42, 46, 53, 69, 79, 80, 104, 108, 109, 128, 129, 210, 226, 421, 437, 443, 444, 445, 446, 447, 448, 449, 451
Al-Saduq, 274, 275, 276, 277, 278, 279, 280, 281, 282, 283
al-Saffar, 440
al-Sahib ibn 'Abbad. Al-Dhahabi, 65
Al-Saqifa, 342, 352, 389, 413
Al-Sawa'iq al-Muhriqa, 15, 16, 17, 23, 24, 26, 27, 31, 32, 35, 36, 39, 42, 44, 45, 46, 47, 48, 49, 50, 54, 55, 56, 165, 166, 167, 182, 183, 185, 186, 187, 195, 219, 225, 227, 231, 232, 234, 237, 238, 239, 267, 269, 297, 305, 307, 418, 439
Al-Sayyuti, 167, 255
al-Sha'bi, 51, 75, 78, 83, 86, 87, 97, 115, 422, 445
al-Shafi'i, 36, 39, 45, 48, 70, 246
al-Shahristani, 84, 87, 90, 95, 98, 352, 389, 449
Al-Sharaf al-Mu'abbad, 32, 36
Al-Shifa, 33
Al-Sira al-Dahlaniyya, 177, 378
Al-Sira al-Halabiyya, 44, 150, 177, 257, 378
Al-Sirah al-Nabawiyya, 248
Al-Siyasa, 150
Al-Sulaymani, 119
Al-Tabarani, 126
al-Tabari, 94, 149, 255, 292, 295, 306, 342, 352, 378, 381

Al-Tafsir al-Kabir, 34, 39, 40, 41, 42, 44, 48, 55, 149, 184, 188, 203, 215, 226, 246, 256, 332
Al-Tafsir Al-Kabir, 179
al-Taqi, 444
Al-Tarikh al-Kamil, 416, 430
Al-Dhahabi, 62, 63, 68, 69
Al-Thari'a, IX
Al-Thikra, 448
al-Tibrisi, 47, 207, 418, 445
al-Tirmizi, 63, 64, 65, 68, 69, 70, 71, 85, 86, 87, 89, 101, 104, 111, 113, 117, 128, 167, 187, 192, 218, 220, 239, 255, 313
al-Wahidi, 43, 51, 53, 202, 238
Al-Wajiza, 91
al-Walid ibn 'Uqbah, 51, 243
al-Walid ibn Harb, 87
al-Walid ibn Jami', 100
al-Walid ibn Muslim, 117, 135
al-Walid ibn Muslim., 117
Al-Wilayat, 255
Al-Yawaqit, 226
al-Zahra', 113, 183, 305, 412, 413, 415
al-Zamakhshari, 207, 306
al-Zubayr, 101, 129, 140, 154, 185, 316, 342, 343, 389, 426, 427, 430
al-Zubayr ibn Bakkar, 429, 430
al-Zuhri,, 98, 106, 222, 317
Amali, 49, 278, 279, 280, 281, 282
Amr ibn Qays, 79
Amr ibn Yathribi, 97
Anas ibn Malik, 42, 48, 67, 84, 89, 116, 133, 175, 182, 217, 250, 273, 392, 443
and Muhammad ibn Talhah, 83
Ansar, 177, 179, 235, 256, 276, 280, 281, 304, 316, 343, 345, 347, 351, 352, 377, 381, 389, 426, 429, 430
Aqil ibn Khalid, 87
Arqam, 22, 89, 150, 240, 241
Asbab al-Nuzul, 43, 51, 202
Asbat ibn Nasir, 63
'Ash'ath al-Hadani, 116
Asid ibn Hadr, 390
Asiya daughter of Muzahim, 312
Asma', 102, 154, 167, 188, 325
Asma' bint Qays, 167
Aswad ibn 'Amir, 153

A'thar Thawat al-Siwar, 430
athbat, 233
Atiyyah ibn al-Ash'ath, 112
Atiyyah ibn Sa'd, 112
Awf ibn Abu Jamila al-Basri, 121
Awn ibn Abu Jahufah, 42
Awsat, 25, 32, 34, 184, 226, 364
Ayesha, 48, 73, 98, 102, 115, 154, 227, 301, 306, 311, 312, 315, 316, 317, 318, 319, 325, 329, 332, 333, 335, 336, 337, 338, 339, 344, 424, 425
Ayesha daughters of Abu Bakr, 154
Bada', VI, 455
Badi'a, IX
Badr, 47, 50, 185, 249, 250, 251, 252, 352, 382, 397, 407, 423, 430
Baghdad, II, XII, 65, 113, 129, 137, 222, 253
Bahrain, 98
Bajir ibn Raysan, 98
Bakir ibn al-Ashaj, 87
Balaghat al-Nisa, 413, 422, 431
Balqa, 378
Bani Sa'idah, 343
Banu Umayyah, 85
Baqiriyya, 447
Bara', 112, 120, 182, 187, 188, 234, 241, 269, 343
Bard ibn Mu'awiyah al, 445
Basrah, 80, 99, 101, 116, 141
Battle of Siffin, 97, 427, 428, 441, 444
Battle of the Camel, 96, 210, 337, 423, 424, 425, 426, 427
Bayan ibn 'Amr, 139
Bayan ibn Bishr, 71
baytul-mal, 440
Bihar Al-Anwar, 91
Bishr ibn Marwan, 119
Bisr ibn Arta'ah, 141
Bughyatul Fa'iz fi Naql, X
Bughyatul Sa'il 'an Lathm Al-Aydi wal Anamil, X
Bukhari, X, 25, 30, 50, 54, 58, 63, 64, 70, 76, 78, 79, 81, 83, 84, 86, 87, 88, 92, 95, 98, 99, 100, 101, 102, 104, 109, 110, 112, 115, 118, 121, 122, 123, 124, 125, 127, 129, 131, 132, 133, 135, 136, 138, 139, 153, 154, 155, 165, 167, 219, 247, 292, 301, 302, 305, 307, 312, 316, 317, 319, 320, 321, 325, 331, 336, 338, 342, 344, 361, 362, 363, 364, 431, 439, 444
Burayd, 39, 48, 445
Buraydah, 41, 93, 188, 192, 193, 194, 198, 222, 256, 292, 295, 307, 379, 419, 421, 422, 431
Caesar, 404
Christian, 48
Commander of the Faithful, 12, 13, 17, 35, 42, 43, 45, 49, 51, 53, 74, 88, 93, 97, 98, 99, 102, 112, 114, 138, 143, 145, 155, 166, 207, 208, 209, 248, 249, 250, 253, 273, 275, 278, 279, 288, 298, 316, 325, 330, 350, 351, 382, 421, 422, 424, 428, 431, 435, 436, 438, 439, 440, 441
Dala'il, 149, 151
Damascus, IV, XI, 135
Dar Qutni, 46, 80, 85, 100, 104, 111, 116, 126, 134, 185, 191, 219, 229, 269, 418
Dawud ibn Abu, 81
Dawud ibn Rashid, 137
diwan, 166, 254, 432, 433
Diya' al-Maqdisi, 150, 292
Du'bal ibn Ali al-Khuza'i, 433
Dujail Battle, 102
Durrat al-Ghawwas, 93
Egypt, V, XI, XII, XVI, 103, 180, 218, 257, 405
Eizah al-Ishkal, 35
Ezekiel, 49
Fadil ibn Ghazwan, 83
Fadil ibn Marzuq, 122
Fadl ibn Marzuq, 122
Fakhrul-Din al-Razi, 184
faqih, 43, 49, 62, 102, 176, 188, 231, 273
Farwah ibn 'Amr, 343
Fath Al-Barari, 154
Fatima, 7, 45, 47, 48, 107, 162, 178, 183, 186, 207, 225, 276, 296, 297, 298, 299, 305, 307, 312, 320, 324, 331, 339, 401, 413, 422, 439
Fatima bint al-Husayn, 413
Fiqh, VIII, 59, 455

firqa, 393
Fitr ibn Khalifah, 123
Fudayl ibn Ghazwan, 112, 126
Furat al-Qazzaz, 100
furu, 144
Gabriel, 38, 184, 204, 217, 220, 248, 274, 281, 335, 338, 412
Ghadir Khumm, 21, 23, 43, 237, 238, 239, 240, 242, 246, 253, 408, 409
Ghanima daughter, 430
Ghayat al-Maram, 42, 43, 45, 48, 50, 56, 202, 255, 279
Greater, 13, 316
Habib al-Najjar, 49, 227
Habis ibn Janadah, 167
hadith, IX, 20, 21, 22, 24, 25, 30, 31, 32, 33, 35, 46, 48, 49, 50, 52, 53, 55, 58, 59, 62, 63, 64, 67, 68, 69, 70, 71, 72, 73, 74, 75, 76, 77, 78, 80, 81, 82, 83, 84, 85, 86, 87, 88, 89, 90, 91, 92, 93, 94, 95, 96, 97, 98, 99, 100, 101, 102, 104, 105, 106, 107, 108, 109, 110, 111, 112, 113, 114, 115, 116, 117, 118, 119, 120, 121, 122, 123, 124, 125, 126, 127, 128, 129, 130, 131, 132, 133, 134, 135, 136, 137, 138, 139, 140, 141, 149, 150, 151, 153, 154, 155, 157, 158, 161, 163, 165, 166, 167, 168, 169, 170, 171, 172, 175, 176, 177, 178, 179, 180, 181, 182, 186, 187, 188, 191, 192, 193, 194, 195, 196, 198, 199, 202, 210, 213, 215, 216, 217, 218, 219, 220, 221, 222, 223, 224, 225, 226, 228, 229, 230, 231, 234, 237, 239, 240, 241, 245, 248, 249, 250, 251, 252, 254, 255, 256, 257, 259, 263, 264, 265, 267, 268, 270, 273, 274, 275, 276, 277, 278, 279, 280, 281, 282, 285, 287, 288, 291, 292, 293, 295, 296, 298, 299, 301, 303, 304, 305, 306, 307, 309, 311, 312, 313, 315, 317, 319, 321, 323, 324, 325, 326, 328, 329, 330, 331, 332, 333, 335, 336, 337, 338, 342, 343, 344, 348, 349, 352, 355, 361, 362, 364, 365, 366, 376, 383, 386, 388, 389, 402, 408, 438, 440, 441, 448, 452, 456, 458, 459

Hajar ibn 'Adi, 426
Hajjaj ibn al-Sha'ir, 110, 122
Hamadan, 426
Hamid ibn 'Abdul-Rahman, 77
Hammad ibn Selamah, 87
Hamran, 80, 108, 109
Hamzah, 46, 47, 50, 68, 79, 80, 127, 135, 149, 176, 429, 444, 445
Hamzah al- Zayyat, 79
Harithah, 120, 183, 377, 378, 389, 424
Harun ibn 'Abdullah, 124, 154
Harun ibn Sa'd, 77, 133, 134
Hasan, II, 16, 34, 45, 48, 51, 56, 69, 77, 78, 79, 83, 88, 91, 98, 99, 110, 112, 113, 115, 116, 117, 118, 120, 121, 124, 126, 127, 133, 135, 136, 137, 138, 162, 177, 181, 293, 307, 401, 412, 413, 418, 421, 426, 430, 435, 438, 444, 450, 451
Hasan al-Hulwani, 83
Hashim al-'Arabi, 150
Hashim ibn al-Barid, 118, 134
Hashim ibn Bashir, 136
Hatib ibn Balta'ah, 397
Heroes and Hero Worship, 150
Hijaz, 141, 250, 447
Hilyat al-Awliya', 30, 216, 217, 228, 230, 329, 332
Hubayrah ibn Maryam, 134
Hudaybiya, 30, 194, 339, 397
huffaz, 53, 125
Humam ibn Nafi' al-Himyari, 105
Humam ibn Yahya, 122
Husayn, 5, X, XII, 16, 45, 47, 48, 71, 83, 85, 88, 92, 98, 103, 112, 113, 120, 126, 139, 141, 162, 181, 275, 277, 283, 307, 324, 401, 413, 418, 433, 435, 450, 451
Husham ibn al-Hakam, 448, 449, 450
Huzayfah ibn 'Asid, 180
Ibn al-hanafiyyah, 53
Isti'ab, 88, 96, 97, 99, 167, 177, 181, 185, 191, 196, 222, 303, 312, 313, 325, 429
Izekiel, 227
Ja'dah ibn Salam, 398
Ja'fariyya, 447
Jabir al-Ju'fi, 70, 229

Jabir ibn 'Abdullah, 168, 179, 188, 218, 279, 329
Jabir ibn Yazid, 69, 422
Jalawla, 97
Jami' al Bazanti, 451
Jami' ibn 'Umayrah, 73
Jarir, 30, 34, 70, 72, 73, 85, 92, 149, 151, 153, 192, 194, 195, 218, 239, 255, 292, 295, 298, 316, 325, 337, 342, 352, 381, 393, 424
Jawad, II, 108, 444, 450
Jazira, 88
Jehmi, 448
Jesus, 226, 227
Ka'b, 54, 329
Ka'b al-Ahbar, 329
kafir, VI, 64, 92, 175, 336
kalima, 404
Kamil ibn Talha, 332
Kashshaf, 207
Kazimiyya, II, XIII, XIV
Khadija, 162, 311, 312
Khalid ibn Mukhlid, 80, 122
Khasa'is, 151, 185, 192, 195, 222, 239, 241, 292
Khashbi, 73, 123
Khazir Battle, 134
khiraj, 348
khums, 192, 194, 315, 336, 397
Khurasani, II
khutba, 15, 22, 180, 379, 409, 410, 413, 428
Khuzaymah ibn Thabit, 343, 419, 423, 428
Kisra, 404
Kufa, 47, 62, 80, 81, 82, 90, 95, 96, 98, 99, 102, 112, 113, 114, 115, 117, 120, 122, 124, 127, 130, 131, 282
Kulthum ibn Habib, 100
kunayat, 99, 124, 134, 139
Lebanon, III, VI
Lesser Camel Battle, 316
Lut, 47, 336
Ma'arif, 8, 63, 64, 70, 71, 74, 76, 77, 78, 83, 84, 87, 89, 90, 92, 95, 96, 98, 101, 103, 105, 109, 112, 115, 120, 121, 123, 126, 129, 131, 135, 136, 137, 138, 140

Ma'adh ibn Jabal, 100, 273
Ma'bid ibn Khalid, 102
Ma'dan ibn Abu Talha, 84
Ma'qil ibn Yasar, 299
Ma'ruf, 24, 100, 127, 129
Ma'ruf ibn Kharbuth, 129
Ma'adh ibn Muslim al-Harra, 141
Mafatih al-Ghayb, 234
Mahmud ibn Ghaylan, 110
Makhduj ibn Yazid, 182
Makrimah, 115
Malik al-Ashtar, 405, 441
Malik ibn al-Maghul, 79
Malik ibn al-Nadar, 175
Malik ibn Anas, 81
Malik ibn Isma'il, 124
Malik ibn Ja'na, 132
Man la Yahdaruhul Faqih, 447
Manaqib, 30, 48, 53, 178, 188, 218, 305
Manhaj al-Maqal, 443
Mansur ibn al-Mu'tamir, 130
Mansur ibn Hayyan, 100
Maqam, 33, 34, 457
Marwan, 88, 137, 444
Mary, 297, 299, 312, 325, 338, 339
Masruq, 75
Matar ibn Maymun, 110
mawali, 259, 439
Mawla, 335, 457
Mawti', 438
Maymuna, 102
Mecca, XII, 85, 98, 99, 100, 106, 130, 148, 177, 220, 247, 320, 408, 438, 455, 458
Medina, 23, 109, 128, 169, 171, 177, 179, 248, 263, 350, 357, 380, 390, 404, 439, 443, 447
Messenger of Allah, 2, 7, 8, 12, 15, 22, 23, 24, 25, 26, 29, 30, 31, 33, 34, 35, 41, 43, 45, 46, 47, 48, 49, 51, 52, 53, 55, 72, 73, 74, 101, 103, 106, 108, 120, 126, 145, 146, 148, 149, 158, 162, 163, 166, 176, 177, 178, 179, 181, 182, 184, 185, 186, 187, 188, 191, 192, 193, 195, 196, 198, 203, 206, 210, 211, 215, 219, 220, 222, 224, 225, 226, 228, 230, 231, 232, 237, 239, 240, 241, 242,

247, 249, 250, 251, 254, 256, 260,
263, 265, 269, 270, 273, 274, 275,
276, 277, 278, 279, 280, 281, 282,
283, 291, 292, 293, 295, 296, 297,
298, 299, 301, 303, 304, 306, 307,
311, 312, 317, 318, 319, 320, 321,
323, 324, 325, 328, 329, 330, 331,
332, 336, 337, 338, 344, 345, 348,
350, 351, 356, 358, 359, 362, 363,
364, 365, 366, 372, 373, 375, 378,
381, 385, 386, 387, 388, 389, 391,
392, 400, 402, 403, 407, 408, 410,
411, 412, 416, 417, 418, 419, 421,
422, 423, 431, 432, 433, 440, 441,
442, 450, 456
Michael, 184
Minhajul Maqal fi Tahqiqi Ahwalir Rijal, 442
Minhal, 76, 97, 131, 154
Mis'ab ibn 'Abdullah, 94
Misar, 76, 79, 122
Mis'ar, 112, 113
Mishkadanah, 102
Mizan, 30, 62, 63, 64, 65, 67, 68, 69,
70, 71, 72, 73, 74, 75, 76, 77, 80,
81, 82, 83, 84, 85, 86, 87, 89, 90,
92, 93, 94, 97, 101, 103, 104, 105,
106, 107, 108, 109, 110, 111, 112,
113, 114, 115, 116, 117, 118, 119,
120, 121, 122, 123, 124, 125, 126,
127, 128, 129, 130, 132, 133, 135,
136, 137, 138, 139, 140, 191, 295,
422
Mizan al-I'tidal, 67, 295
Moses, 49, 99, 162, 163, 166, 169,
170, 176, 177, 178, 179, 180, 185,
187, 188, 203, 226, 227, 270, 305,
308, 313, 409, 418, 432
Mu'ammar, 63, 72, 105, 106, 107,
115, 118, 222, 317, 319, 438
Mu'ammar ibn Rashid, 438
Mu'awiyah, 34, 83, 86, 87, 94, 97, 99,
101, 107, 114, 119, 124, 128, 136,
137, 141, 166, 167, 231, 252, 378,
422, 423, 428, 430, 445
Mu'awiyah ibn 'Ammar, 128
Mu'awiyah ibn Abu Sufyan, 167
Mu'awiyah ibn al-Suwayd, 87
Mu'awiyah ibn Salih, 83

Mu'jam, 126, 182
Mu'tamir, 89, 129, 130, 132
Mu'tazilite, 30, 151, 192, 217, 324,
337, 390, 407, 416, 417, 429
Mughirah, 70, 81, 90, 97, 120, 126,
423
Muhajirun, 177, 179, 235, 276, 281,
304, 347, 359
Muhammad, II, XII, XIX, 6, 7, 12, 13,
14, 16, 24, 31, 33, 38, 39, 41, 45,
46, 49, 51, 53, 54, 55, 59, 69, 72,
74, 75, 76, 77, 78, 79, 80, 81, 83,
84, 85, 91, 92, 95, 96, 102, 103,
104, 105, 106, 110, 112, 113, 114,
118, 119, 120, 121, 122, 124, 125,
126, 127, 128, 130, 131, 132, 133,
136, 138, 139, 140, 145, 150, 154,
184, 188, 191, 226, 227, 229, 238,
243, 246, 247, 255, 256, 261, 273,
274, 282, 293, 295, 312, 321, 329,
332, 344, 345, 351, 357, 386, 393,
404, 405, 410, 411, 413, 415, 421,
424, 428, 429, 430, 431, 432, 433,
436, 441, 442, 445, 449, 451, 454,
455, 456, 458, 459
Muhammad 'Abdoh, 345
Muhammad Ahmad al-Dhahabi, 93
Muhammad al-Baqir, 69
Muhammad al-Muqaddimi, 139
Muhammad ibn 'Abdullah al-Dabi, 125
Muhammad ibn 'Abdul-Rahman, 413
Muhammad ibn 'Ubayd ibn Hasab, 72
Muhammad ibn 'Ubaydullah, 126, 229
Muhammad ibn 'Umayr, 31, 451
Muhammad ibn 'Uthman, 81
Muhammad ibn Abu Bakr, 72, 105
Muhammad ibn Abu Hafs, 133
Muhammad ibn Abu Ja'far, 102
Muhammad ibn Ahmad, 255
Muhammad ibn al-Faraj, 83
Muhammad ibn al-Hanafiyyah, 140
Muhammad ibn al-Hasan, 92, 110, 113
Muhammad ibn al-Munkadir, 443
Muhammad ibn al-Muthanna, 127
Muhammad ibn al-Qasim, 112
Muhammad ibn al-Sabah, 95, 137

Muhammad ibn al-Sa'ib, 444
Muhammad ibn Fudayl, 85, 103, 126
Muhammad ibn Hamid, 295
Muhammad ibn Hatim, 83, 139, 154
Muhammad ibn Ibrahim al-Nu'mani, 441
Muhammad ibn Ja'far, 81, 95, 154
Muhammad ibn Jehada, 79
Muhammad ibn Khalad al-Bahili, 139
Muhammad ibn Khalid, 110
Muhammad ibn Khazim, 124, 125
Muhammad ibn Kuthayyir, 74
Muhammad ibn Muqatil, 138
Muhammad ibn Musa, 81, 128
Muhammad ibn Muslim, 41, 127, 445, 449
Muhammad ibn Muslim ibn al-Ta'ifi, 127
Muhammad ibn Muslim ibn Jummaz, 128
Muhammad ibn Nabahan, 136
Muhammad ibn Namir, 127, 138
Muhammad ibn Rafi', 83
Muhammad Ibn Sa'd, 76
Muhammad ibn Salam, 125, 127, 138
Muhammad ibn Sinan, 451
Muhammad ibn Sirin, 75, 121
Muhammad ibn Sulayman, 118
Muhammad ibn Yazid, 127
Muhammad ibn Zakariyya, 413
Muharib ibn Dithar, 83
Mujahid, 41, 47, 53, 76, 78, 83, 87, 92, 107, 123, 393, 438
Mujma' al-Kabir, 196, 229
Mujma'ul Bayan fi Tafsir al-Qur'an, 45, 47, 207, 445
mujtahid, 456, 459
Mukashafatul Qulub, 326
Mukhlid al-Shu'ayri, 107
Mukhtara, 150, 292
Mukhtasar, 79, 80, 99, 127, 446, 448
Mukhtasar al-Kalam, 80, 99, 446, 448
Mu'min al-Taq, 449
Muntahal Maqal, 79, 129, 442
Muntakhabul Kanz, 151
Murrah al-Hamadani, 51, 83
Muruj al-Thahab, 352
Mus'ab ibn Sa'd, 78
Musa al-Zaman, 125

Musa ibn Qays, 132
Musaddid, 72, 101
Musaylamah, 404
Mushbir, 181
Muslim al-Batin, 87, 92, 134
Muslim al-Malla'i, 86
musnad, 140, 150, 167, 391, 439
*musnad*s, 58, 100, 102, 104, 108, 114, 129, 133, 134, 140, 168, 202, 321
Mu'ta, 193, 378, 389
Muwaffaqiyyat, 429, 430
Na'im ibn Mas'ud, 205
Najasa, 458
Nakhila, 88
Naqd al-Uthmaniyyah, 150
Nasibis, 81, 82, 90, 106, 120, 131, 141, 147, 218, 448
Nisa'i, 41, 68, 70, 71, 73, 74, 75, 77, 81, 84, 86, 89, 98, 104, 117, 118, 119, 127, 128, 133, 134, 151, 185, 191, 192, 194, 195, 202, 220, 222, 232, 240, 242, 292
Nuh, 67, 133, 336
Nuh ibn Qays, 133
nuthur, 409
of al-Ash'ari, 6
Umayyads, 85, 93
Palestine, XII, 378, 389
Persia, 112
Pharaoh, 49, 227, 285, 411
Qa'im, 275, 276, 278
Qatadah, 84, 89, 100, 116, 319, 393
Qatan ibn Nasir, 72
Qays ibn 'Abdullah, 114
Qayyim, 458
Qibla, 144, 145, 458
Qur'an, VI, XIX, 11, 12, 13, 14, 15, 16, 22, 23, 27, 35, 38, 39, 41, 42, 43, 44, 45, 48, 49, 50, 51, 52, 53, 54, 55, 56, 59, 62, 67, 78, 80, 98, 101, 102, 109, 110, 125, 127, 131, 135, 136, 141, 144, 149, 159, 162, 163, 164, 171, 184, 188, 202, 203, 205, 206, 208, 209, 210, 211, 220, 227, 228, 233, 235, 246, 247, 253, 255, 257, 259, 260, 261, 262, 265, 280, 308, 315, 318, 325, 335, 336, 337, 338, 351, 357, 362, 365, 370, 373, 374, 376, 389, 392, 395, 412,

416, 417, 429, 430, 438, 443, 444,
    445, 446
Quraysh, 15, 89, 210, 356, 357, 358,
    393, 409, 410, 411, 415
Qurrah ibn Khalid, 83
Qutaybah ibn Sa'd, 138
Qutaybah ibn Sa'id, 70
Rabatha, 98
Rafidi, 58, 68, 69, 70, 71, 72, 73, 74,
    80, 89, 109, 111, 116, 119, 121,
    125, 132, 133, 134, 137
Rafidism, 72, 100, 287, 296
Rahba, 249, 250, 251, 252, 407
Ramadan, 59, 91, 256, 280, 355, 397,
    460
Ramallah, 378
Ramla, 95
Rashid al-Hijri, 97
Rawdat al-Jannat, 440
Rayy, 66, 70, 86
Rijal al-Shi'a, 127
Risalat al-Huquq, 445
Riyah ibn al-Harish, 256
Sa'd ibn 'Abadah, 351, 352
Sa'd ibn 'Ubaydah, 67
Sa'd ibn 'Ubaydullah, 83
Sa'd ibn Abu Waqqas, 76, 166, 167,
    187, 188
Sa'd ibn Azhar, 138
Sa'd ibn Ibrahim, 102
Sa'd ibn Janadah, 112, 113
Sa'd ibn Mansur, 125, 132
Sa'd ibn Muhammad, 113
Sa'd ibn Tarif, 85
Sa'id al-Jariri, 72
Sa'id ibn Ashwa', 86
Sa'id ibn Jubayr, 51, 76, 78, 87, 92,
    112, 132, 193, 198, 363, 364
Sa'id ibn Khaytham, 86
Sa'id ibn Malik, 186
Sa'id ibn Mansur, 137, 150, 228, 303
Sa'id ibn Masruq, 87
Sa'id ibn Qays, 425
Sa'id ibn Sulayman, 136
Sa'sa'ah ibn Sawhan, 95, 96, 97
sadaqat, 253, 397, 458
Sadfah ibn al-Munthir, 451
Sadr ad-Din al-Musawi, 445
Safiyya, 162, 312, 313, 339

Safwan ibn Yahya, 451
Sahabah, 418, 437, 458
Sahih, *X*, 25, 30, 54, 62, 63, 64, 67, 68,
    69, 72, 76, 77, 78, 79, 81, 82, 83,
    84, 85, 89, 92, 98, 99, 100, 101,
    103, 104, 109, 110, 112, 115, 118,
    119, 121, 122, 124, 125, 128, 132,
    133, 134, 135, 136, 138, 139, 154,
    166, 167, 187, 202, 218, 221, 222,
    226, 231, 241, 301, 302, 312, 316,
    317, 319, 320, 321, 325, 336, 338,
    342, 344, 348, 349, 362, 364, 439
Sahl ibn Abu Khadouthah, 72
Sahm ibn Munjab, 63
Saif ibn Abu Sulayman, 122
Saif ibn Sulayman, 83
Salamah ibn Kahil, 132
Salih al-Jazrah, 101
Salih ibn al-Aswad, 92
Salih ibn Muhammad, 103
Salih ibn Salih al-Hamadani, 77
Salim al-Muradi, 112
Salim ibn Abu Hafsah, 84, 85
Salim ibn Abul-Ja'd, 84
Salim ibn Qays, 441
Salma, 83, 102
Salman, 46, 47, 134, 182, 217, 276,
    277, 281, 295, 304, 343, 363, 419,
    422, 440, 441
Samarra, II, XIII
Sammak, 46, 63, 219, 443
Sammak ibn Harb, 77, 443
San'a, 105, 106, 222, 239, 438
saqifa, 341, 343, 345, 352, 403
Sarij ibn Yunus, 299
Selamah ibn Kahil, 87
Shabar, 181
Shaqiq ibn 'Uqbah, 122
Sharaf daughter of Khalifah, 326
Sharh al-Hashimiyyat, 243
Sharh Nahjul Balaghah, 150, 151,
    153, 192, 216, 217, 226, 286, 293,
    296, 324, 330, 331, 332, 337, 342,
    343, 345, 352, 358, 363, 366, 390,
    407, 416, 417, 421, 428, 429, 430
shari'a, 80
Sharik, 68, 77, 91, 92, 93, 94, 95, 101,
    105, 111, 119, 133, 154, 295
Sharik ibn 'Abdullah, 91, 92

Shayban ibn Farukh, 135
Shaykh Hasan al-Karbala'i, II
Shaykh Rashid Rida, 313
Shi'ah, 201, 393, 418, 435, 436, 437,
    438, 441, 446, 447, 448
Shi'ism, 62, 67, 73, 77, 81, 82, 84, 86,
    104, 105, 109, 112, 114, 115, 118,
    121, 122, 123, 124, 134, 137, 138,
    296
Shihab, 70, 122
Shu'ab al-Iman, 228
Shu'bah, 62, 69, 70, 76, 79, 83, 87, 89,
    92, 111, 115, 116, 119, 120, 121,
    131, 132, 138, 153
Shu'bah ibn al-Hajjaj, 95
Shubayr, 181
Shubuhat, 165
Shura, 185
Shurayh, 136
Sihan ibn Sawhan, 96
Sirah, 150, 206
Siyaq Nisabur, 203
Siyar ibn Salamah, 121
Sufyan ibn 'Ayinah, 62, 108, 122, 139
Sulayman al-A'mash, 76
Sulayman ibn 'Abdul-Malik, 84
Sulayman ibn Bilal, 81
Sulayman ibn Harb, 71
Sulayman ibn Mahran, 90
Sulayman ibn Qarm, 89
Sulayman ibn Sa'id, 87
Sulayman ibn Tarkhan, 88
sunan, 75, 77, 80, 81, 83, 85, 89, 95,
    111, 115, 117, 119, 122, 123, 126,
    128, 132, 133, 134, 138, 139, 161,
    165, 167, 171, 231, 288, 321, 348,
    361
Sunnah, XVII, 6, 8, 11, 20, 27, 34, 36,
    143, 144, 145, 178, 185, 231, 274,
    278, 287, 301, 305, 318, 349, 375,
    376, 400, 435, 442
Sunni, 5, VII, XVI, 2, 9, 15, 43, 49,
    58, 61, 64, 90, 95, 98, 101, 114,
    121, 125, 129, 140, 143, 147, 149,
    150, 153, 154, 167, 171, 187, 202,
    235, 237, 255, 257, 316, 322, 436,
    437
Suwayd ibn Ghaflah, 87, 413

Syria, III, 2, 47, 100, 175, 201, 408,
    419, 447
Tabaqat, 76, 77, 81, 84, 85, 88, 95,
    102, 109, 112, 115, 117, 122, 123,
    124, 126, 128, 130, 138, 140, 184,
    185, 302, 307, 317, 325, 326, 328,
    329, 378, 379, 398, 418, 419
Tabataba'i, II
tabi'in, 8, 73, 75, 76, 84, 102, 116,
    141, 172, 301, 418, 438, 442, 459
Tabuk, 162, 167, 169, 171, 175, 176,
    180, 418
Tafsir, 34, 39, 40, 41, 42, 43, 44, 45,
    46, 47, 48, 55, 132, 150, 179, 184,
    188, 203, 207, 210, 215, 226, 246,
    255, 256, 332, 445, 459
Tahir al-'Alawi, 433
Tahir ibn al-Husayn, 433
Tahthib, 46, 137, 292, 393, 447
Tahthib al-Athar, 292, 393
Taj al-'Arus, 422
Takbir, 459
Talhah, 51, 101, 103, 104, 175, 302,
    309, 316, 389, 404, 451
Talhah ibn Khuwaylid, 404
Talhah ibn Masrif, 302, 309
Talid ibn Sulayman, 68
Talkhis, 22, 52, 151, 163, 165, 181,
    182, 183, 185, 192, 193, 195, 199,
    221, 222, 227, 228, 231, 233, 240,
    292, 293, 303, 305, 306, 307, 325,
    331, 337
Tanzil al-Ayat, 56, 208
Taqiyya, 459
Taqlid, 459
Tarikh al-Khulafa', 255
Tarikh al-Umam wal Muluk, 149
Tarikh Baghdad, 417
Tariq ibn Shihab, 440
tashahhud, 54, 440
Tawatur, 22, 459
Tawbah al-Halabi, 95
Tawus, 76, 98
Tawus ibn Kisan, 98
Tawwabin, 459
Thabit al-Banani, 72, 116
Thabit ibn Dinar, 68
Thanij, 73
    Dharr ibn 'Abdullah, 78, 87

That al Riqa', 206
Thiqat, 72, 460
Thomas, 150
Ubayd ibn, 63
Ubaydah ibn Sulayman, 78
Ubaydullah ibn 'Abdullah, 364
Ubaydullah ibn Abu Rafi', 126, 229, 441
Ubaydullah ibn Aslam, 441
Ubaydullah ibn Musa, 77, 78, 106, 109, 110, 129, 132
Ubaydullah ibn Ziyad, 88, 131
Ubayy ibn Ka'b, 419
Ubna, 378, 379, 381, 385
Uhud, 47, 99, 176, 352, 397
Ulema, 460
Uman ibn Talhah, 86
Umar ibn 'Abdul-'Aziz, 84
Umar ibn al-Khattab, 99, 100, 182, 186, 358, 362, 363, 438
Umar ibn Shakir, 68
Umayr ibn Ma'mun, 86
Umm al-Aswad, 108
Umm al-Khayr, 422
Umm Ayman, 183, 390
Umm Salamah, 132, 167, 188, 221, 222, 225, 306, 331, 332, 333, 335, 339, 349
Umm Salim, 175, 176
Umm Sinan, 431
Urwah ibn al-Zubayr, 352
Usamah, 102, 110, 122, 123, 193, 277, 332, 377, 378, 379, 380, 381, 382, 385, 386, 387, 388, 389, 391
Usamah ibn Zayd, 110, 377, 378, 389
usul, 144, 165, 168, 441
Wafiyyat, 90, 92, 93, 94, 98, 104, 108, 120, 129, 203
Wahab ibn Hamzah, 196
Wajiza, 442
Waki', 41, 69, 70, 71, 78, 116, 123, 128, 137, 393, 445
Waki' ibn al-Jarrah, 128, 137
wali, 24, 73, 162, 163, 164, 185, 188, 191, 193, 194, 195, 196, 197, 202, 204, 209, 211, 216, 223, 224, 238, 239, 242, 251, 254, 259, 260, 261, 265, 267, 274, 276, 277, 281, 304,
305, 306, 316, 322, 339, 409, 418, 423, 426, 432
wasi, 125, 179, 204, 238, 280, 283, 297, 305, 309, 316, 335, 339, 408, 412, 421, 422, 423, 424, 425, 426, 427, 428, 429, 430, 431, 432, 433
Wilayat, 201, 278, 460
Y'aqub ibn Hayyan, 393
Ya'li ibn 'Ata', 95
Ya'li ibn Umayyah, 337
Ya'qub al-Dawraqi, 136, 139
Ya'qub al-Faswi, 117
Yahya ibn, 30, 67, 70, 71, 72, 73, 77, 78, 83, 88, 95, 96, 99, 108, 112, 119, 121, 122, 123, 125, 126, 127, 129, 132, 135, 136, 137, 138, 139, 141, 191, 220, 222
Yahya ibn 'Abbad, 67
Yahya ibn Adam, 77, 119, 122, 123, 220
Yahya ibn Ayyub, 83, 137
Yahya ibn Bakir, 114
Yahya ibn Bishr, 71
Yahya ibn Ma'in, 73, 96, 108, 121, 127, 137, 222
Yahya ibn Sa'id, 67, 95, 112, 138, 139
Yahya ibn Salim, 191
Yahya ibn Ya'li, 30, 126
Yahya ibn Yahya, 70, 72, 125, 127, 129, 137
Yanabi' al-Mawaddah, 188
Yazid ibn Abu Habib, 104
Yazid ibn Abu Maryam, 114
Yazid ibn Abu Ziyad, 86
Yazid ibn al-Rashk, 72
Yazid ibn Arqam, 120
Yazid ibn Harun, 72, 137
Yazid ibn Qays, 62
Yazid ibn Zari', 116
Yazid ibn Ziyad, 139
Yemen, 141, 192, 193, 194, 198, 259, 263, 397, 438
Yunus ibn Muhammad, 95
Yusuf ibn, 110, 120
Yusuf ibn 'Isa, 125
Zafar ibn Huzayfah, 429
Za'idah, 67, 70, 86, 122
Zajr ibn Qays, 427

zakat, 41, 47, 122, 202, 204, 205, 234, 246, 256, 348, 386, 397, 441, 460
Zalim ibn 'Amr, 98
Zararah, 108, 136, 445, 449
Zayd ibn Abu Anisa, 79, 112, 132
Zayd ibn al-Habab, 83, 123
Zayd ibn al-Mubarak, 107
Zayd ibn Arqam, 20, 22, 31, 69, 133, 182, 187, 188, 237, 239, 240, 251, 252, 255, 281
Zayd ibn Ka'b, 87
Zayd ibn Sawhan, 96
Zayd ibn Thabit, 21, 98, 175, 265
Zayd ibn Wahab, 74, 76, 92

Zaynul-'abidin, 442, 445
Ziyad ibn Alaqah, 95
Ziyad ibn Kulayb, 63
Ziyad ibn Labid, 426
Ziyad ibn Matraf, 30
Zubayd al-Yami, 82, 90, 120, 130
Zubayd ibn al-Harith, 82
Zuhair ibn al-Aqmar, 89
Zuhair ibn Harb, 83
Zuhayr, 69, 83, 115, 120, 121, 122, 124, 125, 127, 137, 138, 154
Zuhayr ibn Mu'awiyah, 83, 124, 154
Zurarah, 80

www.ingramcontent.com/pod-product-compliance
Lightning Source LLC
Chambersburg PA
CBHW020246010526
44107CB00002B/118